THE MAN HE BECAME

HOW FDR DEFIED POLIO
TO WIN THE PRESIDENCY

JAMES TOBIN

THORNDIKE PRESS
A part of Gale, Cengage Learning

GALE
CENGAGE Learning·

Detroit • New York • San Francisco • New Haven, Conn • Waterville, Maine • London

Copyright © 2013 by James Tobin.
Thorndike Press, a part of Gale, Cengage Learning.

ALL RIGHTS RESERVED
Thorndike Press® Large Print Biography.
The text of this Large Print edition is unabridged.
Other aspects of the book may vary from the original edition.
Set in 16 pt. Plantin.

LIBRARY OF CONGRESS CATALOGING-IN-PUBLICATION DATA

Tobin, James, 1956–
    The man he became : how FDR defied polio to win the presidency / by
James Tobin. — Large print edition.
        pages cm. — (Thorndike Press large print biography
    Originally published: New York : Simon & Schuster, 2013.
    Includes bibliographical references.
    ISBN-13: 978-1-4104-6550-4 (hardcover)
    ISBN-10: 1-4104-6550-0 (hardcover)
    1. Roosevelt, Franklin D. (Franklin Delano), 1882-1945. 2. Roosevelt,
Franklin D. (Franklin Delano), 1882-1945—Health. 3.
Poliomyelitis—Patients—United States—Biography. 4. Presidents—United
States—Election—1932. 5. Presidents—United States—Biography. I. Title.
E807.T63 2014
973.917092—dc23
[B]   2013040086

Published in 2014 by arrangement with Simon & Schuster, Inc.

Printed in the United States of America
1 2 3 4 5 6 7 18 17 16 15 14

To Leesa

and to

John Bacon
Richard and Dianna Campbell
Jonathan Marwil
Randy Milgrom
Rob and Anne Raymond

CONTENTS

7

"One of the central problems facing anyone dealing with Franklin Roosevelt's
personal history is just what made him the
man he became."

— JOSEPH ALSOP

PROLOGUE

Franklin D. Roosevelt sat in a plain chair, waiting to be summoned to the chamber of the United States Senate. It was eleven thirty in the morning on the day of his inauguration as president of the United States. At noon, he was to watch his running mate, John Nance Garner of Texas, take the oath as vice president. Then he would walk outside for his own swearing-in at one o'clock.

He was waiting in the room reserved for the Senate's Committee on Military Affairs. Several assistants sat with him, among them his eldest son, James, always called Jimmy, twenty-six years old, brawny and an inch or two taller than his father.

At ten minutes to noon someone looked in and said they were ready for him in the Senate.

Roosevelt hitched himself to the edge of his chair, placed his hands on his thighs,

11

and pushed until his legs were straight out in front of him. He felt through the fabric of his trousers for metal locks on the custom-made braces that encased his legs. Then he snapped the locks shut so his knees would not buckle when he rose. Jimmy stood and faced him. Father and son grasped each other by the arms and, with a quick heave, the elder Roosevelt rocked up onto his feet and straightened at the waist. With one hand he grasped a wooden cane. With the other he held Jimmy's arm. Under his trousers, the bars and cuffs and belts of his braces held his legs rigid from his heels to his buttocks. His cane, his son, and his own stiffly braced lower body formed the three legs of a reasonably stable tripod.

Slowly, they moved across the room and into the corridor. There Colonel Edward Halsey, secretary of the Senate, met them and held up his hand. Halsey said he was very sorry, but the Senate wasn't quite ready after all.

Jimmy and his father stopped, pivoted, and ambulated back into the Military Affairs committee room. At the chair, Roosevelt pivoted again, set down his cane, gripped his son, and lowered himself onto the seat, legs locked straight in front. He reached behind his knees, undid the locks, pulled his knees up, hitched himself backward, and rested his hands on the arms of the chair, ready to tighten his grip if he began to tilt and fall to the floor.

After ten more minutes, the Senate was ready.

Jimmy stood. Roosevelt pushed his legs down and locked the braces. Father and son heaved and he was standing.

They moved across the room and into the corridor, where members of the Committee on Arrangements waited to escort him. A voice ahead of him was announcing, "The president-elect of the United States . . ." Then he was inside the brilliantly lit chamber. Senators, congressmen, the justices of the Supreme Court, the military chiefs, members of the diplomatic corps, his children, his mother, his wife in a purple-blue gown, holding an enormous bouquet of violets — all were looking at him. Jimmy escorted him to a new chair, and there, between President Herbert Hoover, whom Roosevelt had defeated in the November election, and Senator Joseph Taylor Robinson of Arkansas, leader of the new Democratic majority, Roosevelt sat again, unlocked the braces, pulled up his knees, and lightly grasped the arms of his chair.

He listened as fifteen new senators and

the new vice president were sworn in, and the Senate of the 72nd Congress was declared adjourned.

Then the Senate chaplain, the Reverend ZeBarney Thorne Phillips, rector of Washington's Episcopal Church of the Epiphany, asked the assembly to rise for prayer.

Every one of the hundreds of people in the Senate chamber stood up except the president-elect.

A reporter in the press gallery saw Roosevelt lean forward for an instant, as if by instinct. Then he settled back.

Senator Robinson, now standing, glanced down at Roosevelt. Robinson was hardly known for courtliness. He had once been suspended from the Chevy Chase Country Club for punching a fellow golfer on the 15th green. But at this moment he did something, as another watching reporter put it, "that should win him a golden mark in the manual of gentlemen." He dropped to his seat beside the president-elect. Everyone else in the room remained standing for the prayer.

The moment came to move outside for the presidential oath of office and the inaugural address. The Capitol's corridors filled with people. The crowd jammed up at the great door that opened onto the Capitol's east plaza. Roosevelt stood behind Herbert Hoover and waited. His bulky upper body pressed down on the joints of his knees. Holding himself upright was a concerted act of strength and balance.

Then Jimmy and he, now in top hats, were out the door into cold, gray daylight under lowering clouds, moving slowly down a long ramp that led to the speaker's platform and the lectern itself. Members of the Hoover administration, Roosevelt's own new Cabinet secretaries, and members of Congress walked in a close-packed formation.

One hundred thousand people were watching. Twelve thousand were seated. The rest stood in a crowd that spread across the plaza and East Capitol Drive and up the front steps of the Supreme Court and the Library of Congress and into the branches of the surrounding trees. A hundred press photographers straight in front of him clicked their shutters. Newsreel cameras whirred.

Roosevelt moved toward them all with a slow, swaying gait, Jimmy next to him, swaying in rhythm with his father. The procession blocked the crowd's view of anything but Roosevelt's shoulders and head. But if Jimmy and he had been walking alone, people would have noticed that with each

15

step he leaned a bit to one side, while on the opposite side he hitched his shoulder just enough to swing the leg on that side forward. The coordinated movements of the shoulder and the leg were smooth and almost simultaneous. Anyone who saw his gait could see he was crippled. But, with help, he was walking.

He reached the lectern, grasped it with one hand, set down his cane, and removed his top hat. Jimmy moved a few steps back. Roosevelt swiveled to face Chief Justice Charles Evans Hughes. With his left hand, he gripped the lectern. As Hughes read the words of the oath, beginning, "Do you, Franklin Delano Roosevelt, solemnly swear . . ." Roosevelt held up his right hand. When Hughes completed the question, Roosevelt lowered his right hand to the Dutch Bible that had been in his family since the seventeenth century. Breaking precedent, he did not, after Justice Hughes posed the question of the oath, simply say "I do." Instead, he recited the entire oath, holding the lectern with his left hand, resting his right hand on the first page of Paul's First Epistle to the Corinthians.

For most of his life he had hoped to become president. For twelve years he had prepared for the task he had just performed:

walking to this lectern before an enormous audience and standing upright to take the oath of office. The performance had been the culminating and indispensable act of the great struggle of his life. It was not an act of deception; he was not trying to fool anyone into thinking he was not crippled. Anyone who read the newspapers knew that. Rather, it was a deliberate show of strength, a silent, symbolic assertion that he could bear the burden of the presidency.

The preceding week had been the worst in the history of the American economy. People felt a collective desperation unknown in the United States since the Civil War. The banking system was collapsing. Indeed, when many in the Capitol crowd tried to draw cash from their hotels later that day, clerks refused; their banks at home had closed during the inaugural festivities. One in four Americans was out of work, and the prospect of many more losing their livelihoods loomed over everyone. Two million people or more were riding freight trains in search of a chance to work. Dairy farmers in Iowa, Nebraska, and Wisconsin had blockaded roads and dumped thousands of gallons of milk on the pavement in an effort to drive up starvation prices of two cents a quart. On the left there was dead-serious talk of the need for social revolution; on the right, of the need for a dictator.

Most people in the Capitol crowd could hardly see Roosevelt. Even those close to the rostrum could see only his shoulders and hatless head darting left and right for emphasis. Loudspeakers broadcast the rich tenor with the upper-crust inflections over the crowd — not all the way to the edges, where people could not hear; but microphones relayed the voice over the radio to the whole country.

He had told his assistants beforehand that he saw little point in using the speech to announce any specific policy. The main thing was to give people reason not to be afraid. So he came to his main purpose promptly.

"This nation will endure as it has endured," he said, "will revive and will prosper. So let me assert my firm belief that the only thing we have to fear is fear itself — nameless, unreasoning, unjustified terror — which paralyzes needed efforts to convert retreat into advance. . . . Our common difficulties, thank God, concern only material things."

By many accounts, Roosevelt's speech exerted a powerful effect on many in the crowd and millions listening to the radio. A man in Cleveland named Raymond Hummel was one of many who wrote to Roosevelt to express his gratitude. "Today sitting among a gathering of the all but 'forgotten men' during your inaugural address," Hummel wrote, "I seen those worried looks replaced by smiles and confidence, eyes fill up with tears of gratitude, shoulders lifted and chest out." In New Jersey, Albert Rutherford wrote: "Never, since the news of the Armistice reached this country, have I had such a vibrant and electric feeling come over me, as when you made your vibrant inaugural address." In Florida, Dorothy Fullinger said: "I felt as if I could stretch out my arms and cry: 'I'm glad I'm an American!' It gave me a new thrill in life, something to live for."

Praise in the press was all but euphoric. The next day's *Cleveland Plain Dealer* voiced the typical view: "Millions will say as they read the inaugural address this morning: Here is the man we have been looking for."

Roosevelt's remark about fear got less play in the papers than his promise of "action now" and his plea for power "as great as the power that would be given to me if we were in fact invaded by a foreign foe." But in the coming weeks and months, as he kept his promise of extraordinary action and people began to think the country might indeed recover from the catastrophe, they remembered the sentence from the inaugural speech — the idea that fear alone could paralyze, and that if one went ahead in spite of fear, the paralysis might recede. "The only thing we have to fear is fear itself" became the epigram of the moment.

Americans knew that Franklin Roosevelt's legs had been paralyzed by the disease that most of them called "infantile paralysis." But only his intimates knew enough to appreciate the parallel between his injunction to the nation — indeed, his entire response to the Great Depression — and his own experience of paralysis, fear, and recovery. Nor have many since fully appreciated that Roosevelt's momentous presidency sprang from a personal drama that began with a virus, then grew and grew until it took the national stage and shaped history.

Roosevelt's gifts and flaws were myriad and mingled. He has always resisted efforts to see him whole. A distant cousin by marriage, the powerful columnist Joseph Alsop, once wrote that "one of the central problems facing anyone dealing with Franklin Roosevelt's personal history is just what made him the man he became." No one has solved that problem; probably no one will. As one of his earliest and greatest biographers — the playwright Robert Sherwood, who worked for FDR and knew him well — wrote: "I tried continually to study him, to try to look beyond his charming and amusing and warmly affectionate surface into his heavily forested interior. But I could never really understand what was going on in there."

So there is no simple solution to Alsop's problem. Poliomyelitis by itself did not make Roosevelt the man he became. The determinants of anyone's life are legion. No single factor explains all. But one cannot see Roosevelt in full without a deep understanding of his encounter with disease and disability. The crippling of his lower body, and his complicated response to that crippling, altered the course of his career, shaped his view of life, and changed his relationships with others, from his intimates to the entire American public. Without the poliovirus and what it did to FDR, the history of American life since the 1920s would not be what it has been. It is a truism to say Roosevelt overcame polio to become president. It is just as accurate to say that Roosevelt would not have been the president he became — probably would not have been president at all — had it not been for the germ that infected him in 1921.

It seems to me that when I was growing up in the 1960s, everybody knew Franklin Roosevelt had been crippled. When I was no older than six or seven, my grandmother told me a tale of a heroic, crippled president who once had struggled bravely across a stage to give a speech. But either I am wrong about what was once common knowledge, or what was once common knowledge has become awfully muddled in the meantime. I believe it's the latter, but exactly how this happened is a puzzle to me.

When I began research, I found that Roosevelt's major biographers, with the exception of Geoffrey C. Ward, had dealt with his paralysis as only an isolated episode. They described it in brief, then left it behind for the larger matters of politics, the New Deal, and World War II. Whether they believed the impact of polio on FDR to be small or great, they didn't say very much about it. That I understood. To tell an entire life story as large as Roosevelt's, even in several volumes, a biographer has to stick to business or find — as several who tried it have found — that his own life may not be long enough to finish the job. Nonetheless, the big books did not answer my questions about FDR's condition.

I came to expect, when someone learned what I was doing, to hear something like this: "He hid it, right?" Or: "Isn't it amazing that it was all covered up?" I read Hugh Gregory Gallagher's book *FDR's Splendid Deception* and suspected that Gallagher's main idea — that Roosevelt and the people around him engaged in a campaign of deceit about his condition — rather outran the hard evidence. Then I went back and sampled the arguments that raged in the 1990s over designs for the Franklin D. Roosevelt Memorial in Washington, D.C., and there I found Gallagher's idea about a "splendid deception" all over the place. Important and popular writers said things such as: *"It is hard to imagine, in this era of journalistic strip-searches, that only sixty years ago a president was able to hide such a huge fact of his daily life from the American public"* (Maureen Dowd). And: *"He relentlessly, obsessively hid his condition from the American people"* (Charles Krauthammer). The evidence shows these assertions to be terribly misleading at best. Yet since that debate in the 1990s, such references to Roosevelt and polio have become commonplace.

23

Whenever I spoke with someone who remembered the 1930s and 1940s, I would ask if he or she knew at the time that FDR was crippled. Everybody said they knew. But some people said this: "We didn't know *how* crippled he was." In contemporary source materials, I found the same remarks made by people who had seen Roosevelt in person when he was president. Many were surprised, even shocked, by the extent of his disability. (This was especially true of people who happened to see assistants carry him up or down stairs.)

Others said: "We knew he was crippled, but people didn't talk about it." Or: "We knew, but we forgot about it." Or: "We knew, but we didn't think of him that way."

People knew but didn't know, knew but didn't think about it. Year after year in the 1930s and 1940s, there was a massive, nationwide drive on Roosevelt's birthday to raise money to fight infantile paralysis, with Roosevelt's picture on posters and appeals over his signature. But people didn't think about the president being crippled.

These were signs that I had a complicated story to tell — more complicated, certainly, than earlier writers had shown it to be. The story would have to take account of a culture in which, as Maureen Dowd put it, the "journalistic strip-search" was indeed not routine, in which much more was kept private and privacy was more respected than it is in our own time. It was not only a matter of what people did not know. It was also a matter of what people did not think they *ought* to know.

In time I came to focus on the period between the onset of Roosevelt's illness in 1921 and his first election to the presidency in 1932. Those were the years when an absurd wager for which no bookmaker would have given odds turned out to be a winning bet with a spectacular payoff. After 1932, his accommodation with disability was a fait accompli. That act in the drama of his life was done.

Franklin Roosevelt said little and wrote less about what he really thought and felt. That was his strategy as a politician and his nature as a person. Not for him the meaty, introspective letters of biographical subjects who wear their hearts on their sleeves. (The *New Yorker* writer Richard Rovere once remarked that as a writer of letters, FDR "was a credit to Western Union and the Bell System. . . . He regarded letter-writing as a nasty chore, to be got out of the way as quickly and painlessly as possible.") He did not keep a diary or write a memoir. One can learn a lot about what he *did* about his disability — including what he said about it to other people, which was itself a form of action. But no one will ever learn exactly how he felt about it. So this is a story pieced together largely from what Roosevelt and the people around him did and said. The mysteries of "his heavily forested interior" remain. But the silences guarding his condition are part of the story too.

This leads me to say a word about the lexicon of disability. After a good deal of thought, I chose to use the words "crippled" and "cripple" in telling this story. In our own era, of course, those words, though still used, are widely regarded as offensive. In Roosevelt's time, it was not so. People of the 1920s and 1930s attached those words to people without understanding that they were applying a social stigma — a scarlet "C" — that was often far more disabling than the physical condition itself. To understand Roosevelt's situation — in his time, not ours — one needs to enter a realm in which the stigma of physical disability was like the presence of oxygen in the air: utterly taken for granted, and therefore terribly powerful. I felt I could not lead the reader into that realm without using the words for his condition that he and everyone else used. "Disability" was in use then too, but "crippled" was more common and more telling. To substitute words we now deem appropriate — such as "handicapped," "physically challenged," and the like — would be, I think, to paper over an essential element of Roosevelt's problem.

■ ■ ■ ■

PART ONE:
VIRUS AND HOST

SUMMER 1921

■ ■ ■ ■

CHAPTER 1
INFECTION
JULY 28, 1921

The virus that causes poliomyelitis entered
Franklin Roosevelt's body in the summer of
1921. At the moment of infection he was a
famous and vigorous young man on the rise
toward national leadership. The virus was
small beyond imagining.

Ten more years would go by before the
first electron microscopes revealed that the
poliovirus resembles a distant planet in-
scribed with tiny canyons. The virus is not
alive in the way a bird is alive or even in the
way a bacterium is alive. It is nothing more
than a little sphere of fat enclosing a smaller
strip of genetic material. It cannot move by
itself. It does not eat or breathe. It is at most
half-alive — a parasite. To reproduce, it
must enter a human body, then survive an
onslaught from the protective machinery of
the body's immune system, then blunder
up against a welcoming cell in the human
intestine. If the virus can burrow inside that

31

cell, its fatty capsule dissolves, exposing the strip of genetic chemicals within. Then a bizarre meshing of genetic equipment ensues. Like the two sides of a zipper, the strip from the virus unites with a matching strip from the intestinal cell, forming an assembly line that begins to duplicate the original virus by the thousand. Overloaded, the cell bursts, the virus's progeny collide with neighboring intestinal cells, and the multiplication spreads.

Even then, the effect of this submicrocosmic production would likely be negligible. Most of the virus's human hosts suffer nothing worse than a headache and a mild fever. The immune system overwhelms the virus and flushes it out of the body, and the human host goes on with life none the wiser.

But in a fraction of those infected — fewer than one percent — the virus escapes from the intestinal tract into the central nervous system. It has an affinity for certain cells in the spinal cord that govern the movement of muscles. If the virus finds these cells, it destroys them — sometimes only a few, sometimes a great many. The number of spinal-cord cells destroyed determines the fate of the human host. If only a few cells are destroyed, the host might be only temporarily hobbled, then recover completely.

If a great many cells are destroyed, depending on their number and location, he might be left badly damaged or dead.

Outside the human host, the virus can escape disintegration for as long as six months. To propagate — its only purpose, if it can be said to have a purpose — it must find its way into a susceptible human being. Its best chance of doing so comes in the heat of summer.

The whole Northeast had been roasting for days. In Rochester, New York, police were attributing a double murder and suicide to "heat-craze." In New York City, the chief clerk of the Edison Electric Company collapsed of heat prostration and died. Inside Manhattan's Traffic Court, the magistrate allowed boys to roam through the courtrooms to sell lemonade. On 10th Street in Greenwich Village, members of Fire Engine Company 18 filled their portable water tank and waved the kids in — dozens of sweaty boys in woolen pants, jostling and dunking each other, spitting and swallowing the cloudy water.

So it was a good day to get out on the Hudson River, where at least there might be a breeze. And Franklin Roosevelt would seize any chance to get afloat. He loved the water. On his mother's side he was the scion of an old seafaring family. He had grown up sailing small boats on the mid-Hudson and among rocky islands of the northern seacoast. As a teenager his great ambition had been to attend the U.S. Naval Academy and command ships at sea. But his parents had said no, that his future lay among men like the ones he was joining for today's outing on the river: well-dressed, well-educated, well-heeled men of business, law, and government. All were friends of the Greater New York Council of the Boy Scouts of America, of which Roosevelt had just been elected chairman.

He found them gathering just after lunch in the clubhouse of the Columbia Yacht Club, a pleasant, low building with broad porches and big windows on Riverside Drive at the foot of West 86th Street. They mingled in paneled rooms hung with lovely old naval prints like the ones in Roosevelt's own collection, one of the finest of its kind in the country. Soon the men moved to the pier outside, then boarded small boats to be ferried to the steam yacht *Pocantico,* pride of Barron G. Collier, the largest landowner in Florida and one of the richest men in New York. Just after 2 o'clock, the yacht slid away from the city's edge and began to glide north up the river. It was bound for Bear Mountain State Park, forty miles north, where the men would join hundreds of Boy Scouts for a tour of inspection and a big dinner.

Scouting was all the rage, with a heavy concentration of members in New York and its suburbs. Among these boys, the summer outing to Bear Mountain was the focus of the entire year. Throughout the fall and winter, Scouts attended weekly meetings to learn skills to apply on the annual campout — fire making, forestry, astronomy, mapping, compass reading, signaling, outdoor cooking. The whole point of the Scouting year was to prepare for this trip. The boys earned the right to go.

Roosevelt heartily approved of the Scouts. His oldest son was a Scout already, and he wanted his three younger boys to join when they could. He believed city boys should hike forest trails and learn to build a fire without matches. He himself had grown up tramping the woods and wetlands of his family's home up the Hudson, shooting and stuffing birds. That, to his mind, was a proper boyhood. A city-bred Boy Scout may be "a product of the streets and of artificial conditions of living," he wrote, yet he "discovers that the woods, the birds, the fields, the streams, the insects speak a language he understands."

But he was taking today's trip to Bear Mountain not just for the sake of the Scouts, nor just to escape the sweltering city. It was the sort of event he attended these days as often as he could, for political purposes.

From 1913 to 1920 — exhausting years of rearming, war, and demobilization — he had been assistant secretary of the U.S. Navy under President Woodrow Wilson. Then, just a year before, in July 1920, the Democratic Party had nominated him to run for vice president. (At thirty-eight, he had been two years younger than Theodore Roosevelt, his uncle by marriage and distant cousin by blood, when the latter had been nominated for vice president in 1900.) Roosevelt and his presidential running mate, Governor James M. Cox of Ohio, had been beaten badly by Warren G. Harding and Calvin Coolidge. But Roosevelt had sealed his status as a rising star, and now he was cultivating the associations he would need for a statewide race in New York.

He might run as early as the following year, in 1922, when he would be just forty years old. He might make a bid for the U.S. Senate seat occupied by William Calder, the

Republican real estate developer who had built much of Brooklyn but made no discernible mark in Washington. Or he might challenge Nathan Miller, the Republican governor who had barely nudged the popular Al Smith out of Albany in the Harding-Coolidge landslide of 1920. Al Smith was Roosevelt's ally and friend — of a sort; if he decided to run for governor again, Roosevelt would defer to him. If not, Roosevelt would make a highly plausible Democratic candidate for governor of the Empire State — and thereby become, quite automatically, a potential candidate for president.

There was no need to decide any of that now, in the summer of 1921. For the moment, after eight years entrenched in Washington, Roosevelt was simply reestablishing himself as a New Yorker — thus the chairmanship of the local Boy Scout council and a list of other good works for worthy local organizations. Each endeavor meant more opportunities to make new friendships and bolster old ones. On this day trip to Bear Mountain, for instance, every handshake, every quiet chat, every photograph for the newspapers might do a little good toward the greater goal. He was only thirty-nine years old. He possessed one of the great names in American politics. He planned to do a great deal.

Aboard *Pocantico* he was a tall figure telling stories and shouting with laughter (". . . I *love* it . . ."). As a student at the exclusive Groton School and Harvard, he had not excelled in sports, but he certainly looked like an athlete. He stood an inch or so above six feet but somehow seemed larger, perhaps because of his especially large head and jutting chin and his habit of quick and incessant movement. In Washington he had hurled himself into weekend matches in golf, tennis, baseball, and field hockey. During the world war he had plunged into exercises and cross-country runs organized for government men by the great Yale football coach Walter Camp, who called Roosevelt "a beautifully built man with the leg muscles of an athlete." At his family's summer home on the island of Campobello, New Brunswick, he loved to lead his five children through a risky chase game called Hare and Hounds, which involved racing up and down rocky escarpments. Instead of walking he often jogged or ran. An associate during the war remembered him flying down the steps of the Naval Observatory, "two, three, or four at a time, bobbing up and down like a man jumping rope." At his home in upstate New York he chopped trees, sailed iceboats, sledded with his children, and charged back up the slopes at full tilt.

Yet for all his vigor, something made him not quite the quintessential "man's man." In his twenties he had been rather staggeringly handsome. At the time of his engagement in 1904, his nineteen-year-old fiancée had blurted to a friend: "I can never hold him; he is too attractive!" But he had been handsome in a slightly prissy way. A reporter who compared his looks to those of his world-famous cousin, then the president of the United States, said that while nature had left Theodore Roosevelt's blocky head "unfinished," it had lavished perhaps a little too much loving attention on Franklin Roosevelt's face. One of Theodore Roosevelt's nieces, Corinne Roosevelt Robinson, later likened Franklin's youthful looks to the *beau ideal* of the Victorian commercial artist. "There used to be satin handkerchief boxes," she remarked once, "and on top of them there were painted figures with a gentleman dancing a minuet with a handkerchief in his hand. . . . In our family we called a certain type 'handkerchief box-y'," and that was Franklin in his early twenties. "Franklin wasn't effeminate," she said, "but he wasn't rugged." Theodore Roosevelt's daughters liked to point out that their sturdy brothers, as young men, had *rowed,* while Franklin had *sailed;* they thought that was a revealing difference. They had always said, with titters, that their distant cousin's initials might have stood for "Feather Duster." And if Corinne Roosevelt Robinson insisted FDR was "not effeminate," her acid-tongued aunt, Alice Roosevelt Longworth, had referred to him as "Miss Nancy" — slang in society circles for "homosexual." That was pure calumny; Roosevelt's preference for women was obvious throughout his life. Yet others too saw some thread in his fabric that struck them as vaguely feminine. The journalist Marquis Childs would later say he had "a kind of feminine intuition . . . the quality of the actor . . . who could be photographed and who could speak always with just the right camera angle." An associate of later years remarked that he was "the most androgynous man I ever knew." No man acted more hale and hearty, but he used language that a conventional "man's man" might hesitate to use — when he was ill, for instance, he might say he felt "weak as a kitten." He seemed a little more at ease with women than he did with men. His father had been twenty-five years older than his mother, who had the more powerful personality of the two parents. Indeed, Roosevelt had been dogged since youth, even among relatives and good friends, by the assumption that he was a "mama's boy." In fact, though his mother tried to make his decisions and determine his course, he had been defying her and setting his own course since his teenage years.

By now, nearing the age of forty, the slim dandy of the handkerchief box had grown thicker and ruddier. He no longer took care to dress snappily, but, as a woman friend said, "You couldn't make him unattractive, whatever you did."

His smile and his habits of speech made the deepest impressions. His smile was massive and winning, with none of the lock-jawed frigidity of the upper-crust stereotype. It was an expression that "quiver[ed] with animation," shifting from delight to surprise to warmth in the space of seconds. His tenor voice and superb enunciation identified him instantly as a man of American society's highest echelon, though in his refined accent some also heard a hint of the remote coastal villages of Maine where, as a privileged boy fascinated by the sea, he had made friends among fishing-boat captains.

When introduced, he seemed merely to fit "all the categories of the Good Fellow," as a writer would put it later. "He was a back-slapper, a mixer, . . . and all the rest of it — the kind of undergraduate who would, and did, make a fine permanent chairman of his class committee." But his charm far exceeded ordinary good fellowship. He seemed perfectly delighted to be who he was and equally delighted to bring everyone else in on the sheer fun of being Franklin D. Roosevelt. You knew immediately you were dealing not with an ordinary person but with a personage — a presence larger than others and more alive, as if surrounded by a sparkling aura. He regarded himself as someone who ought to be recognized and reckoned with. Even as a young boy he had signed letters to his parents with his initials: "FDR."

In his early adulthood, that quality had struck many people as sheer arrogance. As a rookie state senator, barely out of his twenties, he affected an air of such upright gentility that he reminded veteran pols of a snooty young Episcopalian clergyman. If they asked him to compromise, he would toss up his chin and say: "No! No! I won't hear of it!"

But ten years in politics had sanded off the haughty shell. The personality he displayed now was all but irresistible. The word "charm" invariably came up in conversations about him. But it was a strange admixture of forces. There was supreme self-confidence, as if no one could possibly doubt his sincerity, goodwill, and ability. Yet there was also an extraordinary determination to please, as if he were driven by an inner demon that would not quit until he was liked and admired. One who did admire him referred to "the amiably insistent force of his personality." After a while in his presence, some got tired of it.

He seemed supernaturally capable of tuning to the frequency of other people. His wife later said he was always "particularly susceptible to people," so he "took color from whomever he was with, giving to each one something different of himself." Among bookish people he would display his knowledge of American history, while among natural scientists he could recount experiences in ornithology and forestry. "He was fantastically sensitive to people around him," said a woman friend who had known him for many years. "Almost like a compass needle he would turn to people. . . . Like a chameleon he changed colors with the person he was talking with." Anyone meeting him would encounter "a big friendly smile," an observer reported, "and the glint of intense interest in his sparkling eyes." He would encourage his new friend with "little laughs, and goads, and urgings such as 'Really? Tell me more!' . . . 'Well, what do you know!' . . . 'Same thing's happened to me dozens of times!' . . . 'Oh, that's fascinating.' " If you liked him, this treatment indicated a genuine and winning sensitivity to your ideas and desires. If you weren't so sure about him, the effect was more like that of a well-performed show, a deliberate exhibition of traits calculated to gain favor.

He had developed these skills as a child — an only child — with adults, especially women, but not so much with peers. As a young boy he had taken his schooling from tutors in his home. Then, when he was thirteen, the age at which other boys of his social class were leaving home for prep school, his mother held him close for another year. So he started at Groton School outside Boston when his classmates already had endured their first-year trials together, and after this late start he never caught on with the popular crowd. At Harvard he remained outside the "in" groups. His deepest ambition in college was to be chosen for Porcellian, the most exclusive of the social clubs, but he was anonymously blackballed

— a slight that a relative thought was "the bitterest moment of Franklin Roosevelt's life" — and one of the complaints about him at Harvard was simply that he tried too hard to be liked.

He was still doing so, though he was better at it. Never quite "one of the boys" in his youth, he seized every chance to be one of the boys now.

This afternoon, for instance, aboard the yacht *Pocantico,* he was plunging headlong into fraternal revelry. With Prohibition dominating the headlines, the men aboard were staging a well-lubricated mock trial of Richard Enright, New York's commissioner of police, who had been comically "caught" transporting a suspicious-looking walking stick that turned out to contain a prohibited "amber liquid." FDR took the role of the outraged prosecutor, roaring with mock alarm, playing the part to the hilt.

The men laughing along with this burlesque came from two spheres of power. The first was Roosevelt's native sphere. These were men of Wall Street and Park Avenue, born to wealth and influence, such as William M. Chadbourne, Harvard '00, one of Manhattan's leading corporate lawyers. The other sort included self-made scramblers like Police Commissioner Enright, the first

New York cop to work his way all the way to the department's top post, thanks to the friendship of Mayor John Francis ("Red Mike") Hylan, a brawler in the wars of Tammany Hall, the city's Democratic machine.

Roosevelt had embarked on his political career as a young man wholly of the first sphere. Now, in 1921, he had one foot planted in the second sphere of power. He had made many friends among politicians and promoters of lesser social rank but greater political wisdom. To his long head start in life he had added their techniques and tools. He knew now how to hustle and maneuver, how to plan and plot without divulging his intentions, how to give and withhold.

But he kept that bag of tricks hidden under the polished veneer of the old families and the Ivy League. Upon meeting him for the first time, people beheld simply — as Josephus Daniels, his chief at the Navy Department, once put it — "as handsome a figure of an attractive young man as I had ever seen." He exhibited all the qualities of a prize show horse. It was sheer pleasure to be in his company. He had every advantage that family, money, good schooling, and good luck could provide, and ever since the mild social hardships of Groton and Harvard, his connections had brought him positions of prestige and power. His mother had gotten him his first job in a Wall Street law firm. The power brokers of his home county in upstate New York had invited him to enter state politics. He had been named to Woodrow Wilson's subcabinet at the age of thirty-one without even asking for the job. He had won the nomination for vice president without raising a finger for it. The odds had always favored him.

The poliovirus was at hand. It always had been at hand, circulating anywhere human beings lived together. In recent times it had become more dangerous. But the new danger lay in the humans, not in the virus.

When Franklin Roosevelt was growing up in the 1880s, hardly anyone even knew that of all the lame children in the world, a scattered few had been crippled by an infectious microorganism. Their number was inconsequential compared to the throngs of children brought down by the far more dangerous microorganisms that caused scarlet fever, yellow fever, typhoid fever, cholera, smallpox, tuberculosis, whooping cough, and diphtheria. The poliovirus could kill and maim. But for most of its history it seldom did so.

The reason seems paradoxical. Until the twentieth century, the poliovirus had caused so little harm because it had been so common in the human community.

The poliovirus passes from person to person via specks of human waste, and before the coming of modern sanitation in the late 1800s, specks of waste were practically as common as dust. In a nineteenth-century metropolis such as New York, for example, the soaring population overloaded leaky privies, the contents of which often drained into the water supply. The pits beneath the privies were supposed to be cleaned out regularly, their contents hauled away by "night soil" men and dumped in the rivers. But this makeshift system left plenty of fecal matter in haphazard circulation. The existence of infectious micro-organisms — germs — was essentially unknown, so hand washing was not the habitual practice it would become in the twentieth century. Only the wealthy had running water inside their homes. Everyone else had to haul whatever water they needed, which meant there was little to be spared for cleaning. In many households laundry was done infrequently and indifferently, usually with dirty water, and daily bathing was a luxury few could afford. From hand to hand, hand to food, and hand to mouth, specks and smears of feces were heedlessly passed around on every street and in every home. The poliovirus rode along.

To propagate, it needed to get inside people. Naturally, it found most of its hosts among infants and young children, the sloppiest members of the human tribe. Only a rare child grew up without ingesting the poliovirus. It moved from child to child, as the medical historian John R. Paul put it, "almost in the same manner that air rushes into a vacuum or water seeks its own level."

But the vast majority escaped serious illness. Their immune systems saved them. A child infected in infancy would likely be protected by antibodies passed through the placenta from his mother. If infected later in childhood, other agents in the immune system were likely to keep him safe.

Whenever a tiny intruder enters the human body — a grain of pollen sniffed up the nose, a bacterium or virus that goes down the throat, a sliver poking into the skin — immune cells rush to the scene. First come the cells called *phages,* from the Greek root "to eat." They are blunt weapons that recognize only one distinction among the objects they encounter — the distinction between "self" and "nonself." Anything

49

they find that is "nonself," they consume and destroy. But some bits of "nonself" survive this defense.

The next line of cellular defenders, the *lymphocytes,* are slower to react but more sophisticated. They enjoy a marvelous ability to adapt to specific intruders. Locking with a poliovirus, for example, the lymphocyte will clone itself over and over again, creating a legion of new, specialized cells whose sole function is to lock with any new poliovirus and destroy it. These cells remain in the human system for good. They guard against any new infection. They *immunize* the host.

So went the quiet career of the poliovirus in the era of ubiquitous human waste. A viral particle surviving outside the body in its fecal vessel would inevitably wind up in the mouth of nearly every baby. It would multiply in the child's intestine. But the immune system would suppress any severe infection and generate lymphocytes to immunize the child against all future infections. Copies of the virus would be shed in the child's feces and get into other children. But most of them, too, would shed the virus with no harm done. And here another benefit emerged.

In the feces of an infected child, there

would be intact, or "live," copies of the poliovirus as well as copies destroyed by the immune system. Yet these "killed" copies, as they are called, if *they* entered a human host, would provoke the defensive reaction of lymphocytes just as a healthy virus would. The "killed" virus could not make a person sick. But it could stimulate a lifelong immunity. The poliovirus spread through sewage. But — incredibly — so did immunity to the poliovirus.

A few developed poliomyelitis, but only a few.

Then came the American Civil War and a tidal wave of death by disease — far more deaths than were caused by cannonballs and bullets. This prompted calls for a revolution in sanitation. The germ theory of disease was not yet widely accepted. Diseases were generally understood to be the result of accumulated filth and the "miasmas," or smelly clouds, that filth produced. So the obvious remedy was cleanliness, both in the management of daily life and in the running of cities and towns. When cleanliness crusades were seen to work against certain diseases, more and more cities and towns took on the expense of installing sewer systems. By the 1880s and 1890s, many American communities had toilets to flush, and as the germ theory of disease became well known, many Americans were keeping themselves cleaner.

With this, the situation of the polivirus began to change. In one community after another, as privies and cesspools gave way to flush toilets and underground pipes that whisked feces away to be decontaminated, the poliovirus became less common, in both its "live" and its "killed" state. More and more children reached school age without encountering it. So they never developed the lymphocytes that would protect them against it. Gradually, here and there in Europe and North America — and often in the most sanitary communities — clusters of children grew up without the usual cadre of defenses against the poliovirus. Sanitation in these places had not extinguished the virus but merely excluded it. If the virus got loose here, among people lacking the usual immunities, it would be far more dangerous than before.

These facts about the poliovirus were unknown even to the best doctors practicing during Franklin Roosevelt's boyhood in the 1880s. By 1921, scientists had discovered that poliomyelitis was caused by a contagious virus. But how the virus was transmitted from person to person remained a mystery.

Thanks mostly to medical pioneers such as Louis Pasteur and Joseph Lister, doctors now accepted the germ theory of disease. But in many cases they knew little about how a *particular* microorganism passed from one person to another. They didn't know, for instance, whether the poliovirus was transmitted by droplets from a sneeze or from hand to hand. They didn't know if it was carried by insects or by tainted food or water. They didn't know if a germ could survive on a tabletop and they didn't know why an epidemic arose in one town but not in another.

So in 1893, doctors in and around Boston were at a loss to explain twenty-six cases of paralytic poliomyelitis — several times the number they had seen in any previous year. The following summer, the town of Rutland, Vermont, saw 132 cases — a genuine epidemic in that small town — and most of the victims were not babies but older children. The disease had become known as "infantile paralysis" because so many of the victims had indeed been infants. But in Rutland, a number of adults were struck as well. Year after year, more outbreaks occurred, but the numbers remained insignificant compared to the great killers.

Then, in the summer of 1916, the disease struck with bewildering force. Some 27,000 Americans were diagnosed. More than 6,000 died; many more were paralyzed. The epidemic was worst in New York City, where more than 9,000 were paralyzed, including large numbers of babies. Frightened parents rushed their children out of the city. Public health officials imposed quarantines. But none of these measures seemed to do any good. Health officials could give parents only commonsense advice about protecting their children: prevent overfatigue; keep them away from large gatherings and from persons with colds, since it was possible the infecting agent was expelled from the nose or throat in coughs and sneezes; avoid ice cream parlors, soda fountains, and restaurants suspected of uncleanliness; keep children's fingers out of their noses; keep them away from dust raised by the sweeping of streets, sidewalks, and homes; swat flies. How any parent could hope to do all this was a perplexity. The result was rampant anxiety.

In the summers of 1917, 1918, 1919, and 1920, outbreaks were smaller and more isolated. Influenza was a much greater danger in those years, and the fear of infantile paralysis faded. But doctors could no more explain why "the infantile" had receded than they could explain why it had attacked so brutally in 1916.

Now, in 1921, the disease's summer season was beginning again.

New York's first cases were reported in the last week of July in upstate Utica. Then several children were struck in Westchester County, just north of New York City. Three cases, all children, were reported in nearby Paterson, New Jersey.

The numbers were small. Public health officials saw no need to fear a recurrence of 1916; and even if they had, they would not have known how to prevent it.

Epidemiology and history are nowhere near precise enough to trace the exact events that led to Franklin Roosevelt's infection. But one can map the most likely possibilities.

One of the stronger possibilities is that somewhere in New York or northern New Jersey, in late June or early July, the poliovirus entered a particular boy who was bound for the Boy Scout campsites at Bear Mountain. Down in his small intestine, the virus was snagged by a crooked projection that protruded like a tiny tree branch from the wall of an intestinal cell. Virus and cell interlocked. Then the virus penetrated the cell wall and began to make copies of itself.

Over the next few days, the boy may or may not have felt ill. If he did, it was probably no more than a slight stomachache or headache, and certainly not severe enough to make him tell his mother. He would not have wanted to miss that trip up the Hudson River.

That was one possible source of infection — a Boy Scout infected at home.

Another possible source was associated with the terrain of Bear Mountain itself. The park sits in the Hudson Highlands, the rumpled ridge that shoulders up to the river between New York City and West Point. The mountain and the lands nearby had become a public preserve by the generosity of Mary Averell Harriman, widow of the banking and railroad magnate E. H. Harriman. As a boy in the 1850s, E. H. Harriman had often hiked through the woods of the Highlands. In 1885 he purchased a chunk of forest southwest of Bear Mountain to protect the land from encroachment by lumber and mining interests, and he built a summer home there. Over the years he added more tracts to the original to create one of the great natural preserves in the northeastern United States. After Harriman's death in

1909, Mrs. Harriman arranged to give thousands of acres to the state as a woodland retreat for New York's millions, provided the state give up its plan to move the Sing Sing penitentiary to Bear Mountain and instead make that property a public park as well. So these sprawling tracts of forest became the first of America's great state parks — two adjoining parks, actually: Bear Mountain State Park along the western shore of the Hudson; and Harriman State Park, in the rolling woodlands southwest of the mountain.

In the 1910s, construction crews swarmed through the woods, damming streams to make lakes and building pavilions, campgrounds, docks, icehouses, and a network of roads and trails.

Then crowds of New Yorkers came, and by 1920 the park's boosters were calling it "the greatest playground in the world," with more visitors annually than all the national parks combined. It had been conceived as a place of escape from the city, but in fact, on the busiest days of July and August, the whole city seemed to have come to the park. Catching the Hudson Day Line steamer in Manhattan for a trip to Bear Mountain was a highlight of the season for thousands of New York families. Many visitors were sponsored by settlement houses and philan-thropists in the belief that fresh air and rustic pleasures were good medicine for the poor and their children — delinquent children, crippled children, working boys and girls, orphans. Then there were the Boy Scouts, who came in packs of roughly two thousand at a time, with a staff of fifty, each group staying for two weeks at a string of sixteen permanent campsites built around three lovely man-made lakes — Upper, Middle, and Lower Kanawauke Lakes. So on any given day of the summer, the population of a fair-sized city was hiking the trails, roaming the woods, eating lunches out of picnic hampers, wading in the streams, and swimming in the lakes and ponds.

This was the Harrimans' dream come true. But the park's popularity came too quickly. Almost no one knew it, but by 1920 the water at Bear Mountain was dangerous.

In the fall of that year, at the request of New York's Public Health Council, the state Department of Health sent its water-quality expert, Earl Devendorf, a civil engineer, to make an inspection of sanitary conditions throughout the park. After a thorough survey, Devendorf concluded that the human invasion of the Bear Mountain and

Harriman forests had outpaced the authorities' ability to keep the park's drinking water clean. At some bathing beaches and campsites, he reported, chemical toilets had been installed, but there were not enough of them, and waste was being disposed of improperly. At many sites the pit privies were "in an insanitary condition." The danger of contamination was not confined to the campsites. Down in the ground below the Highlands, spurts and sheets of molten lava had long ago penetrated the ancient beds of granite. The native granite and the lava now formed something like a petrified sandwich of many layers, shot through with cracks and fissures. Through these long, wandering cracks, groundwater could move for miles. No one really knew where a bucket of water drawn at the Boy Scout camps had come from. For this reason, Devendorf said, all those springs and wells were to be "viewed with suspicion." As the engineer pointed out, "With the very large summer population, consisting mainly of young boys and girls and numbering at times over 75,000 which roam promiscuously over the entire park area, any supply derived from a stream, pond or spring is subject to the accidental, incidental or chance pollution from such a population."

In plainer words, children playing outdoors in the summertime are apt to shit in the woods. And, as Devendorf said, "the probability of [disease] carriers being present in such a large population is very great."

In fact, Devendorf had discovered that nearly every spring and well in the camping region of the park contained specimens of coliform bacteria. This indicated the presence of unfiltered human waste in the water. So the poliovirus was in the water too.

It was late afternoon when *Pocantico* deposited its passengers at the Bear Mountain docks. Buses carried them around the mountain and down Seven Lakes Road through "keen country," as a brochure described it; it was "wild, big, away from everywhere, with inspiring heights." At the camps, under old stands of oak, ash, and hemlock, Roosevelt and his party found 2,100 boys: 1,200 of them from New York, the rest from New Jersey.

Boys and men convened at the mess hall for what the newspapers called "a regular old-fashioned southern chicken dinner." Franklin Roosevelt was chosen as toastmaster. With four sons at home under the age of fourteen, he had no trouble making a bunch of boys laugh. His yearning to charm an audience, whether a crowd of a thousand or a single soul he had just met, was inexhaustible.

He was always quick to shake hands.

Like a seed, the virus had come into being as one of millions, nearly all of which would miss their marks, fall apart, and blow away. Survival of the line depended on just one finding a host cell and beginning anew the process of re-creation.

If the virus came by water — that is, from one of the tainted wells or ponds somewhere in the park — it was now at the campsite. Perhaps it was suspended in a bucket of water or a pitcher of lemonade. It might have been floating in a basin where the forks were soaked after dinner; then the forks were gathered quickly and placed on a picnic table next to pieces of pie set out for dessert.

Or the virus may have stuck to the finger of the infected boy from New York or New Jersey. Maybe he had run from the privy to the mess tent without washing his hands. Maybe he had picked up an apple from a bowl or a piece of fried chicken from a platter and then, when a friend called him away, put the apple or the piece of chicken back.

Perhaps he had run up to greet the famous man.

Whether it came by the water or the boy or by some other unknowable route, the virus was now directly at hand. From the tainted cup or the dirty fork, or from the boy's hand to Roosevelt's hand, from the red surface of the apple or the crispy skin of the chicken, from Roosevelt's hand to his tongue, the virus passed into Roosevelt's mouth. He swallowed.

CHAPTER 2
SYMPTOMS

Pocantico delivered FDR back to Manhattan that night in time for him to sleep at his home at 49 East 65th Street. Only the servants were there; his wife and children were up at the family's summer home on Campobello Island, just off the eastern tip of Maine. In the morning he went downtown to his office, where he had paperwork to clear off his desk. He was assisted by Marguerite A. LeHand, a tall young woman of twenty-three with an extraordinary combination of intelligence, efficiency, good cheer, and wit. She had worked in the Navy Department, then in the offices of the Cox-Roosevelt campaign, where FDR's wife, Eleanor Roosevelt, noticed her ability and suggested that FDR hire her as his personal secretary.

Miss LeHand and FDR finished the work in a few hours. He was set to spend several days at the family's estate at Hyde Park,

63

New York, two hours north of New York by train, where a mass of disorganized personal papers from the Navy Department needed his attention. Then he would spend a couple of weeks with family and friends at Campobello.

Marguerite LeHand, who was perhaps already half in love with her new boss, watched him leave the office. Years later, when she was far into her tenure in Roosevelt's closest circle, she was asked what made a good secretary, and she replied: "The first thing for a private secretary to do is to study her employer." She had studied her employer well already, and a few days later she wrote Mrs. Roosevelt: "I thought he looked quite tired when he left."

If the poliovirus entered Roosevelt's body at Bear Mountain, it probably infected others there too. Yet there is no evidence of an outbreak among the Boy Scouts. Reported cases of polio in New York State mounted for several weeks. But the numbers were highest more than two hundred miles away, in and around upstate Utica, not in the region of New York City, where most of the Scouts lived. If any others were infected that night at Bear Mountain, it appears that all or nearly all fought off the virus and remained healthy.

Maybe the terrible events that overtook Roosevelt in the following days and weeks were the result of sheer bad luck, a one-in-a-million chance. Maybe the virus eluded every agent of his immune system purely by accident. But it is hard to avoid the suspicion that he was especially vulnerable.

If so, why?

Several factors might have played a part, acting alone or in concert.

The first factor was the condition Marguerite LeHand noticed on July 29. Roosevelt was indeed tired. He had been driving himself without a pause for many months. And a few days earlier, in the middle of July, he had undergone an ordeal that shook his confidence and taxed his remaining stamina.

It had arisen from an old scandal at the naval training station at Newport, Rhode Island. Two years earlier, in 1919, newspapers had printed allegations of homosexual liaisons among sailors and civilians there. Roosevelt was then the navy's assistant secretary, or second in command, in charge of the enormous department's day-to-day affairs. He had authorized an investigation at Newport, though whether he had authorized the particular surveillance methods — which included the use of young sailors to entrap others into sexual encounters — was a matter of dispute. Without evidence, the *Providence Journal* accused Roosevelt of personally directing the whole operation, thus imperiling the morals of the sailors used as bait, some of them teenagers. Roosevelt denied it. He said he had done no more than order officers to clean up vice at the station. The moment he learned about the admittedly outrageous methods, he said, he had ordered them stopped.

The hubbub faded, then flared again during the 1920 campaign as Republicans looked for ways to embarrass the Cox-Roosevelt ticket. After the Democrats were defeated, Republicans in the U.S. Senate continued to gather evidence. Then, in mid-July 1921, Josephus Daniels, Roosevelt's old chief at the Navy Department and a leading Democrat, heard that senators were about to release findings "libelous" to both himself and FDR. He urged Roosevelt to mount a defense in person.

FDR rushed to Washington. When he reached the capital, his accusers gave him a single day to read and prepare a response to some six thousand pages of testimony. In the poisonous Potomac heat he paged through the volumes to find renewed charges that he "must have known" about and likely approved "most deplorable, disgraceful and unnatural" acts. He scribbled a forceful denial and issued it to reporters that evening, but it was too late. The Republican majority had released its report to the press without waiting for his response. The coverage was embarrassing, including a front-page headline in the next morning's *New York Times.* But it was not as heavy as FDR and Daniels had feared, and, much to their relief, there had been no follow-up in the two weeks since.

Still, FDR was unnerved. He seethed over the affair for days. He was especially angry at Senator Henry Wilder Keyes of New Hampshire, chairman of the investigating committee, a fellow Harvardian whom Roosevelt believed had misled and maligned him. FDR vented his fury in a letter, chastising Keyes for his "despicable action" and calling him the only Harvard man he had ever known "to be personally and wilfully dishonorable. . . . My only hope is that you will live long enough to appreciate that you have violated decency and truth, and that you will pray your maker for forgiveness."

At first glance, the depth of Roosevelt's anger at Senator Keyes is a little hard to fathom. After all, FDR was not running for office just then, in 1921, so the old scandal posed no immediate danger. And whatever investigative tactics he had authorized or not authorized, it was pretty clear the Republicans were simply recycling old stuff in the running warfare between the parties. That FDR was so badly shaken can be understood only if one appreciates that the stakes, in his eyes, were enormous. He was not just playing a short-term game for statewide office in New York. He was playing a long-run game for the presidency. In that game, every precaution must be taken to protect one's good name.

The notion of running for president occurs to some men only when they are well into their careers, and it dawns on them that they are at least as bright as the other fellows running, so why not give it a try? For others the presidency beckons much earlier and guides their steps for many years. Roosevelt was one of the latter. Near the end of his life, with intimates, he "spoke of the presidency as having been the controlling guide to all his career." He later told a British reporter: "For twenty years I had a perfectly natural and laudable ambition to become president, and was obliged to behave like a man who wants to be elected president."

He certainly had conceived of the goal by

the time he was a student at Harvard, from 1900 to 1903. Spinning tales of his future to the family of Alice Sohier, a gorgeous Boston debutante whom he courted hard for a time, he had said that "he thought he might one day be President." (One of Alice's cousins had made the company laugh by asking: "Who *else* thinks so?")

He spoke in more detail a few years later, as a junior law clerk at the New York firm of Carter Ledyard & Milburn. One day in 1907, when the clerks were sitting around talking about their plans, FDR confided that he didn't intend to stay in the law for long. According to a colleague, Grenville Clark, he told the fellows that he meant to enter politics. Not only that, but "he wanted to be and thought he had a real chance to be president." He planned to follow the exact path taken by his distant cousin, Theodore Roosevelt, then occupying the White House. First he would win a seat in the New York state legislature, just as T.R. had. Then he would go to Washington as assistant secretary of the navy, also like cousin Theodore. Next he would run for governor of New York (T.R. had been elected to that post in 1898), and "anyone who is governor of New York has a good chance to be President, with any luck." ("I do not recall that . . .

any of us deprecated his ambition or even smiled at it as we might perhaps have done," Grenville Clark wrote later. "It seemed proper and sincere; and moreover, as he put it, quite reasonable.")

Reasonable or not, he took the first of these steps in 1910. His late father, James Roosevelt, had been a friend of the last Democratic president, Grover Cleveland, and although the courtly James Roosevelt had been no politician in the strict sense, he had done his civic duty as a leader in the village of Hyde Park in upstate Dutchess County, where Franklin was raised. Now FDR himself, at age twenty-eight, began to attend civic meetings in Hyde Park, and soon politicians from the neighboring city of Poughkeepsie, recognizing the value of the young man's name, asked him to run for a vacant seat in the state senate. He agreed, and, quite to the surprise of everyone in Republican Dutchess, he was elected. In Albany he promptly made his name as a reform-minded opponent of New York City's corrupt and powerful Democratic machine, universally known by the name of its meeting place, Tammany Hall. He also joined progressive Democrats who were backing Governor Woodrow Wilson of New Jersey for the presidency.

Then came the second step in his pursuit of the presidency. At the Democratic national convention in Baltimore in 1912 — the convention that nominated Wilson — FDR became friendly with Josephus Daniels of North Carolina, editor and publisher of the *Raleigh News and Observer,* a William Jennings Bryan man who, with the Great Commoner three times defeated for president, had become Woodrow Wilson's most influential supporter in the South. Though Daniels was never known to have set foot on the deck of a ship, Wilson asked him to be secretary of the navy; and then Daniels, considering choices for his second, thought of the energetic New Yorker he had met in Baltimore — in part, no doubt, simply because the only well-known assistant secretary of the navy before that time had been Theodore Roosevelt. On the morning of Wilson's inauguration in Washington, Daniels and FDR ran into each other in the lobby of the Willard Hotel, and the older man asked the younger how he would like the job. Roosevelt said he would be delighted.

"I always thought he had this in mind," Daniels said later — that "Theodore Roosevelt had gone up that way."

Indeed, the example of Theodore Roosevelt, the largest figure in American society since Lincoln, was one of the most powerful forces in FDR's life. Many people revered him from afar as a paragon: virile, courageous, brilliant, far-sighted. But to FDR he was no distant idol. The two were fifth cousins and a generation apart, but, more important, the older man had been a good friend to both of Franklin's parents. FDR's father had once courted T.R.'s older sister; and T.R.'s brother, Elliott Roosevelt, had been Franklin's godfather. In letters to Franklin, his mother called cousin Theodore "your noble kinsman." (He was perhaps the only politician of her generation whom Sara Roosevelt did not regard with haughty distaste.) FDR carried vivid memories of boyhood visits to Sagamore Hill, the dark house on the north shore of Long Island where T.R. led his five children and their friends through rugged hikes and games (so noisy and outsized compared to FDR's quiet rides on horseback with the elderly James Roosevelt, a good-natured and loving father, but so gray, even feeble, by contrast to the volcanic T.R.). As a teenager at Groton School, FDR had been best known for his connection to the great Rough Rider of 1898, and he had ordered pince-nez spectacles just like his cousin's.

His vaulting ambition to tie his own life to the example of his "noble kinsman" took its most extraordinary turn when he married the girl T.R. called "my favorite niece," Anna Eleanor Roosevelt.

FDR had known her vaguely for years as a distant and younger cousin. But in 1902, just back from school in France, she was a new creature to him, very different from most of the girls he knew in New York and Boston — and she was now the favorite niece of the fabulous president of the United States. She was tall, reflective, kind, vulnerable, not beautiful by conventional standards but vividly appealing, with "a very good mind," as he put it. He wooed her, then convinced his mother he meant to marry her, and in 1905 he did so. President Roosevelt gave her away at the wedding, substituting for the girl's father, who had died of alcoholism years earlier. "Well, Franklin," the president said, "there's nothing like keeping the name in the family." FDR hung a portrait of the president in his bedroom near a Thomas Nast cartoon depicting T.R. as a young state legislator conferring with President Grover Cleveland, the Democratic hero of Franklin's father — three paternal models linked in a single image. FDR now could comfortably refer to

T.R. as "Uncle Ted."

By the time Theodore Roosevelt died in
1919, FDR's ambition for the presidency
was no longer an adolescent's dream. It was
a matter of pragmatic planning on the part
of a credible young politician rising toward
prominence on the national scene, tempered
by striving and setbacks. He had tried for a
U.S. Senate nomination in 1914 and lost.
When the country went to war in 1917 he
had asked repeatedly for a battle assignment
— an important credential for any postwar
political campaign — but Woodrow Wilson
had insisted he stay at his Navy Department
post in Washington. In the campaign of
1920, most people perceived that bland
James Cox of Ohio was destined to join
what one writer called "the ghostly procession of Democratic presidential nominees
who have run for the Presidency without a
chance of being elected." But as Cox's running mate, FDR made the most of the opportunity, campaigning well and making
friends with hundreds of party leaders
across the country. Afterward, he helped his
campaign aides to find jobs, and he signaled
them to be ready when the trumpet sounded
on some morning to come. One of these
friends, Tom Lynch, a Poughkeepsie florist
and part-time pol who had been boosting

FDR since the first state senate campaign, was heartbroken over the loss. "Tom," FDR assured Lynch, "1932 will be our year."

He was no longer so reckless as to speak of his presidential hopes with anyone but close associates. But he was utterly dedicated to the goal. So it was no wonder that when the Republicans resurrected the homosexual scandal at Newport, FDR was alarmed, especially when senators made it so difficult for him to put his own case before the public. His life's purpose was at stake. When the newspapers dropped the affair after one day's dose of headlines, it appeared that he had escaped a catastrophe. He kept the draft of his furious letter to Senator Keyes on his desk for a while, then filed it away, jotting on the envelope: "Not sent — what was the use?" But to a man of his temperament, with his ambitions, the incident was deeply disturbing — disturbing enough, quite possibly, to put a chink in the armor of his body's immunities.

Emotional stress can weaken the body's immune system. Medical scientists and physicians are not sure precisely why or how this happens. But they have little doubt that a link exists. Somewhere in the body's intricate cellular architecture, signals sent by the brain under stress can radiate through the endocrine and immune systems to confound the body's response to danger.

Of course, it may be far-fetched to think that a few Republican senators got so thoroughly under Roosevelt's skin that they disturbed his immune system. But anyone who looks through FDR's long history of medical troubles before 1921 will suspect that his immune system was anything but robust to begin with. This too may help to explain his particular vulnerability to the poliovirus.

At the age of seven, he had typhoid fever. At Groton School and Harvard, he suffered from scarlet fever, measles, mumps, and chronic sinus infections and colds. On his honeymoon in 1905, he had lumbago and persistent hives, which can indicate a malfunctioning immune system. In 1911 he developed severe sinusitis and fever, losing ten pounds in a few days. In 1912 a second dose of typhoid fever forced him to forgo campaigning for reelection to the state senate. He had stomach trouble in the summer of 1913; appendicitis in 1915; a severe throat infection in 1916; and another throat infection in 1917 that put him in the hospital for several days. In 1918, leaving Europe near the end of the war, he caught the Spanish influenza, developed double pneumonia, and nearly died. In 1919 he had tonsillitis. Josephus Daniels said his assistant secretary seemed to pick up every bug that came down the pike.

If his immune system was weak, why might that have been so?

Strong immune systems are most likely to develop in a city, a town, a dwelling, or a school where there are lots of babies and children. All day long, within inches of each other, they cough and sneeze and wipe their noses and scratch their bottoms. They don't wash their hands. They share food, drink, and toys. They put things in their mouths. In their play they touch each other, jostling and pushing. Germs spread and the children get sick, but their immune systems gradually gain strength.

But at the home of James and Sara Delano Roosevelt in the 1880s, there was only one child, and he spent very little time with other children.

The Roosevelts raised Franklin in a large, comfortable house on a tranquil estate that sloped down to the majestic mid-Hudson through quiet forests and fields. The boy did not have a cossetted, indoor childhood. He roamed the woods, rode horses, and shot birds. But he did these things alone or

with his aging father, and his frequent illnesses caused his mother to keep a tight
rein on his dealings with other children. His
only sibling was his half-brother, James
Roosevelt Roosevelt, called Rosy, who was
James Roosevelt's son by a previous marriage. Rosy was a year older than Franklin's
mother, so the brothers were hardly play-
mates. Sara allowed Franklin to play with
only a handful of other children: chiefly Ed-
mund and Archibald Rogers, sons of a mil-
lionnaire who lived on another estate half a
mile away; and Mary Newbold, a little girl
who lived at the estate next door to the Roosevelts. Sometimes Franklin went sledding
with other boys, mostly the sons of workers
on the river estates, but these were not the
close and constant contacts of city boys running in packs all year long. There were no
overnight visits. "I never should allow a
small boy to visit a friend over night,
especially in the same town," Sara declared.
"It is always a mistake." She brought in tutors to teach her son in the home — nothing unusual for a wealthy family like the
Roosevelts, but it was another circumstance
that kept young Franklin away from other
children. Hyde Park was not remote from
civilization — the main road for horse-
drawn traffic between New York and Albany

ran right outside the front gates of the property — but it was not the sort of place where infectious microbes spread quickly from person to person. And water for the Roosevelt kitchen and baths came from the family's own springs just a few yards from the house.

In all likelihood, FDR never encountered the poliovirus before the outing at Bear Mountain. If so, he never developed the specific immunity that would have protected him from it. So even if the shock of the Newport scandal had no effect on his immune system whatever, he was almost certainly a textbook "susceptible" — by genetic inheritance or by the circumstances of his upbringing or both.

Roosevelt combed through his old Navy papers at the family home at Hyde Park for the last days of July and the first days of August. Then he returned to New York City and prepared for his vacation far up the New England coast at Campobello Island. He was going with his friend and employer, Van Lear Black, aboard Black's oceangoing yacht.

Black was a sportsman, a *bon vivant,* and one of the wealthiest men in Maryland. (His holdings included the powerful *Baltimore*

Sun.) He was also an active Democrat. He had met Roosevelt in 1912 at the Democratic convention in Baltimore, where the two discovered a mutual love of sailing and fishing. When FDR found himself out of work after the Democrats' defeat in 1920, Black invited him to take charge of the New York office of his insurance firm, the Fidelity & Deposit Company of Maryland. The "F & D" insured contracts between major entities, public and private — hardly a glamorous business for the likes of FDR, but, as Black perceived, his friend's contacts in government, labor, and industry could generate deals. So Black offered FDR a salary of $25,000 a year — five times his navy pay — and said he could divide his days between the F & D and the law firm he had formed with two old friends, Grenville Emmett and Langdon Marvin. And it was understood he could take whatever time he needed for politics. His associates at both firms gave him that time for the sake of including his very prominent name on the office door and the letterhead.

It was now the high season for ocean cruising, so Roosevelt invited Black, with his family and friends, to spend a few days in the waters around Campobello. On Friday, August 5, they departed New York

80

aboard Black's yacht, *Sabalo,* and enjoyed two marvelous days on the Atlantic. Later FDR remembered that he had "never laughed as much as we all did on the cruise up the Coast of Maine in 1921."

Campobello Island is a conifer-dotted fragment of rock some ten miles long by three miles wide. It belongs to the Canadian province of New Brunswick, though only a few yards of water separate the island from the fishing village of Lubec, Maine, at the easternmost point of the continental United States. James and Sara Roosevelt had chosen it as a summer retreat when Franklin was two years old, partly to escape the summertime risk of malaria in the Hudson River Valley. In the 1880s, many wealthy New Yorkers were building summer places in Maine that were not quite so remote, at Bar Harbor or Kennebunkport, but the Roosevelts chose Campobello for its stark beauty, its superb climate, and its reputation for extraordinarily clean air. Hay fever and asthma were said to be unknown there. That appealed to the parents of a toddler prone to getting sick. For a year or two they rented rooms at the new hotel on the island. Then they built a house where the little family spent parts of many summers. After

Franklin and Eleanor Roosevelt were married, the family's next-door neighbor on Campobello offered to sell her place to Sara Roosevelt, provided she give the house to the young couple. It stood on ten acres, a broad red house with a barnlike mansard roof, substantial and inviting, a pleasant agglomeration of gables, chimneys, and windows. From the wide porch the family looked out across miles of blue-gray water to the western horizon, where the sun set over scattered islands, the forested mainland, and the tiny white buildings of Eastport, Maine. There was no electricity, no telephone. At night the family lit gas lamps and candles.

Approaching the narrow Lubec Channel, Van Lear Black's crew surrendered the tiller to Roosevelt. He had been sailing in these waters since, as a boy, he learned about the dangerous local tides and reefs from the island's fishing captains. He loved to exercise the keen coordination and acute sense of timing that were essential to the sailor. He took risks. He made passengers shudder as he skimmed through tidal shallows and skirted boulders and cliffs. Once, in 1916, he had piloted a U.S. Navy destroyer through these same narrows. The commander had been Lieutenant William F.

Halsey Jr., later commander of the U.S. Third Fleet in World War II. Entering the Grand Manan Channel in a dense fog, Halsey gave the tiller to the assistant secretary only with reluctance. A yacht-club sailor might know his way around a buoy in a catboat, Halsey remarked later, but a high-speed destroyer in a dangerous passage was an entirely different matter, for a turn swings a destroyer's stern in a much broader arc than its bow — too tricky for a mere weekend yachtsman. But as Roosevelt steered the ship into its first turn through the fog, Halsey saw him glance over his shoulder to check the swing of the stern. "My worries were over," Halsey said. "He knew his business."

Now Roosevelt steered *Sabalo* through the same passage, then emerged into Passamaquoddy Bay and around the point of Friar's Head toward his anchorage.

Eleanor Roosevelt's summer household was already busy. The Roosevelt children ran in two pairs with an unruly fifth in the middle. The older pair were Anna, the only girl, who had turned fifteen in May; and James, who was thirteen. Anna attended a private school in New York City; James had entered Groton the previous fall. The two youngest boys were Franklin Jr., soon to turn seven; and John, who was five. In the middle stood the lone wolf, eleven-year-old Elliott, named for Eleanor's adored father, Theodore Roosevelt's brother.

The children's governess, Jean Sherwood, was with the family for the summer. Miss Sherwood's mother, who had become friendly with Eleanor, was visiting. Also there were FDR's aide, Louis Howe; Howe's wife, Grace; and the Howes' young son, Hartley.

The children were anticipating a trip by canoe up the nearby St. Croix River for fishing and a stay of one or two nights in some cabins on the river. They had endured several weeks at the cottage with their mother, who prescribed long hours of study every day. The fun began whenever FDR came. They had scarcely seen him at Campobello for several summers. In 1917 and 1918, the war had kept him in Washington except for a few stolen days. In 1919, both Franklin and Eleanor spent most of the summer at the Paris Peace Conference. FDR joined the family on the island in 1920 but then left for the Democratic convention at which he was nominated for the vice presidency.

Eleanor recalled later that FDR said he

felt "logy and tired" during his first couple of days on the island. But he was not going to let Van Lear Black and his party leave without a fishing expedition. Supplies were packed on the tender of *Sabalo.*

Eleven days had passed since the picnic at Bear Mountain. Symptoms of poliomyelitis usually appear between seven and fourteen days after infection.

As the virus incubates in the intestine, it often causes various combinations of symptoms that look like an ordinary "stomach flu." These include fever, headache, sore throat, and vomiting. It is terribly difficult to distinguish one infection from another in the first days. The only doctors really qualified to do so were those who had treated lots of acute infantile paralysis patients in the epidemics of recent summers.

One such doctor, as it happened, was Franklin Roosevelt's personal physician, an old Harvard friend and a neighbor on Manhattan's Upper East Side. He was Dr. George Draper, "Dan" to his friends, author of a leading text on poliomyelitis, a work he had written based on intensive work on Long Island during the 1916 epidemic. Draper had known many a good doctor to examine a child just coming down with poliomyelitis; see the symptoms of fever, drowsiness, diarrhea, and inflammation of the upper throat and tonsils; and diagnose a simple summer bug. Yet there were distinct and "delicate manifestations" in the polio patient, Draper wrote, a "subtle and striking difference" that was difficult to put into words but discernible to an experienced observer. These signs, in Draper's observation, included a "peculiar expression" and puffiness around the eyes, a "glazed porcelain quality" in the cornea, and often "a look of mingled apprehension and resentfulness, quite unlike the alert, bright and shining eye of other fevers."

In cases like this, Draper and other veterans of 1916 had learned to watch closely for the sudden emergence of another and more startling set of symptoms and signs. Only a small number of those infected with the poliovirus would exhibit them. Often the symptoms would begin with stiffness in the neck and backbone; the patient would report pain when bending at the waist or inclining the head. Doctors called this the "spine sign." Malaise and restlessness appear. The patient "seems to be busily and actively resisting some incomprehensible disturbance of its usual comfort," Draper wrote. "The whole organism seems to be composed of tensely drawn wires — a universal overstimulation." Muscles may twitch involuntarily. In some cases the doctor sees a clumsy tremor as the patient reaches to grasp an object. Many patients notice an uncomfortable sensitivity in the skin, sometimes ticklishness or numbness, more often an acute exaggeration of sensations in response to the normal stimuli of mere touching, pressure, heat, and cold.

In these cases, the virus has penetrated the tough membrane protecting the spinal cord and brain — the meninges — and entered the central nervous system. No one has ever determined precisely how or why this invasion occurs. It is not in the virus's evolutionary interest to do so. It's better for the virus to stay in the intestine, where it will eventually be flushed out of the body. Better for the human host too, since if the virus gets inside the spinal cord, with its cables of nerves running up and down the body, it may do grave damage to the nerves that govern movement — that is, the ability to stand, walk, and run.

When the brain wants a muscle to move — say, a muscle of the big toe in the right foot — it sends signals to a region of the spinal cord called the anterior horn. There, special cells pass the signal to long nerve fibers reaching down through the leg to the toe. When all goes well, the muscle in the toe receives the signal and obeys the brain's command to move. But the poliovirus wreaks havoc in the line. For reasons lost in some distant epoch of evolution, the virus has an affinity for anterior horn cells. If the virus bumps into such a cell, it sticks to it and gets inside. The result is partial or complete cellular destruction. Any brain signal that reaches the destroyed cell is simply lost, and the muscle in the toe never receives the brain's command to move.

In an even smaller number of those infected, the virus ascends to the upper spinal cord and the lower parts of the brain, where the devastation can paralyze muscles of breathing and swallowing. This is the disease in its worst form, the usual cause of death from poliomyelitis.

An autopsy discloses that the gray (*polio-*) marrow (*myel-*) of the spinal cord has become severely inflamed (*-itis*) — thus the term that appeared in medical texts. By 1921 authorities agreed that neither "infantile" nor "paralysis" properly defined a disease that caused paralysis only in a minority of the people infected by the virus, and one that struck not only infants but children of all ages as well as people in young adulthood — very few in their thirties, but some. But it would be years before the abbreviated "polio" replaced "infantile paralysis" as the common term for a disease that was more and more widely feared as its yearly visitations expanded.

If the rare doctor of George Draper's experience and insight had been along on *Sabalo*'s voyage; if FDR had spoken to him frankly about the symptoms he recalled later, not only fatigue and sluggishness but an odd hypersensitivity in the skin; if that doctor had examined Roosevelt closely and questioned him about other sensations he might have been feeling — stiffness in the neck, especially — he might have become alert to the possibility of poliomyelitis, and he might have intervened with the speed essential for any of the possible remedies. But of course no such doctor was along.

Off the coast of Campobello Island, FDR assigned himself the job of baiting hooks for Van Lear Black's fishing party. They were using the yacht's tender, the boat that ferried passengers and cargo between the yacht and a pier. The boat had two cockpits, one fore and one aft, with the hot engine in between. Only a narrow, varnished plank connected the two. Roosevelt had to scoot back and forth along this slick board, taking care not to fall against the engine. On one of these tricky passages, he lost his footing and fell into the ocean. A moment later he was up and out, dripping water and making jokes at his own expense: Wasn't it silly for an "old salt" like himself to fall in the drink while the landlubbers stayed safe on board?

It *was* odd for him to fall. He moved nearly as comfortably on the deck of a boat as he did on the carpeted corridors of his mother's home in Hyde Park. His coordination was normally excellent.

Roosevelt had swum many times in these waters, which averaged 51 degrees Fahrenheit in August — too cold for most swimmers to stay in for more than a few minutes. But he said later the water that day had been "so cold it seemed paralyzing." It felt colder than any water he had ever felt in his life.

Among the anterior horn cells in his spinal cord, the virus was now replicating.

At this early point, there was no way to predict the ultimate effect of Roosevelt's infection. From one victim to the next, the destruction of cells in the anterior horn varies widely. In some the number of cells destroyed is vast, causing total paralysis of all four limbs, with no hope of recovery. In others the cell damage is mild; few motor nerve cells are destroyed, and the undamaged cells compensate for the loss. Most cases fall somewhere in between. Certainly there are many cases in which paralysis comes on and then goes away. Why the damage is severe in one case and mild in the next has never been fully understood. Probably a number of factors are interwoven: the dose of virus received, the virulence of the particular strain, the strength of the infected person's immune system.

In cases that could go either way — severe or mild, permanent or passing — one factor has been clearly established: If a person has had the virus in his central nervous system for a few days, and he then engages in strenuous physical exertion, the risk of permanent paralysis rises.

As a teenager, FDR had eagerly accepted invitations to join the family of Theodore Roosevelt at Oyster Bay, Long Island, where T.R. led his children in his own domestic version of "the strenuous life," his ideal for American civilization. Now, at thirty-nine, FDR was about the age T.R. had been during those visits in the 1890s, and he followed T.R.'s example with his own children, especially during precious weeks at Campobello. "Father loved life on the island more than any of us," Jimmy Roosevelt recalled later, "but got to spend the least time there." He often rounded up every available child and no small number of adults for strenuous games and hikes around the island's edge. For the next couple of days they had "a wild, whooping, romping, running, sailing, picnicking time with him," Jimmy remembered. FDR's native exuberance and his urge to make up for frequent separations from the children pushed him to go absolutely all out.

His activities on Wednesday, August 10, would have exhausted a man half his age.

That morning, he said later, he continued to feel oddly depleted, as he had during the cruise up the coast. He hoped that exercise would revive him. So he resisted whatever impulse he felt to stay in and rest, and instead he set out for a day of sailing with Eleanor and the older children. Early in the afternoon, they caught sight of smoke rising from one of the heavily forested islands nearby. Roosevelt steered the twenty-foot, single-masted *Vireo* that way, anchored the boat, and led the children to pitch in with other volunteers to fight the fire. They beat at the flames with evergreen boughs and stamped on sparks that crawled through the spongy bed of needles at their feet. They worked in a haze of smoke. Anna remembered standing by a tall spruce, then recoiling as it caught fire, hearing "that awful roar of the flames as they quickly enveloped the whole tree." The Roosevelts labored in the blue haze and heat for much of the afternoon.

At length they broke away from the work, returned to *Vireo* and sailed home, grimy and tired, speckled with spark burns. They climbed the long slope from the rocky beach to the house — and then someone suggested a swim. Eleanor stayed behind, but the rest of them, after hours of sailing and firefighting, set off at a trot.

Because the ocean at Campobello is so terribly cold, the best place to swim is a long, narrow pond called Lake Glensevern, about a mile and a half across the island from the Roosevelt house. Despite the late-afternoon heat, FDR and the children jogged along a dirt road to reach the pond. They plunged into the water and swam across, a distance of about a hundred yards. On the far side of the pond, just over a rise, lay the island's southern beach and the ocean. FDR ran over the rise and plunged in for a dip in the ocean too. Then they all swam back across Lake Glensevern and dog-trotted home to the house.

FDR had failed to shake off his lethargy. "I didn't feel the usual reaction" to hard exercise, he said later, "the glow I'd expected."

Inside, he sat down to look at the mail and the newspapers.

The house was spacious and comfortable. Eleanor's taste in decorating was more casual than her mother-in-law's, so the cottage was free of the hulking Victorian furniture that crowded every room of the house at Hyde Park. Corridors lined with dark woodwork led to rooms full of light. The long central living room facing the water was furnished with cushioned wicker chairs and a window seat for surveying the sloping lawn and the great bay.

The children ran upstairs to change. Eleanor urged FDR to change into dry clothes too, but he said he just wanted to sit. He was "too tired even to dress," he remembered. "I'd never felt quite that way before."

When Eleanor called them all to the dining room, he said — "very quietly," Anna recalled — that his lower back ached and he felt ill. He thought he would skip dinner. If he had a cold, he didn't want it to get worse so that he would have to miss the camping trip with the children. He said he wanted to "get thoroughly warm." "There was no fuss," Anna remembered. Her father rose, walked across the polished hardwood floor of the living room, and climbed the stairs.

One of the earliest names given to the acute form of poliomyelitis was "paralysis of the morning," since so many of the stricken seemed perfectly well when they went to bed one night, then awoke the next day unable to move one or more of their limbs. The first hint that something is wrong with the muscles is often overshadowed by more troublesome symptoms — a severe headache, nausea, pain. Rubbery legs can be attributed to the usual weakness of a fever. An ache or a pain can have a thousand causes. Then, at some point in the midst of this, the patient goes to shift his foot or reach out a hand. Something is wrong. The limb fails to do as it's told. There may be a feeling of simple puzzlement, like the momentary confusion one feels when flipping a switch and a light fails to come on.

The chill lasted all night. In the morning he swung his legs out of bed and stood. His right knee felt odd. Some muscular problem seemed to have developed. Had he slept on it wrong? Injured it in all the running around of the day before? He put his weight on it, tried to walk off the sensation. He crossed the hall to the narrow bathroom and shaved, feeling considerably worse than he had the night before.

When Anna came upstairs with his breakfast on a tray, he smiled and joked with her. In the Roosevelt family, one did not "whine about trouble." But he couldn't possibly go on the camping trip and he had to tell Eleanor why: It wasn't just a minor muscle ache but really quite severe pain in the back of his legs — "stabbing pains," his son Elliott remembered him saying. Eleanor took his temperature: It was 102 degrees. He felt "thoroughly achy all over."

Eleanor decided the older children should go ahead with the trip as planned. She and the other adults would stay home with Franklin and the two younger boys. Supplies were packed into the boat of their island helper, the fisherman Franklin Calder. Eleanor directed Calder to stop in the village of Lubec and ask the doctor there to come over to the island.

Only one treatment in the early stage of poliomyelitis had yielded promising results.

Blood would be taken from a person who had survived the infection and thus developed antibodies to the poliovirus. The blood would be spun in a centrifuge to produce serum — a watery extract containing the virus-fighting antibodies. Then the serum was injected into the patient's spine once a day for three days. In some cases, this appeared to have arrested the paralysis creeping up a patient's body and saved motor nerves. Doctors were divided on the treatment's reliability. But to have even a chance of working, it had to be given as early in the disease process as possible. As Dr. George Draper pointed out: "When the anterior horn cells are finally destroyed no one imagines that they can be revived by serum or anything else." So any hope for such a treatment depended on the earliest possible diagnosis. But that was not to be.

Back across Lubec Channel came Dr. Eben Homer Bennet. He was a general practitioner, a graduate of Jefferson Medical College in Philadelphia. He cared for Lubec's fishermen and their families and for any of the summer people who got sick or had an accident. He had known the Roosevelts for years — "our faithful friend," Eleanor called him.

He found the recent nominee for the vice presidency in his bed upstairs complaining of a chill and aches and pains. A thermometer under the tongue showed a temperature of 102 degrees. There seems to have been little if any discussion of the weakness in the right knee. If the knee was mentioned, it would have been natural to attribute the problem to the highly strenuous exercise of the day before. In his remote village, Dr. Bennet probably never had seen a case of infantile paralysis, and cases among adults were rare enough that such a diagnosis, if it occurred to him at all, would have seemed far-fetched and certainly premature. That day, at least, he apparently thought the problem to be no more than a nasty summer cold.

Colonies of the poliovirus were now creeping upward through the spinal cord. The ensuing war between these viral invaders and the body's immunological defenders resulted in severe inflammation inside the spinal cord. The roaring inflammation, in turn, aroused the sensory nerve cells. For Roosevelt, the result was shooting, shocking pain in every one of the affected muscles. Adult patients have compared the sensation to having nails hammered into one's flesh, or to having one's teeth drilled without an anesthetic. Hallucinations and nightmares are not uncommon.

During the afternoon of August 11, FDR leaned forward, began to stand up, then stopped. His right knee now seemed too weak to support his weight on that side. He lay back down. By evening he was feeling the same weakness in his left knee.

When he awoke the next morning, Friday, both legs felt rubbery and flimsy. It wasn't that he had lost sensation. He could feel the fabric of his pajamas against his skin, and when he put his hands on his knees he could feel his hands. But when he willed his legs to move, they were listless. Rays of pain spread through his back and legs and feet. As the hours of Friday passed, more muscles seemed dormant. He couldn't tighten his buttocks or clench the muscles of his gut. By evening he realized he could not hold a pencil. There was something the matter with his thumbs. By the time he tried to go to sleep that night, he was unable to stand up at all.

CHAPTER 3
DIAGNOSIS

AUGUST 12 TO AUGUST 25, 1921

Eleanor Roosevelt knew basic skills in nursing, and she now put them to use on the second floor of the cottage, in the bedroom overlooking the bay. She helped her husband to eat, lifted and shifted his body to ease the ache of stationary limbs, helped him to relieve his bladder and bowels, and washed him afterward.

A spouse does such things out of love or out of duty. Even her closest friends could never be sure which motive predominated in Eleanor's mind after sixteen years of marriage, the birth of six children (one of them dead in infancy), and the discovery that her husband had fallen in love with another woman. "She had been hurt, cruelly hurt," her friend Marion Dickerman said. "She said she had forgiven but could not forget." Eleanor once told her friend Esther Lape "in very clear terms" that she no longer loved her husband. "That was her story,"

Lape said later. "Maybe she even half believed it. But I didn't. I don't think she ever stopped loving him."

That summer she was close to thirty-seven years old. She was unsettled and unhappy. Lately she had been searching for some safe harbor where she might feel fully useful and thus fulfilled. Her early life had been dominated by the traumatic losses of her cold and negligent mother, a younger brother, and her adored but alcoholic father, all dead between her eighth and eleventh birthdays. She was educated at a fine girls' school in England, where she showed glimmers of spectacular potential. Then she had married her charming fifth cousin (once removed), only to find herself under the thumb of a well-meaning but powerful mother-in-law who dominated the Roosevelts' home life and all but took over the rearing of the Roosevelt children.

Eleanor's intelligence was acute but largely untapped. She was capable of working extremely hard but so far had found little opportunity for work outside of her family. She felt and showed deep affection toward those close to her — except her husband, who had forfeited her trust; and, tragically, her children, who found her distracted and distant. She was a daughter of New York society who understood the rituals of that world but largely disdained them; a mother who supervised her children's activities closely yet worried that a woman should not seek fulfillment through her children; a woman with a strong social conscience but too many domestic responsibilities to exercise it.

As for the sad crisis in her marriage, there had been much gossip but only a few undisputed facts. They are as follows.

In 1916, when the Roosevelts were living in Washington, D.C., a young, unmarried woman, Lucy Mercer, had been introduced to them by Eleanor's aunt, Anna Roosevelt Cowles, Theodore Roosevelt's sister. Eleanor hired Miss Mercer as her social secretary. Over the next several years, Miss Mercer and Franklin were seen together in public several times. In 1918, when Franklin returned with pneumonia from a trip to Europe, Eleanor discovered love letters from Miss Mercer in his luggage. Relatives said later that Eleanor offered to divorce Franklin, but that Sara Roosevelt, who controlled the family fortune, warned her son that if he abandoned his family she would give him no more money, ever. The marriage survived, and in 1919 Miss Mercer married a wealthy widower.

In the three years since the crisis, Eleanor and Franklin had gone about the business of living their busy, complicated lives — together in name, but at arm's length from each other. The older children sensed tension between them and saw that they no longer shared a bedroom.

Five children and three households — a townhouse in Manhattan, the family estate in Hyde Park, and the summer house on Campobello — absorbed most of Eleanor's time and energy. Yet early in 1921 she had taken decisive steps into a sphere apart from her routine as wife, mother, and daughter-in-law. She already had decided to have little to do with the social world she had known before the war — Sara Roosevelt's sphere of society women who paid calls on each other, attended charity luncheons and teas, and gave expensive dinner parties. "The war had made that seem an impossible mode of living," Eleanor wrote later. She was powerfully drawn to the work being done by progressive women in the wake of the 19th Amendment, which extended the vote to women in 1920. Eleanor was indifferent to Franklin's nomination for vice president that year, but she agreed to join his campaign train. Then — tentatively, at first, but with increasing interest — she took up political activities of her own.

In the spring of 1921, she accepted an invitation to join the board of the new League of Women Voters. (These were nonpartisan activists who wanted the nation's enfranchised women to assert their political power, whatever their party.) And at the League's national convention that May, she was enthralled by the speeches of Carrie Chapman Catt and other leaders. She became friendly with the writer Esther Lape and the attorney Elizabeth Read, who were influential in the League and prototypes of the era's "New Woman" — that is, they were feminist and progressive in politics, defiant of domination by men, and unconventional in their domestic arrangements. Some were lesbians, like Lape and Read. Eleanor accepted their unconventionality, declaring that "no form of love is to be despised," and her circle of friendships with independent women began to broaden.

Then came her annual summer trek with the children to Campobello and her husband's illness.

Now, on the morning of Friday, August 12, she became "very anxious," and she summoned Dr. Bennet back to the island. The doctor took note of Roosevelt's increasingly obvious muscular symptoms but was "mystified," Eleanor recalled later. Her husband too was now in a state of desperate anxiety. They all agreed that more expert help was needed. Someone would have to find another doctor. They turned to Franklin's assistant, Louis Howe — "who, thank heavens, is here," Eleanor said, "for he has been the greatest help."

Louis Howe had been the man closest to Franklin Roosevelt for ten years, perhaps his one true intimate, but to say the two were friends misses the odd complexity of their relationship. Howe acted simultaneously as FDR's errand boy and as an older brother; he was both Roosevelt's employee and his senior advisor. Howe hectored and lectured a man ten years his junior whom he addressed as "Boss."

In 1921 Howe was a fifty-year-old ex-newsman in a body that appeared to be just about at the end of its string. People trying to be nice described his physique as "gnomelike" or "elfin," but the plain fact was that "he was a very little and very ugly man," as one who knew him at the navy said, with bulging dark eyes in an oversized head. He "looked like a singed cat," a New York pol once offered, and Howe himself bragged of being the "third ugliest man in

New York" — a defensive maneuver he deployed at who knew what cost. He was sloppy and he looked literally unclean, because as a youngster he had fallen off a bicycle onto his face and come away with specks of gravel permanently embedded in his cheeks. His looks made people uncomfortable on first impression, and his acid manners won few of them over — though the few people who became his devoted friends said he was loyal, thoughtful, and generous. He had once been an accomplished amateur actor, with a voice that was "astonishingly deep and dignified."

He insisted that people pronounce his first name *"Loo-ee"* because, he said, it was French. It was one of his offbeat little affectations, like his aromatic Sweet Caporal cigarettes. They were remnants of his upbringing around the rough edges of resort society in upstate Saratoga Springs. His father had been a newspaper editor and postmaster in that racetrack town when Ulysses S. Grant and Republican bosses rubbed shoulders with the Democratic kingpins of Tammany Hall at hotels, tracks, and theaters. Howe learned stage acting, politics, and newspapering in the same few square blocks.

As a statehouse reporter in Albany in

1911, he already had reached the point at which he was no longer content (as another member of the forlorn brotherhood of aging newsmen would later put it) "to wear out his hams sitting in marble corridors waiting for important people to lie to him." He grabbed the coattails of a promising politician on the rise, Thomas Mott Osborne, but Osborne soon found Howe irritating and fired him. Then Howe chanced to meet Franklin Roosevelt, newly arrived in Albany as a very young and naive state senator. Howe claimed later to have spotted a future president in the youngster, though it is more likely that he simply spotted a new chance for a regular paycheck. In any case, he began to tutor Roosevelt in the finer points of state politics, and soon the relationship bore fruit. FDR hired Howe to handle press contacts for the Woodrow Wilson organization in New York State, and it was Howe who ran — and won — FDR's campaign for reelection to the state senate when the candidate was flat on his back with typhoid fever in 1912. The little man had left newspapering behind. He was now what a later generation would call a political operative, and he was to become very good at the game.

When Roosevelt went to Washington,

Howe went along, taking the office next to FDR's in the State, War, and Navy Building, next to the White House. His title then and later was "secretary," but FDR referred to him simply as "my man." Josephus Daniels said Howe was one of the strangest men he ever met, but also one of the smartest — "much abler" than a run-of-the-mill Washington gofer. During the war, Secretary Daniels often asked Howe to write speeches and fix problems all through the Navy Department. But he became convinced that Howe would sabotage any interest of Daniels, the navy, or Woodrow Wilson himself if it would help advance Franklin Roosevelt's prospects for high office.

Howe was the key man in FDR's campaign for the vice presidency in 1920, heading up the band of aides who went on the campaign train to pound out press releases, line up rallies, and stay up late for poker with the man they called "the Boss" and "the Chief." He was FDR's speechwriter and press agent. He wrote fast and well, if quality is measured by mastery of the persuasive prose a politician must deploy in written documents ranging from thank-you notes to press releases to major speeches.

Howe and the four or five other men whom FDR gathered around himself were "harder, racier, more down to earth" than men of the Groton-and-Harvard sphere. Several were Baptists or Catholics, not upper-crust Episcopalians or Presbyterians, and generally of Irish or Scotch-Irish ancestry. They had risen by hustle and talent, by their knowledge of who needed what and who else could deliver it. Howe was the senior member of this little circle. He was Roosevelt's guide, and he kept Roosevelt's secrets.

Now, in Dr. Bennet's office in the village of Lubec, Louis Howe placed long-distance telephone calls to the oceanside towns at the southern end of Maine, where wealthy families from New York, Boston, and Philadelphia spent much of every August. In Bar Harbor, the poshest of all the summer towns, Louis located Dr. William Williams Keen of Philadelphia. Keen had been on the faculty at Jefferson Medical College when Dr. Bennet was a student there. The doctor was eighty-four years old now but still well known and much respected. By the afternoon of Saturday, August 13, he was motoring north to see the Roosevelts. Howe met him in Lubec, and Captain Calder ferried them over to the house on the island at about seven thirty.

Dr. Keen had been practicing medicine for a long time. Valedictorian of the Brown University Class of 1859, he had treated his first patients in 1861 at the Battle of Bull Run. His examination of a dying soldier whose face had been pierced by a Minié ball at Gettysburg started a lifelong interest in damage to the nervous system. After the war he became a practicing surgeon and professor at Jefferson Medical College, where he performed one of the first successful removals of a brain tumor. Dr. Keen knew his way around famous patients and their need for privacy. In 1893 he took part in a secret operation to remove a cancerous lesion from the mouth of President Grover Cleveland on a private yacht in Long Island Sound — an operation that, if revealed, might have exacerbated the financial panic of that year. And he kept the secret.

Short and slim, with a neatly trimmed beard and "a genial simplicity" of manner, Dr. Keen made a striking contrast to the large young man whom he found sprawled in the bed upstairs, unable to move his legs and struggling against what Eleanor said was, at that point, "great discouragement." She watched as Keen made "a most careful, thorough examination." Then everyone went to bed.

In the morning Keen repeated the entire "excruciating" procedure of bending Franklin's limbs and prodding his muscles. At the end of this second examination, Keen declared that Roosevelt was suffering from a sudden congestion of the blood — a clot — that had lodged in the lower spinal cord, where it had compressed or injured motor nerves. Keen blamed the "chill and exposure" of August 9 and 10 — the cold dunking FDR had taken from Van Lear Black's yacht tender, then the exertion followed by cold swims on the day of the forest fire. The condition would be temporary, he told the Roosevelts. Franklin's ability to move the toes of one foot was a "very encouraging" sign that his bloodstream was already beginning to reabsorb the clot.

Then, in another room, Keen gave Eleanor graver news. Reabsorbing the blood clot might take a long time. Her husband might be paralyzed for months. Keen said Franklin must rest at Campobello for several weeks, and he might need stretchers and a wheelchair for the move down to New York. A professional masseuse must be summoned from the city, and, in the meantime, Eleanor and Louis Howe must rub Franklin's legs vigorously to encourage circulation, which in turn would help to break up the clot.

Dr. Keen was revered as the dean of American surgery. Upon his retirement fifteen years earlier, a colleague had remarked that "his judgment seems at its very best when the surgical situation appears at its very worst." But the problem he encountered at Campobello was a matter of diagnosis, not surgery — and in the case of Franklin Roosevelt, Keen's judgment was wrong in almost every detail.

The patient was quite obviously suffering from fever and chills along with paralysis. Fever and chills are responses to agents of infection — germs — not to clots in the bloodstream. Keen had been retired since 1907, when poliomyelitis was still very rare. Like Dr. Bennet, he may never have seen a case. But he should have known the common signs of infection when he saw them. Instead, he pronounced an illogical diagnosis that meant more crucial days would pass without the only treatments that offered the only slim chances of arresting the virus's march.

Eleanor could not bring herself to tell Franklin that Dr. Keen thought he would be immobilized for months, with hard consequences for his new positions in law and business, not to mention the pursuit of political office in 1922. So she told him only that Dr. Keen had said he "could surely go down [to New York] the 15th of September." She told the children their father was ill upstairs and must not be disturbed.

Next she sat down to compose letters to those who must be told the news: Franklin's business associates, his law partners, and the closer Roosevelt and Delano relatives.

She went at these letters with some anxiety — "I hope you will think I am doing right and have done all I could," she told Franklin's half-brother, Rosy — but also with astute judgment about who must know what. She and Louis Howe surely pondered the consequences of telling everyone that Roosevelt might be trapped in bed for much of the lead-up to the 1922 elections. She certainly did not "want the particulars in the newspapers," and if she passed Keen's prognosis to all the Roosevelt and Delano uncles and aunts and cousins, someone in those vast and well-connected circles was sure to spill it.

So to most members of the family she simply reported Dr. Bennet's hazy first diagnosis: that Franklin was "ill from the effects of a chill and I hope will soon be better." She told FDR's secretary, Marguerite

LeHand, that her husband "had a severe chill last Wednesday which resulted in a fever and much congestion and I fear his return will be delayed."

She then weighed the much larger problem of what and how to tell her mother-in-law.

Sara Delano Roosevelt was on her annual summer holiday in Europe. On August 25, eleven days from now, she was due to embark for New York on the White Star liner *Olympic.* Eleanor believed it was probably too late for a letter to reach Sara explaining the circumstances, the diagnosis, the treatment, the prognosis, what she had done to address all the details, and so on. Sara had asked FDR and Eleanor to send her a cable just before she was due to sail, but a terse transatlantic cable could convey only the bare facts, not the nuances. This "would simply mean worry all the way home. . . . She will have enough once here but at least then she can do things." So, Eleanor told Rosy, "I have decided to say nothing."

This still left the tricky issue of how to meet her mother-in-law at the dock in New York and how to convey the news. Sara always counted on being received by Franklin and Eleanor themselves. She would be disappointed, even alarmed, not to see them, and whoever went in their place would have to explain about Franklin. The elder Mrs. Roosevelt was still in the habit of telling her thirty-nine-year-old only child, who had overseen the movement of fleets in wartime, that he must wear galoshes in the rain. Eleanor could imagine her panic upon learning that her son lay paralyzed in his bed.

Eleanor asked Rosy to take on the job of telling Sara. If he couldn't be in town to do it, she said, she would ask Frederic Adrian Delano, one of Sara's brothers and Franklin's favorite uncle. Eleanor would compose a brief letter to be given to Sara and leave the job of explaining to the men.

"The doctor feels sure he will get well," she told Rosy, "but it may take some months."

She and Howe began to massage Franklin's legs, as Dr. Keen had ordered. The pain was excruciating.

Franklin's bedroom on the second floor was now a sickroom containing a prostrate, helpless patient, sedated by a mild opiate, struggling with once-routine matters of evacuation and the effort to find physical comfort. He was occasionally delirious with fever. In the rest of the house, as if in a nursing station, the other adults held quiet conversations. Eleanor and Louis Howe closely guarded what they said to FDR. They did not want him to know how worried they were. In a letter to the Reverend Endicott Peabody at Groton School — a family friend who had married the Roosevelts — Eleanor wrote: "We have really had a very anxious time about Franklin, far more so than he knows."

Howe began to answer the mail on Franklin's desk. He used the same careful approach as Eleanor, even the same words. He made no mention of paralysis or blood clots or spinal cords. He said FDR had "a severe chill," was "very weak," and thus was under doctor's orders "not to so much as look at the postage stamp on a letter for some time."

But on Monday, the day after Dr. Keen left the island, Louis wrote a letter to Franklin's uncle Frederic Delano, a much longer letter than the brief and even breezy notes he was sending to others. Howe's letter has been lost; only Fred Delano's response survives. The latter makes it clear that Louis harbored doubts about Dr. Keen's diagnosis of a blood clot in the spinal cord.

Howe's own health had always been fragile. He had heart disease, asthma, and chronic bronchitis. He wore a truss. During the war he had told Roosevelt he believed that "sooner or later I [will] ignore the danger signals too long and drop out like a snuffed candle." He had spent a lot of time with doctors, and his respect for them was guarded at best. He was certainly not intimidated by professional credentials or a big reputation like Keen's.

Howe saw that some of the Roosevelt children were showing symptoms like the first ones their father had reported — fever and chills. Surely none of them was suffering from a blood clot in the spinal cord. So some infectious agent must be responsible. If so, what was it?

He likely wondered whether Dr. Keen, at eighty-four, could still be at his best. Howe had spent many more hours with Franklin over the last few days than Keen had in his single overnight visit. He was also a devoted reader of the newspapers, which were brought to the island daily, and he may have seen something Dr. Keen probably missed during his vacation at Bar Harbor: news in the New York papers about cases of infantile paralysis in the Northeast.

Howe concluded that yet another opinion was needed. Someone would have to find yet another doctor, an expert on infantile paralysis. Howe couldn't leave Campobello to search for such a doctor himself; the Roosevelts needed him. Franklin's half-brother, Rosy, was a fine fellow at a party but not much good in practical affairs. So Howe composed his long letter to Fred Delano, the most worldly and best connected member of Sara's clan. He explained the situation in detail and asked Delano to help them figure out what to do as quickly as possible.

Howe decided to tell Fred Delano of his suspicions about infantile paralysis without discussing the idea with Eleanor Roosevelt. If Howe had told her he thought they needed an authority on that disease, she surely would have said that the Roosevelts' own family physician in New York, Dr. George Draper, happened to be one of the nation's leading experts — and not only on the disease itself but on its treatment in the early phase.

W. W. Keen's misjudgment already had delayed a proper diagnosis by a number of days. Now, by failing to contact Dr. Draper in New York, Howe, with the best intentions, caused a second delay. If Howe had telephoned Draper immediately, it is highly likely that Draper would have dropped everything to locate the closest anti-poliomyelitis serum and have it rushed to FDR, or to have him rushed to it. Instead, Draper knew nothing of the matter for many more days.

On Wednesday, August 17, a week after the onset of obvious symptoms, Eleanor opened a long letter from Dr. Keen. Along with a bill for $600 — the amount startled her — Keen was sending a revised view of what was wrong with FDR. After leaving Campobello, he said, he had reflected on the matter further and concluded that the problem was probably not a blood clot in the spinal cord. He now believed an inflammation of the spinal cord, not a clot, was damaging the nerves, and thus recovery "might be a longer business" than he had predicted at first. The possibility of poliomyelitis still had not occurred to him.

At Campobello Keen had estimated the recovery would be a matter of several months. Now it was to be an even "longer business" than that?

"I dread the time when I have to tell Franklin," Eleanor wrote to Rosy, "and it wrings my heart for it is so much worse to a man than to a woman . . ." Still, of course, the doctors agreed that "he will be eventually *well* if nothing unfavourable happens in the next 10 days or so and at present all signs are favourable so for that we should be very thankful."

She found Franklin feeling a bit better. After a week of fever, his temperature had returned to normal; and though he still suffered "times of great discouragement," he was "getting back his grip & a better mental attitude." He was testing his legs for signs of the recovery Dr. Keen had predicted. He told Eleanor he was quite sure he was moving his toes slightly more than before.

At his home in Washington, D.C., on Friday, August 19, Fred Delano received Louis Howe's long letter. He dropped everything to do what he could for the nephew he loved almost as a son.

Delano was fifty-eight years old. He had been born in Hong Kong when his formidable father, Warren Delano II, was making his fortune, chiefly by providing opium to the enormous Chinese market. After the family returned to the United States, Fred was educated as an engineer and rose swiftly to lead a succession of railroads, then served on the founding board of the Federal Reserve. In the world war he went to France as an army major to help build railroads.

Then he launched an entirely new career in urban planning. He was smart, practical, and good-hearted — a favorite in the family. Even before the death of Franklin's father in 1900, Delano had assumed the role of a wise older brother in FDR's life. He was well aware of the privileged circumstances of Franklin's boyhood — a doting mother, tutors in a cloistered country home, servants in the house and grooms in the stable, summer voyages on Cunard liners, leisurely stays in German spas — and he did not want the boy to drift into an adulthood among the idle rich. Once, when Franklin was seventeen and preparing for Harvard, Fred had written to remind his nephew of "how often we see young men of more than ordinary talents, having wealth and position, either 'going to the dogs' or becoming indolent spendthrifts, neither happy themselves or making others happy, simply for want of necessity to make them work and develop themselves." And he urged Franklin to read the recent speech of Theodore Roosevelt on the need for young men of Franklin's class to embrace "the strenuous life." This was the speech in which T.R. said: "Far better it is to dare mighty things, to win glorious triumphs, even though checkered by failure, than to take rank with those poor spirits who neither enjoy much nor suffer much, because they live in the gray twilight that knows not victory nor defeat."

Delano digested Louis Howe's doubts about Dr. Keen's diagnosis, then called his son-in-law, Alexander Grant, a physician, who referred him to a Washington doctor named Parker. Dr. Parker said the case did indeed sound like infantile paralysis. He told Delano the best authorities in the country could be found in Boston, at the Harvard Infantile Paralysis Commission at Peter Bent Brigham Hospital. Delano hurried to Union Station near Capitol Hill, caught the Federal Express, and arrived in Boston the next morning.

During the epidemic of 1916, so many cases of poliomyelitis were reported in Massachusetts that Harvard recruited two young physicians to help with the enormous caseload. One of these was Samuel A. Levine, then just out of medical school. That summer and fall, Levine visited the bedsides of some three hundred children and young adults throughout the state. He had gone on to become a cardiologist, but his experience in 1916 taught him as much about poliomyelitis as any physician in the country.

He happened to be in his office at Brigham Hospital on the morning of Saturday, August 20, when Frederic Delano rang him on the telephone.

Delano said he'd been told that the senior physicians of the Harvard Infantile Paralysis Commission were all out of town but that Levine might be able to answer questions about a possible case. The patient, Levine learned, was Franklin D. Roosevelt, the recent Democratic nominee for vice president. Dr. Levine asked Delano to meet him immediately at his private office on Bay State Road, overlooking the Charles River.

Delano showed Dr. Levine the letters and telegrams he had received from Campobello, including Howe's detailed review of the particulars: "the initial general malaise and limb pains, followed by weakness and then paralysis of the limbs and the fever of 101 which subsided in a few days." From these details, combined with the occurrence of other cases in the region, Dr. Levine wrote later, "it seemed clear to me that Mr. Roosevelt was suffering from acute poliomyelitis." He told Delano that Dr. Keen's diagnosis "could be definitely dismissed." Levine pointed out that, as a surgeon, Keen "probably had very little if any experience" with infantile paralysis.

Fred Delano asked if it would do any good for Dr. Levine himself to go to Campobello that day.

This placed the young physician in a difficult spot. It was one thing for a thirty-year-old doctor to challenge a diagnosis by the highly regarded W. W. Keen from a distance; it would be quite another to do so at the bedside of Keen's patient. And Levine was hardly accustomed to an upper-crust patient like FDR; as an immigrant boy in Boston, he had hawked newspapers all through his school days to help pay his family's bills and he had gone through Harvard on scholarship. But the deciding factor in Levine's mind was speed.

He told Delano he had only one urgent recommendation. A lumbar puncture, or spinal tap, should be performed on Roosevelt that very day. In this procedure a physician pierces the spine with a needle and draws out cerebrospinal fluid. In a healthy person, the fluid is clear. Cloudy fluid means high numbers of white blood cells, which indicates an infectious process in the spinal cord. Considered along with other symptoms — fever, chills, hypersensitivity of the skin, followed by motor paralysis — such a finding would all but confirm the diagnosis of poliomyelitis. More important,

Levine believed that a lumbar puncture sometimes triggered an abrupt improvement in the patient's condition. He had seen the procedure appear to bring immediate relief to a severe headache in some patients, while in others it seemed to trigger a break in the fever and even the recovery of muscle function. Levine could recall performing the spinal tap on a young girl who could not move her toes; the moment he finished, her toes began to wiggle. He suspected the relief of pressure in the spine at the right moment could save critical nerves and even, if the timing were right, reverse paralysis.

Levine said such an outcome was at least possible in Roosevelt's case, but it would take at least a day for him to make the 350-mile trip to Campobello. So Delano would be better advised, the young doctor said, to reach a qualified physician by telephone — perhaps in Bangor, the nearest city of any size — who could go to the island and perform a lumbar puncture on Roosevelt immediately.

There the meeting ended. Fred Delano telephoned Campobello, where Eleanor had to be summoned to the village to take the call. Uncle Fred told her what Levine had said about the likelihood of poliomyelitis. (It was the first she had heard of it; Howe had kept his suspicions from her.) Uncle Fred followed up with a letter advising Eleanor to stop massaging Franklin's legs and to disregard the advice from Dr. Keen, whom Fred's advisors said was "a fine old chap but he is a surgeon and not a connoisseur of this malady. I think it would be very unwise to trust his diagnosis where the Inf. Paralysis can be determined by test of the spinal fluid."

Eleanor relayed all this to Dr. Keen, who resisted the infantile paralysis theory "very strenuously." As a result, no immediate lumbar puncture was ordered. But Keen did contact Dr. Robert Lovett, one of three directors of the Harvard Infantile Paralysis Commission, whom he knew. Keen asked Lovett to go to Campobello to examine Roosevelt.

So for many hours Eleanor and Louis Howe could only wait in miserable uncertainty, pondering two possible explanations for what was happening, both of them dire — and one a good deal more dire than the other.

Many years later, Dr. Samuel Levine, who became one of the leading cardiologists of his era, reflected on the events of that day in a private note. He was troubled by the thought that a prompt lumbar puncture might have arrested the progress of FDR's paralysis, and he blamed himself for being "so timid and self-effacing." He wished he had gone to Campobello himself or at least pressed his point about lumbar puncture. But, he reflected later, "I had not been in the practice of medicine very long at that time and was inexperienced. There were some things not mentioned in Osler's textbook on medicine." One of these was the question of how much a young doctor should say about the case of a famous man when an eminent superior held a contrary opinion.

It is hard to know whether Levine's regrets were justified. A lumbar puncture, on that day or even earlier, might have done nothing to help FDR. In 1925, two doctors writing in the *Journal of the American Medical Association* reported the same sort of benefit Levine had seen in his 1916 patients. But in the worsening polio epidemics of later decades, lumbar puncture, though it remained a standard diagnostic test, was not generally regarded as a potential therapy, and no prospective clinical trials were conducted. Still, Levine had seen what he had seen in 1916. He remembered the little girl who could suddenly wiggle her toes, and he always wondered whether things might have turned out differently if Franklin Roosevelt had received the same treatment.

On Monday, August 22, two days after his meeting with Fred Delano, Dr. Levine received his second telephone call about the Roosevelt case. It was from Dr. Robert Lovett, the expert called to Campobello by Dr. Keen. Levine and Lovett knew each other through the Infantile Paralysis Commission, and Lovett had been Levine's professor in medical school. The older man told the younger about the summons to Maine, and he asked Levine to join him for dinner at the Harvard Club that evening.

Lovett was sixty-one years old but his mustache and heavy eyebrows remained coal-black. He was a sober, diligent, straight-to-the-point orthopedist — a bone doctor — with impeccable credentials. Raised near Boston, trained at Harvard, he had been practicing in Boston since 1886. He had been president of the American Orthopedic Association, consultant to the New York State Department of Health, and a major in the Army Medical Corps during the war. He had developed expertise in the care of infantile paralysis patients in the period after the acute stage. That is, he used corrective surgery and braces to make the best of permanently paralyzed limbs. And he had worked with a cadre of physical therapists — a new profession born to help soldiers disabled by war wounds — to create new methods in physical rehabilitation and exercise.

Over dinner at the Harvard Club, Lovett asked Levine how to distinguish a paralysis caused by poliomyelitis from a paralysis caused by a clot or lesion in the spinal column — Dr. Keen's theory of the case. Lovett knew perfectly well that lumbar puncture was the standard test for poliomyelitis; he had written about it. He must have been double-checking his ammunition in case W. W. Keen put up a fight for his own view of Roosevelt's case. Lovett and Levine reviewed the protocols. The next day, Lovett went on to Maine.

On Wednesday, August 24, Dr. Keen met with Dr. Lovett in the fishing town of Eastport, across the bay from Campobello. Lovett questioned Keen closely. Upon hearing the older man's answers, Lovett was quite sure Dr. Levine's long-distance diagnosis of poliomyelitis had been correct.

The doctors were taken over to the island,

and Lovett made his examination — a "more or less superficial" one, he admitted, since FDR remained highly sensitive to touch in many spots. Nerves that regulated breathing — which, if affected, could lead to death — had escaped the attack. The bladder was paralyzed but not infected, a common danger when a catheter is used. The arms were somewhat weak, the abdominal muscles "pretty normal." The ball of the left thumb showed signs of atrophy — a cardinal sign of infantile paralysis — but none of the limbs had been deformed. The patient could not stand or walk, of course, and in the legs Lovett found "scattered weakness, most marked in the hips." Yet some muscles seemed to be recovering already, and in those there was "a pretty fair degree of power after two weeks."

From what Dr. Samuel Levine learned later, a lumbar puncture was indeed performed, though not as promptly as Levine had urged. (On this point, Levine's private note says: "I learned that when Dr. Lovett saw the patient the lumbar puncture had not been done and it was not done till Wednesday [August 24, the day of Lovett's arrival], four days after I advised it. I did not find out the cause of the delay.") Administered at this point, nearly a month after the initial infection, the procedure had no good effect on FDR's paralysis, as Dr. Levine had hoped it might. But it was the more or less definitive test to indicate poliomyelitis, given the presence of other signs and symptoms.

Anna Roosevelt, waiting nearby, heard the adults say they would confer in her bedroom. She sped down the hall and slipped into her closet to eavesdrop.

Dr. Lovett believed the matter was "perfectly clear," and Dr. Keen, conceding Lovett's greater experience with the disease, did not protest.

Anna could make little sense of the doctors' medical terms, but she understood enough to know they were convinced it was a case of infantile paralysis.

Lovett reentered Roosevelt's room and told him the diagnosis.

Near the end of her life, Eleanor Roosevelt was asked how her husband responded when Lovett spoke to him. She said she could recall only one other time when she saw the same expression on his face. It was on the day twenty years later when he was told that Japanese warplanes had attacked the U.S. fleet at Pearl Harbor.

CHAPTER 4
"TO KEEP UP HIS COURAGE"
AUGUST 25 TO SEPTEMBER 15, 1921

Dr. Lovett stood before the collective gaze of FDR, Eleanor Roosevelt, Louis Howe, Dr. Keen, and Dr. Bennet and detected "some uncertainty in their minds about the diagnosis."

That was understandable, even in the case of Howe, who had suspected infantile paralysis in the first place. Was it really possible for a thirty-nine-year-old Anglo-Saxon Episcopalian in excellent health, a man who lived in the best surroundings with the highest standards of cleanliness and safety, to contract infantile paralysis? Wasn't this a disease that struck only children, especially poor, unfortunate children of the slums?

Probably no one in the room posed any such question out loud. The Roosevelts were not in the habit of discussing either physical imperfections or class distinctions, let alone any subject that combined the two. And Dr. Lovett was of the same mind; he was "by instinct an aristocrat," a close friend said, "and not a man given over to ready intimacies." So he could only state what he knew to be facts. Adults did sometimes contract the disease, and in his view the "physical findings" — that is, the evidence gleaned from the examination and the lumbar puncture — made the diagnosis "perfectly clear."

The inevitable next question was whether Roosevelt would be permanently paralyzed. Lovett was well prepared for it. From all over the Northeast he had gathered data from recent epidemics to determine rates of recovery. But he had learned it was all but impossible to examine a patient at this early stage, especially a patient who was only partially paralyzed, and predict the future with any confidence. Lovett simply did not know, *could* not know, whether Roosevelt would be able to walk again.

The reason was the maddening inscrutability of the virus.

The poliovirus spreads through the spinal cord with all the predictability of a steel ball in a pinball machine. It seldom destroys all the motor neurons. It just destroys some, and the number and location make all the difference.

Again, think of the big toe of the right foot. If the poliovirus destroys *all* the anterior horn cells that control the muscles in that toe, then the toe will never move again, because dead motor nerve cells never come back to life. But if only one of those cells is destroyed, or only a handful, the surviving cells can compensate — they sprout multiple new nerve endings to supply signals to the muscles — and the toe can still be moved, though it may be weak. Other cells will be damaged but not destroyed. The muscles they control may be paralyzed only for the moment. As the inflammation in the spinal cord gradually recedes, the damaged nerves may come out all right and the muscle can resume its work. The toe that was paralyzed can curl again. This was called "spontaneous recovery." But you could only wait and see whether the affected toe would recover spontaneously or be lost for good.

There were other imponderables. Some muscles that failed to recover on their own could be revived with proper exercise — just a little, or a lot — but no one could tell which muscles might come back that way, and no one could tell how much exercise would be needed. A recovering patient could try to move a paralyzed toe every day for three months with no success, then get a flicker of movement. Would three more months restore more strength and more motion? Maybe, maybe not.

Nor was it possible for a doctor to predict the grimmest effect of infantile paralysis: the limb that bent or twisted under the continual pressure of a good muscle pulling against a bad one. That was called a "contracture." When you saw a little girl with a twisted leg, or a boy stuck in a permanent bend at the waist, you were seeing untreated contractures. An orthopedist like Robert Lovett had ways of reversing contractures once they started, but he could not predict which patient would develop a contracture and which patient would not.

Lovett had studied patients who were severely paralyzed at the onset of the disease, patients who were only mildly paralyzed at the onset, and patients in between. He had found that even the severity of the original paralysis allowed no sure bet as to the likelihood of either spontaneous recovery or recovery with exercise. Mild cases tended to do better. But he had seen patients with severe paralysis at the outset who recovered completely, and he had seen patients who started with very mild effects who developed severe and permanent paralysis.

Everything depended on cellular processes unfolding inside the spinal cord at a level invisible to the era's most powerful microscope.

So in the moment of greatest agony for the patient and the family, the doctor could not honestly give the only thing that might bring relief: a promise that the patient would regain power in the paralyzed parts of the body. It might happen; it really might. But there was no way to know. "In the present state of our knowledge," Lovett had advised his fellow doctors, "the man of experience will, in the early days of the disease, express himself with great reserve in the matter."

Yet here was another family asking Lovett the inevitable question. What should he say to them? What was his best judgment about what would happen to *this* patient? And how should he phrase that judgment to this desperate little audience: the patient himself, a famous man with an even more famous name, highly educated and intelligent; his wife, the niece of a president; and two other physicians, one of them eminent?

Lovett's answer would influence a good deal that happened in the coming weeks, and those events would have large consequences for the rest of Roosevelt's life.

But what, exactly, did he say?

Several days after leaving Campobello, Lovett put his confidential view of the case in a letter to Dr. George Draper, the Roosevelts' physician in New York.

He listed his findings: no harm to respiration (meaning Roosevelt had escaped the life-threatening form of the disease); some pain but "not excessive"; some weakness in the arms but "not very severe"; abdominal muscles "pretty normal"; the bladder paralyzed but so far not infected; and "scattered weakness in the legs, most marked in the hips." Lovett thought "spontaneous improvement" was already under way. All in all, from a doctor's point of view, it was not too bad, considering all the cases he had seen that were much worse.

"It seems to me," Lovett advised Draper, "that it was a mild case within the range of possible complete recovery. . . . It is dangerous to speak from impressions at the end of the second week, but my feeling about him was that he was probably going to be a case where the conservation of what muscular power he has may be very important, and it looked to me as if some of the important muscles might be on the edge where they could be influenced either way — toward recovery, or turn into completely paralyzed muscles."

His letter to Dr. Draper continued:

"I told [the Roosevelts] very frankly that no one could tell where they stood, that the case was evidently not of the severest type, that complete or partial recovery to any point was possible, that disability was not to be feared, and that the only cut about it was the long continued character of the treatment."

But how could Lovett possibly say "disability was not to be feared," given everything he knew about the danger of predicting the degree of recovery?

By "disability" (if that was indeed the word he used with the Roosevelts) he may have meant complete immobility, with no chance of regaining any sort of independent locomotion. Here he would have felt on safe ground. Lovett was accustomed to the long-term treatment of infantile paralysis. The core of his work was to perform the surgeries and provide the apparatuses — splints, braces, crutches, canes — that helped partially paralyzed people get around and do their work. And in all his years of dealing with the aftermath of this disease, Lovett had seen "no more than two or three cases that could not be made to walk in some form or other, and these cases were of the severest possible type — a really bedridden case of infantile paralysis should almost never occur." So he may have meant simply that Roosevelt need not fear spending the rest of his life on his back. He would be able to get around somehow.

If Lovett's report to Draper is accurate, then he told the Roosevelts nothing more or less than what his clinical experience and his data from many other cases showed. Roosevelt was not going to get any worse and he was not going to wind up completely immobilized. Other than that, anything might happen, from a poor outcome to a good one, and only time would tell.

That is what Lovett told Dr. Draper, who would understand that Lovett really and truly meant the case might go "either way," that it was "on the edge."

But was Lovett really that frank, that agnostic, that detached in his judgment with the agonized people he faced at Campobello, for whom "on the edge" meant the line between salvation and disaster for a man who wanted to be president of the United States? Is that what he said to the Roosevelts?

It can't be known for sure. Accounts of the discussion left by Lovett and the Roosevelts are fragmentary. But somehow the Roosevelts took something from Lovett that allowed them to hope.

Possibly Lovett soft-pedaled. Even a great and experienced doctor may weaken under the spell of a famous name; may feel the urge to please people of substance and power. And Lovett was delivering news that was much worse than what Dr. Keen had told the Roosevelts; the urge would have been strong to soften it just a bit. Even if his words were completely frank, an inclination of his head or the tone of his voice may have hinted that although he was administering harsh medicine, all would be well in the end.

He was saying, after all, that it was *a mild case . . .* and *complete or partial recovery to any point was possible . . .* and *disability was not to be feared.*

That is what the Roosevelts remembered Lovett saying: All was not lost. There was a hard time ahead, but with work and determination, Franklin and the family might look forward to a full recovery or something approaching it.

Lovett also said — and this the family and the other doctors remembered clearly —

that Roosevelt could expect "considerable" improvement within about two weeks.

Then Lovett gave his lesser directives. For the time being there must be no more massage, he said. Dr. Keen had been wrong about that, since, of course, he had also been wrong about the clot in the spinal cord. Lovett believed massage would exacerbate sensitivity and pain without benefit to the damaged muscles. (Eleanor always reproached herself for her role in the early massage, though of course she had only been acting on Dr. Keen's instructions. In fact, later studies tended to vindicate Keen. Evidence cropped up that deep massage might diminish the chance of life-threatening blood clots in cases like Roosevelt's.)

Eleanor asked about the children. She was deeply worried that her own five and the Howes' son, Hartley, might be infected. Uncle Fred Delano had told her such cases must not "be treated lightly, the disease is too serious to trifle with."

Dr. Lovett told her the children almost certainly were out of danger. He said he himself took the precaution, after examining a patient with infantile paralysis, of changing his clothes before he saw his grandchildren, but this was probably "an entirely useless thing to do." The children may indeed have been infected with the poliovirus, but since they were showing no signs of muscular weakness, it was clear they had fought it off. At this news, at least, Eleanor felt "great relief."

Lovett congratulated Eleanor on the fine care she had given so far, but he insisted that a trained nurse be brought up to the island. He recommended a young nurse he knew, Edna Rockey, and she was sent for.

As for returning home, Lovett said FDR should rest at Campobello until the middle of September, then enter a hospital in New York for an extended convalescence. He suggested that Dr. George Draper, the expert on infantile paralysis who happened to be the Roosevelts' own doctor, take charge of day-to-day care, with Lovett consulting from Boston.

The thing now was to rest and wait. They would see how many muscles remained active when the acute stage was over. Then there would be exercises to preserve those muscles and increase their power.

Before Lovett left the island, Louis Howe pulled him aside for a private word away from the family. Louis wanted the honest odds. Was his boss ever going to walk again?

Now Lovett became more pointed, Howe reported later. Any improvement in Roosevelt's condition "would be very slight unless he had the most extraordinary will and patience — and that hours, days, weeks, months and years of constant effort would be needed to bring the muscles back." Lovett said he had known few people with sufficient courage and determination to make such an effort, "but if Mr. Roosevelt's interest in resuming active life is great enough, his will to recover strong enough, there is undoubtedly a chance."

With Lovett gone and the diagnosis finally settled, others must be told. Howe took the lead. "The handling of [FDR's] mail and the newspapers all fell entirely into Louis's hands," Eleanor said later, though she played her own part in informing others.

But what to say, and to whom, was a highly delicate matter.

Three more weeks on the island was plenty of time for reporters to form a vulture's watch over the life of a famous young politician. Total secrecy was unsustainable, since people in New York already knew something was wrong; and with a long delay in FDR's return to the city, questions could become ugly rumors. As Dr. Keen put it, the need was seen to announce "the fact of his illness . . . to the press in order to prevent misinformation being spread about a prominent man."

But it was not the right time to tell the whole truth. Eleanor hoped to hold the news of Lovett's diagnosis as closely as possible "until we knew something definite about the future," and that might take many weeks. Once FDR was back in New York and better able to make decisions, Howe and he could devise a larger strategy for dealing with the press. But right now, if the words "infantile paralysis" were coupled with "F. D. Roosevelt" in the headlines, Eleanor would face agonized queries from the family's sprawling circles of relatives and friends: *Is Franklin dying?* Worse still, that abbreviated report might reach Sara Delano Roosevelt aboard her ocean liner. That likely settled the matter right there: Franklin's mother must not find out through the press that her son was paralyzed.

So Howe and Eleanor steered a cautious course between secrecy and full disclosure. On the day after Dr. Lovett left Maine, Howe released a statement that on its face was perfectly accurate. The *New York Times* published it on page 7 in the edition of August 27: "Franklin D. Roosevelt, former assistant secretary of the Navy, has been seriously ill at his Summer home at Campobello, N.B. He is now improving." In Howe's view, that gave the story its first nudge in the proper direction, a positive one, before the word "paralysis" (let alone "infantile") saw print. And if the report reached Sara Roosevelt aboard her ship, the word "improving" might keep her anxiety in check.

Then, Howe went to New York, where he conferred with Roosevelt's associates at the insurance company and the law firm. To most of them he said the problem was no more than a bad cold, "nothing serious." He was more honest with Langdon Marvin, FDR's old friend and partner in the firm of Emmett, Marvin & Roosevelt, who wrote to Eleanor immediately to ask if he might come to Campobello.

FDR dictated a reply — probably his own first reference in writing to his problem:

Dear Lang —
Thank you very much for your offer of coming up to see me but you wouldn't be allowed to see me if you came! After many consultations among the medical fraternity my case has been diagnosed by Dr. Lovett as one of poliomyelitis, otherwise [known as] infantile paralysis.

Cheerful thing for one with my gray hairs to get. I am almost wholly out of commission as to my legs but the doctors say that there is no question that I will get their use back again though this means several months of treatment in New York.

Eleanor, writing in her hurried, hieroglyphic hand, scribbled the truth to a few other close relatives and friends, but she asked them to repeat it to no one for the time being.

"It is perfectly marvelous how you have kept the secret," replied Annie Delano Hitch, a favorite aunt of Franklin's, "and we will be very careful to say nothing to anyone."

For the moment, the patient was "remarkably cheerful." After the morbid uncertainty of two weeks in the dark, it may simply have brought relief, as Eleanor put it, "to feel that we know what is the trouble." No doubt he was also doing his best to put on a good face, especially for the children, who were allowed "only a few glimpses of him, a hurried exchange of words from a doorway," Jimmy Roosevelt remembered later. "He grinned at us, and he did his best to call out, or gasp out, some cheery response to our tremulous, just-this-side-of-tears greetings."

But he did not improve.

Dr. Lovett had predicted he would see definite improvement within two weeks. But after one week had gone by he was no better at all; in fact, he was worse. He could now hold and manipulate a pen, and he felt some strength returning in his trunk. That was all. His thighs and calves were shrinking. He couldn't sit up by himself. He could move his toes and feet less than he had a week earlier. Caustic pain persisted. (For a patient at this stage of poliomyelitis, even the weight of cotton sheets on one's thighs can be intolerable.) Dr. Keen had warned about the need for strict antisepsis in the use of the catheter, "the most dangerous instrument in surgery," and sure enough, FDR now came down with an infection in his bladder. He had diarrhea and he couldn't urinate without his wife's help.

Dr. Bennet now reported that FDR was becoming downright "unnerved."

Had anyone ever said such a thing of Franklin Roosevelt? Had he ever been unnerved, even seriously frightened? At Groton and Harvard he had known the sting of exclusion from the higher echelons of schoolboy prestige and popularity, and surely the crisis of his marriage in 1918 had jolted his steady path. But that is what his path had been — a steady, confident ascendency from one plateau of achievement and power to another. Now his future was being stolen — the everyday pleasures of sailing and golf, of "hare and hounds" and riding horses with his children, the plans for new campaigns, the glowing hope of the presidency. It was all in the gravest doubt.

Dr. Bennet listened to FDR's plaintive queries. Hadn't it been foolish to abandon massage? Wasn't that decision, and not the disease, the most likely cause of the sponginess he felt in the muscles below his waist? Bennet was pondering the same questions.

So, perplexed and increasingly worried, Bennet wired Dr. Lovett in Boston:

"ATROPHY INCREASING POWER LESSENING CAUSING PATIENT MUCH ANXIETY. . . . CAN YOU RECOMMEND ANYTHING TO KEEP UP HIS COURAGE AND MAKE HIM FEEL THE BEST IS BEING DONE OR TELL HIM THOSE CHANGES ARE UNAVOIDABLE. HIS WIFE ANXIOUS TO AVOID WORRY ON HIS PART."

Bennet followed up with a letter to Lovett

asking: "When you stated that the improvement in 2 weeks would be considerable, did you mean *above* or *below* waistline? If the *former* it is working . . . if the *latter* not so. He seems to think that something more could be going on. It is easy to imagine how he feels."

Dr. Lovett's reply from Boston gave no reassurance. "CANNOT ADD ANYTHING," he wired. "REGARD CARE AS ROUTINE AND WOULD ADVISE AGAINST ADDITIONAL TREATMENT."

Lovett must have felt he had made himself clear. He had told the family that "no one could tell where they stood." He had been through innumerable cases like this. The only thing to do was wait for the end of the initial period of recovery and see which muscles still worked.

So Roosevelt lay in bed as Louis Howe read aloud to pass the time: news story after news story from New York, Albany, Washington . . . his world proceeding without him.

It was just at this point, on the first day of September, that FDR's mother arrived at Campobello. Her brother Fred had met her at the pier in New York and given her the news. She had rushed to the island.

Franklin knew what to do. When Sara

reached his bedroom — so she wrote one of her sisters that night — she found "a brave, smiling & beautiful son" who cried: "Well, I'm glad you are back, Mummy, and I got up this party for you!"

Sara "controlled herself remarkably," Eleanor recalled later. She saw him lying on his back, able to move only his arms. It touched her to see that "he had shaved himself" and seemed "very bright and very *keen.*" He charged into the usual buzz of homecoming talk, insisting that she recount the details of her summer trip. "He looks well and eats well," she told her sister, "and is . . . full of interest in everything."

Everyone took a role in this determined performance, including, Sara said, "dear Eleanor," who "is not tired"; the new nurse, Miss Rockey, who was "perfect"; and Dr. Bennet, who exclaimed, "This boy is going to get well!"

Sitting alone that evening, Sara wrote her brother: "I hear them all laughing, Eleanor in the lead." She thoroughly approved. "He and Eleanor decided at once to be cheerful and the atmosphere of the house is all happiness. So I have fallen in and follow their glorious example."

She was no fool. She did not look away from the central fact. "Below his waist he cannot move at all," she wrote Fred. "His legs (that I have always been so proud of) have to be moved often as they ache when long in one position. . . . They have *no* power."

And yet Dr. Lovett was "the greatest authority we have on Infantile Paralysis," she asserted, and he had declared that Franklin "*will* get well."

As Sara sat in the house at Campobello writing to her sister, her brother Fred was passing an uncomfortable night many miles away in Stockbridge, New York, where his daughter was preparing to be married the following weekend. He was ruminating about Franklin, trying to think what more he might do to help. In a letter the next day, he struggled to assemble "some 'fatherly' advice."

The sympathy of loved ones surrounded FDR, Fred told his nephew, "and if prayers can save you, you do not need to lift your hand . . . but I do think there is more truth than poetry in the saying, 'God helps those who help themselves'!"

Since passing the age of forty, Delano wrote his nephew, he had determined that for himself at least, all the world's wisdom came down to "taking things as they are, analyzing the facts, above all not *fooling* yourself." One need not be a Christian Scientist to accept "the kernel of truth in their dictum" that a sufferer can render an affliction powerless by refusing to acknowledge its power. As for the pursuit of recovery, Fred said, the doctors and nurses could help, but "the construction work of getting *well* depends largely on your own character. . . .

"I realize you are up against a hard problem, and hard, cruel facts. . . . And yet I feel the utmost confidence that you will emerge a better and a stronger man. It will give you time for reflection and that alone is worth a good deal. In your rushing and busy life you have not had that. . . .

"I feel so confident of your background of health and good habits, and of your courage and good temper, that I refuse to be cast down."

So, on the same day, many miles apart, a sister and brother of the Delano clan expressed the creed of pragmatic self-mastery on which they had been raised. Much the same thing had been said by Theodore Roosevelt's father when T.R. suffered debilitating asthma as a boy, and when T.R.'s sister Anna struggled to overcome tuberculosis of the spine. T.R. had followed the same code when his first wife, Alice, died in childbirth.

"Courage and good temper" — nothing more nor less. The creed came down to FDR from both great branches of his family tree.

As usual, the Delanos made things happen. Eleanor and Louis Howe had been debating whether to have Franklin taken to New York by boat or by the usual long train journey. Either would be exhausting. Sara settled the point: She would not allow her son to be manhandled from one train to another across crowded public rail platforms, nor to be lifted from a boat to a teeming Manhattan pier. With help from another of her brothers, Lyman Delano, executive vice president of the Atlantic Coast Line Railroad Company, she simply hired a private car that would take Franklin straight through from Eastport to Grand Central Terminal, where he could be carried off the train in privacy.

Sara had timed her return from Europe to be present for the wedding of her niece, Fred Delano's daughter, Louise. Eleanor and Franklin insisted she must go as planned, and she finally agreed. (Anna went with her, the first of the children to leave Campobello. Jimmy, the eldest boy, left for

Groton a few days later.)

As soon as Sara reached New York City, she made an appointment to see her son's doctor, George Draper. "Her history of the case was very vague," Dr. Draper told Dr. Lovett, "and I did not get a clear idea of it."

Dr. Draper knew FDR would be in New York shortly, so he needed a quick response from Lovett. Draper asked for "as complete a story as possible of the early stages of this unfortunate malady, and any directions which you have to give in the matter of temporary splinting, or massage, or rest, please include it in the letter, so I shall have it before he arrives."

One thing Sara had gotten across to Draper quite clearly.

"I was glad to hear Mrs. Roosevelt say that you [Lovett] felt he would make a hasty recovery."

This was evidence that Eleanor, when speaking to her mother-in-law, had been squeezing as much optimism out of Dr. Lovett's prognosis as she possibly could.

If Sara's report to Draper was foggy, she was downright misleading a day or two later, when a reporter came to inquire about her son. Based on their conversation, bulletins reported that FDR had suffered a kind of "trouble with his legs which has interfered with their normal use," though "there was no suggestion of paralysis"; and that the source of the trouble, though "not . . . diagnosed to the complete satisfaction of his physicians," was "a form of rheumatism."

On September 14, just over a month since the onset of symptoms, FDR was prepared for the trip home to New York. Captain Calder and five other islanders were sent upstairs with an improvised stretcher. Down the stairs they lugged him — six steps to the first landing, six steps to the second landing, six more to the ground floor — then out the door and down the sloping lawn to the rocky beach and the dock. They lowered him into Calder's launch. Eleanor and Howe and Dr. Bennet and the nurse, Edna Rockey, looked on, then stepped into the boat themselves. Then the boat crossed Passamaquoddy Bay to Eastport, Maine, where they would catch the train for the overnight trip to New York.

Louis Howe knew that newspaper reporters were waiting in Eastport. He wanted them to get a specific impression of Roosevelt's situation, and to that end he had arranged the details of a tableau. First Howe let it be known among the reporters that

Calder's boat would take Roosevelt to one end of Eastport; then he directed Calder to steer the boat to the other end of town. Upon reaching the mainland unobserved, the party loaded Roosevelt onto an old baggage cart and pushed him to the depot. By the time the reporters caught up, a window of the railroad car had been removed and FDR had been hoisted through and settled. The window was put back in place, and Howe handed his friend a lit cigarette to give the appearance of casual relaxation.

As the train was prepared to leave the depot, Dr. Bennet spoke with the reporters for a few minutes. His summary of the case was anything but straightforward. According to the *New York World,* he "said that some weeks ago Mr. Roosevelt suffered a severe chill, which was followed by great muscular pains in his back with considerable temperature. This condition lasted for some time and the exact nature of his illness was a matter of considerable difficulty of diagnosis. His patient is now convalescent, he declared, but the weakness of his back may be expected to continue for a short time longer."

FDR smiled and smoked as he chatted through the open window, giving reporters the precise impression that Howe desired.

He struck them as a man who had been quite ill but now was "feeling more comfortable," as the *World* put it.

This news reached New York by telegraph long before the train.

Anyone who had been following the story of Roosevelt's illness in the press — friend, associate, or casual reader — was now surely in a state of bewilderment. The malady had been reported variously as a cold, "a severe chill," "a form of rheumatism," and pneumonia. A federal judge had heard it was influenza. It was no longer a secret that something was amiss with Franklin Roosevelt; what it was remained mysterious and misunderstood. This was all due to the scrambling efforts by Eleanor, Louis Howe, and Sara Roosevelt to tell a small circle of people that Franklin was ill without saying what the illness was, then to dampen the news, to soften it, to temper it, to say something other than that the family was facing the possibility of a cataclysm.

The younger Roosevelt boys, Franklin Jr. and John, ages seven and five, knew their father was very ill, but no one had told them precisely what was wrong. Franklin Jr. retained a memory that one of his older brothers, James or Elliott, had said it must be a heart attack — a very serious illness, they knew. But when their father was being carried on the stretcher across the beach to Captain Calder's boat, his head lower than his feet, adults hovering all around, John saw that "he managed to wave to me, and his whole face burst into a tremendous sunny smile. So I decided he couldn't be so sick after all."

All this confusion among the people involved, from Roosevelt's orthopedist down to his five-year-old son, set the pattern for what would happen to Roosevelt's condition in both the short term and the long. At the purely physical level, of course, it would remain what it had been since the infection at Bear Mountain: a cut-and-dried matter of a virus and its human host, of "hard, cruel facts," of nerve cells and muscle fibers that either did or did not function. But at another level it was becoming an ambiguous and intangible thing that assumed first one appearance and meaning, then others, depending on who was talking about it and to whom. That would go on. And it was a necessary condition for all that followed. The ambiguity would allow FDR, once he took back the reins of his destiny, to define his condition by his own lights, shaping the meaning of his situation to his own needs with astonishing dexterity.

■ ■ ■ ■

The journey by rail carried FDR some six hundred miles from one of the most remote points in the United States to the heart of its greatest city. Dr. Bennet rode along and reported that his patient "stood the journey finely and did not seem at all exhausted." The train reached Grand Central Terminal at 3:20 P.M. on the fifteenth of September. An ambulance was ready to move FDR to Presbyterian Hospital at Madison Avenue and 70th Street.

Dr. Draper stood on the platform with a few other friends of the family. One of these was Tom Lynch, the politico who had assisted FDR's vice-presidential campaign in 1920. Lynch watched as the window was laboriously removed from the passenger coach, then as a team of porters lifted the stretcher and eased it out — and there was the figure of his friend, a man he had hoped would be president, flat on his back and immobile as a piece of freight.

Lynch called out to the porters, warning them to be careful. FDR, staring straight up at the sky, heard Lynch's voice.

"Hello, Tom!" — the familiar tenor voice, rich and clear. "Come on and ride up with me! There are some things I want to talk to you about!"

It was a characteristic summons, a small thing, but charming — the invitation not just to talk but to talk about unspecified particular items of interest to you and only you.

Then Lynch saw the paralyzed legs. He stood still as the porters moved off, hefting their load toward the freight elevator. In a moment Eleanor Roosevelt came hurrying back. She told Lynch to come along; Franklin was saying he wouldn't let the ambulance leave until Lynch joined them.

Lynch turned his face away.

"Tell him you can't find me," he said. "I'll go up to see him tomorrow."

These sixty disastrous days in Roosevelt's life left a string of might-have-beens and if-onlys.

What if Josephus Daniels, instead of Roosevelt, had gone to Washington to fight the Newport charges, thus sparing FDR the physical and emotional ordeal that wore him out in the last weeks of July 1921? Or what if, on the morning of July 28, some minor emergency had cropped up at Fidelity & Deposit, forcing Roosevelt to miss the Boy Scout excursion to Bear Mountain? Or, having gone to Bear Mountain, what if he had decided to cancel his trip to Campobello in order to clear up the remains of the Newport scandal? Then he would have been in New York City when he began to feel the first strange symptoms of his illness, within blocks of Dr. Draper and excellent hospitals stocked with anti-poliomyelitis serum. Or what if, when he felt ill upon arriving at Campobello Island, he had taken to his bed instead of racing around the island for several days?

What if Louis Howe had known that Dr. Draper was an authority on the early treatment of infantile paralysis; called Draper instead of William Keen; and followed Draper's advice to find a hospital nearby with serum? What if Dr. Samuel Levine had been more insistent with Fred Delano about the need for an immediate lumbar puncture?

The exhaustion, the serum, and the lumbar puncture, alone or in combination, might not have changed the course of events at all. And yet, however long the odds in each case, these factors might have made a difference. If any of these mischances had gone the other way, Roosevelt might have avoided the virus altogether, or he might have wound up much less crippled than he became. He might have been able to walk again.

But these mischances, in their utterly unpredictable and mysterious way, set in motion a twisting chain of events that led to the White House. If they had gone the other way, as we shall see, FDR probably would not have become president at all.

■ ■ ■ ■

Part Two:
"He's Through"

FALL 1921 TO WINTER 1924

■ ■ ■ ■

CHAPTER 5
"THE PSYCHOLOGICAL FACTOR IS PARAMOUNT"
SEPTEMBER 15 TO OCTOBER 28, 1921

Louis Howe had been earning his livelihood in politics for ten years, but he remained a newsman to the tips of his small, tobacco-stained fingers. As the train bearing his boss rattled down through New England toward New York City, he thought about what Roosevelt's doctors should say to the press. After all the contradictory bulletins in the papers, a minor mob of newspaper reporters would be at the hospital demanding to know what was wrong with Roosevelt. Once they learned the correct diagnosis, their next question would be: *Will Mr. Roosevelt be crippled?* If the answer was no, Roosevelt had been quite ill but was recovering well, Howe knew that would make a story, but only a minor one — a few column inches of type that editors would insert somewhere inside the news sections, not on the front page. If the answer was yes, it would be highly newsworthy. It would affect not just

165

the fortunes of a famous family but the future of the Democratic Party in the state of New York, perhaps even the national ticket in 1924. Howe could visualize the words his old comrades would deploy in the next day's editions as clearly as if he were typing them himself: "invalid" . . . "paralyzed" . . . "cripple." Any of those words held the power of a bomb if tossed into the career of a major politician.

And Howe knew what images the words would kindle in readers' minds: the soldier amputee behind a closed door in his mother's apartment; the little girl with stunted legs jammed into a carriage for easy ambulation; the "dirty, unkempt urchin" scuttling for garbage in the alley. The word "paralysis" might trigger rumors of meningitis, with hints that FDR's mind had been affected. Doctors often heard laypeople insist, contrary to all evidence, that "such a serious illness of the central nervous system must surely have ill effects upon that part of it which is called the mind." A report of paralysis might even arouse suspicions that the Roosevelts were covering up a case of syphilis. Americans who had grown up before penicillin knew that syphilis in its advanced stages could not only paralyze limbs but drive people mad.

And that word "cripple." The world war and the great polio epidemic of 1916 had damaged the bodies of so many people that the word had a new currency, and movements to help "the crippled child" and disabled war veterans were active and earnest. But a realist like Louis Howe, whose own life had been shadowed by bad health and an ugly physique, knew that the public's dread of abnormal bodies came out of deep springs in the past.

Fear of the cripple was as old as history. In earliest times, it surely had come out of fear for a family's well-being. In cultures based on hunting and gathering or agriculture, a severely crippled man could not support or protect his kin. A child who could not work drained his family's resources. Human communities had sanctioned the abandonment or killing of deformed and crippled children in every age and in many places: ancient Rome, Sparta, the Antilles, the South Pacific islands, sub-Saharan Africa.

But the dread also arose from something deeper than anxiety over mere subsistence. To Christians before the modern era, human deformity was understood as a penalty for sin. The cripple was regarded as an alien. The Old English word *crypel,* the Old

Norse *cryppil,* and the German *Kruppel* had evolved from some even more ancient word that meant "to creep," "to crawl." In early times, that was how the paralytic had moved across the ground — like a beast. Indeed, some medieval Christians detected signs of *the* Beast, regarding cripples as the product of Satan's lust for virginal girls. Martin Luther was only one of many sober believers in the existence of changelings — deformed offspring that "diabolic mothers" swapped for healthy babies. Luther once advised that a twelve-year-old boy with twisted limbs, probably a victim of rickets, be drowned in the River Mulde.

Of course, no one in New York City in 1921 was going to pitch Franklin Roosevelt into the East River. Few people of the modern era saw physical abnormality as evil. But the cripple was still cursed with "otherness." Henry VIII had made it legal for cripples to beg for alms and food, thus creating a connection in the public mind between disability and the lowest rung on the social ladder. The Church established asylums for the crippled, thus associating them with grim sanctuaries set off from normal life, like prisons. The cripple of post-medieval times was no longer the devil's spawn. But he was pitiable, pathetic, embarrassing, and still shunned.

Since the American Civil War, long strides in orthopedics had made it possible to repair many damaged limbs and ameliorate many impairments. The occasional home for crippled children provided fine care and a sound education, even if the curriculum slighted English and mathematics in favor of handicrafts. Many homes were shabby or worse. At least one such institution in the United States had recently been raising money by putting its children on display in the style of a P. T. Barnum freak show. Most disabled people spent their lives either as shut-ins in the homes of relatives or beggars on the streets.

The physically impaired adult of the 1920s, raised in such circumstances, was fully accustomed to regarding himself as the natural object of pity, scorn, and repelled fascination. The effect on one's emotional well-being could be devastating, and even those who retained a healthy sense of self confronted a widespread assumption that cripples were unpleasant, self-pitying people. "Physical weakness or inferiority creates a peculiar state of mind," wrote a professor of orthopedics — a strong advocate for the disabled — in the early 1920s. It encouraged "a mind on the defensive and desiring to obtain . . . that which a poor physique renders impossible. The unfortunate seems always imbued with the idea that he has been unfairly treated in the distribution of bodily favors, that society is opposed to him, regarding him as a useless being with no place in the economic structure. He becomes touchy, spiteful, vindictive and even malignant." If that was more perception than reality, it was a powerful and pervasive view.

And who would hire someone like that to fill a responsible job? Not many. A survey of 600 major U.S. employers in the 1920s found that half would not employ a disabled worker under any circumstances; another 25 percent would think of doing so only if the individual had been disabled while working at the firm. "We naturally do not employ the afflicted when we have sound material at hand," a manufacturer of steel products told researchers. "Taken as a whole, even when fitted to the job, they are apt to prove less satisfactory, due to an accompanying mental state of depression or nervousness often to be observed."

"The repugnance and distaste with which the cripple has been regarded throughout history still prevail," a scholar of the era wrote. "Although modern society has become humane to the extent of feeling called upon to provide care and even education for all of its disabled members, it has not yet progressed so far as to overcome entirely a reaction of repulsion to all departures from the normal of human kind."

Even if Roosevelt were to make a partial recovery, Louis Howe could imagine the dark cloud of doubt, speculation, and rumor that would seep into any conversation in which his name arose: *"Wasn't Roosevelt terribly ill? Isn't there something wrong with him?"* Maybe no one but a crazy zealot still believed in a connection between disability and the devil. But virtually everyone equated disability with weakness and incapacity. The cripple was not whole, not a real man. Certainly not a man to be entrusted with power.

When people heard the words "infantile paralysis," they did not think of just any child. They thought of an immigrant child living in rags in a filthy tenement. During the great epidemic of 1916, rumors had filled the city about cases clustered in crowded Italian neighborhoods, and about epidemics in the distant debarkation ports of Genoa and Naples. The historian Naomi Rogers found the words "congested" and "infected" were virtually interchangeable descriptions of the immigrant slums that summer. As death tallies rose, public health officials plastered slum buildings with anti-polio posters in Italian, Yiddish, and Slavic and spread chloride of lime in the streets. When Catherine Sefton Page, the twenty-five-year-old daughter-in-law of the U.S. diplomat Walter Hines Page, came down with "the infantile" and died in the wealthy and presumably sanitary enclave of the Upper East Side, it was taken as grim evidence that the germ had crept out of the slums. When a young man of Philadelphia's posh Main Line died, that too was taken as a sign "that infantile paralysis had penetrated to that exclusive section where immunity should seem certain if it were possible at all."

How could this happen? It was quite simple. Blame the housefly, that malevolent carrier of germs — as one cartoonist put it — "from gutter pools and filth of streets, from stables and backyards neglected, slovenly homes — all manner of unclean places."

Later, when statistical tables were published in obscure public health reports, they showed that polio cases per capita in 1916 had been higher among native-born children than among Italian newcomers. But in

1921, amid a swelling outcry against European immigrants, the memory persisted that infantile paralysis was a slum disease attributable to ignorant, backward people who would not keep their homes or their children clean. The victim of infantile paralysis was dirty.

Dirty, sinful, useless, repellant — all these half-conscious associations in the public mind somehow must be quashed or at least quieted before Franklin Roosevelt's name could ever again be placed on a ballot.

Louis Howe knew the hard labor of physical recovery could be done only by Roosevelt himself. But he, Howe, could help with this other work — the deft, delicate job of shaping public perceptions. Like the process of physical rehabilitation that Dr. Lovett had foretold, this work of Howe's in the murky fields of press relations and social psychology would be difficult and lengthy.

For both jobs, the physical and the perceptual, one ally would be essential: Dr. George Draper, FDR's personal physician. Draper was about to take responsibility for Roosevelt's day-to-day care, and it was he who would give the first authoritative statement of the patient's condition to the New York press. Neither Roosevelt nor Howe could have found a better ally.

The ties between George "Dan" Draper and FDR went back to Groton School and Harvard. Their families moved in the same social circles. On his mother's side Draper was the grandson of Charles Anderson Dana, founding editor of the *New York Sun,* and his father was a prominent doctor in New York. In fact, Draper had just missed becoming a shirt-tail relative of the Roosevelts. In 1906, a year after Franklin and Eleanor were married, he was engaged to Eleanor's first cousin, Corinne Robinson, another of then-President Theodore Roosevelt's nieces. But Corinne broke it off when — her son reported later — she decided Draper was "a little too loose around the edges." Apparently she had caught on to a central fact about her fiancé: Draper had an open and original mind that ranged beyond the walls of traditional Western science in search of truths about the human condition.

Draper was tall and thin with a long, narrow head and piercing dark eyes. He looked like a strict, cerebral army officer, and in fact he had been a lieutenant colonel in the Army Medical Corps during the war. But he had also been analyzed by no less a figure than the pioneer Swiss psychiatrist Carl Jung. In his office on Manhattan's Upper East Side, just a few blocks from the Roosevelts' townhouse, Draper had hung an ancient scene of an aged Chinese physician at the edge of a lake, gazing skyward at the rising moon. The inscription read: "If I could only collect the moonbeams, I could cure all the ills of mankind."

Draper was not chasing moonbeams, but he did believe that in many cases disease and recovery turned on forces beyond the reach of conventional medicine. Few doctors of the era believed as strongly as he did that a patient's state of mind could tip his chances toward success or disaster. He had founded a clinic at Presbyterian Hospital for the advancement of "constitutional medicine," a branch of the healing arts that would wane to obscurity until, decades later, it reemerged with new vigor under the name "holistic medicine." Draper was one of its leading American advocates. He believed deeply in what a later generation would call "the mind-body connection." He was wholly in sympathy with the scientific advances that had revolutionized medicine in the nineteenth century — germ theory, pathology, bacteriology, physiological chemistry. But he and a few like-minded colleagues were convinced that physicians of their generation — trained in the new scientific medicine, armed with microscopes, zealous to reduce disease to matters of pathogenic microbes and lesions — were losing sight of the true object of their work: the human being, in all his or her imponderable complexity. "We must subject the individual who comes for advice and relief from suffering to an analysis that is directed . . . toward an understanding of his personality," Draper wrote, by which he meant not only the patient's psyche but his entire "constitution" — that particular combination of physiology, chemistry, immunological equipment, genetic inheritance, experience, and environment that made up a whole life.

In the modern era only charlatans and quacks peddled "mind cures," Draper later wrote. But he believed the physician must always "remember that the healing force of appropriate suggestion remains as strong as it was when the original medicine men first cast out devils. . . . The insistence of laboratory science upon absolutism has overawed clinical (bedside) science and almost persuaded physicians to set aside the powerful agences of faith and hope."

So when Louis Howe spoke to Draper

about how the press should be told about FDR's condition — as surely Howe did, either by telephone or in person, given what followed — he could not have found a doctor more attuned to the nuances of Roosevelt's situation.

Howe's chief concern was immediate. Draper must not lend one ounce of unnecessary fuel to the grim associations attached to the words "infantile paralysis." Every effort must be made to amplify the good news that the Roosevelts had inferred from their talk with Dr. Lovett: that the case was only mild and that FDR would not be permanently paralyzed.

Even without instructions from Howe, Draper faced a delicate task. Roosevelt was a famous and important man. Any public statement about his condition would appear in the newspapers for the persual of thousands of people. It had to be given with great care. Draper was also a personal friend of his patient, which always complicated doctor-patient relations. And Draper would have felt conscious that Roosevelt was still, in one sense, the patient of Robert Lovett, who was senior to Draper and much more prominent. Draper had no time to make a thorough examination, and he thought FDR too tender for it anyway. All he really had to go on was Dr. Lovett's short letter about the case, based on an examination already three weeks in the past.

Louis Howe may also have told Draper that Roosevelt remained exhausted and emotionally fragile. Even if Draper refused to let political considerations influence his remarks, he must think of the impact that terrible headlines might have on Roosevelt himself. It might devastate Roosevelt to read pessimistic accounts of his case in the newspapers, and that could hurt his chances of recovery.

But what precise words should he use to estimate those chances? Every doctor knew that some poliomyelitis patients got better. But would Roosevelt?

Like Dr. Lovett, Draper was well aware of the facts. Rates of recovery from poliomyelitis had varied from one outbreak to another. In 1916, one of every three patients who had been wholly or partially paralyzed in the acute stage of the disease had recovered the use of the affected limbs. Another study put the recovery rate at close to 50 percent. (Still another found that only 6 percent had come back from paralysis, but Draper thought that number was skewed.) The best estimate was that one-third to one-half of those paralyzed in any given epidemic would recover all or nearly all the use of paralyzed muscles. In other words, one-half to two-thirds would be permanently crippled.

But what about a *particular* patient's chances? Again, like Lovett, Draper knew there were no grounds for a definite prediction, not at this stage. In poliomyelitis, as Draper would write, the "paralyzing injury" was "completely hidden from view in the microscopic cell deep in the spinal cord." So there was "no possibility of knowing about the concealed damage." No test, no X-ray, no manual examination of the patient's limbs could determine the likelihood that muscles damaged and lifeless today would regain their vigor in a day or a week or a year. So "any honest doctor," Draper wrote, "when asked by an anxious parent about the chance of a child's recovery, must say: 'I do not know.' "

Yet there the reporters stood, asking that very question. If he sent them away without a clear answer; if he said he did not know; if he told them to ask again in a week, after he had observed the patient thoroughly, then the next day's headlines — as Louis Howe may well have warned him — would declare:

Draper had to say *something* definitive. But he could not tell the definitive truth, which was that he had no idea what would happen to Roosevelt.

So Draper followed the course that must have seemed the only one available to him. He announced the diagnosis and prognosis that Robert Lovett had provided in his letter to Draper — but he delivered the news with a maximum of reassurance and a minimum of the nuance and tacit acknowledgment of contingency and chance that physicians take for granted when they speak with each other, and which Lovett had used in his letter to Draper.

Franklin Roosevelt, Draper said, was suffering from infantile paralysis and was temporarily unable to walk. Yes, this was a shocking diagnosis for a man in early middle age, especially for a man of Roosevelt's standing and social type. But it was only a mild case (so Lovett had said). Furthermore the patient was "much improved." He was "feeling very well." He was already "regaining control of his legs."

"Power is already beginning to return to the affected muscles," Draper was quoted as saying, "power of control is returning, and this is a promising sign. His general condition is exceedingly good and he is in the best of spirits."

Then he gave his most reassuring declaration.

"I can say definitely that he will not be crippled, and no one should have any fear of permanent injury in any way from this attack."

Late in the day, reporters from the *World* and the *Times* knocked on the door of the Roosevelts' New York City townhouse on East 65th Street.

If the attack was so mild and the patient was doing so well, one of the reporters asked, why was Mr. Roosevelt in the hospital?

Only to give him special treatments that "would hasten the return of control of his legs," he was told — probably by Louis Howe, though the papers did not say who spoke for the family.

What about all the confusion about the diagnosis, the conflicting reports in the papers?

The answer was that "the attack was so slight that the physicians had been loath to designate the ailment."

So the papers of September 15 and 16, 1921, did not foretell disaster. Instead, Draper's promise — no permanent disability — was emphasized.

F.D. ROOSEVELT HAS INFANTILE PARALYSIS; SLOWLY NEARING RECOVERY
(Washington Post)

UNABLE TO WALK, BUT HIS PHYSICIAN IS CONFIDENT OF HIS ULTIMATE RECOVERY
(New York World)

IT WAS SAID THAT MR. ROOSEVELT WOULD NOT BE PERMANENTLY CRIPPLED.
(New York Times)

It was a story of the disaster-narrowly-averted genre, as if two ships had just missed a collision, a reassuring story about a popular and prominent man for whom everyone wished the best. No one wanted to learn that such a man could be cut down in the middle of his life by a crippling disease of childhood, his promising career destroyed; and now, thank God, it was not so.

The early, conflicting reports in the press had put relatives, friends, and associates in a state of agonized suspense. So the newspaper stories now brought enormous relief. "My dear Eleanor," wrote Adolph Miller of the Federal Reserve Board, a close friend, "Dr. Draper's statement made after Franklin's arrival at the hospital was right to the point — gratifying and reassuring — and in line with what doctors here tell me with regard to the prognosis in cases of infantile paralysis with mature persons. I'm sure Franklin is going to get well — completely well." Miller's wife was equally confident. "I simply cannot bear to have beautiful active Franklin laid low even for a time," Mary Sprague Miller wrote. "Of course he will regain the use of his limbs, and I don't believe he will even be lame." Van Lear Black, head of Fidelity & Deposit, delivered the good news to Roosevelt's staff in the New York office with relish. "I thought it would please both you and [FDR]," Black wrote Eleanor, "to know the general relief and gratification expressed when I was able to pass the word . . . as to his physical shape."

Friends and family observed a certain delicacy about the nature of the malady. After all, if a man went down in the prime of his life, it was not supposed to happen like this. This was not an accident while hunting or boating, nor a manly heart attack or the kind of exotic infection that Theodore Roosevelt had contracted on a tributary of the Amazon. One or two boneheads made cracks about a "childish disease." But it was more typical to use the genteel discretion exercised by Eleanor's cousin, Corinne (now married to Joseph Alsop, father of the columnist of the same name) who was "terribly distressed" but "thankful that it is not so serious as it might be with an illness of that kind." To such a lady, it was apparently distasteful even to pen the words "infantile paralysis," with their quiet and dreadful connotations.

No visitors were allowed except Eleanor, Sara Roosevelt, and Louis Howe, who came each morning to handle a little mail. A stream of flowers, books, candy, and calling cards flowed up from the lobby below.

"I hope this will keep green and cheerful in your room."

"Good news you are coming home so soon!"

"Please ask Eleanor to let me know if there is anything I can do."

The card in Uncle Fred Delano's firm hand said simply: *"Semper Virens."* Perhaps it accompanied a woody plant for FDR's bedside; in horticulture the term means "evergreen." But the literal translation from the Latin is "always strong." Delano would have known his *double-entendre* sent the right message to his forest-loving nephew.

"I appreciate your little note more than you can possibly imagine," FDR wrote to Daniel Roper, commissioner of Internal Revenue under Wilson, "unless you have in the past had the misfortune to be flat on your back in the hospital, with nothing particular to do, and strict orders not to think of anything important."

Not to think of anything important — there was slim chance of that. More likely Draper simply told Roosevelt not to worry about the office work he was missing downtown. The doctor would have known that a man in FDR's situation could hardly help but think about elemental matters of existence.

The brute fact of paralysis itself commanded attention. Again and again, you tell the limbs to do their routine work — the toes to curl, the thigh to flex, the buttocks to clench — but the limbs are no longer yours to command. "You drive the thought of it with all your might down from your mind toward the lifeless leg," one man struck by polio wrote about the early time

185

in his paralysis. "But the thought doesn't get there. Some deadly barrier lies between." The familiar flesh of your leg flames with pain. But you cannot make the leg move. The leg is no longer *you* at all.

Roosevelt, of all men — because he was so richly endowed with advantages of family, education, money, and personality — had always lived with the unconscious pleasure of shaping his own fate. Now this disease was threatening to rob him of that pleasure. He had always been the actor. Now he was the one being acted upon.

The only direct evidence of Roosevelt's state of mind during his first few days in the hospital is the note he dictated to Adolph Ochs, publisher of the *New York Times;* the two were on friendly terms. After reading the *Times* story about his condition, FDR wrote Ochs: "While the doctors were unanimous in telling me that the attack was very mild and that I was not going to suffer any permanent effects from it, I had, of course, the usual dark suspicion that they were just saying nice things to make me feel good, but now that I have seen the same statement officially made in the New York Times I feel immensely relieved because I know of course it must be so."

It was meant as a joking dig at the "Old

Grey Lady's" pride as the newspaper of record. But it also suggested that FDR was not entirely persuaded. Whatever Dr. Draper had told reporters or Roosevelt himself, only Roosevelt could feel the dead weight below his waist, and the "dark suspicion" no doubt was real. Following Draper's orders — and he could do nothing else, anyway — he lay flat on his back, testing his lower limbs and waiting for his pain to subside. At Campobello he had regained control of the muscles controlling defecation and urination, so the enema tube and catheter were no longer needed. Instead there was the bedpan. Nurses lifted him to insert the pan, waited, removed it. They spooned food into his mouth, moved his legs this way and that. He was learning the deep loss of dignity that fell upon adults struck by incapacitating disease. Adults struck by polio, perhaps men in particular, looked on helpless as their physical standing in the world was degraded day by day. "In their own eyes, and often in the attitudes and words of their nurses and attendants, they had been reduced to the condition of babies," the historian Daniel Wilson has written. "Like babies, they could do little for themselves, but they never completely lost their sense of manhood, and the incongruity between their treatment and a sense of self added to their pain."

An adult's first response to the lightning strike of poliomyelitis was often a reflexive and simple *No.* "The idea that you — you, yourself — have polio is at first almost unbelievable," wrote the journalist Jim Marugg, who contracted the disease as a young man. "Then the usual reaction is, 'Well, I'll be pretty sick for a few weeks but I won't have any lasting effects; John Smith didn't.' " Marugg compared it to the common reaction to a serious automobile accident: "You see a man gather himself up from the wreck and come out holding his guts in his hands and yet protesting, 'I'm all right. I'm not hurt.' "

That was Roosevelt in his hospital room as he and Louis Howe began to write letters to his friends and well-wishers. For a time, Dr. Draper informed Dr. Bennet up in Lubec, FDR had passed through "that state of nervous collapse in which all these cases find themselves for some little time after the acute attack." But now, citing the guarded assurances given by Lovett and Draper, FDR told everyone that he was going to be fine. Note after note carried the same message of cheery defiance. Every recipient, from close friends to well-wishing strangers, learned of his wonderful progress toward "a very rapid, and very complete, recovery" from "a very mild attack." He promised "a record for speed and completeness in my recovery from this youthful disease." "You will be glad to learn that the doctors are most encouraging," he told Henry Morgenthau Jr., his neighbor and friend in Hyde Park, "and that up to date I am well ahead of the record-breaking schedule I have set out to maintain in recovering." To a golfing partner he said he would soon be back on the links. He declined a speaking invitation from the Democratic governor of Arkansas but promised a quick return to active party duty. To a banker friend he said he was "still just as optimistic as ever, and I appear to have inspired the doctors with a certain amount of optimism as well, as they are most encouraging as to the future." Walter Camp, the Yale football coach who had led high-placed Washington men through strenuous workouts during the war, reminded FDR of their times "double-quicking" along the Potomac with Fred Delano and William McAdoo, secretary of the treasury. "I can assure you," FDR replied, "that if I could get up this afternoon and join with Messrs. McAdoo . . . and Delano in a sprint for the record, I would consider it the greatest joy in the world. However, the doctors are most encouraging and I have been given every reason to expect that my somewhat rebellious legs will permit me to join in another course of training sometime in the future."

When Dr. Draper permitted a few visitors, they found FDR bright, talkative, and utterly dismissive of sympathy. On the day Josephus Daniels came, FDR motioned for him to bend close, then tossed a punch at Daniels's chest. "You thought you were coming to see an invalid!" he cried.

It was a persuasive performance. But for a man too paralyzed to get out of bed, let alone walk, it simply was not reasonable to feel certain of a full recovery. His mind was rebelling against facts — an instinct of self-protection that psychologists call *denial.* He was building a shield against panic.

Dr. Draper was seeing the same manic enthusiasm when he visited Roosevelt every day. Any trace of paralysis in his patient's face had vanished, so the jaws were in their usual vigorous working order. FDR was making increasingly "cheerful and hopeful" assertions that in two or three weeks he would be ready to walk out of Presbyterian on crutches, then embark on the strenuous exercise program that would build him back up to full health. About this plan, Draper saw, Roosevelt had entirely "made up his mind."

While the patient talked away, lying flat on his back, the doctor carefully, even stealthily, examined Roosevelt's muscles and observed his movements. By September 24, nine days after FDR had entered the hospital, Draper had seen enough to be deeply worried.

In a mild case bound for a good recovery, such as Dr. Lovett had described, Draper would expect to find pain and tenderness much diminished. Below the waist, where the paralysis had been profound when FDR was at Campobello, he would see some degree of power returning — at least the power to twitch the affected muscles. Dr. Lovett had told Draper he saw only "scattered" effects in the arms at Campobello, so by now they should be well on their way back to full power.

A few signs above the waist were encouraging. Roosevelt could manipulate a pen well enough to make "a very trembling signature," awkward though it was to sign letters while flat on his back. The biceps were strong enough that he could grasp a heavy strap that hung over his bed and hoist his trunk a few inches off his sheets as the nurses shifted his body for sponge baths and bedpans. This show of strength, Draper said, was affording Roosevelt "a great sense of satisfaction."

Otherwise, Draper could see nothing to give hope of a strong recovery. Contrary to expectation, Roosevelt was still suffering considerable pain and abnormal tenderness to touch. Draper noted privately that his legs and feet made up "a most depressing picture." But what really startled the doctor were indications of much more damage in the abdomen, shoulders, and arms than Dr. Lovett had foreseen. Roosevelt insisted he felt no weakness in his arms and hands, so Draper, hesitant to challenge him, refrained from a thorough examination of those parts. But the doctor could see by the patient's movements that there was, in fact, "marked weakness" in his left shoulder, "very marked weakness" in the upper right arm, and "an unusual amount of gross muscular twitching in the muscles of both forearms." In the thighs, Draper saw not "even slight power to twitch the muscles." Elementary tests of the lower legs and feet were nearly as discouraging. Roosevelt could twitch the muscles of his hamstrings just a little, but he could not obey commands to extend his feet or move his toes more than a fraction of an inch.

Every day, very gently, so as not to cause more pain, Draper palpated the muscles of the buttocks and the lower back on either side of the spine. And every day the flesh there felt less substantial than it had the day before.

Draper's fingers were detecting the result of billions of cellular proteins dying by the day. To thrive, muscle tissue needs blood, oxygen, and the electrical impulses conveyed from the brain by healthy nerve cells. If a nerve cell is disrupted, the muscle it supplies with electrical instructions rapidly loses the power to do what a muscle does — that is, contract. Without regular contraction, healthy proteins in the muscle soon collapse. Dry, fibrous scar cells take their place, no more useful to their human host than stone. The muscles congeal into a shrunken mass.

By the objective signs, Roosevelt was not getting better. It was perfectly obvious to Draper that below the level of the navel, his body was essentially useless. Above that level, it was hard to say. But the prospects were frightening.

Roosevelt remained in too much pain to be raised to an upright position in the bed.

But the doctor's intuition told him that when FDR was ready to try sitting up, the results might be very grave. "What I fear more than anything else," Draper wrote Dr. Lovett, "is that we shall find a much more extensive involvement of the great back muscles than we expected." If so, then a moment was coming when the nurses would lift Roosevelt's torso away from the bed and slowly bend him upward at the waist; then, when they eased their hands away, the torso would simply collapse back to the mattress. Roosevelt would realize not only that he could not stand and could not walk, but that he could not even sit up.

This possibility presented Draper with an excruciating problem in medical management. His patient and friend was constructing a castle in the air, and chances were good that he was about to discover the castle had no foundation.

The doctor's new fear was not simply that Roosevelt would never walk again; that seemed all but inevitable. It was worse than that. If he could sit up, at least he could spend time at a desk. He could write and work. He could be wheeled from place to place in a wheelchair, indoors and outdoors. With his family's resources, he could enjoy some of the pleasures available to a man of leisure on a country estate. But if the major muscles of his back were deteriorating and dying, then Roosevelt faced the fate of a true invalid, of a mind in cold storage, trapped in a bed until death.

Draper posed his dilemma to Robert Lovett in a letter. "I am much concerned at the very slow recovery," he wrote. If Roosevelt were forced to confront "the frightfully depressing knowledge that he could not hold himself erect" even in a sitting position, then his will to fight back could be shattered, and a devastating depression could ensue. That, Draper knew, was by no means an uncommon response in a patient just awakening to the gravity of this kind of loss. To make any gains at all in muscular power, large or small, he would have to undertake a prolonged and terribly difficult program of exercise. The will to do so depended largely on a patient's belief that he could return to his old life. And if that belief were destroyed, the patient might well lapse into a torpor, and even the redeemable parts of his musculature would deteriorate into a completely hopeless state. Protecting his expectations for the future was as important as treating his injured body.

In Roosevelt's case, Draper feared, hope for anything close to a full recovery might not be justified. Yet hope was indispensable for any kind of recovery at all.

So once again Draper faced a difficult problem about what to say, just as he had when FDR arrived in New York from Campobello. What should he tell his determinedly cheerful patient? Should he share the whole truth as he saw it? But what was the truth? That was no easy question for a physician who believed disease was shot through with imponderables. And what effect would his observations have on the patient's determination?

Among Draper's colleagues in the 1920s, it was common to tell critically ill patients little or nothing about what ailed them. Most doctors were short of time. Many were short of the patience it took to make a layman understand what was wrong with him. "They assume a Papa-knows-best attitude and expect the patient to accept such paternalism without questioning, and many patients do accept it," wrote a contemporary of Draper's, Isidore Snapper, a Dutch-trained doctor renowned as "the champion of bedside medicine." "What is it that may make telling the whole truth so brutal?" Snapper continued: "There are few people who will continue to fight . . . once they know that they are lost. A shipwrecked sailor who survived the ordeal of drifting out on limitless ocean for days or weeks owes much . . . to his abiding faith that rescue will come." Few could "live bravely" with a devastating truth; many would succumb to "despair and hopelessness."

But which was Roosevelt: the one who would break, or the one who would endure?

"I feel so strongly after watching him for over a week that the psychological factor in his management is paramount," Draper wrote Dr. Lovett. "He has such courage, such ambition, and yet at the same time such an extraordinarily sensitive emotional mechanism that it will take all the skill which we can muster to lead him successfully to a recognition of what he really faces without utterly crushing him." The very qualities that boded well for the immediate future — Roosevelt's unusual buoyancy and optimism — were also putting him at risk of a crashing descent into depression.

Draper decided he could not put Roosevelt's ambition at risk, not yet. So he asked Dr. Lovett, a master of orthopedic support devices, to devise some sort of strong brace for Roosevelt's back. They could get it on him just before they tried for the first time to move him into a chair. That way, Draper explained, "he will not realize too suddenly that his back will not hold him. I thought that we might explain the preparation of such a brace or corset as being merely a conservative method to prevent the inevitable strain on muscles set to work again for the first time."

When Lovett's reply came, Draper saw no response at all to his heartfelt plea for a ruse that might preserve Roosevelt's courage for a while longer. Robert Lovett was a fine doctor and an innovator, but he fit the classic pattern of the orthopedist as mechanical engineer of the human body, attending to bones and joints and muscles as if they were the parts of a machine. When the machine breaks, the mechanic is called to fix the break, repair the joint, mend the tear. The cause of the break, much less the personality of the patient, has little to do with the repairs. Practically Lovett's first words about the case to Draper had been: "I never find the history [that is, the origins of the case] of much use." Bone and muscle and how to make them work correctly — that was what Lovett worried about. So he said nothing about Draper's idea for a back brace, and nothing about the patient's "extraordinarily sensitive emotional mechanism."

Lovett did want to get a close look at Roosevelt, and he could not do so until the pain of the acute phase had passed. So he made a simple suggestion to Draper: "I do not know whether you use it or not, but I have found immersion in a strong saline bath to be of value at this stage, as I believe it hastens the disappearance of the tenderness and allows some muscular action. . . . I have no definite engagements ahead and can come on at any time."

Draper said no more about his idea for a brace, and he followed Lovett's advice. On each of the next ten days, he directed nurses to lift Roosevelt into a tub filled with hot water mixed with salt. There he sat soaking, and the procedure, Draper reported, brought "great comfort to the patient."

Finally, Draper decided it was time to test the muscles that Roosevelt would need to sit up: the upper thighs, the pelvic girdle, and the great back muscles.

Draper watched closely. He squeezed limbs here and there to detect the mass and texture of muscles. As he had feared, the pelvic muscles, thigh muscles, and most of the muscles of the lower legs were "in poor shape." But to the doctor's surprise and delight, Roosevelt "had much more power in the back muscles than I had thought." Weakly, painfully, he could now hold himself erect in a sitting position.

In later years, neither Draper nor Roosevelt nor anyone in the family remarked on the significance of that moment. But it made all the difference for what was to come. If Roosevelt could sit up straight, he had a chance, however small, of returning to the world he had known.

Dr. Lovett came over from Boston, got FDR into a wheelchair, and said he could go home from the hospital when he wanted. "There is power in practically all of the hip muscles," he noted, "and when he starts on muscle training I believe that things will start along." As usual, Lovett's remark was guarded. He did not comment on Roosevelt's hope of recovering fully and walking again — not to Draper, anyway; he simply said the time had come when improvements could be pursued.

By the end of October, the worst of the muscular pain had subsided. The acute stage of the illness was over.

The virus was gone.

On October 28, Roosevelt was taken to his home on East 65th Street. He directed that the move be made after dark, so that in the transfer from the car to the house, neighbors and people passing on the street would not see how he was.

Robert Lovett and George Draper had performed no miracles. But the two doctors, especially Draper, had rendered a great service to their patient. In the period of shock and dawning awareness that followed the disaster, they gave him a margin for hope.

Lovett and Draper well knew the odds against a full recovery, but they kept their expectations to themselves. Lovett told Louis Howe it was possible that his boss, with great difficulty, might regain the ability to walk. Draper detected few if any real signs of a spontaneous return of muscle power in FDR's legs — and so much had been lost that walking again must have seemed inconceivable to Draper. Yet he withheld his fear from FDR. Both doctors were doing no more than adhering to the best medical insight. The peculiar nature of polio's effects — the uncertainty of how much muscle power would return with exercise — meant that disability was not, in fact, a complete certainty. The possibility of progress, however slight, would persist.

If Draper and Lovett had gone the other way — if they had despaired and told FDR their pessimistic expectations — then Roosevelt and his family too likely would have despaired. By keeping the degree of his disability indefinite, the doctors created an opportunity and a precedent. If they would not acknowledge disability as inevitable, then FDR need not acknowledge it either. If they would not say he was out of luck, that he must prepare to face facts, then he could spin his own scenario of the future. He could preserve a fragile bubble of hope and expectation, an interior realm where he could lay plans.

Two thoughtful students of Roosevelt's career, Amos Kiewe and Davis W. Houck, have noted that "a physical impairment's meaning is never fixed." Dead cells cannot be restored to life; the physical realities of a loss may be unchangeable. But the person who has suffered the loss, if allowed to do so, may determine for himself what the loss will mean. The doctors allowed Roosevelt to do that. They allowed him to shape his own story of what had happened and what was to come, a story he would tell himself and everyone else over and over.

Chapter 6
"Perfectly Definite in My Determination"
NOVEMBER TO DECEMBER 1921

Sara Delano Roosevelt had been keeping herself "very cheerful," Eleanor remarked later, though Eleanor suspected "it must have been a most terrific strain for her, and I am sure that, out of sight, she wept many hours."

While her son was still at Presbyterian Hospital, Sara left the city for her home on the Hudson River in upstate Dutchess County. She felt sure that when he was ready to be released, he would want to convalesce in serene Hyde Park. New York City was no place for an extended rest, and she wanted to prepare the house and servants for a new task: to make life as easy as possible for an invalid.

By this point Sara had discarded her faith in Dr. Bennet's promise that "this boy is going to get well!" This, at least, was the sense of Franklin's condition that she apparently conveyed to an old friend, Mrs.

Lily Norton, who stayed with Sara at Hyde Park for a few days that fall.

"It's a lovely region," Mrs. Norton wrote to a friend, "but tragedy rather overshadows this once so happy & prosperous family, for Mrs. R's only son, Franklin Roosevelt, was struck down in August with a terribly serious case of infantile paralysis. He is only 39 — both too young and too old for such a fell germ to disable him. He's had a brilliant career as assistant of the Navy under Wilson, & then a few brief weeks of crowded glory & excitement when nominated by the Democrats for the Vice-Presidency. Now he is a cripple — will he ever be anything else? His mother is wonderfully courageous & plucky, but it's a bitter blow."

A terribly serious case: If Sara had ever believed the doctors' contention that it was "only a very mild case," she wasn't saying that to her friend now.

And: *Now he is a cripple — will he ever be anything else?*

The question sounds less like a question and more like a settled judgment: Once again, life had lowered a cruel burden upon an undeserving victim. If the comment reflects Sara's own dawning sense of Franklin's situation, as it probably did, then it suggests she was having none of her son's optimistic chatter about getting up on crutches soon and exercising his way back to a full recovery. Sara was no dreamer. She was sixty-five years old, highly intelligent, with a broad experience of the world. She had run a large estate without a husband for twenty years. She knew what made sense and what didn't. She knew, certainly, that her son must now have a long, proper rest in the country. First he could enjoy the silent, soothing upstate winter; then, when the spring came, there would be long after-noons of fresh air and sun out in the garden, near the stables, where he could look down the forested slope and out to the distant river.

But when FDR was about to leave the hospital in New York and Sara told him the house at Hyde Park was ready for him, he said no, he would not be going to Hyde Park. He was returning to the house in town, on East 65th Street, where he would be close to his doctors and the nurses who would supervise his program of exercise. Once again, the man whom others had privately derided as a mama's boy overrode his strong-willed mother's wishes without a second thought.

Roosevelt had strict orders from Dr. Draper.

Any patient recovering from the acute phase of poliomyelitis, Draper noted, would feel the "most natural insistence . . . that he start at once to 'do something' for the paralyzed muscles." Indeed, Draper told Dr. Lovett, FDR was "exceedingly ambitious and anxious to get to the point where he can try the crutches." But until the pain was gone, "doing something" could only make matters worse. The patient must resist the urge. "There is no question that the subsequent recovery of weakened muscles is seriously jeopardized by overt treatment at this early stage," Draper would write. "The physician should stoutly maintain an attitude of masterly inactivity." Roosevelt must stay immobile in bed for twenty-three hours of every day for several weeks. For a single hour every day he could sit up in a chair.

So he waited.

The Roosevelts' adjoining town houses — 47–49 East 65th Street, three blocks east of Central Park — comprised one of the loveliest residences on one of the most elegant blocks in one of the most desirable residential neighborhoods in all of New York City. Sara Roosevelt had commissioned their design and construction as a belated wedding present for her son and his wife in

1907–1908, though, to be precise, only one of the town houses was to be for the young couple. The other was for Sara herself, with interior doors connecting the residences on three floors. It was not unusual in the Roosevelts' era for a widow to live with a married child. But in this family the invisible screen between generations was porous indeed — a fact made plain by those interior sliding doors. And the doors rumbled open a great deal.

In choosing the Upper East Side, the family had been following the trend of many well-to-do New Yorkers migrating north from Gramercy Park and Washington Square to the city's newest zone of prosperity and taste. Sara ordered the demolition of four old brownstones on the property and hired Charles Platt, a leading designer of country estates and landscapes, to be her architect. At Sara's direction, Platt modeled his design on the Ludlow-Parish house at 6–8 East 76th Street. (This was the home of Eleanor's cousin, Susie Parish, where Eleanor and Franklin had been married in the company of the president of the United States, Theodore Roosevelt, who gave away his niece as the bride. It was of occasions like this that the president's daughter Alice once remarked that T.R. wanted "to be the bride at every wedding, the corpse at every funeral, and the baby at every christening.")

High above the street, etched into the limestone, Platt carved the Roosevelt coat of arms — three roses sprouting from a grassy mound, a *rose field.* Under this he placed matching front entrances that opened into mirror-image layouts. There were dark-wood balustrades, floor-to-ceiling windows over the street, fireplaces in the main rooms, and a deep well that came down from the roof, bringing sunlight to the lower floors. The houses were narrow, with no windows along the sides, yet there was a feeling of space and light. If the decorating was not chic, it certainly created an air of comfort and hospitality. Servants' quarters were on the upper stories and the kitchen in the basement, with a small elevator in each house to make the seven stories (basement to sixth floor) easier to negotiate.

FDR lay in his bedroom on the third floor at the rear. The broad window gave out on a small yard and the backs of brownstones on East 66th. For his one hour out of bed, a wheelchair was purchased. Using the chair was a minor ordeal. First, Nurse Rockey would help him to a sitting position. Then, with someone to hold the wheelchair steady

— one of the servants or Eleanor or Louis Howe — she would manhandle FDR from the bed onto the seat of the chair. Then she would push the chair and its load down to the elevator near the front of the house. In the elevator there was barely room for FDR and the chair, so he would descend alone to the first or second floor, where Rockey would meet him and push him to a place to sit. If it was afternoon, when Rockey took her break, Eleanor performed the job. "He was tall and heavy to lift," she said later, "but somehow both of us [Rockey and she] managed to learn to do whatever was necessary."

The children were kept at a distance. Marguerite LeHand, whom the children had begun to call Missy, came in for an hour each day to take dictation. Only a few close associates and friends were permitted brief visits. Franklin must have spent much of his time alone during these weeks of waiting, since even Louis Howe was spending a good deal of each weekday handling Roosevelt's affairs at Fidelity & Deposit downtown. His mother was gone. There were few distractions, and he had time to think.

Anyone who seeks the subterranean streams of Franklin Roosevelt's mind comes up against stony shields, chiefly his lifelong habit of happy chatter in nearly every circumstance, even with those closest to him, and his disinclination to tell anyone what he was really thinking.

As to physical pain, he did say later that during this time in the city, although he no longer was suffering the "extreme discomfort" of the weeks at Campobello, "the leg muscles remained extremely sensitive," the calves being the worst.

As to his state of mind, there are two kinds of testimony: that of his friends who popped in for a few minutes at a time, and that of other adults who have suddenly lost the ability to walk. In the 1920s few people with disabilities recorded frank memoirs. But in later decades, because of the mounting polio epidemics themselves and the openness encouraged by the disability rights movement, more people wrote about what it was like to lose the use of their limbs. From their writings, we can learn a good deal about things that FDR probably was feeling but kept hidden.

According to a reporter who later asked questions about these weeks in FDR's life, his friends all gave the same story "in tones of wonder." He "gaily brushed aside every hint of condolence," they said, "and sent them away more cheerful than they could make a pretense of being when they arrived." They heard him express not "a complaint or a regret or even acknowledge that he had had so much as a bit of hard luck." His letters gave the same impression. He made no reference to the dreadful reprise of high fever that hit him three weeks after leaving the hospital, or the frightening pain in his eyes. On the contrary, he wrote a Democratic Party friend in Ohio, "I am back in my own house again and getting on extremely well, though it will be some time before I am able to get down to the office again. The doctors say, however, that my progress is excellent and even more rapid than they had hoped!"

But the experiences of other traumatically disabled people run so contrary to these reports that we cannot help suspecting Roosevelt of a smiling diversionary campaign. Indeed, his happy talk with friends may signal that he was developing a battery of skills familiar to many disabled people. The anthropologist Robert Murphy, struck by a congenital disorder of the spine when he was forty-eight, wrote: "The price for normal relations" with the able-bodied is that the disabled "must comfort others about their condition. They cannot show fear, sorrow, depression . . . or anger, for this disturbs the able-bodied. The unsound of limb are permitted only to laugh. The rest of the emotions, including anger and the expression of hostility, must be bottled up, repressed, and allowed to simmer or be released in the backstage area of the home. . . . People have been surprised to learn that my paralysis preys so heavily on my mind, as I rarely show it. But it does, and on the thoughts of all the deeply impaired."

There are parallels too between Roosevelt and the writer Hugh Gregory Gallagher, arrested in young adulthood by a severe attack of polio. Like FDR, Gallagher had been raised by an ebullient mother to work hard to please and impress the adults around him. He found that his catastrophe did not diminish this deeply ingrained habit but actually enhanced it, even while he was still in the hospital. But his happy mask covered a dark chasm. "As cheerful of demeanor as my mother," Gallagher wrote, "I continue[d] pleasant and helpful, certainly the most popular patient on the floor. It is a wonder I did not turn catatonic with suppressed rage and grief."

An adult who is suddenly disabled enters a realm unknown and ultimately unknowable to the able-bodied, a prisonlike place where "everything look[s] big and menacing" and "even familiar things [seem] strange." More than a few people struck by a severe disability have likened their situation to that of Gregor Samsa, the young man in Franz Kafka's *Metamorphosis* — written just a few years before Roosevelt's illness — who awakens one morning to find himself transformed into a giant insect.

Disastrous as polio was to the young children who were its usual victims, the disease treated adults even more harshly. "When the small child is suddenly robbed of his ability to walk, a door slams shut on a very brief experience of active play, and the new world of the cripple is soon all he holds within his memory," wrote Turnley Walker, who contracted polio in early adulthood. By contrast, "the brand-new polio of thirty-five is overwhelmed with anguish for all he has lost." For victims in the early months after the acute stage, the loss was complicated by agonizing uncertainty about the future. They had entered a hideous lottery: *This* cripple would recover but *that* cripple would not, and no one could predict which would be which.

In the able-bodied, one's legs are taken for granted as "mine" and "me." They are not separate, inanimate objects but parts of oneself, ready instruments of the mind and will. "Each person simply accepts the fact that he has two legs and can walk," Robert Murphy observed. "He does not think about it or marvel at it any more than he would feel gratitude for the oxygen content of air." But in someone like FDR, the legs had become all-but-inanimate lumps, still attached to the rest of the body by muscle and bone but not under his control. In fact, some people with polio or spinal-cord injuries have said the affected limbs seem as if they have joined an enemy force in rebellion against the sovereign mind: "The alien intruder and the old occupant coexist in mutual hostility in the same body." The mind is caught off guard, still unconsciously assuming the body can walk, hop a fence, make love. But "this other body — the Now-Me — does none of these things, does not even belong to Me," another person with polio wrote. The person recovering from polio often began to remove the possessive pronoun from references to affected limbs, as FDR now did when he began to speak not of "my legs" and "my leg muscles" but of "*the* legs," "*the* leg muscles," "*the* calves," "*the* right knee," "*the* left knee." In such cases he may have been echoing the physician's habit of referring to body parts as independent entities. But that too suggests a view of one's own body as a thing apart from the self.

Before his illness, Roosevelt had been blessed with a superb way with people. His friends' stories from the months after his homecoming show that he retained his social gifts as he lay paralyzed. But there can be little doubt that his relations with others were changing.

Reason tells the adult who has suddenly been disabled that he is not to blame for his affliction, that he is the same person he has always been, a perfectly good person worthy of others' respect. But reason is often overwhelmed by deepening suspicions that he is, in fact, *not* the same person — not as good a person, that he has lost essential value, especially in the eyes of others. He may feel embarrassed, and he senses embarrassment in the people around him. They don't know what to say. One friend of Eleanor's must have spoken for others in the Roosevelts' circle when, after apologizing for her long failure to get in touch following the news of Franklin's illness, confessed: "I have tried hard to write you but I simply did not know how to express my feelings." If one's condition inspires speechlessness, then the logical inference is that one must have an unmentionable flaw.

Self-consciousness may knot itself into guilt. The sufferer has grown up in a culture in which bad deeds are supposed to be followed by shame, then punishment. Now he finds himself the victim of a particularly terrible punishment, and to many an unconscious mind it stands to reason that one must have done something very bad to deserve it. Freudians have posed an Oedipal theory — that the disabled son may think he is being punished for unconscious desire for the mother. To a man like FDR, the only child of a powerful mother and an ailing, elderly father, it is not inconceivable that this theme struck a dismal chord in his unconscious mind.

The disabled may spin an invisible cocoon and withdraw even in the midst of what seems to be normal conversation. The instinct is to protect oneself and one's loved ones, but the tactic can be wounding. Robert Murphy described aloneness as "a fixture of the consciousness of all disabled persons. . . . I had visitors constantly every day that I was in the hospital, and I was surrounded by family at home, but I nonetheless was invaded by a profound sense of removal. My family felt this acutely, and their concerns for me became tainted by hurt and bewilderment." Eleanor once remarked on the solitude behind her husband's jolly extroversion. "It was a kind of inner reserve which I think at times made it very difficult for him to actually become very close to many people," she said. "There were certain things that he never really talked about — that he would just shut up, and it made him very, very much alone in some ways."

Yet the person who now may feel profoundly alone also becomes "a person without privacy," as Hugh Gallagher put it. To accomplish the intimate and now unwieldy acts of urination, defecation, and bathing, Roosevelt had to depend on his nurse and his wife, not just for a brief stay in the hospital but every day, week after week after week. One depends on others for every need, from making money to making a phone call. The sense of obligation can become crushing. "It's hard to ask those around us, even those who love us, to do things for us, intimate things, over and over again," wrote the polio activist Lorenzo Wilson Milam. Most people, Milam observed, will not grasp the psychic costs of dependence — "a word so meaningless to those who can move and walk and dance . . .

(and, most sacred of all, can jump up and run away)" — until they lie on their death-beds. The inability to perform an act as simple as dressing oneself reminds one of being a helpless child. "If you require the help of someone else to put your shirt on," Gallagher wrote, "you lose your personal identity, your physical oneness during that period of time that the act is taking place. You cease to be you; you become a part of someone else in that instant of assistance."

All these changes — the perception of body parts as alien, the altered relations with others, the damage to self-esteem — roll together in a broad assault on one's whole sense of self. The assault forces "a diminution of everything I used to be," as Murphy put it, and, perhaps even worse, of everything one had hoped to become.

What, precisely, is the "self"? Modern students of the mind say it is Murphy's "everything-I-used-to-be" plus everything one expects to be — a kind of unfinished autobiography carried around in the head. It is always being revised and extended, with unwritten chapters outlined vaguely or even in detail. From an early age, Franklin Roosevelt had composed a life story like that of Uncle Ted and followed its chapters quite fabulously: service in the New York legislature, assistant secretary of the navy, even the nomination for vice president. Unlike T.R. he had lost the 1920 race for vice president, but the campaign had made him a national figure in the Democratic Party. The Democrats were in for a spell in the wilderness now; anyone could see that. But he was not even forty! He would have time to make money of his own and get free of his mother's purse strings; time to help build the party; time to make more friends where he would need them; time to serve in statewide office. "Thank God we are still young!" he had exclaimed to his aide Steve Early after the defeat in 1920.

And now what? By Thanksgiving 1921 Roosevelt had been incapacitated for more than a quarter of a year. Whatever hopes his doctors had allowed him to entertain, whatever promises he had made to himself, he was not yet even walking on crutches. Hopes for spontaneous recovery in the muscles below his waist had gone a-glimmering. It was now obvious that if there was to be any recovery, it was certainly not going to be the spontaneous and speedy business discussed in the early weeks of the illness. They all knew it now. When Herbert Pell, chairman of the Democratic Executive Committee, wrote to invite FDR to attend the committee's next meeting, Louis Howe passed the letter to Roosevelt with a note in the margin: "Mr. Pell had better wake up & hear the birdies!"

For many people who come under this psychic assault, there can be no response but despair and surrender. That is what Dr. Draper had feared would happen when Roosevelt's "extraordinarily sensitive emotional mechanism" collided with "what he really faces."

But some who come under this assault on the self mount a counterattack. During these first weeks at home, by some process Roosevelt never described in any detail, he appears to have done just this. It was an act of sheer defiance. No, he would not be crippled. No, he would not relinquish the life story he held in his mind. He would do whatever it took to walk again and resume his pursuit of the presidency.

But he must have help. More than ever, he would need a "man Friday" to help him work, to speak and write for him, to act as his eyes and ears.

But would Louis Howe do it?

In the year since the defeat of the Cox-Roosevelt ticket in 1920, Howe had been stewing about what to do next. Few men would have needed a year, but few men conceived of their choices quite as Howe did.

In some buried recess of longing, Howe was a disappointed dramatist. As a young reporter for his father's newspaper, barely out of school, he had entered the theatrical world of Saratoga Springs, a summertime haven for Broadway actors. He acted, directed, designed sets, published programs, wrote plays. Any hope of a career in the theater was cut short by his marriage. From then on he had to scramble to make a living, with no time for a larkish pursuit of the stage. Ever since, he had played at theatricals as a hobby, writing and directing skits for parties. But his love of drama — of directing characters through intricately contrived plans and designs — was transmuted into a fascination with politics in general and, in particular, with the idea of stage-managing some great talent to fame.

When Roosevelt had first joined the state legislature in Albany, Howe had sized him up and seen the makings of a leading man, or so Howe claimed later. They had met in the library of the big house the Roosevelts rented, just down the street from the capitol. Louis noticed the coat of arms on the wall over FDR's head; it happened to show a fist holding a club, and Howe made a quick comparison to Uncle Ted's famous "big stick," a connection the young FDR must have relished. "I was impressed at once by his sincerity and earnestness," Howe told a reporter later. "Almost at that first meeting I made up my mind that he was of presidential timber and that only an accident could prevent him from attaining that office."

Whether Howe really had such an early vision, the remark showed his tendency to imagine himself into the role of director and stage manager.

Much later, it occurred to the economist Rexford G. Tugwell, who observed Roosevelt and Howe at close quarters, that the contrasting physiques of the two men must have played some important part in their relationship. Howe's "bony body," Tugwell wrote, was "more appropriate to a preadolescent boy than to a full-aged man. It was as though progress toward adulthood had been arrested along in the early teens and a kind of withering process had set in. How this contrasted with the handsome and well-articulated younger man can be imagined."

For ten years Howe had pinned his enormous hidden ambition to Roosevelt's. As FDR's campaign aide in 1912, with the candidate bedbound with typhoid fever,

Howe had single-handedly saved Roosevelt's seat in the state senate. From 1913 to 1920 he was FDR's man at the Navy Department, skimping along on a bureaucrat's salary, his wife and children forced to live in Grace Howe's hometown of Fall River, Massachusetts, because Louis couldn't afford a decent place in Washington. He was the "confidential assistant" whom Roosevelt trusted to guard the office door against unwanted visitors; to answer letters and draft speeches; to clean up messes and brainstorm plans for the long pursuit of the big prize. He was perhaps the only person who fully grasped and shared FDR's deep ambition for the presidency. Howe could never play the leading man himself, but the game of Pygmalion was an absorbing substitute, especially when it involved a man whose comradeship, once given, was so fulfilling.

In smoky political headquarters in Albany and Washington, the social worker Frances Perkins watched Roosevelt and Howe work side by side for years. Perkins respected Louis but pitied him. She believed he had been twisted by the burden of carrying a first-rate mind and a sensitive temperament in that hacking little frame, the face marked up by wrinkles and moles, the bulging black eyes throwing suspicious glances around the room. "He couldn't be . . . natural and easy and relaxed . . . because of his very peculiar appearance," Perkins said later, "which must have been an awful thing to cope with all his life." She conjectured that "as a boy he had been repulsive to many people," so as an adult "he wanted to be loved by something great . . . something outside himself" — and to Howe even a wife could not provide that. Roosevelt could. "His first view of Franklin Roosevelt was of a beautiful, strong, vigorous, Greek god king of an athlete," Perkins said, "so gay, so everything that Louis never had been. He seemed to be the kind of a person that Louis had always been looking for, kind of from another world.

"Franklin Roosevelt represented hope to him. Louis was fulfilled through Franklin . . . in the way that some people are fulfilled through their children who turn out to be great and shining and beautiful creatures up from the muck and mud of their mother's life or their father's life which has been lowly, scrabbly and hardworking. I'm sure that was the case with Louis."

But now, with Roosevelt out of political office, Howe confronted a difficult choice. During his years at the Navy Department, despite his eccentricities, he had impressed a number of influential men. Some were newspaper editors. Some were business executives now looking to cherry-pick talented Wilsonians with Washington connections. Finally, he had the chance to make a good living, and that might make amends for the collapse of his relationship with his wife.

His marriage had been stone-cold for years. It's not clear what the root problem was — perhaps Grace Howe's sense that she had married beneath the station of her prominent family, perhaps the half-baked career that kept Louis away most of the time — but by the time they had two growing children in the 1910s, some deep disillusionment on Grace's part had left the two emotionally estranged and miserable. Louis's wanderings among the back rooms of newspapering and politics in Albany, New York, and Washington had made their lives unstable and their finances precarious. Once, in mid-1915, when Louis was working in Washington while Grace raised the two children all but alone in Fall River — "this stupid way of living," he called it — he had been astonished to hear her speak fondly of their youthful outings to pick flowers together. He could hardly believe she recalled any happy times. "Is it possible," he wrote after ruminating about the fleeting moment for several days, "that I am wrong in thinking that it is only your sense of duty that keeps you by my side? . . . I have felt so sure that I have lost your real love, that all life held was to try and make life just endurable for you, with no hope of making you really happy, that I have tried to bury my love for you deep in my heart. I thought that every time I kissed you I could feel you wince and draw back. . . . But oh dear heart if I am wrong — if you really want loving — let me know dear and you and I will go flower hunting many, many times like the old days." But the estrangement remained. Just before the family went to Campobello in the summer of 1921, Louis reminded his wife later: "You told me . . . that you hated my touch."

His health was so fragile that doctors had told him a cold might trigger a crisis in his lungs or his heart and kill him before he was sixty.

But "I cannot die," he told Grace, "until I feel sure you and Kiddens [daughter Mary] and Bub [son Hartley] will be at least modestly provided for."

Now he had a chance to accomplish that aim.

When the Harding administration took over the government, Howe had stayed on at the Navy Department to help with the transition. Then he accepted FDR's invitation to join him as an aide at Fidelity & Deposit — another subordinate job with a salary to match. But he was getting bigger offers. One of the New York dailies wanted him as city editor. He turned that down. Then Arthur Patch Homer, a big-talking entrepreneur, offered him big money — FDR told Josephus Daniels it was $20,000 a year, far more than Howe had ever made — to take an executive job in a new oil-exploration concern. Homer's project was hardly General Electric, and Howe may have thought he was a risky man to bet on. But an offer like that, along with the others he got, must have opened his eyes to the sort of position he might now find in the business world.

But that would take him out of Franklin Roosevelt's service.

If Howe in 1911 had looked in the mirror of Roosevelt's knightly countenance and seen his own gnomish self glorified, now, in the fall of 1921, he saw Adonis crippled, the prince humbled. Overnight, Howe had shape-shifted into the able-bodied member of the pair. Suddenly Roosevelt was the weakling, far more in need of a friend and a helper than ever before. Howe could play the role of the strong man.

So there was Howe's choice: to save his family, or to save Franklin Roosevelt. He could not do both at once, not with the degree of devotion that FDR's all-consuming career demanded.

In the Roosevelt family, a story was later told that at Campobello, Eleanor had urged Louis not to let the Roosevelts' problem interfere with the life of his own family any longer. He must attend to his job at Fidelity & Deposit and resolve the issue of other job offers.

"This is my job," he was said to have told her. "Helping Franklin."

That autumn, when Roosevelt and Howe discussed the matter again in New York, with the prospect of a long haul against the longest odds, Howe made the same choice. He gave up the chance at a livelihood that would have relieved his wife of the insecurity they had lived with for many years. She and the children would live near Hyde Park in Poughkeepsie, where Mary attended Vassar College. FDR himself told Grace that he would let Louis loose every weekend but that he must have him close all week long, since he would need Louis at odd hours. So it was decided that Louis would live on indefinitely at East 65th Street.

To those who knew the Howe family, Louis's decision was not an inspiring act of self-sacrifice for a friend. "It was the closest thing to desertion I've ever seen," Jimmy Roosevelt would say later.

Years later, Howe liked to claim credit for Roosevelt's decision to remain in politics. As Howe told the tale, he had "flung [a] challenge" to FDR. He must decide whether to retire as an invalid to Hyde Park, where he could take up "a useful life engaged in literary work, and other things that required no personal agility"; or to "gather up your courage and plunge forward as though nothing had happened. You are a man of destiny, and I will go along with you every inch of the hard way, if that is the way you choose. Besides, this makes it certain that you'll be President. My reason? You'll get the sympathy of the public and you will be spared the handshaking, the platform stumping, the bazaar openings — in short all the political nonsense that ruins so many men."

According to Howe, Franklin listened closely, then "flashed a smile" and said: "Well, when do we begin?"

But this yarn has the sound, once again,

of Howe conjuring the image of himself as dramatist. This was not the way things went with Franklin Roosevelt. Before and after he became ill, it was FDR, not Louis, who made the decisions about his career, and he did not need Howe to define this critical choice. In fact, no surviving evidence suggests that Roosevelt ever allowed himself to think seriously of quitting politics. The fact that he asked Howe to stay with him reinforces the point. For the path FDR saw ahead, he needed Howe as fixer, messenger, and sounding board more than ever.

There is no record of whatever discussion occurred between FDR and Eleanor Roosevelt about the prospect of Louis Howe living with them until further notice. During the 1920 campaign, she had gotten over her distaste for Howe. On Campobello a bond between them had formed, and in the coming months a true friendship would develop. For now, Howe's presence simply meant a new problem in managing the household: She would have to reassign bedrooms. "The house was not overlarge," she said later, "and we were very crowded." Nurse Rockey had needed a room. Now Howe needed a room. Counting the servants, at least a dozen people now needed beds in the side-by-side town houses. So some of the children would have to be moved around.

The easy ones were the two little boys, Franklin Jr. and John; she put them on the fourth floor of Sara's house along with their nurse. The hard one was Anna, the oldest of the children, at fifteen, whose bedroom was on the third floor at the front of the house — the nicest of the bedrooms, really, since the windows overlooked the passing scene on the street.

Eleanor gave Anna a choice: stay in her room but share it with the nurse for several hours each day, or take a small room all to herself on the fourth floor at the back. Anna chose the latter. So Howe was installed in Anna's room. Nurse Rockey could station herself there when Howe was at Fidelity & Deposit during the day.

All the shuffling left Eleanor with no room of her own. So "I slept on a bed in one of the little boys' rooms," she wrote later. "I dressed in my husband's bathroom. In the daytime I was too busy to need a room."

On the first day of December she needed to accommodate yet another regular visitor to the house: Kathleen Lake, the physical therapist who would supervise FDR's first course of exercise. She was to come most mornings and spend several hours.

This was about the time when Eleanor's mother-in-law returned from Hyde Park to spend the winter on East 65th Street.

More than any other member of the family, Sara had been deeply frightened by the disease. She seemed never to understand that after the first few days of the virus's assault, Franklin's life was not at risk, and she continued to fear that he was in mortal danger. Eleanor said later: "Her anxiety over his general health was so great that she dreaded his making any effort whatsoever."

So when Sara was given to understand that her son meant to recover the ability to walk and then resume his pursuit of political office, she was dumbfounded. Then she discovered that the slovenly Louis Howe, whom she could not abide, was ensconced in her granddaughter's bedroom. And her son's body was being manipulated by a strange woman. It was bedlam.

She took the position that the time had come to face facts. The safe and intelligent thing for Franklin to do now was to retire to the house at Hyde Park. There he could rest indefinitely and fully recover his health — not his ability to walk, which she thought quite evidently impossible, but the rest of his constitution, which had been so gravely weakened by the disease.

Later, people inside and outside the family would say Sara's position was nothing more than the selfish willfulness of a "domineering Tartar," an overbearing mother who wanted her beloved boy back among her apron strings.

But that judgment was too harsh. Sara's wish for FDR to retire to the calm safety of Hyde Park was, first, the natural instinct of a parent whose only child had been badly hurt. It was also mature, sensible, and realistic. For how could he possibly have the life of a politician now? Even if the Democratic Party could somehow be persuaded to nominate a crippled man for office, it was preposterous to think he could undertake the physical demands of an important public position, let alone of a campaign. To a paralyzed man, the hectic cityscapes of New York and Albany and Washington, D.C., presented obstacles and embarrassments at every turn. His infirmity — an entirely private matter — would be fully exposed to public view. A demanding schedule would only weaken him further. He would risk not only defeat and disappointment but humiliation and additional risks to his health.

Consider the alternative: Sara knew that, of all people, her son was in a position to enjoy a pleasant and rewarding life despite being crippled. Without the use of his legs he still could do a great many things he loved. He could develop his collections of stamps and rare books and naval prints. He could read. He had spoken often of a wish to write, and now he would have the leisure to do so. He could develop and manage — at least from a distance — the estate and its farms and forests. He could be a leader in the village of Hyde Park and at St. James Church, as his father had been. The family had the means for all the assistance he would need. He would not want for a thing.

There was much to be said for Sara's view of the matter. For people with property and means, the secluded world of the Hudson Valley estates was one of the most comfortable fragments of civilization that Americans had ever created. The life Sara loved at Hyde Park, and which she knew Franklin loved, was a placid cycle of quiet afternoons and pleasant evenings with neighbors; of picnics on rustic pavilions in summer and reading and games by the fire in winter. Tables were laden with the produce of one's own garden and dairy. Down the shaded driveway was the Albany Post Road, which led to the lovely homes of relatives and old friends. All along the majestic Hudson were reminders of the family's past. Franklin loved to tell stories of those days; perhaps he would gather them into books. He loved the old Dutch farmhouses and churches; these too he could study at leisure. All these pleasures would still be available to him. And of course the difficulties of paralysis could be managed in near-total privacy. Why would he not make the inevitable bow to misfortune and accept the compensations of this rich and full life in the country?

Sara pressed her arguments often during the first weeks of her return to the city.

Eleanor, working desperately to keep the household moving from day to day, wanted to do what was best for her husband, though both alternatives — returning to an active life in politics or retiring permanently to Hyde Park — struck her as equally implausible.

She sought out George Draper to ask his opinion. The doctor told her that a vigorous resumption of normal activities, insofar as was possible, would not endanger Franklin; that "even if it tired him, it was better for his general condition"; and that if FDR retreated into the sanctuary of Hyde Park, it would be "a terrible waste." Believing as always in the mind's influence on the physical constitution, Draper said Franklin would likely make a better recovery if he believed in his own destiny as a politician.

Eleanor took this to heart. Privately, she had reached the conclusion that her husband would never again walk unaided, and thus an actual candidacy for office would be impossible. "She had faced that," said Frances Perkins, who would become close to both Roosevelts. "She never fooled herself about his getting back the full use of his legs, which he did believe in. [But] she thought he would die spiritually, die intellectually, and die in his personality, if he didn't have political hope." Perkins said she heard Eleanor say: "I do hope that he'll keep in political life. I want to keep him interested in politics. This is what he cares for more than anything else. I don't want him forgotten." At the very least, he could stay in touch with political people and keep up to date on the issues he cared about — and that meant staying in New York City for most of the year. Surely too it appalled Eleanor to think of spending the rest of her own life as helpmate to a crippled man in the remote Hyde Park house that remained her mother-in-law's domain. And it was quite the contrary of what her husband wanted.

"If it had been a necessity he could have done it and not been unhappy," she said later. But Dr. Draper said it was *not* a necessity.

So she took Franklin's side against her mother-in-law.

Outnumbered but undaunted, Sara refused to join what she regarded as an astonishing flight from reality. She became "vociferous in her demands," Anna Roosevelt recalled later, that Franklin give up all thought of returning to politics. She offered to provide all the money necessary for the family's support at Hyde Park. And she fomented trouble. She spoke privately to Anna about the injustice of Louis Howe's privileged position in the house. She told Anna her mother had been wrong to allow the man to sleep in Anna's own bedroom, whereupon Anna went to Eleanor to insist that her mother no longer cared about what was best for her. Eleanor then followed her tendency to "shut up like a clam" when family matters grew tense.

Sara spoke to Louis Howe himself. Surely, she said, Howe had the good sense to realize that Franklin's political career was over.

Howe, by his own account, looked at her levelly and replied that he still expected her son to be elected president.

But Howe and Eleanor were merely following FDR's lead, and he was presenting his mother with his invincible "No." In all things he meant to behave as if his condition were temporary, even though the prospect of a quick recovery had evaporated. Eleanor would later say: "He has never said that he could not walk." That was not literally true — he did say it occasionally, in the sense that on any given day, right at the moment, he could not walk and knew it — but what she meant by it was true. He made no concession to the growing likelihood that he would never again walk without assistance, and he signaled that he would tolerate no such talk in the family. "Ever since I got this fool disease . . ." he would say later, "I have been perfectly definite in my determination to throw away the crutches." Starting with the two people closest to him, Eleanor and Sara themselves, he must deter doubt. *Any* talk of being permanently crippled might hinder his ability to persuade others — and there would be many others to persuade — that he would be all right in the end. Discussion of the eventual outcome must *all* be positive. He would do his best to make a full recovery, but in the meantime he would make it *seem* as if a full recovery was only a matter of time. He would behave as if he were the protagonist of a drama in which a happy ending was assured. If he confessed fear or doubt or even uncertainty, the whole performance might collapse. He would give no one, least of all his mother, an opportunity for turning his own doubts against him. He would give her no ammunition for an argument that began *"Franklin, as you have said yourself . . ."* If this was a further impediment to true honesty with the people closest to him, so be it. He would pay that price. And he insisted that everyone else play by the same rules. Howe said later that FDR "treated the entire affair as a soldier would a wound and went along making plans as if nothing had happened."

So it was that Franklin Roosevelt — and his family, by the force of his own insistence — perpetuated and widened the margin of hope first offered by Dr. Lovett and nurtured by Dr. Draper. His mother had threatened it. To follow her direction would be to give in to despair. She was not to speak of it; he would not hear any more such talk. "Franklin had no intention of conforming to my quiet ideas for his future existence," Sara wrote later. "He was determined to ignore his disability and carry on from where he had left off."

It became an article of faith in Roosevelt lore that, as the journalist John Gunther wrote as early as 1950, "what really happened during these agonizing months was a battle to the finish between these two remarkable women [Sara and Eleanor] for Franklin's soul." It wasn't so. The decision had been wholly his from the start, and he had made it by the time he asked Louis Howe to move in, before Sara even started the petty battle over Anna's bedroom.

Eleanor Roosevelt and others said polio changed Roosevelt, that it made him more compassionate. That may be so. But the first impact of the disease was to call forth elements of his nature that no one had seen before — elements that even he may not have known he possessed. His decision to defy polio was a critical moment in his life — perhaps *the* critical moment — and it is frustrating to have no direct documentation of it. But the evidence is perfectly clear that he made this decision, whether it was the epiphany of a moment or a realization that crystallized slowly over several days or weeks.

Richard T. Goldberg, a rehabilitation psychologist who made a careful study of Roosevelt's illness and recovery, concluded that "many men and women," if faced with the crisis that FDR endured, "would have broken under such an intense strain," and "not one in a thousand would have returned to combative political life."

Why did he choose to do so? Where did the strength to do so come from? No one really knows.

Perhaps "the infantile" seemed to him the ultimate epithet, the crowning insult about being a perpetual child under the thumb of his mother. And that is not what he was. By defying the disease, he would fight those who had called him "Feather Duster" and "Miss Nancy" . . . the Porcellians who had blackballed him at Harvard . . . his mother, who thought politics and the use of power were unsuitable for a gentleman . . . and the tough politicians who thought he was a spoiled prig.

He seemed to decide on some deep level of instinct and will that now he was going to show them all.

CHAPTER 7
"A TOWER OF BLOCKS"
DECEMBER 1921 TO DECEMBER 1922

The virus was long gone from Roosevelt's body. Yet new dangers to his paralyzed limbs were rising up. The doctors had chosen Mrs. Kathleen Lake to defend against them. She was an orthopedic nurse trained in the new techniques of physiotherapy, developed largely to help disabled soldiers in the wake of the world war. Not much is known about her — just that she had worked with many crippled children under Robert Lovett and other orthopedists; that she was by the book and businesslike (so much is clear from her reports to Lovett); and that she knew how to deal with the damage done to FDR.

One sort of damage was beyond repair. This was the damage done by the poliovirus in the original attack: the killing of nerve cells by which the brain commands muscles to move. Once destroyed, a neuron is gone for good, and Roosevelt's paralysis proved that many, many neurons were gone. But there were millions of motor neurons below his waist. The fact that he could not make a particular appendage move did not mean all the motor neurons in that appendage were dead, nor that all the muscles were shot, only that enough neurons had died to make normal movement impossible right now.

But that was where the next danger lay — in his immobility.

When Mrs. Lake began coming to East 65th Street in early December 1921, FDR's legs had been all but motionless for nearly four months. This is disaster for muscles. In a functioning limb, the movements of everyday life are accomplished by muscles contracting. That contraction, in turn, exerts a pumping action on the body's circulatory system. In other words, the body's movements summon blood into the vast river system of arteries and arterioles that distribute nourishment to muscle cells. When motion stops, pumping stops. If the pump is stopped long enough, cells die of starvation. They collapse, then shrink into hard, irredeemable scar tissue. Muscles that might have been saved are then gone for good.

There were several ways for a therapist such as Mrs. Lake to invite the benefits of contraction to muscles that could not contract on their own. She could massage the muscles. She could apply heat. She could manipulate the limbs herself, bending joints without the patient's help. But the best chance of recovery lay in arduous effort that only the patient himself could undertake. In Boston the physical therapist Wilhelmine Wright, an associate of Robert Lovett and a pioneer in the new techniques, had recently written the authoritative instructions to therapists. "Wherever there is . . . the ability to contract the muscle even slightly by an effort of the will," she said, "the muscle cells are more favorably affected. . . . When not used, the muscle cells degenerate, and the only way to increase their nutrition is to make them work."

To contract the muscle even slightly by an effort of the will: That was a challenge guaranteed to appeal to either a Roosevelt or a Delano. The creed of willpower was a fixture in both families. "Please tell him I am an admiring aunt," the redoubtable Annie Delano Hitch, Sara's older sister, had written to Eleanor, "and that I love to think that he has not only faith, but pluck and a courageous determination to conquer the enemy even if he fights hard to do it."

But there was a second new threat to his limbs.

The poliovirus often strikes like a tornado that leaves one block of houses untouched and the next block in ruins. Say the virus kills the nerves in one bundle of muscle fibers near a particular joint — the knee, for instance — and leaves the next bundle healthy and strong. The lifeless muscle has lost the strength to counterbalance the healthy muscle. So the healthy muscle, doing its work as usual but with no force to resist it, continues to contract and pull, while the fibers of the stiff, nerve-damaged muscle collapse, die, and wither. Slowly, and wholly out of the patient's control, the healthy muscles pull or twist the limb out of its normal position. The process is called "contracture." If nothing is done to check the process, only surgery can repair the damage. Depending on the degree of imbalance between the counterposed muscles, the contracture can be mild — just enough to make normal walking difficult or impossible — or severe. At the ankle, the result was called "foot drop" — difficulty in raising the front of the foot. In the severest cases, untreated limbs became locked in a grotesque and permanent dogleg. This was the kind of crippling that made people look away when they encountered a polio victim on the street, and it was the prospect, in Roosevelt's case, that Robert Lovett was most concerned about. He directed Kathleen Lake to take strict measures to prevent it.

Mrs. Lake went to work.

A wide wooden plank longer than a man was laid on Roosevelt's bed on the third floor of 49 East 65th. (FDR began to refer to this makeshift gymnasium as "The Morgue.") Then Mrs. Lake and Nurse Rockey and the patient, all working together, would lift and pull and push to maneuver his body onto the board.

The early movements of paralyzed limbs in a still-recovering patient bring startling pain. A lower leg that once had yielded effortlessly to the unconscious will now reveals itself as a raging, resisting enemy, even when simply being manipulated by the nurse. "My body was still rigid with muscular adhesions," one young man with polio wrote of this stage of his treatment. "The least deflection of my limbs from the horizontal produced intense, exquisite pain. I had not been aware, until I was moved, just how painful and sensitive my body still was, nor did I expect the extreme fatigue that overcame me."

Mrs. Lake commanded FDR to flex one muscle, then another. He tried. The big toe of his left foot might not move right now. But if he tried and tried and tried again to make it move, even to twitch it, it *might* twitch, maybe on the fiftieth try, maybe on the five hundredth, and if it did, then a rivulet of blood would flow; and if the toe could be made to move often enough, the flow of blood might redeem the muscle. So it might proceed, conceivably, muscle by muscle, limb by limb. It was an exploratory mission to discover which of the unmoving muscles might really be all right, just dormant and ready to be reawakened. Any tiny gain would inspire hope for more gains.

Roosevelt still reported pain through regions of his legs and feet — less pain than in October and November, but still troublesome, despite the hot baths he was given each day. Persistent pain was a signal that a muscle was still recovering from the trauma of the virus's onslaught, and that meant the muscle could be damaged anew by massage. So massage, though important later on, was forbidden for now.

Mrs. Lake ran exercises in the lower back and the abdomen, with good effects. She saw signs of contracture in the hamstrings, so she got to work stretching them out, extending the patient's knees again and again.

In the muscles of the arms she detected a "marked gain," she told Lovett. Here, as in the abdomen and lower back, there had been spontaneous recovery, and FDR took advantage of it, doing pull-ups with the straps above his bed day after day. This was the start of a process that would make his upper body unusually powerful. If his legs remained limp, at least he could take pride in this new strength above the waist. "He himself is quite pleased with the way he is getting on," Mrs. Lake wrote Dr. Lovett in the first week of January, "& a friend of his told me he wouldn't have believed he was the same man he saw in November."

Mrs. Lake was very serious about her work, even prepared to be stern with a patient who failed to buckle down to the hard regimen. But she found no need to be stern with her new charge, not at first. "He is a wonderful patient," she told Lovett, "very cheerful & works awfully hard & tries every suggestion one makes to help him."

But as the bleak days of January passed, Mrs. Lake grew puzzled. One day there would be signs of progress: The incipient contracture in Roosevelt's hamstrings would ease and the pain in his calves would recede.

Then, a day or two later, the ankles and calves would be swollen and acutely painful to the touch, and Roosevelt would seem fatigued and irritable.

Dr. Draper, who dropped in now and then, noticed the same pattern. He thought Mrs. Lake had overworked the patient and chided her for it. But she retraced each step of the treatment in her mind and concluded she could not possibly be to blame. Indeed, she had been very careful not to overdo, and she began to suspect "there was more to it than met the eye."

Away from the Roosevelts, she "did a little private detective work."

She considered Edna Rockey, the nurse-masseuse who got along so well with the patient. She seemed to have his sort of sense of humor. The two of them were always laughing.

Mrs. Lake drew Miss Rockey into conversation.

Had Mr. Roosevelt been doing much exercise when Mrs. Lake was away from the house? she asked.

Oh, yes, Miss Rockey said. "She remarked with some pride [Lake told Lovett] that she was doing some 'quite heavy manipulation' (her own words) on the patient at night."

Mrs. Lake went to Roosevelt, who admitted, under Lake's questioning, that nurse Rockey had been administering massage when Mrs. Lake was away. How much? she asked.

"Oh," he said, "just a little to rub the oil in to build up the muscles!"

An oil to build up muscles? There was no such thing.

For how long, she asked, and what sort of massage?

Perhaps ten minutes each time, he supposed — Swedish massage. This was the deep kneading of the damaged muscles that Dr. Lovett, Dr. Draper, and Mrs. Lake had specifically forbidden.

Didn't Mr. Roosevelt know it was risky to begin massage too early? she asked. He must not rush things.

He assured her "again and again that he does not wish to hurry, but wants to do what is absolutely the best thing for his ultimate recovery."

No more rubdowns by night, she ordered. By the end of another week, the pain in the legs had eased and the patient seemed less worn out.

Mrs. Lake had caught FDR in an error that many patients make in physical therapy: They push too hard and do too much. It was the first sign that, however often he promised to do so, he was not going to be content to follow his doctors' orders — not when the orders seemed to be directed toward paltry goals. Dr. Lovett's exercise regimen was aimed at small, slow improvements that might — *might* — allow FDR to get up on crutches. This was not the ambitious plan that Roosevelt himself had in mind. He was not interested in simply re-awakening scattered muscles that had gone dormant. He wanted, as he had said to Mrs. Lake, to "build up" his legs — to restore them to full working condition, so that he could get up, walk out the door, and get back to his work.

Nurse Rockey, who was in the house at all hours and heard more of the family's conversations than Mrs. Lake did, had her own opinions about the patient overworking. She confided them to Mrs. Lake. "The nurse seems to think there is a good deal too much pushing forward done by the wife & Mr. H.," Mrs. Lake told Dr. Lovett. "That I know nothing of, but am putting it down to you for what you think it is worth."

Mrs. Lake concluded the patient could no longer bear the exercises to stretch his hamstrings. Each effort to straighten the leg tore tough adhesions that had formed in his musculature. There is nothing wrong with the sensory nerves of a polio's legs, only the nerves that control movement, and when tissue tears the sensory nerves rage. "The stretching of his knees is causing a good deal of discomfort & is I think really getting on his nerves, although he would probably tell you it is not," she told Lovett. She also thought she saw signs of foot drop on the right side. She thought it was time for Dr. Lovett to pay another visit. Dr. Draper agreed.

This meant a new ordeal.

Lovett came over from Boston at the end of January 1922. Upon examination, he wasn't so worried about contractures in the lower legs; it was the muscles just below the waist that concerned him. They were drawing tighter. If the atrophy there went unchecked, Roosevelt's body would be permanently bent at the waist. This was now "the most important feature in the case," Lovett declared. "Every effort ought to be concentrated on getting those legs out straight."

He prescribed a body cast.

A New York orthopedist, Dr. Arthur Krida, was brought in. Krida encased Roosevelt's legs in a sheath of plaster from the waist to the ankles, with hinges at the joints. This would address the problem of incipient contractures in both the hamstrings and the hips.

For two weeks Roosevelt lay rigid. Day by day, Krida straightened the joints by pounding wedges into the cast.

While this went on, Mrs. Lake took a few days off. When she returned, she found Roosevelt distraught. "He appeared extremely relieved to have me back," she told Lovett. "The patient was extremely worried about his left leg." After their weeks of hard work together, Roosevelt now reported "a complete loss of power in all the returning muscles of that leg, which did not occur in the right leg." With the cast still in place she was unable to palpate the muscles, but she "convinced him that he could still get the muscles [back], and the power has since been slowly returning again, which has helped to clear up the situation."

On February 13, Mrs. Lake watched as Dr. Krida sawed off the body cast. Then she went to work on a regimen of soothing massage.

Next Dr. Lovett directed her to try to get Roosevelt up on his feet for the first time in half a year.

To the able-bodied, standing is the automatic response to the day. Motor nerves call

253

the muscles and joints to work; the skeleton rises and balances on a foundation of two stable feet in a splendid collaboration of muscles in the abdomen, the back, the hips, the knees, ankles, feet, and toes. Proprioception — the sense of where one's limbs are in space — provides an unconscious system of physical reckoning, like a compass in three dimensions.

But when muscles are weakened or knocked out, the act of standing becomes far more precarious, even dangerous. It requires considerable strength just to keep the joints of the knees and hips from collapsing under the body's weight. And if one has been out of the habit of standing, one's proprioception is rusty and skewed.

A cautious attempt or two made it obvious that Roosevelt no longer possessed the strength he needed for standing, at least not now. His muscles would need mechanical help.

Dr. Krida took careful measurements, then fabricated a pair of braces. Each brace weighed thirteen pounds — a sudden increase of more than ten percent in Roosevelt's weight. With the braces locking him into board-straightness at the waist and the knees, he was hauled into the standing position. His first crutches were brought into the room and inserted beneath his armpits.

A recovering polio patient approached the task of standing upright with a different set of tools than the ones he had used when he first stood as a child. "It depressed me to find it so difficult," a patient wrote of the first time he tried to stand with a brace on one leg. "I had not known that the weakness of my hips, only slightly involved, would so completely destroy my feeling of security. Even with my back to a wall, my brace locked at the knee, I would feel brittle and vulnerable, at least ten feet tall; thinking that if I fell I could shatter on the floor like a tower of blocks." Others trying to stand for the first time found themselves trembling and sweating. They stood like weightlifters under the burden of their massive dumbbells. Charles Mee, paralyzed at the age of fourteen, recalled the repetitive process of "pulling myself up out of my wheelchair to my feet and trying to stand there holding on, my midsection swaying from side to side, my knees giving out from time to time, as I learned to bring myself back to equilibrium with the muscles that were ordinarily used for this purpose and with whatever other muscles my body could imagine calling into play to compensate for those that were gone.

"This was the new equilibrium," Mee recalled, "a bizarre, jury-rigged system of muscular checks and balances that could not be taught. The body had to learn this on its own through days and days of trial and error."

Roosevelt would fall, then be lifted back to his feet, then begin again and fall again.

Meanwhile, he talked and talked about other things to try. He continued to do too much when Mrs. Lake was not around — though she suspected as much and tattled to Dr. Lovett.

"Counsel him not to try new methods," the orthopedist urged her, "but to trust us to give him the maximum dose that he can stand for, and above all things caution him to look out for hip flexion contraction. . . . He cannot be too careful."

At one level FDR understood, even agreed. Yet his instincts appear to have been telling him that on another level Lovett was wrong, that he *could* be too careful.

All that winter and spring of 1922 there was commotion and tension in the house. Eleanor and Louis Howe invited a parade of Democratic friends to talk politics with Franklin night after night. Dr. Draper was aware of continuing strains among the family and the nurses.

First, the sober Mrs. Lake. FDR apparently found her — not that he would ever say so directly — a bore. An "interesting thread in the complex tapestry is the fact that Mrs. Lake does not seem to fit perfectly smoothly into the picture," Draper informed Lovett. "She is admirable as far as her technical work is concerned, and is accepted with the greatest satisfaction from this standpoint. As far as I can make out, the difficulty . . . is merely that she lacks the bubbling sense of humor which Miss Rocky [sic] possesses, and which has been the main stay of the whole outfit ever since the beginning." But Miss Rockey set off her own discordant hum. Draper observed that she "occasionally gets on the nerves of Mrs. R," who may have believed, as Mrs. Lake apparently did, that the nurse was unduly chummy with her patient. (Mrs. Lake confided to Dr. Lovett that she kept an eye on Miss Rockey "for various reasons. If you have seen her you will perhaps understand." No photographs of the cheery nurse survive, but Mrs. Lake's prim note, plus one or two other clues in the family papers, suggest that she was something of a knockout.)

Meanwhile, Sara Roosevelt smoldered in disapproval. Despite Franklin's insistence that she drop her objections, she would not be entirely silent. Dr. Draper became her new target. She told Draper repeatedly that the exercises were overtaxing Franklin's strength. Draper took to dropping in as seldom as possible, just to avoid the senior Mrs. R. (Indeed, it may have been a plea from Draper to Dr. Lovett — whom Sara continued to revere — that induced Lovett to invite her over to Boston for a confidential chat. "I am writing without any talking to Mr. Roosevelt about it," Lovett said. "I thought perhaps it might be a comfort to talk things over with me, because I have not seen you for some time, and I know how anxious you are.")

FDR himself made tensions worse all around by announcing that the family must take dramatic action to reduce expenses. He had been telling people for weeks that his treatments were draining his funds. Whatever the truth of this claim, he used it as a pretext to push away friends trying to sell him bonds; to turn down requests for loans from former servants; to refuse requests, some of them desperate, for help with medical costs. "I have had such enormous doctors' bills for the past year that I simply have not got anything to spare," he told one such supplicant, "and have to be extremely careful myself in order to make both ends meet." To a stranger overwhelmed by bills for his diabetes treatment, FDR wrote: "I am inclosing [*sic*] a small check which I hope will be of some assistance. I wish I could make it larger, but I, myself, have been under very heavy expense in getting over an attack of infantile paralysis." This was not just a handy excuse. He meant it. His mother had offered to pay for everything, but he said no — then felt terribly pressured.

Now he declared that when summer came, they must economize by letting both Miss Rockey and Mrs. Lake go and assigning all of the two nurses' combined tasks to Eleanor.

This struck Dr. Draper as plain silly. "Obviously this is an impossible plan," he wrote Lovett. "In the first place Mrs. R. is pretty much at the end of her tether with the long hard strain she has been through, and I feel that if she had to take on this activity, that the whole situation would collapse." Not to mention that Eleanor, however capable, had no training in orthopedic nursing.

Evaluating Roosevelt purely in medical terms, Draper concluded he was nowhere near the point where he could do without professional nursing — not if he meant to continue a dedicated course of physical therapy. And yet Draper also believed the time had nearly passed when one could hold out a realistic hope for anything approaching a full recovery.

"Below the knee I must say it begins to look rather hopeless," he wrote Lovett in March 1922, "but I know that even at this stage one cannot tell."

Eleanor Roosevelt was, indeed, near the end of her tether. When people asked her later how she felt about her husband's condition, she would say she never "stopped to analyze my feelings. There was so much to do to manage the household and the children and to try to keep things running smoothly that I never had any time to think of my own reactions. I simply lived from day to day and got through the best I could." She was contesting daily with the demands of two teenagers, two little boys, an invalid husband, a semipermanent houseguest, two nurses — one of whom was too friendly with her husband — and, most trying of all, her mother-in-law, who considered herself in charge of the family and opposed Eleanor's wishes for the central project at hand: getting Franklin back to an active life. She could go out in the mornings when Nurse Rockey sat with Franklin, but when the nurse took her break in the afternoon Eleanor had to serve her husband as nurse.

One day, when she was reading aloud to the younger boys, she began to weep. She fled to another room and wept on and on, unable to stop.

It was, she conceded, "the most trying winter of my entire life."

Before long, she would have enough of it.

Finally Dr. Lovett decided he must see for himself whether Roosevelt was confounding the recovery program by doing too much. "I should judge that he was going ahead a little too fast mentally," he told Draper. And it was time for the patient to learn — really learn — how to use those crutches. So Lovett asked Roosevelt to come to Boston for ten days in late May and early June. He was to stay at Phillips House, the patient-care home attached to Massachusetts General Hospital, where Wilhelmine Wright, the authority on the new physiotherapy, could test his progress and teach him new techniques in mobility.

Crutches and canes and braces had been used for centuries, of course, but in the late nineteenth and early twentieth centuries, many more people needed them than before, thanks to industrial accidents, the Great War, and infantile paralysis. In Boston, Robert Lovett and a group of orthopedic nurses formed a coterie of innovators who developed the first systematic approach to testing muscle strength and putting orthotic aids to better use. As Lovett's senior assistant, Miss Wright ran a "gymnasium" clinic at Boston Children's Hospital, and she developed a system for rating the strength of damaged muscles. High expectations for what patients might achieve prevailed among Miss Wright and her colleagues, one of whom was Laura Henrich, another pioneer in physical therapy. The physician Pauline Stitt, who was treated in the Wright-Henrich clinic after coming down with polio as a youngster in 1918, recalled the atmosphere among the therapists: "They gave us self-respect and a whole new outlook." When Pauline told Laura Henrich she hoped to become a doctor and her mother called the notion "preposterous," Henrich turned to the young girl and said: "Keep right on with ideas like that. Those are the things that grown-up doctors are made from. You have to have ideas like that and have to have them early."

Roosevelt arrived in Boston reporting difficulty with the braces Arthur Krida had fabricated for him in New York. Dr. Lovett quickly saw why: The braces were made of a flexible material that bent under FDR's weight, making them not only ineffective but painful. The doctor decided they were "pretty hopeless," threw them out, and ordered a new set that "worked beautifully, and which [Roosevelt] likes very much." (This was FDR telling the doctor what he hoped to hear. If he liked the new braces at all, it was the only pair he ever owned about which he felt that way. He came to detest braces and wore them as seldom as possible.)

Thus equipped, Roosevelt submitted himself to the curriculum of Wilhelmine Wright.

Lovett said Miss Wright's job was to teach Roosevelt "tricks in handling himself." That offhand phrase made the work sound trivial. In fact, it encompassed difficult techniques that could transform an invalid's mobility. Wright had examined the terrain of everyday life with the eyes of a cripple. She knew that to someone with FDR's damaged legs, the distance of fifteen feet from one side of a room to the other posed the prospect of utter exhaustion. She knew the miniature ballet of unconscious movements that make up the simple act of rising from a chair, and how hard it was to accomplish that task without the full armament of muscles in the feet, knees, hips, and trunk. She knew that a single stairstep, let alone a staircase, might just as well be an ice-covered cliff unless one learned a new way to climb stairs. And she knew that before you could try to help a patient to master these maneuvers, you had better be sure his muscles could take it. You could crush a patient if you encouraged him to learn crutch-walking, only to find that his shoulders lacked the strength to swing the crutches forward. "It is hard to tell a patient that nothing can be done," Wright wrote, "but it is more discouraging for the patient to fail after sincere effort."

Miss Wright had observed that some little children with polio quickly became whirling dervishes on crutches. She had seen a boy approach a street corner and spin around it through the air on one crutch, neither his feet nor his other crutch touching the ground. But it was different with an adult who had walked on two feet for many years. "To furnish the timid adult who has recently lost the use of his leg muscles, possibly of his trunk muscles also, and tell him to walk is useless and absurd. He doesn't know how to begin, and there are few persons who know how to instruct him."

The act of standing up with braces came first. On a solid chair with arms, preferably braced against a wall, Miss Wright demonstrated the intricate series of steps. First, you pushed your buttocks up to the edge of the seat. Grasp one braced leg — say, the right . . . lift it . . . set it down across the top of the left leg, also braced. Then twist your trunk toward the left leg, the left underneath the right. Twisting hard at the waist, reach with both hands for the back of the seat . . . then, with a push and a flip, spin yourself completely over. Now you look as if you're doing a push-up against the seat, with your legs sticking out behind. Walk your hands up the back of the chair until your toes and feet reach the floor. From that position, Miss Wright said, "it is an easy matter to push the hips back and straighten the body while balancing with the chair, and finally to place first one crutch and then the other under the arms." You've stood up by yourself. It's easier if one leg is unbraced, but it's possible with braces on both, as long as you have enough strength above the waist. Possible, but hardly easy.

Then — walking with crutches. Here again, the choice of technique depended on how much strength the virus had left behind in the shoulders, arms, and elbows — especially the depressor muscles of the shoulder girdle, the downward rotators of the scapula, and the extensors of the elbow — and how much you were bent by contractures.

Then — climbing stairs. You needed a strong rail on one side. Place one crutch — say, the left — on the stair ahead of you. Hold the second crutch in the fingers of the left hand, or use two crutches side by side as if they were one. With the right hand, reach far ahead on the rail, bracing the elbow on the inside of the rail, then push with the crutch arm and pull with the rail arm to lift your feet to the next step. Repeat to the top of the stairs, where, running out of rail, you must thrust the rail arm behind you and push rather than pull.

"To go up and down stairs which have no rail without leg muscles is work for the intrepid mountaineer," Miss Wright confided, but it was not impossible. With sufficient strength and a certain amount of courage, it could be done backwards — that is, by facing the bottom of the stairs and pushing off the crutches step by step, lifting the weight of your entire body each time, and leaning forward over the descending stairs.

Going *down* stairs required similar sequences of movement in reverse, knowing that if you slipped, you were likely going to fall all the way down the stairs face-first.

These "tricks" were not for the faint-hearted, and they were impossible without significant strength in the upper body. Learning them by heart, so they could be done quickly and confidently, required many hours of trial and error. "The safety of the patient should be guarded at every moment while learning to walk," Miss Wright declared, "but his freedom of independent motion should not be interfered with. He must have absolute confidence in the strength and watchfulness of the instructor." This required experts. A family member could not do it without extensive training. Miss Wright preferred to work with an aide. She and the aide would clasp hands around the patient's middle, not touching him. That way he could move freely, but he knew that if he fell he would be caught. On stairs she added a second assistant.

When FDR's ten-day visit came to an end, Lovett declared himself satisfied. He had wanted, he told Sara by letter, "to get hold of him alone and observe him and see whether I thought he had been persistently overdoing at home and see what his resistance was, as in this way I felt I could control him better." To Draper he said: "I think [he] has made some gain. He enjoys Phillips House, and Miss Wright has taught him some tricks about getting up and down and walking that are going to be of use to him. . . . I think the thing turned out very well."

Lovett judged FDR by the norms of recovery to which he was accustomed. Roosevelt seemed to be on track. He may have been pushing too hard, but that was nothing unusual. Now he had a better pair of braces, and he seemed to be taking to crutch-walking pretty well. Lovett sent his patient home with instructions for a strict regimen of practice with crutches for the rest of the summer. Crutch-walking — that was the thing now, in Lovett's view.

But his hopes for the case were more modest by far than his patient's.

Franklin's distant cousin Theodore Roosevelt Jr. was the Roosevelt riding high in New York politics now. He was serving in the Harding administration as the third Roosevelt to become assistant secretary of the navy, and he was being spoken of as a Republican candidate for governor. In 1920 the papers had made much of the antagonism between the Oyster Bay (Republican) and Hyde Park (Democratic) branches of the family, quoting T.R. Jr. to the effect that FDR did not enjoy "the brand" of Teddy's part of the clan. But now the feud was moot. Franklin Roosevelt's name had all but disappeared from the newspapers. He was just beginning to broaden his network of private correspondence with Democrats near and far, but many people who had known him were puzzled or downright in the dark about the state of his health. After the optimistic news stories of the previous fall, and his cheerful letters to friends about a speedy and full recovery, it was now understood that he had *not* made a speedy recovery. But hardly anyone knew more than that.

An odd fragment of writing from the spring of 1922 survives in Roosevelt's vast collection of personal papers. It appears to be the draft of a newspaper article, unsigned and handwritten on stationery of the National Press Club. It apparently was never published, and the writer got a few facts wrong, but it showed how much was *not* known about FDR's situation at the time of his treatment with Wilhelmine Wright. It began: "Considering the long illness of former Assistant Secretary of the Navy

Franklin D. Roosevelt, it is singular how few of his friends seem to know about his condition. He has been removed from his home in this city [New York] to Boston. Since his removal his condition has improved but he is still a very ill man."

If some were short on details, others were downright befuddled about what had happened to FDR. James Cox, the newspaper publisher and former governor of Ohio who had headed the Democratic ticket in 1920, was quite undone when he visited his running mate. As FDR told the story years later: "Jim's eyes filled with tears when he saw me, and I gathered from his conversation that he was dead certain that I had had a stroke and that another one would soon completely remove me. . . . Jim Cox from that day on always shook his head when my name was mentioned and said in sorrow that in effect I was a hopeless invalid and could never resume any active participation in business or political affairs."

But in another political neighborhood, few tears were shed over FDR's misfortune. Indeed, quiet rejoicing was the likely reaction among the sachems of Tammany Hall; their dour chief, Silent Charlie Murphy; and Tammany's machine allies in the bigger cities across New York State. Poliomyelitis had solved a problem they had not been able to solve themselves.

For ten years, Roosevelt had been an irritation, then a rising threat, to the state's machine Democrats. This had begun the moment a very young FDR took his seat in the state senate in 1911. His only political identity then was as a member of the "Cleveland Democrats," vaguely known as opponents of bossism and sponsors of "good government" in the style of President Grover Cleveland himself, the former mayor of Buffalo who had taken "good government" to mean chiefly that he should say no to any new idea. The idea of a "progressive," or "liberal," Democrat awaited the administration of Woodrow Wilson.

In the meantime, a towering obstacle stood in the way of any ambitious Cleveland Democrat in Republican-dominated New York State. He might cling to an isolated seat in the assembly or the senate. But if he meant to win statewide office, he must play ball with Tammany Hall and Silent Charlie Murphy, since most of the state's Democrats lived in New York City, and Tammany Hall exerted extraordinary influence over how their votes were cast — or at least how they were counted. Yet the independent upstate

Democrat who made deals with Murphy would be independent no more. He would lose any reputation he had for integrity. That, in turn, would sour his chances of attracting votes from independents and Republicans — votes that Democrats needed to win statewide, especially in this time of rising disgust with Tammany and its imitators.

But Silent Charlie was due for a comeuppance.

For the Democratic nomination to succeed the retiring Senator Chauncey DePew, a Republican, in 1911, Boss Murphy pointed at William Francis Sheehan of Buffalo and New York City. Sheehan had been out of the headlines for some years, but he was still known around Albany by his old nickname, "Blue-Eyed Billy," a remnant of his years as the charming young boss of Buffalo (actually co-boss, with his big brother, John); then as the right-hand man of Governor David B. Hill, one of the dirtiest grafters of the era; and as the intra-party foe of Grover Cleveland himself, who swore never to run on a ticket that included "that man Sheehan."

By striving for years to ensure the well-being of New York's railroads, utilities, and liquor interests, Billy Sheehan was able to pull himself well above the poverty of his boyhood in the Irish-Catholic wards of Erie County. Then in 1894, after one term as New York's youngest lieutenant governor, he moved to New York City, where he served his friends in business via the private practice of law. Behind the scenes, he kept his hand in politics, running Judge Alton B. Parker's presidential campaign against Theodore Roosevelt in 1904 (a failure) and soliciting large contributions from his utility clients for Boss Murphy's Tammany Hall (a success).

In 1910, still relatively young at fifty-one, Sheehan decided the time was ripe to cap his career in the U.S. Senate. This was in the last years of the era when most U.S. senators were chosen by the legislatures of their states. So Billy asked his friend Charlie Murphy to make the necessary arrangements in Albany, and Murphy agreed.

In some other year the nomination of Blue-Eyed Billy might have sailed through. But in the 1910 election, the electorate's disgust with bossism had sent a cadre of reform-minded legislators to Albany, Roosevelt among them. As they gathered for the first days of the 1911 session, the prospect of a rogue like Blue-Eyed Billy representing the Empire State in Washington seemed a final offense against public decency — and a tool, perhaps, to pry open Tammany's grip on the statewide Democratic Party. So a rump faction of Democratic rebels, most of them young, announced that they meant to deny Silent Charlie the caucus quorum he needed to secure Sheehan's nomination. FDR joined the rebels immediately; he was a rank rookie of twenty-eight, new to everything in Albany. He offered the fine house he and Eleanor were renting near the capitol as rebel headquarters, and FDR became, if not the leader of the rebels, at least their public face and voice, a good-looking and well-spoken youngster with a name like gold. (It was during the Sheehan fight that Louis Howe spotted Roosevelt as a comer.)

After a long fight, Boss Murphy was compelled to drop Sheehan, and FDR secured statewide fame as an up-and-coming man of integrity who had tilted against Tammany. That enabled him to scrape past his Republican opponent in the November 1912 election. Then Woodrow Wilson's victory and the offer of a post in the Navy Department gave FDR his ticket out of the trap of the upstate, "good government," Cleveland Democrat, at least for a while.

But the battle over Blue-Eyed Billy made

Roosevelt's name anathema in Tammany Hall, especially within earshot of Silent Charlie Murphy. Indeed, though Josephus Daniels always claimed that FDR was his own selection for assistant secretary of the navy, it has been said that Murphy had a hand in Daniels's choice, just to get young Roosevelt the hell out of New York politics. FDR jumped back in when he tried for the U.S. Senate nomination in 1914, but Tammany pushed him back out.

In 1920 Tammany struck at him again, this time with a golden axe.

The story was told by Walter Myers, a Democratic underling in 1920 who published the tale long after the death of all the main players. If true, it was a plot worthy of an emperor's salon in the declining years of Rome.

In 1960, Myers published a claim that he was present during a last-minute rush to make Roosevelt the running mate of James Cox — not because FDR might help the Democrats win but because the Democrats were sure to lose, thus tainting FDR as a vote getter.

Cox had been nominated for president after a deadly struggle for delegates with William Gibbs McAdoo, secretary of the treasury under President Wilson and Wilson's son-in-law. After eight years of Wilson and war, the country was sick of Democrats, and Cox was no star. Democratic pros could see their man was going down. But in New York City, Tammany was thinking about the future of its own true rising star, the canny and capable city boy who had been elected governor in 1918: Alfred Emanuel Smith.

Al Smith talked to New Yorkers in the raspy patois of the Lower East Side, where he had come to maturity hawking newspapers, cleaning fish, and running errands for the local ward boss. His father had been Italian-German, but it was his Irish-Catholic mother, Catherine Mulvihill, who raised him from the age of thirteen, when Al's father died and he had to drop out of school to work. Tammany men spotted him as a good kid, and smart, and in 1903, when he was about to turn thirty, they sent him to Albany as a state representative. At first he could barely understand the bills he read. But he stayed up nights to master them, and by 1913 he was speaker of the New York State Assembly, the smartest and most powerful figure in Albany, with admirers even among upstate Republicans. He liked his beer and he liked his pals, but he was also a practicing Catholic devoted to his wife, Katie, their five children, and a menagerie of household pets. He wore loud suits and talked with his mouth full. At the rostrum he was frank and genuinely funny. When men above Al's station mentioned their college degrees — B.A., L.L.D., Ph.D. — he liked to say his own degree was "F.F.M.: Fulton Fish Market." He was in love with his city; he said he "would sooner be a lamp post on Park Avenue than governor of California." And although he was a man made by the Tammany machine — indeed, the favorite protégé of Silent Charlie Murphy — Tammany's enemies had come to acknowledge that Al Smith was also a true progressive. Unlike do-gooding upper-crust reformers down through the decades, Smith actually got things done for the immigrant poor. After scores of women workers were killed in the Triangle Shirtwaist sweatshop fire of 1911, it was Smith who championed legislation to protect workers' safety. When Smith was pushing a bill to mandate one day off each week for working women and children, the owners of canneries lobbied for an exemption; Smith listened, then said: "I have read carefully the commandment 'Remember the Sabbath Day, to keep it holy.' I am unable to find any language in it that says, 'Except in the canneries.' "

By 1918, reformers had come to appreciate the advantages of having a master of the deal on their side, and they helped make him governor. Charlie Murphy, dreaming of the presidency for his boy, helped to steer Smith clear of Tammany's less legal operations. So he now was coming to national attention as a rare politician indeed: He had the power of the bosses behind him, but he was clean.

But in 1920, Governor Smith expected a very tough fight to retain his job. He would face Nathan Miller, a leading attorney and former judge who had presided at the birth of U.S. Steel, an upstater well placed to oust Smith in a Republican year. So the pros came up with their intricate, Machiavellian scheme: If Franklin Roosevelt were on the ticket, his name — then still associated with the hero Republican, Uncle Ted, only months in his grave — would certainly pull some Republican and independent voters to the Democratic ticket. That could give Al Smith the edge he needed for reelection as governor. This could never happen unless Boss Charlie Murphy said okay — and Murphy still hated Roosevelt. But the pros saw an angle to urge upon Silent Charlie. Think about it, they said: If FDR ran for vice president and lost, especially if the

Democratic ticket lost in New York State, then he would have lost two statewide campaigns: first in the 1914 Senate primary, and now in 1920. He'd be finished. Yet his name might pull enough votes to help Al Smith to keep the governor's chair.

And then, they said, in 1924, Smith might just become the first Tammany man to reach the White House.

Boss Murphy bought it. The pros — so wrote Walter Myers — proposed Roosevelt to Governor Cox, who said if Roosevelt was all right with Tammany, he would go along.

The plan did not work: Cox and Roosevelt were defeated — as expected — but so was Governor Smith, though not by much.

And Franklin Roosevelt, early in 1921, had started right up with an informal thrust toward a new campaign in New York, even to the extent of mending fences with Tammanyites. He was the fair-haired-boy, Groton-Harvard, Protestant threat to the ascendency of the cigar-chomping, uneducated, Irish-Catholic Al Smith.

Then poliomyelitis appeared to solve Tammany's Roosevelt problem for good.

Whether friend or enemy, whether they knew a lot or a little, no one thought FDR could seek office ever again. At this point, Eleanor remarked later, "My husband seemed to be out of politics forever." That much everybody knew.

"Of course the word had spread around," Frances Perkins remembered. It was: " 'Poor Roosevelt, he's through. Too bad about Roosevelt, he's through. Too bad.' "

Then, in the middle of 1922, Al Smith got in touch with FDR.

Smith was in a difficult spot. Since losing the race for governor in 1920, he'd finally been able to make some real money as the head of a trucking company. With his big family, real money after many years on a politician's salary — and Al didn't take graft — was darned nice. He wanted to be governor again, but if he ran, he wanted to be sure he would win. He had to have the state party firmly with him, so he needed to be asked to run — prominently and publicly. And who better to make this request than the pillar of good-government, progressive, upstate Democracy — the man with the golden name, but also a man who could not possibly pose any further threat to Al, since he was a cripple? That wasn't how Smith put it to FDR, but he did ask FDR to ask. Roosevelt did so, praising Al as an honest man of the people who must reclaim the governorship from the Republicans. And

Smith went on to take the nomination and win the race in the fall of 1922.

It was not much, but it was something — a stroke that got FDR's name in all the papers as a kind of young elder statesman, out of the game himself, yet still able to wield influence on behalf of the new star of the Democratic Party. It was the start of an odd but powerful alliance: the Hudson River Harvard kid, crippled but such a great speaker; and the scrappy Irish boy from the Bowery, looking beyond Albany toward the White House.

After the nominating convention at Syracuse, Smith wrote Roosevelt a note of thanks — a little patronizing, maybe, but that was Al being nice.

"I was really sorry that you could not be there, but take care of yourself," he said. "There is another day coming."

George Draper may not have understood the precise emotional mixture that was roiling inside 47–49 East 65th Street, but he suspected it was having a toxic effect on FDR. When Roosevelt returned to New York from Boston in early June 1922, Draper recommended a shake-up. Soon Sara was off to Europe with the two oldest children, Anna and Jimmy; and FDR was in

Hyde Park to spend much of the summer more or less on his own, with Louis Howe and Nurse Rockey and the servants to help him. Draper wanted FDR to get away from "the intense and devastating influence of the interplay of those high-voltage personalities."

FDR relished the prospect of summer on the Hudson. New York City had been his home only for a few years of his life, and only during the workweek. He disliked life in Manhattan — "this vile burgh!" he called it that spring — and identified in nearly every way, even fanciful ones, with the country village of his youth. He took every chance to spend weekends in Hyde Park. "I wish you would change my address . . . to Hyde Park, Dutchess County, New York," he wrote to an association to which he belonged, "as I never have been and never will be a resident of New York City."

He exercised indoors and out. At the bottom of a staircase, he would turn his back to the stairs and have himself lowered to a sitting position. Then he would reach behind his back with both hands and push himself up to the next stairstep, then the next, and so on all the way up the stairs, with a turn at the landing. He did this many times.

One exercise routine his wife found difficult to watch. He had been practicing sliding out of a chair and dropping to the floor, facedown. Then he would pull himself along, using only the strength of his arms and trunk. He said it was a matter of safety. But it disturbed Eleanor. Many years later she told a friend that the only time she had cried in his presence — after he had contracted polio, she noted — was once when he had called family members into his bedroom and said: "Look what I can do." He slipped out of the bed onto the floor, then pulled himself across the floor and out of the room by his elbows. To him, it represented the ability to escape a fire. But Eleanor had broken into tears and walked from the room.

Out in back, by the big garden between the house and the stable, the estate men set up two parallel bars, ten feet long, one set at the height of the hips, the other head-high. With the braces under his trousers to hold his legs straight and a corset strapped around his waist to keep him unbent at the waist, he would grip the wooden bars and slide one hand forward, then the other, taking the weight with flexed arms and shoulders and pulling his legs along.

As the summer months passed, with these exertions inside the house and out, he gained a great deal of strength in the upper part of his body. Visitors who hadn't seen him since before the onset of his illness were astonished at the new barrel chest, the thick upper arms and neck.

An old navy friend who saw a photograph of him after the expansion of his upper body said the picture made it appear that he was "passing from the Battle Cruiser to the Dreadnaught class." Was he getting fat?

"Don't worry about my getting fat," FDR shot back. "The upper part of me weighs, of course, more than it did before, but that is because my arm and shoulder muscles have developed tremendously in this effort of getting about with crutches."

He had visitors. He liked to have people out on the lawn with him as he did his exercises; without company the routine was suffocatingly dull. While his guests sat in garden chairs, he would move slowly and painstakingly from one end of the bars to the other, then turn and go back, talking incessantly.

One person who came often had been invited by Sara Roosevelt. She was Margaret Suckley, a distant cousin ten years younger than Franklin, single, a quiet, pleasant young woman whom her family and friends called "Daisy." She lived up the road a few miles with the remnants of her old Hudson River clan at a great, rambling manse called Wilderstein, which sat on a rise at a bend of the Hudson near Rhinebeck. She loved the Hudson Valley as much as Franklin did. They didn't know each other very well, but they had grown up among the same old families, remembered who had married whom, knew which road led past whose property. Sara had realized that Daisy Suckley might make a good companion for Franklin during these long sessions. Her time was her own. She had few responsibilities and asked nothing. She listened to him chatter, laughed, said not much.

Among the old stories and exchanges of local news, Daisy heard him say often: "I'm not going to be conquered by a childish disease."

A friendship began between them that would grow, years later, into one of the most important in FDR's life.

On some long afternoons, Louis Howe and he sat on the back porch and constructed model sailboats. Sometimes one or more of the boys would join them. Depew, the chauffeur, would drive them down to a dock on the river, and as Depew rowed the boat, Louis and Franklin would sail their boats up and down the Hudson. On other days he would go over to trade stories of old days in Dutchess County with Benjamin Haviland, the Hyde Park town historian. FDR wanted Haviland's job and soon got it. Draper had advised him to develop new activities to absorb his interest — something without the nervous strain of politics — and this was one of them.

Twice a week Louis Depew would get FDR into the car and drive to the house of another friend in Rhinebeck, this house a good deal grander than the Suckleys' house, which was grand enough. It belonged to Vincent Astor, scion of one of the wealthiest families in America, kin by marriage to Franklin's half-brother Rosy. Astor had dug a swimming pool near the tracks of the New York Central. As Dr. Lovett had advised, FDR got in the water and did exercises there for an hour or more at a time. In the water his weak legs would float, so he could exercise them more easily. The water was good for the stronger muscles too, providing resistance as he pushed his limbs in and out, up and down.

At home he began to do these exercises in a pool the Roosevelts called "the ice pond," where the stream ran down the wooded slopes between the house and the river and clattered over a little stone dam in deep shade. Men would carry FDR to the edge of the dam, then help him slip into the pool where he had swum as a boy and where he had taught his older children to swim. Sometimes by himself, sometimes with the younger boys splashing alongside, he would exercise.

"Well," he called to Louis Depew one day, "the water got me where I am, and the water has to bring me back."

That was an odd and striking remark.

Did FDR believe his accidental immersion in the frigid Bay of Fundy the previous summer had somehow caused his illness? Another such hint came several years later, when, telling the Bay of Fundy story to a journalist, he said: "I'd never felt anything as cold as that water! . . . [T]he water was so cold it seemed paralyzing."

The chill he had felt that day may have been a *symptom* of polio — he was probably experiencing the hypersensitive nerve response characteristic of the acute stage of the infection — but the cold water could not possibly have been the *cause* of the infection, as he surely knew. By mid-1922 FDR had a sophisticated layman's understanding of his disease. He was well aware that the cause of his problem had been a viral invasion of his central nervous system. He would have known that ocean water, no matter how cold, could not have made him sick.

It is just barely possible, though he never referred to it, that when he said "water," he meant the tainted water of Lake Kanawauke at the Bear Mountain Boy Scout camp.

But it seems more likely that the remark Louis Depew heard — the connection that FDR drew between water and polio — was a kind of purposeful whimsy, a mental magic trick, a playful, daydreaming way of trying to conjure a miracle. One day he had plunged into water and come out paralyzed. Now, or someday soon, he would reenter the water and come out walking.

Roosevelt needed help to get into the swimming pool, into the ice pond, and back out. He needed help to get from the house to the parallel bars and back again. He needed a spotter to catch him if he fell. He needed help to get in and out of the car, in and out of bed, in and out of his chair, in and out of his bath. He needed someone to lower him down onto the seat of the toilet and to lift him up again. He needed help every hour he was awake, and at night he needed someone strong nearby in case he needed to use the bathroom or to rescue him in case of a fire.

Probably the one who helped him most that summer was LeRoy Jones, the character in this story about whom the least is known because he was an African-American servant. It's not clear when the family hired him, but at about this time he became Roosevelt's personal attendant, a body man. FDR called him "Roy." He was probably from New York City, since Dutchess County counted few African-Americans in its census. All that remains of Jones now is a photograph and his name in a few surviving letters. He was one of the assets that a family like the Roosevelts could afford to hire in order to cope with the difficulties imposed by traumatic disease. Jones's presence at FDR's side is one of the ways in which Roosevelt's case, though similar in some ways to every other polio case, was also quite different.

Many years later, members of Roosevelt's family would remember his saying repeatedly that summer that he must walk with crutches "to the end of the driveway" — a distance from the house to Route 9, the Albany Post Road, of about a quarter-mile. He did a lot of exercising; there's no doubt of that. The proof appears in photographs that show his newly beefy arms, shoulders, and chest. And he seems to have made it to the end of the driveway on crutches at least once. But the evidence suggests that FDR did not try terribly hard to follow his doctor's orders about walking with crutches.

His wife and his nurse gave him away. The first to tell on him was Eleanor. She and Dr. Lovett spoke in Newport, where both spent time that summer. After their chat, Lovett wrote to chastise his patient — diplomatically — saying: "I rather inferred from what she said that you had not been using your crutches and splints as much as I think you ought to. . . . It is very important for you to do all the walking that you can within your limit of fatigue. . . . Walking on crutches is not a gift, but an art, acquired by constant practice, just as any other game and you will have to put in quite a little time before you get about satisfactorily. . . . I am sure that you will see the point of this, and constantly try new things and acquire the art of walking by keeping at it."

FDR's response was all reassurance. "I am glad to be able to report that I have faithfully followed out all the walking," he told Lovett, "and am really getting so that both legs take it quite naturally, and I can stay on my feet for an hour without feeling tired."

He may have been able to stand on crutches for an hour, but what he said about walking was at best an exaggeration, if Nurse Rockey is to be credited. Six weeks after FDR promised Lovett he was doing just as he had been told, the nurse confirmed Eleanor's tattletale report.

With the last warm weeks of fall passing away, the family finally decided to let the nurse go. The patient had LeRoy Jones to help him around, and the responsibility of supervising the physical therapy would revert entirely to Mrs. Lake.

Just before leaving, Miss Rockey described a situation in which every factor seemed to militate against Roosevelt's progress.

The patient, she said, allowed himself to be distracted by a dozen other interests — and so many visitors! He was doing entirely too much of the "mental work" Dr. Lovett had discouraged him from doing. Without Miss Rockey to push the exercise regimen, Mr. Roosevelt "will make excuses and put off going to bed until very late, etc." And she was the only one, through "constant attention," who could "get him to do things." Certainly his wife could not: "She is too busy and away a great deal or entertaining."

The result was that when he did attend to his walking exercises, he was dangerously unprepared. Just the other day, she said, "he was compelled to walk one quarter of a mile which completely took him off his feet for about four days." Pain had returned on the left side and even on the right, his stronger side.

In fact, she said, "I feel Mr. Roosevelt has not attempted any of your suggestions to date. All this lovely fall has gone with only a few minutes devoted to walking, not every day."

Why was Roosevelt not complying with his doctor's instructions?

Nurse Rockey blamed the patient's mother, since the elder Mrs. Roosevelt was always urging Mr. Roosevelt "to take advantage of the country and space" at the expense of serious exercise — in other words, to sit in the sun and rest.

But, like others, Nurse Rockey mistook Sara's attempts to control her son for actual domination. She had not been able to tell him what to do for many years, much as she may have tried.

It certainly wasn't a case of physical laziness. Hiking himself up the stairs on his rear end; doing pull-ups with the trapeze rings over his bed; working on the parallel bars in the garden — it was demanding physical labor that he performed endlessly that year. Perhaps he did this work so diligently because he *could* do it, and because it paid quick dividends in the form of greater ease in the daily business of maneuvering between chairs.

Walking with crutches was something different. It required him to go through the elaborate fuss of putting on his braces, which he detested, and wearing them, which caused him discomfort — and probably they were a constant, pressing reminder of the condition he could forget for fleeting moments when the braces were off.

Every struggle to walk with crutches brought only the barest incremental improvements, and to do what? To walk a bit better with crutches.

He meant to do more than that — *had* to do more.

One morning in lower Manhattan in October 1922, a young lawyer named Basil O'Connor was approaching 120 Broadway, the building where his fledgling law practice occupied a couple of rooms on the first floor. There O'Connor saw a little crowd of people bunched up at the entrance. They were watching a crippled man, well dressed, moving slowly into the building on crutches. Another man, a chauffeur or servant, was helping him. O'Connor trailed behind, waiting to board his elevator.

O'Connor was thirty years old. Raised in Taunton, Massachusetts, he had snapped up a bachelor's degree at Dartmouth and a law degree at Harvard — not bad for the son of a down-on-his-luck Irish tinsmith. After brief apprenticeships at two of Manhattan's leading corporate firms, he had struck out on his own. As a youngster he had gone by his first name, Daniel, but when he checked the Manhattan phone book he found far too many listings for "Daniel O'Connor." He needed to be known. So he was "Basil" thereafter.

O'Connor recognized the crippled man from newspaper photos — it was Franklin Roosevelt. He'd heard about Roosevelt's encounter with infantile paralysis, but he had no idea the politician was unable to walk on his own.

He watched as Roosevelt set out toward the elevator across the polished stone floor of the lobby. With the chauffeur hovering just at the left, the pole-straight body and the two crutches formed the three legs of a tripod. Hips and knees were locked. The muscles of the thick neck strained; the head thrust forward; the stiff body followed. Then the head reared backward, pulling the weight of the body off the crutches for an instant so they could be shot forward. It was an awkward, heavy, straining progress. It did not look right — the thick neck and trunk of a football player hunching along above flapping trouser legs.

Roosevelt's left side was apparently the weaker one. With each thrust forward, the chauffeur planted his foot just ahead of the left crutch to block and hold the tip as it came down on the slick floor.

O'Connor could see perspiration shining on the back of Roosevelt's neck.

He was partway across the lobby when the footing went wrong. The tip of the left crutch, coming down hard, shoved the assistant's foot to the side. Roosevelt canted and began to fall. The chauffeur lunged to catch him, but Roosevelt was falling too fast, and he went all the way down, straight as a pole, crashing to the floor in a clatter of crutches and braces, his hat flying.

O'Connor saw Roosevelt twist and try to sit up as the chauffeur grabbed him under the armpits and heaved, but the weight was too great and there was no leverage.

People in the lobby moved toward him but hesitated. Roosevelt saw them.

Nothing to worry about! he called.

O'Connor remembered his voice as "pleasant and strong," with "a ring in it."

He'd get out of it all right: "Give me a hand there . . ."

O'Connor reached to help. Roosevelt beckoned to another young man, told him where to put his hands. Get hold, he said. "All right, now, all together!"

They got him up. He leaned hard on the crutches. His legs splayed wide. He pushed himself to his full height.

O'Connor heard him say: "Let's go."

CHAPTER 8
"THE LIMIT OF HIS POSSIBILITIES"
FALL 1922 TO SPRING 1924

The stone floor of the lobby at 120 Broadway may have been slippery that day, but at least it was flat. Yet he had fallen. He had fallen too on the well-worn wooden floors at East 65th Street and at Hyde Park. He ran the risk of falling every time he left his bed. He could quite easily fall out of a chair. In his current condition, if he kept trying to walk, he was going to fall over and over and over.

But a man who crashed to the floor with any regularity could not expect to have a role in public life.

A man in Roosevelt's condition in the early 1920s scanned the habitat of the working politician as an able-bodied man scans a steep slope strewn with rocks. A politician pursued his ends in meetings, and meetings took place beyond steps and staircases and the quarter-inch-high sills of doorways. A politician climbed steps to the porches of private homes. He climbed steps to clubs and hotels and stages and temporary platforms built for speakers and ceremonial dinners. He stood in taverns and leaned over to greet old ladies on verandas. He danced at parties. He moved in crowds where people jostled and backed up unexpectedly and beckoned to him to lean far over to shake hands. He jumped in and out of taxicabs and private cars. He hurried along sidewalks crowded with pedestrians and slick with snow. He traveled from city to city by train; before his illness Roosevelt spent countless hours on the railroads between Washington, New York, Hyde Park, Albany, and Maine. But to reach a railroad platform, you generally went up or down a staircase. The only way to reach the interior of a railroad car was to climb a steep little set of stairs. To walk through a moving railroad car without falling took at least a little strength and coordination. Even to sit still in a swaying rail car required strength in the trunk, buttocks, and thighs that Roosevelt simply no longer had.

So if he couldn't negotiate these obstacles on his feet, why not use a wheelchair?

He had had a couple of plain, armless kitchen chairs converted into simple wheelchairs. (Commercial wheelchairs of that era were too big for the confined spaces of a private home, and certainly too big for the tiny elevators at 47–49 E. 65th Street.) He used these chairs at home every day. But he used them only to be pushed from one room to another. With his atrophied buttocks, it was uncomfortable to sit on a wooden seat for more than a few minutes. When he reached the room he was going to, he immediately shifted from the wheelchair to a roomier chair with arms and a pad or a cushion. He could not travel any distance in these wheelchairs by himself. Someone had to push.

There was little point in using a wheelchair outside the privacy of his homes. If he were pushed out in public in a wheelchair, he would come to a stop at the same steps and staircases that blocked him if he tried to walk with his crutches. He had ramps built at the house at Hyde Park. But there were no ramps for wheelchairs in ordinary buildings, and there were elevators only in tall office buildings and hotels.

Anyway, no politician could be seen in a wheelchair. To disabled people of a later era, the wheelchair would symbolize a certain degree of liberation, but in Roosevelt's time it was seen as something like a rolling prison. One was said to be "confined to a wheelchair." Wheelchairs were not for people leading normal lives. They were for sick people in hospitals and sanitariums. With an attendant always standing behind him, the man in a wheelchair was by definition not an independent human being who could care for himself. He was assumed to be sick. Roosevelt was not sick, not any more. But every person who saw him in a wheelchair would assume he was not at all well, and a man who was not well could not work — could not work at anything, let alone the vigorous job of a leader.

Of course, there was one more way to get up and down steps. He could have men pick him up and carry him. In private, he was having men who worked for the family do that now, at home and at his offices in Manhattan. But Kathleen Lake told Dr. Lovett he did not even want to be seen being helped into a car on East 65th Street. If it was bad to be seen in a wheelchair, it was worse to be carried up steps while people watched.

To stand was an act of manhood, especially in the upper crust of American society that Roosevelt inhabited as a fish inhabits water. In Emily Post's *Etiquette in Society, in Business, in Politics and in the Home* — first published just at this point, in 1922 — one command after another dealt with a man's obligation to stand:

A gentleman always rises when a lady comes into a room.

When any woman addresses a remark to him a gentleman at once rises to his feet as he answers her. In a restaurant, when a lady bows to him, a gentleman merely makes the gesture of rising by getting up half way from his chair and at the same time bowing. Then he sits down again.

When a lady goes to a gentleman's office on business he should stand up to receive her, offer her a chair, and not sit down until after she is seated. When she rises to leave, he must get up instantly and stand until she has left the office. . . .

It is not necessary to add that every American stands with his hat off at the passing of the "colors" and when the national anthem is played. . . . Also every man should stand with his hat off in the presence of a funeral that passes close . . .

If he gets on a street car . . . he must not take a seat if there are ladies standing. . . . If a very old woman, or a young one carrying a baby, enters the car, a gentleman rises at once, lifts his hat slightly, and says: "Please take my seat." . . .

The man who as a child came habitually into his mother's drawing-room when there was "company," generally makes a charming bow when grown . . .

In every form of bow, as distinct from merely lifting his hat, a gentleman looks at the person he is bowing to. In a very formal standing bow, his heels come together, his knees are rigid and his expression is rather serious. The informal bow . . . is easy and unstudied, but it should suggest the ease of controlled muscles, not the floppiness of a rag doll.

And so on.

Franklin Roosevelt could do none of these things, not without the help of a strong assistant. He could not rise when a lady entered the room, "instantly" or otherwise; could not rise halfway from a chair; could not board a streetcar or stand for the American flag; and any attempt at a bow, formal or informal, would send him full length to the floor.

If he was going to resume his career in politics, he was somehow going to have to stand and walk. There was no other way to do it.

But so far he could not rely on himself to cross a lobby without falling down.

Dr. Lovett's treatments simply were not working as FDR needed them to work. He must find some new therapy — something he could do to vault past Lovett's tedious implication that the best he could hope for was to master the art of walking with crutches.

The second winter of his ordeal descended on New York. Nothing much was keeping him in the city — not his two jobs, anyway. His casual understanding with Van Lear Black at Fidelity & Deposit remained in place. FDR continued as the putative head of the New York office at $25,000 a year, and he was putting in a few hours a couple of days each week. But Black put no pressure on him to work more than that and raised no objection when he stayed away. It was much the same at the law firm of Emmet, Marvin & Roosevelt, though in that case he apparently received no compensation when he did no work.

If these arrangements were not quite a matter of charity, they certainly did not constitute a real occupation. "It was his friends giving him an office," Frances Perkins said, "a place to hang his hat, a stable relationship to professional activities."

So FDR decided to hire a houseboat and crew and sail around the Florida Keys for a few weeks. Swimming was the best form of exercise for his legs. So he would go where the water was warm in the wintertime.

Eleanor needed to be persuaded that the expense was justified. When he made his case to her, she said later, it was the only time she could remember when he referred to his disability with anything less than optimism.

"He never complained," she said. "The only remark that I can remember that was in a way of complaint was . . . when we were discussing whether we would take a houseboat in Florida for the winter — because of the expense — and he said, 'Well, I think I might as well do as much as possible in order to improve as much as I can, because I shouldn't be any greater burden than is necessary."

If Eleanor's memory of this moment was accurate, then FDR's remark implied more than it said on the surface. This once, at least, he was acknowledging the difficulties he was imposing on his wife and children. And despite all his confident talk about a recovery, the remark hinted that he knew he might never be independent again.

Eleanor's memory of his comment as a "complaint" opens the door — at least a crack — into the emotional sphere they shared. It was in the inherited code of both their families not to dwell on misfortune. Alice Roosevelt, the first wife of Eleanor's uncle Theodore, had died when the two were in their twenties, and T.R. had never spoken her name again, or so it was said in the family. To ruminate on bad luck, even with one's spouse, was to "complain." To be silent about trouble was to exercise strength. Franklin and Eleanor discussed his condition in terms of practical arrangements, the way a couple might discuss the difficulties involved in moving a piano from one floor of the house to another. But they apparently never opened their hearts to each other about it. One can call that repression, or see it as a sad sign of the loss of intimacy in their marriage. But it also reveals the emotional armament that kept both of them going. By the habits of his upbringing and a sustained act of will, FDR defied the temptation of despair.

In any case, he took his trip. He chartered a sixty-five-foot houseboat called *Weona II* and invited a virtual household of friends to join him for a leisurely cruise from Miami through the Florida Keys, then north and west along the Everglades coast and back. He looked forward to deep-sea fishing and lots of swimming in the warm seas of the Gulf of Mexico. Eleanor did not care for winter vacations, but she agreed to come along for the first few days.

Weona II left Miami for Long Key in the middle of February 1923, and after a few days FDR and his company were cruising and fishing among the Ten Thousand Islands, a wilderness maze of twisting waterways and dense green mangrove and grass. The "fascination" of the terrain held his gaze. He had seen the train cars of the Florida East Coast Railway "absolutely jammed" with northerners, the latest wave in the great Florida land rush, and as he scanned this virginal coastline, he wrote to a friend: "I only wish it were possible to get some portion of it, possibly that lying between Cape Sable and Marco [Island], set aside as a wildlife refuge. There is still time if the right people would get to work and do it, as civilization has not yet got into that portion."

On the deck of *Weona II* he had leisure "to settle the affairs of the world" with friends who did not know or care much about politics, to read books that he never could get to at home. "I read the History of the Christian Church," he told a friend, "until I got so angry with the people who squabbled about doctrine that I felt like starting a new sect to be called 'Aboriginal Christians.' " He swam when he could — they had to look out for sharks — and he fished from the deep-sea fisherman's swivel chair. With practice he caught quite a few, at least one weighing some forty pounds. The new power in his upper body was obvious when he was able to fight and reel in big fish. At first he used the heavy strap on the fishing chair to hold his chest in place, but soon he found he could discard the strap and "hold heavy fish on a large rod without much difficulty."

It had been nearly two years since he had engaged in a vigorous, physical sport, and he was delighted to do so again. But he was just as pleased by his experiments with mobility around the houseboat.

Weona II did not welcome a man who couldn't walk. Passageways belowdecks were much too tight for a wheelchair. The staircase between decks was narrow and steep. He surveyed the quarters carefully, then, during the weeks afloat, "worked out a number of mechanical problems."

To climb the stairs, he resorted to the method he had practiced at home so that he could escape an upper story in a burning building: He sat on the third step from the bottom and hitched himself up with his hands, stair by stair.

In the passageways, he set aside his crutches and reached for the overhead beams. Grasping the beams, he could keep his balance while hauling himself forward step by step.

On deck, he devised a simple exercise for his quadriceps. He sat in "a small, light, low, rocking chair without arms. . . . The tendency at first was to cheat by rocking with the body, but within a few days I could rock back and forth by using only the knee and the lower left leg and foot muscles."

The biggest problem was how to get from the deck down to *Weona*'s motorboat or into the water for swimming — and out again. The surface of the deck was a full ten feet above the waves. But he devised a solution.

"On the top deck where we sat most of the time I had a section of the side rail cut out and hinged," he wrote. "The forward davit [a small crane] swung around to a position just off this opening. From this davit I suspended a plain board, like the board of a swing. I then sat on the deck, put my feet through the swing, pulled it under me. The davit was then swung out and I was lowered into the motor boat or, in going in swimming, into the water. It was perfectly simple once in the water to slide out of the swing and to get back into it."

Nearly two months of swimming, fishing, rocking in his chair, and sunbathing left him feeling marvelously fit. "The result has been most satisfactory," he wrote, "and I am convinced that there is a vast improvement in the leg muscles. I am tremendously keen about life on a boat, especially in Florida waters."

FDR told all this in some detail to Robert Lovett. He enclosed a separate memorandum describing his new mobility tricks in case they "may possibly be of assistance in other similar cases." It's unlikely that Lovett had many other cases of well-to-do men paralyzed below the waist who might need a device to get from the deck of a houseboat to a motorboat below. But FDR, like an enthusiastic teacher, loved to develop specialized knowledge and share the results.

But there was something he withheld from Lovett. Always the student of his own body, attentive to even the tiniest change in his limbs, he believed he had stumbled upon a new kind of therapy.

"I have found . . . for myself one interesting fact which I believe to be a real discovery," he wrote another man recovering from polio, "and that is that my muscles have improved with greater rapidity when I could give them sunlight." In Florida, he said, he had been "much in the open air under the direct rays of the sun with very few clothes on, and there is no doubt that the leg muscles responded more quickly at that time than when I am at home when I am, of necessity, more in the house."

He was not ready to present his claims for the therapeutic power of sunlight to his sober, skeptical orthopedist in Boston. But sunlight, like water, was giving him a reason to keep up his hopes.

Mrs. Lake was not the type to be "tremendously keen" about anything, but she was impressed by what she saw at her first meeting with FDR back in New York.

"He came back immensely improved from his trip south, in all ways," she informed Dr. Lovett, "looking at least ten years younger."

He could now set his right knee — keep it firmly fixed in the unbent position — a goal she had been pursuing for months, "and with slight assistance is able to sit up from [a] lying position." His ability to move his feet had improved too.

These advances were nothing like walking, of course, but they were real improvements nonetheless — certainly enough to justify his belief that if he just kept working at it, he could make more gains.

But Mrs. Lake had observed that whenever FDR made progress during a period of disciplined exercise — at Phillips House in Boston or away from the family at Hyde Park — he tended to lose the gains as soon as he got back to the distractions of New York. And it happened again this time, after his excursion on *Weona II*. Because he felt so much better, Mrs. Lake told Lovett a few weeks later, he had "plunged headlong into work" and entertained guests at dinner every night. Within a couple of weeks he had a bad cold, "looked a perfect wreck," and lost nearly all the gains he had made in his legs.

Mrs. Lake watched him in this state for another week. Then she all but ordered him to Hyde Park with only LeRoy Jones to help. He was to do absolutely nothing for ten days.

The rest cure worked, but then, she said, he carelessly "sat out in the damp, & the quadriceps which was coming back has once more disappeared." And he could no longer set his right knee.

Mrs. Lake blamed Eleanor.

"If only his wife could be persuaded that he does not need urging on all day, & entertaining all evening, I think he would not be so tired & would do better physically," she told Lovett. "You would not believe that two weeks [in New York] could have made such a difference. [H]e himself begins to understand how the city affects him, & the knee going back like that was a real surprise, but he is so surrounded by family, all giving him advice & ordering him round, that he gets quite desperate."

But any desperation was largely his own doing. He simply could not concentrate on one thing for any extended period. Recovery may have been his main pursuit, but he had a hundred others that lured him away from a single-minded focus on Mrs. Lake's precise regimen of exercise and rest. He had people to see, letters to write, ideas to promote. To a friend of his who hoped to make a living by writing full time, FDR sent encouragement but also a word of caution: "I can't help feeling that you are built a bit like me — that you need something physically more active, with constant contact with all sorts of people in many kinds of places." That was one of his rare attempts at self-assessment, and it was on the money. "I have never specialized in any one thing," he told a reporter. "I am interested in too many things."

The catalog of such things was long.

At Hyde Park, he built model sailboats to race on the Hudson and took up a careful study of how to increase their speed, experimenting with his own designs of cutters, double-keeled craft, and catamarans. He reduced the time it took to send one of these thirty-eight-inch boats the five-eighths of a mile across the river from sixteen minutes to ten minutes and fifteen seconds.

He bought farmland in Hyde Park and resumed work on an earlier program to plant trees on the family's growing acreage. Over the next several years he purchased and oversaw the planting of some thirty-seven thousand seedlings: tulip poplars, white pines, red pines, Scotch pines, black walnuts, hemlocks, and Norway spruces. He deplored the destruction of the American forest and embraced reforestation as a matter of good stewardship of the land, smart farming, and sheer love of trees. He acknowledged his presidential cousin's leadership in conservation, but said: "T.R. was the Roosevelt who chopped down trees. I like to plant them." (By the time of his death, the total number of new trees planted at Hyde Park would reach nearly half a million. His aide Samuel Rosenman remembered only once when FDR frankly expressed regret about his disability. He had driven Rosenman and a couple of others into the woods to show them some trees. "He could not drive his car close enough to see them," Rosenman remembered, "and as we got out to walk into the woods, he said: 'I'm sorry, I can't go with you, I'd like to see those trees again after all these years, but' — and he sadly pointed to his wasted legs.")

He became an accomplished amateur archivist and regional historian. He not only cultivated extensive knowledge of the genealogy of the Roosevelt family; he also became the official historian of the village of Hyde Park and an expert on the colonial Dutch architecture of the Hudson Valley. In the summer of 1923 he had to apologize to an old associate for failing to answer a letter: "We are so busy working up historical material that I have got way behind on my correspondence."

He expanded his collections of stamps, rare books, and naval prints. It was hard to attend auctions and visit his favorite antiquarian shops, so he educated Louis Howe in how to read dealers' catalogs and sent him on bidding and buying expeditions. He wrote to the great Americana dealers in New York, Philadelphia, and Boston. He prized his stamps especially. Sorting stamps was ideal for a man who had been compelled to give up most outdoor activities. Sitting at a table with a magnifying glass and tweezers in his hands, he could engage in the minute study of these beautiful miniatures for hours. "It dispels boredom," he would write, "enlarges our vision, broadens our knowledge of geography and in innumerable ways enriches life and adds to its joy."

He read a great deal. In fact, Roosevelt apparently read and learned more during these years after polio than he ever had in school. "I have always liked books of travel and adventure the best, especially those relating to the sea," he said, but somehow he also amassed a vast mental storehouse of facts and stories from the nation's past. "Roosevelt was a walking American history book," Frances Perkins said. "He knew exactly how the troops went here and there, and exactly where the Indian massacres were and why. He knew exactly what the trading towns were and the trading routes across the valleys." She thought such lore had come down to him through his family, but much of it must have come from books too. He would pick up anything to read. According to Louis Howe, he read every number of *The Federalist Papers* purely for pleasure, and he once spent an entire morning absorbed in *Sturtevant's Notes on Edible Plants.*

He was also a leader in the alumni affairs of the Harvard Class of 1904; chairman of the campaign to raise funds for construction of the Cathedral of St. John the Divine in New York City; vestryman of St. James Church in Hyde Park; and chairman of the New York Boy Scouts. (These were the main service activities left after he and Howe scrutinized all the things he had been doing in 1921 and struck many off the list.)

This is not to mention the voluminous correspondence he carried on with Democrats across the country, nor the ideas for businesses and investments that he pursued.

If he was distracted from the hard job of recovery, it was hardly Eleanor's fault.

In the spring of 1923, Dr. Lovett brought FDR over to Boston again. He saw what Mrs. Lake had seen. "I am very well satisfied with Mr. Roosevelt's progress," he told Eleanor. "He handles himself definitely better than he ever has, he shows gain of power, and I think his progress is most satisfactory."

But now, thanks to his informants on East 65th Street — Mrs. Lake, Nurse Rockey, Eleanor, and Sara — Lovett was well aware of his patient's on-again-off-again devotion to his exercise routine. And, unlike Mrs. Lake, he thought Eleanor was right to urge him on. According to Geoffrey C. Ward, Lovett's wife would later "recall her husband having said that whatever progress Roosevelt made toward recovery was due more to Eleanor's exhortations than to his own efforts. She and Louis Howe were 'the taskmasters' and he would have greatly increased his mobility had he listened to them more often."

But Lovett's choice of words shows why FDR was frustrated with the doctor's advice. Lovett was paying attention to Roosevelt's "mobility," to how he "handled himself." Those were references to his ability to move around a room in his current condition. But FDR was not content to be an efficient and effective invalid. It was his current condition that he wanted to improve, not his ability to walk with crutches.

So, soon after Lovett's exam in Boston, FDR made arrangements for two osteopaths to come and see him — one named Starr, the other Barrett. As FDR well knew, Lovett would scoff; in his circles, where allopathic medicine had reigned for decades, the osteopathic claim to heal by manipulation of body parts, and to treat "the whole person," gave off the smell of quackery. But Dr. Starr used light to treat his patients, and FDR wanted to hear more about that. So he invited the osteopaths without telling Lovett what he was up to.

They praised the progress he had made and endorsed his exercise regimen. But they agreed with FDR that much more could be done. "They insist . . . that as I am going at present, the process of muscular development will be very long drawn out, and that the only method of hastening matters is by going to the seat of the trouble — i.e., the nerve cells — and building them up faster than they are building at present. They therefore suggest that I start up here at Hyde Park with a simple light machine . . . i.e., taking an artificial sun bath in my room all over the body for about an hour every morning."

FDR told all this to Mrs. Lake for her "personal and confidential information." He liked the osteopaths and he liked their advice, as it was "absolutely in line with the undoubted fact which I discovered for myself, that the sun down in Florida, and since I have been up here, has done much to keep the circulation going. For instance, it is absolutely a fact that the mornings I am able to sit in the sun for an hour or two my legs do not get cold in the evening, whereas if the day is cloudy and I do not get my sun bath, the legs freeze up from about 5 p.m. on." But he wanted Mrs. Lake's opinion: "Don't you (in your purely private and non-professional capacity) agree that it can do no harm to try [the sunlamp] out at least for a month or two[?]"

Mrs. Lake's reply, if she sent one, does not survive, but FDR did try the light, and he reported good results.

He had been looking into every possibility of a breakthrough. He had sought information on the "aero-therapeutic" method developed by Dr. Orval J. Cunningham, of Kansas City, who put patients in a pressurized steel tube the size of a railroad car with an interior to match: toilet, shower, and enough Pullman car furniture to seat up to thirty-six patients at a time. He listened to friends pitch exercise contraptions of ingenious design, such as the motorized Whiteley Exerciser, which pulled the legs back and forth with rubber cables. He let his mother buy him a giant tricycle. He ordered up "an old-fashioned children's double-swing" that seemed, at least for a time, "to develop the knee muscles in a splendid way." He exchanged ideas with others recovering from polio, especially a young man named Paul Hasbrouck, who lived in nearby Poughkeepsie, also a patient of Lovett's. When Hasbrouck told Roosevelt about spring-loaded leg braces invented by a French orthopedist named Gabriel Bidou, FDR let off a little steam at Lovett: "There is no question that the French are far ahead of us in their mechanical appliances. If you and I do not greatly improve this coming winter [1923–1924] we shall have to get together and work out something along the line of Dr. Bidou's springs."

After all this, and a great deal of exercise, he had found only two things that seemed to offer any real promise of more progress: swimming and sunlight.

So, buoyed by his experience on *Weona II* the previous winter, he went in with an old Harvard friend, John Lawrence of Boston, who also needed exercise in the wake of an illness. They bought a Florida houseboat in the fall of 1923 and christened it *Larooco* (for Lawrence, Roosevelt & Co., and pronounced *la-ROW-co*). FDR went south for its first cruise in February 1924.

It was the sixth or seventh time in two years that FDR was leaving his family for an extended period, and there would be many more such absences.

Anna Roosevelt said later that FDR's paralysis created "an entirely new life for the whole family." If her father and mother seldom discussed his paralysis with each other, they discussed it with the children even less. Yet the disability had transformed the household into an enterprise devoted to FDR's recovery. This meant the children saw their father less than ever. Before 1921 he had been preoccupied with politics; now he was preoccupied with his recovery, though this was worse for the children, since he often left home for treatment and rest. Eleanor too was often away, increasingly absorbed in Democratic Party politics. Sara Roosevelt often stood in; she was a devoted grandmother, and the children were devoted to her in turn. But they longed for their father. Each needed him in different ways. Anna was nearly done with high school. James and Elliott were at Groton School, where Elliott had continuous difficulties. Franklin Jr. and John were grade-schoolers at home. None can be said to have received the attention they deserved. A series of letters from Franklin Jr. in particular reveals a pattern of loneliness:

Dear Father,
I hope you are well. I hope you are coming up here soon. Elliott is a good boy. [The parents often doubted that.] John has helped me to get the hay for my goat. John wants mother to come next week with you. (1922)

Dear Mother and Father,
I hope you are well. The night that John came here he cried for you. I hope that you are coming soon. (1922)

Dear Father,
I hope you are having a good time down south. (1924)

[To Anna:]
Chief [Anna's dog] is very well but seems to grow more and more lonesome just like me and Johny [*sic*]. The house seems just like an emty waistbasket [*sic*]. Now that father has left, mother seems allways [*sic*] to be on the go. (1925)

The Roosevelts' marriage too had entered

a new stage. By 1924, with FDR well beyond the early and most difficult part of his recovery, the two were living increasingly independent lives.

Eleanor Roosevelt was emerging as a powerful voice in Democratic politics. She was on her way to leadership in the New York Women's Democratic Committee; the state and national Democratic committees; in women's trade unions; in the National Consumers League; and in the gubernatorial campaigns of Al Smith. She often described these activities as an effort to keep FDR in touch with politics. But her own social conscience and her desire to be useful in her own right were surely motives just as powerful — and probably more powerful.

Since 1922, she had been spending much of her time with two other Democratic activists, Nancy Cook and Marion Dickerman. The two were life partners who became the close friends Eleanor never had as a girl, and they were, for a time, the center of Eleanor's emotional life — a second family. Soon FDR would help the three women to plan and build (on a piece of his own property) a wholly separate house at Hyde Park — the stone cottage called Val-Kill — where Eleanor and her friends could live out from under Sara Roosevelt's shadow. The three women would also soon buy the Todhunter School for Girls in New York, where Eleanor began a part-time career as a teacher.

Meanwhile, her relationship with FDR was evolving into something different than a conventional marriage, happy or unhappy. They still spent weeks at a time in the same house, either in New York City or Hyde Park, and they were always together for holidays. They discussed the children and politics; they consulted each other about finances and family problems. They traded stories about Sara and kept each other up to date on their various enterprises. But they now were less like spouses and more like a pair of unmarried, middle-aged siblings. They led their own lives and pursued their own ends along parallel tracks, tied to each other by a shared past and mutual devotion. It was no longer the devotion of a happily married couple, but it was strong. They cared for each other's welfare and helped each other. They soldiered on, no longer lovers but allies.

In the meantime, FDR's secretary, Marguerite LeHand, became his full-time companion — more like a wife than Eleanor, in the opinion of some who knew the family well, though no one can know if their closeness extended to physical intimacy.

As she became a daily presence in the house at East 65th Street, one or more of the Roosevelt children began to call her "Missy," and the nickname stuck. She was thereafter even more a member of the family than Louis Howe.

She was, first, a superb secretary who took on more and more responsibility for FDR's day-to-day affairs. She was efficient, hardworking, highly intelligent, and shrewd. Everyone liked and respected her, from Sara Roosevelt to Eleanor to FDR's political associates. She was endlessly smiling — an antidote to Eleanor's occasional glooms — and she had a wonderful sense of humor. "She was always so cheerful and so vigorous that she made everyone else feel good," said a friend. "What amazed me always was the amount of wit and laughter that flew around in her presence." Raised in a working-class family near Boston, she absorbed the Roosevelts' upper-class manners, so she could soon deal comfortably with anyone in her boss's circle of friends and associates, from navy admirals to Tammany politicians. (Daisy Suckley, another Hudson Valley upper-cruster, once remarked on the excellent manners Missy

displayed "without any background at all.")
Though she was said not to have head-
turning looks, she had a combination of
glamour and sassy charm that captivated
many men. One later recalled her "lovely
throaty voice," "the quick upturn of her
face," and her "strange secret smile, com-
pound[ed] of cunning and innocence."
Certainly her boss became deeply fond of
her and reliant on her. She anticipated his
needs and channeled his mood. When he
got down, an associate said later, she had a
way of "banishing distrust and bitterness"
from his mind. Each made the other laugh,
and she was the only person apart from
Louis Howe and Eleanor who had the
standing to warn "F.D," as she alone called
him, when he was about to make an error.

Missy dated but never married. Two
sisters who had known her well since childhood believed "she was just too devoted and
interested in FDR. She'd never meet anybody that would come up to Roosevelt."

So it was Missy, not Eleanor, who spent
long weeks with FDR — along with friends
and the crew — on the leisurely cruises of
Larooco in 1924, 1925, and 1926. It was
Missy who most often shared cocktails and
dined with FDR, Missy who took dictation
at his bedside, Missy who spent her days at

his beck and call and played cards with him in the evening.

Eleanor apparently voiced no objection. She liked Missy very much, even treated her as a daughter. As for the obvious closeness between Missy and her husband, she seems to have shrugged and looked away. She was busy; so was he. Perhaps, as has been suggested, Missy's constant attendance upon FDR allowed Eleanor to go her own way without feeling her husband was being neglected. Anna Roosevelt once proposed that Missy did not threaten Eleanor as Lucy Mercer had; Lucy had been of Eleanor's social class, while Missy was not. That, of course, was sheer speculation about a question that no one could answer — even, perhaps, Eleanor herself.

As Dr. Draper had said, the family was "a complex tapestry" indeed.

A couple of days before FDR went south to try out his new houseboat in February 1924, Dr. Draper gave him a thorough examination. He detected nothing in the lower extremities to justify FDR's hope that he still might discard his crutches and walk. He wished his patient a fruitful trip and sat down to write a confidential note to Robert Lovett in Boston.

"I am very much disheartened about his ultimate recovery," Draper wrote. "I cannot help feeling that he has almost reached the limit of his possibilities."

Perhaps Draper gently said something of the kind to his patient. And perhaps that was why, as Missy LeHand later told a friend, "there were days on the *Larooco* when it was noon before he could pull himself out of depression and greet his guests wearing his lighthearted façade."

In 1920 Roosevelt's famous name brought him the Democratic nomination for vice president. Just thirty-eight, he campaigned with extraordinary vigor.

It was the first active campaign for Eleanor Roosevelt (at top right) with FDR; his mother, Sara Delano Roosevelt; and the five Roosevelt children.

The poliovirus probably infected FDR at a Boy Scout campout at Bear Mountain State Park on the evening of July 28, 1921. Before and after the attack, his chief aide and closest friend was a gnarled, cranky ex-newsman, Louis Howe.

FDR recovered at two homes the family shared with Sara Roosevelt: the twin townhouses at 47–49 East 65th Street in Manhattan and the estate at Hyde Park on the Hudson River. The image above, showing FDR exercising on the lawn at Hyde Park, was the work of a neighbor, the artist Olin Dows.

The elderly William Keen (top left) botched an early diagnosis. Samuel Levine (top right) urged a crucial test for polio. Two polio experts then took over: Robert Lovett, who predicted "possible complete recovery"; and George Draper, FDR's old friend and personal physician, who pondered how to tell the patient "what he really faces without utterly crushing him."

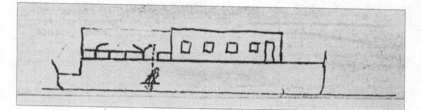

On the houseboat Weona II in 1923, FDR improvised a small crane to lower himself into the ocean for exercise. He drew the sketch above in a letter to Dr. Lovett.

Roosevelt rose from the political graveyard with a stunning address to the Democratic convention in 1924, when his alliance with New York Governor Al Smith deepened. Note that in this staged photo with Smith, FDR took no trouble to hide his braces.

Photographers competed for pictures of FDR (on crutches) at Hyde Park with the 1924 Democratic nominee for president, John W. Davis, and Governor Smith (at right).

With exercise in the mineral-rich water at Warm Springs, Georgia, FDR believed, "it will be only a matter of time till I can walk again." Above, the atrophy of his legs and the buildup of his upper body are obvious.

The resort became a sanctuary where he felt fully at ease with his disability. Above, he fishes near Warm Springs with leg braces over his trousers.

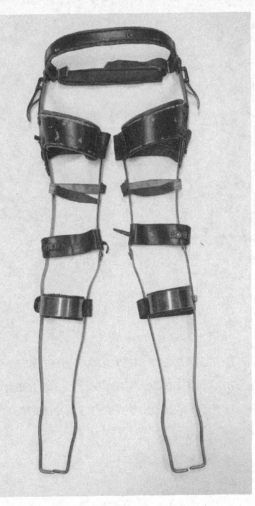

One in the series of at least four
sets of custom leg braces that FDR
used from 1922 on.

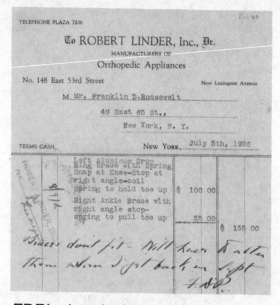

FDR's handwritten note on a receipt for braces purchased in 1926: "Braces don't fit. Will have to alter them when I get back in Sept. FDR"

FDR wore braces chiefly to stand and walk in public (always with assistance), as shown above on January 1, 1929, at his first inauguration as governor of New York. Here, he walks with Eleanor and Guernsey Cross, one of his aides, who was hired partly for his strength.

FDR was most vulnerable to falls and embarrassing postures when he was entering or leaving a car, so he asked photographers not to take his picture in those moments. A few did, as the photo above shows.

FDR was often photographed standing and walking, as in the image above, taken during the 1932 campaign, with Jimmy Roosevelt escorting his father. Contrary to claims that FDR "hid" his condition, any of the thousands who saw his gait in settings like this one could not possibly fail to recognize that he was disabled.

■ ■ ■ ■

Part Three: Resurrection

SPRING 1924 TO FALL 1932

■ ■ ■ ■

CHAPTER 9
"IF YOU WILL GET RIGHT"
SUMMER 1924

In 1924 Al Smith ran for president with the rising power of the cities for fuel. He ran as the voice of the Catholic immigrant and the working man left out of the postwar business boom, of the Irish-American and the German-American who could no longer buy a beer in the neighborhood tavern because the Prohibitionists had gotten their way.

Opposing Smith was William Gibbs McAdoo, who was marshalling the old stalwarts of the Democratic Party for a last stand against the rise of the city. McAdoo was corralling the aging Populist farmers and their children — people for whom William Jennings Bryan, scourge of the northeastern banker and the Darwinian heresy alike, remained the hero of the age. McAdoo had the southerners who distrusted the brash, Catholic, Tammany-tainted governor of New York. With Prohibition the dominant

331

issue of the era, he stood firmly "dry" against Smith, the symbolic face of the "wets," who wanted to repeal the ban on liquor. McAdoo also was playing a quiet game of diplomacy with the Ku Klux Klan, the semi-secret fraternity of xenophobes and racists that wielded political power in the 1920s across a gigantic swath of the country from Georgia through the Midwest to California.

With the country prosperous and at peace, and the staid but popular Calvin Coolidge in the White House, the Democratic nomination in 1924 would be no great prize. But control of the party in the future was at stake. Smith represented the forces on the rise among the Democrats but not yet supreme. If he made a respectable run in 1924, the 1928 nomination would be far more likely, and the presidency itself might really come within his reach.

Smith's men snagged the Democratic convention for New York City and prepared to do battle with the drys and the "hicks" on Al's home turf. New York's electoral votes were crucial to Smith's strategy. So his first job was to shore up his base, and Franklin Roosevelt could be used for the purpose. Just as in 1922, he was the clean, Protestant, antiboss patrician whose support might reassure people like himself that Smith was okay, that it really was all right to vote for an Irish-Catholic wet for president. (FDR himself took an inoffensive middle ground on Prohibition; personally wet, he preferred to get past the fight altogether and simply concede the need to enforce the law.) Smith asked FDR to be the national chairman of his campaign. FDR would not be required to oversee day-to-day operations in campaign headquarters; Al had plenty of men to handle that. Roosevelt could serve as the titular chair with phone calls and meetings at East 65th Street. He would be on the outskirts of the campaign — a pleasant figurehead.

But with the convention looming at the end of June, his role in Smith's drive for the nomination suddenly became not only more important but more visible.

Precisely how he was chosen to give the main nominating speech for Smith at Madison Square Garden became a matter of dispute. In the bitter years after Smith and "Frank" had fallen out, when it was clear that the 1924 convention had been a turning point in Roosevelt's career, Smith would say that FDR "begged" him for the chance to speak at the convention. But Smith's close advisor, Joseph Proskauer, who had no love for FDR, said the speech was not FDR's idea but his own. In Proskauer's version, when he suggested Roosevelt, Smith said: "For God's sake, why?" and Proskauer replied: "Because you're a Bowery mick and he's a Protestant patrician and he'd take some of the curse off you."

So Al asked and FDR agreed, but with private misgivings. The jostling crowds, the banks of slip-sliding chairs with narrow aisles, the steep staircases and steps presented endless obstacles and dangers. But he could not pass up the chance to give a major address to the national party. In Madison Square Garden, the biggest arena imaginable, he was going to display his condition to the world.

He decided that he must contrive to walk. Most of the time he could use a crutch on one side and grasp the arm of a helper on the other. But when the time came to cross the platform to the speaker's rostrum before fourteen hundred delegates and thousands more spectators, he would use two crutches and walk alone. And he must not fall.

He asked his eldest son, Jimmy, now sixteen, to act as his aide. Besides giving the speech, he planned to attend sessions on the floor and other meetings, so the work of getting seated and standing again would be nearly as important as walking. He and Jimmy rehearsed. They found out how far it would be from the top of the stairs to the speaker's platform and the lectern. Then, in the library at East 65th Street, they measured off the distance and FDR practiced again and again, just with crutches.

Madison Square Garden — the second of the Garden's four incarnations, the Beaux-Arts cavern at Madison Avenue and 26th Street — had once been the architectural pride of the city. But that had been thirty years earlier. Now it was about to be torn down, and the Democratic convention of 1924 was to be its last big event. The next to last had been Barnum & Bailey's circus, and the odor of elephants still hung in the air as workers stripped the interior of aging ornaments and installed thousands of new seats. The delegates would sit in chairs on the Garden's floor, while the giant galleries would be opened to spectators — especially to local fans of Governor Smith, who would push through the turnstiles with placards, banners, noisemakers, and thousands of free tickets provided by the governor's men. It was to be the first national party convention to seat women delegates — a cause of some unease among the men accustomed to running these shows.

Two gigantic posters hung at either end of the cavernous room: Grover Cleveland and Andrew Jackson on one side, Woodrow Wilson and Thomas Jefferson above the speaker's platform. Thirty-five hundred American flags of varying sizes decorated the hall, and ten thousand more flags, tiny ones, were crammed into traps in the ceiling, ready to be dropped in a shower of red, white, and blue. A sprawling platform was built to hold seven hundred and fifty reporters and photographers, and engineers of the American Telephone and Telegraph Company set up equipment to broadcast the proceedings by radio, the first time ever for a national political convention. The audience for the principal speakers would be enormous.

On the first day, June 24, the mercury hit 83 degrees by noon, and that was outside. Inside, the heat was worse, and a fight over tickets between the Smith and McAdoo forces poisoned the atmosphere.

The second day's work broke down in an ugly battle of demonstrations for and against the Ku Klux Klan, with Smith's partisans yelling: "Ku, Ku, McAdoo!" McAdoo's name was placed in nomination by James Phelan, the Democratic boss of California, McAdoo's home state, but Phelan's appallingly bad speech was all but buried in the thunder from Smith's adoring battalions in the galleries.

They were behaving much as they would at any other important event in the Garden — say, a heavyweight boxing championship. No delegate was fonder of Smith than Frances Perkins, one of several high-ranking women in his administration, but as she sat in her seat, she began to question the wisdom of bringing in so many of the kind of "people that make up the Brooklyn Dodgers fans." It was obvious, as she looked around, that the spectators' heavy use of "the lingo of the Bowery . . . sort of sickened the delegates," many of whom were Bible-believing small-town southerners. What was more, Perkins said, many in the galleries apparently believed the convention's purpose was simply to name their man as the Democratic nominee, so they greeted speeches in support of any other candidate with alternating expressions of frustrated boredom and outraged anger.

Roosevelt's nominating speech was scheduled for the morning of the third day, Thursday, June 26. The streets of Manhattan were unusually quiet; people without tickets to the Garden stayed inside next to radios.

FDR had arrived at the arena early, but even so, Jimmy Roosevelt remembered, "the process of getting into his seat was an ordeal for Father. We [had] practiced the awkward business of standing together by a chair, with me supporting him and taking his crutch from him as he lowered himself into his seat; he became quite proficient at it."

He began to go about his business, moving in and out of the main hall for meetings, greeting delegates, chatting with Smith lieutenants. At times he used a wheelchair. As the morning went on and the crowd grew, more and more people noticed him and pointed, and little rackets of applause began to rise whenever he came and went. He was scheduled to speak for Smith at ten thirty in the morning, but the McAdoo forces worked a switch and grabbed the time. FDR waited. "Outwardly he was beaming," Jimmy said, "but I could sense his inner tenseness."

Finally, through the hanging pall of tobacco smoke, delegates and spectators alike could see two men lift Roosevelt by the arms and carry him up the flight of stairs from the floor to the speaker's platform. The crowd quieted to watch. Now Roosevelt was standing at the top of the stairs. With his right hand he held a crutch wedged under his armpit. His left hand held the arm of a teen-aged boy.

"His fingers dug into my arm like pincers," Jimmy said later. "I doubt that he knew how hard he was gripping me." The heat was awful, and sweat rolled down Roosevelt's neck.

Joe Guffey, national committeeman from Pennsylvania, was standing a few feet away. FDR called to him in a loud whisper, asking him to go to the lectern and give it a shake. Guffey looked at him quizzically. Go and shake the lectern, FDR said again, "almost fiercely." He wanted to know if the speaker's stand was bolted to the floor. Now Guffey understood. He sidled over and gave the lectern a shake. It was all right.

A moment or two more and the crowd heard Roosevelt's name announced.

Delegates fixed their eyes on the man whom they had first seen at the Democratic convention in San Francisco four years earlier. In the summer of 1920 he had been "a young man in the flower of his manly vigor," as one reporter put it. At a key moment that year, he had pushed opponents aside to seize the standard of the New York delegation and rush it forward to signal praise for the stroke-stricken president, Woodrow Wilson. Soon afterward, the hall had nominated him for vice president.

Now they saw a different figure, thick in the shoulders and chest but flimsy in the legs, the body oddly straight. He turned to the boy and took the second crutch. He started toward the lectern alone.

An Associated Press reporter detected something happening in the crowd. On the floor, he wrote, "it seemed as though the size of the convention itself had mysteriously doubled. The passageways and aisles were choking with humanity although all the seats for the delegates and alternates had long been filled."

Frances Perkins sensed a collective shiver in the hall — a sudden sorrow over this public exhibition of what had been lost. "There was a hush and everybody was holding their breath," she recalled. "Everybody was sort of weeping inwardly. The old-line politicians remembered him as a very vigorous young man at the previous convention. Here was this terribly crippled person . . . getting himself to the platform somehow, looking so pale, so thin, so delicate."

He reached the lectern. With both hands gripping the handles of his crutches, he could not wave. So he threw his head up and grinned.

"It just tore the place to pieces," Perkins said.

When the noise subsided, the voice that emerged from the weak figure on the platform was superb. "It was a surprise to hear him begin to speak and see that his voice was strong and true and vigorous," Perkins remembered, "and that what he had to say had been not only well thought out but was delivered in a very convincing and dramatic kind of a way." The accent and enunciation were of the High Church Episcopal pulpit and the Wall Street boardroom — *guh-vah-nuh* for "governor," *lay-bah* for "labor" — but the words were plain and blunt, and there was a note of fellow feeling that discouraged any suspicion that the speaker, however highborn, was a snob. The pace was stately, unhurried, with pauses deftly timed.

Perkins sat close enough to see another level of the performance. "While he stood there and while his voice was so vigorous and strong," she remembered, "he was literally trembling. The hand that was on the paper was literally shaking, because of the extreme pain and tenseness with which he held himself up to make that speech. Not everybody saw that, but I did. Where our seats were you could see everything."

He cited Al Smith's enormous popularity among ordinary New Yorkers: "Ask the woman who serves you in the shop; the banker who cashes your check; the man who runs your elevator; the clerk in your hotel." He spoke of Smith as a champion of progressive ideals and an efficient and honest manager of government. In a veiled swat at the Klan and its sympathizers in the party, he urged delegates to put away "every sordid consideration, every ignoble personal prejudice."

He cited Smith's prowess as a vote-getter — "This governor of ours is the most dangerous adversary that the Republican Party ever had to fear" — and asked delegates to imagine "his thrust and his genial sarcasm burning out the truth where all men can see it. . . . He is the happy warrior of the political battlefield . . . this man of destiny whom our state proudly dedicates to the nation — our own Alfred E. Smith!"

"In one huge burst," a reporter wrote, "galleries, Smith delegates and Smith cohorts crowding the aisles let go. From either end of the far galleries, the rising, ear-piercing shriek of fire sirens wailed high above the tumult, never to cease their unearthly yelling for an instant until more than an hour had passed."

Afterward, the party's leaders convened backstage. Roosevelt received nearly as many congratulations as Smith himself did. "He was just shaking . . . like a leaf," Perkins recalled. "He was sitting down by this time in some little room back of the stage. He sat down there and was wringing wet — perspiration streaming off his face. He mopped his brow. He was very cheerful, very pleasant, very smiling . . . [but] he was as weak as a rag."

Eleanor and her friend Caroline O'Day, associate chair of the New York State Democratic Committee, had scheduled a reception that evening for the New York delegation at East 65th Street. Eleanor's friend Marion Dickerman left the convention early and ran uptown to help with the party.

When she got to the house, Sara Roosevelt's butler told her that Mr. Roosevelt was resting upstairs and would like to speak to her for a moment. She ran up and found FDR sitting up in his bed. He stretched his arms wide and said: "Marion, I did it!"

In the next day's papers, there was astonishment. "Everybody had thought that he was near to dead," Frances Perkins said, yet there he had been, full of life.

Kyle D. Palmer, the blatantly partisan political correspondent of the Republican *Los Angeles Times,* was one of the few who emphasized the extent of Roosevelt's disability. "He is hopelessly an invalid, his legs paralyzed," Palmer wrote, "obliged to prop himself against the speaker's desk once he had been lifted to his feet. . . . Wheel chair, crutches and attendants are with him wherever he goes."

But most reports emphasized the comeback instead of the deficit.

"There was nothing at the Democratic Convention more inspiring than the heroism of Franklin D. Roosevelt," said the *Louisville Courier-Journal.* "It was the nominator that loomed large in the picture, an invalid on crutches, perhaps in pain, who conquered the frailties of body by sheer power of will. . . . The world abhors the quitter who in his full strength goes down and will not get up. It admires the man who fights to the last and dies with his boots on. Franklin D. Roosevelt showed that this was the stuff he was made of." The appraisal of the veteran columnist Mark Sullivan, a major voice in Washington, was typical. "It was one of the very best nominating speeches this writer has ever heard and he has heard, oh Lord, how many?" Sullivan wrote. "There was art in it and true eloquence. . . . One got the idea that the convention would make no mistake if it should name Roosevelt himself."

Others had the same idea, especially as the ugly battle between Smith and McAdoo snarled into a deadlock. "As the tense hours passed," a reporter wrote, "more and more the word was heard that Roosevelt should take the nomination." But "to every friend who pressed this message that he should lead his party and disregard his own health and crippled condition, Mr. Roosevelt returned the reply that he was for Al Smith."

The struggle between the enemy forces of Smith and McAdoo dragged through day after day and dozens of inconclusive ballots, and as more names were added to the list of formal nominees, with no sign of a break in the impasse, the talk about Roosevelt continued.

A familiar figure at the Garden's press tables was a fellow named Jimmy Montague, a veteran scribbler of light newspaper prose and poetry from the school of Edgar Guest and James Whitcomb Riley. Long of the Hearst tribe, now at the *New York Herald-Tribune,* Montague, like Louis Howe, had once helped the thirty-year-old Roosevelt write speeches as a fledgling state senator. Five days after FDR's big address at the Garden, Jimmy Montague now fed the convention chatter with a front-page report in the *Herald-Tribune:* "The one man to whom the contending factions could turn and at the same time save their faces and keep square with the folks at home" was "sitting in the exact center of the great hall." His name, Montague claimed, "would stampede the convention were he put in nominaton." Yet he not only did not want the honor; he "actually would be alarmed if he knew what people were saying about him in the delegations and in the lower labyrinths of the building. . . . More than once it was found expedient to hush a little delegation which was talking about sending up his name, lest unforeseen results might happen."

Answering a common view outside the convention hall, Montague insisted the surge of interest was "not because of his name" alone, for "there are many Roosevelts. It is because, without the slightest desire or intention to do anything of the sort, he has done for himself what he could not do for his candidate."

At the end of sixteen days, on the 103rd

ballot, the delegates, exhausted, settled on an obscure Virginian, John W. Davis, for president, then limped out of New York. It was clear that the disastrous Democratic convention had done a good deal for the Republican incumbent, Calvin Coolidge.

Jimmy Montague of the *Herald-Tribune* may have written his story about the clamor for Roosevelt more to do a good turn for a pal — and with prodding, quite possibly, from Louis Howe — than in the spirit of strict accuracy. But his account of Roosevelt's surge in popularity surely contained a potent dose of truth, since delegates afterward told their own stories of wishing FDR had been available. "Like the overwhelming majority of the delegates who attended the convention," an Arkansan wrote, "I became an ardent admirer of yours, and had your physical condition permitted, you would have been nominated." An Oregon delegate told him: "I have the utmost confidence in you, and wanted to say that I supported you four years ago and would be glad to support you again, if you will get right." "I have heard it on every hand during the trying days of the convention from men and women from many states," a Louisiana state representative told FDR. "One of your enthusiastic admirers said to me 'Hell it's not legs we want in the White House! It's brains.' "

Those were just ordinary delegates. But Boss Tom Pendergast of Kansas City, one of the three or four most powerful men in the national party, was saying the same thing. "I met your friend Franklin Roosevelt in New York," he told an ally. "You know I am seldom carried away . . . but I want to tell you that had Mr. Roosevelt . . . been physically able to have withstood the campaign, he would have been named by acclamation the first few days of the Convention. He has the most magnetic personality of any individual I have ever met, and I predict he will be the candidate on the Democratic ticket in 1928."

Press accounts like Montague's created their own reality. They shaped a collective memory that in this chaotic and bitter convention, there had been a single shining moment when one of the "higher types in the Democratic party" — not a Bowery brawler or a southern rube — had combined eloquence with physical courage in an act of valor. It was even recalled soberly in years to come that when Roosevelt reached the lectern that day, the overcast sky had cracked open to let a broad ray of sunshine through the skylights to illuminate his smiling face.

Whether the heavens had beamed into the Garden or not, Roosevelt's moment had recreated a figure to reckon with in national politics. It was Franklin Roosevelt, yes, but a new version. In the eyes of the onlookers, the crippling had somehow not diminished him but enhanced him. This was no longer merely the fine-looking Harvard boy with the golden name. It was that boy tried and tempered, his face creased with lines, yet somehow joyous. He was crippled, of course — and yet to see his face and hear him speak, you just would never know it. Everyone remembered how he had called Al Smith "the happy warrior," and the phrase seemed even more apt for Roosevelt himself.

He was having the same effect on people who spoke with him in person. One of these was Isabella Greenway, a delegate to the convention who had been a schoolgirl with Eleanor, a bridesmaid at the Roosevelts' wedding, and was still one of Eleanor's closest friends. When Greenway's husband contracted tuberculosis, the two had moved to Arizona for the dry climate, so she had not seen FDR since the onset of polio, and she knew better than most people what invalidism could do to the life of a family.

The man she sat and talked with now was in every way the same charming friend she had known years earlier, holding forth with stories of the convention and laughing uproariously. As long as she sat talking with him — she told him in a letter after leaving New York — she "could not realize that your life had in any way become handicapped — you have created so normal an attitude."

It was only afterward, out of his presence, that she could think it over and realize the striking contrast between his condition and the way he behaved. "Eleanor had prepared me for your great courage," she said, "but, even so, I didn't realize to what an extent you had mastered the discouragement of it all. Please accept the admiration of an old friend & the faith that the quality of your life is only strengthened — for us all, you are doing something that it is not given many to do."

What makes Isabella Greenway unusual among the family's friends is that she was one of the very few — after the flood of stock expressions of concern and sympathy in 1921 — who spoke frankly and directly to FDR about his paralysis — one who left a written record of such a comment, anyway. He simply did not want to talk about it, and if you missed the message more than once or twice, you were not long for his company — unless you too had had polio or were a professional concerned with the treatment of polio.

Another friend later remembered that once, when she was alone with FDR in some momentary situation in which his physical difficulty was obvious, she had said, impulsively, "You are so brave." He smiled at her, said absolutely nothing, and moved on.

One of FDR's common expressions, when some embarrassing matter came up in conversation, was to label it *"infra dig,"* a Harvardian abbreviation of the Latin *infra dignitatem,* "beneath one's dignity." He found it no less *infra dig* to discuss his legs with people than he would have found it to discuss defecation. He loved gossip about other people — to receive it and to give it — but his own body was not up for discussion.

Frances Perkins once told a story about Al Smith to illustrate the difference in how the two men — and their respective social classes — defined their privacy.

The same summer as the convention, Smith's eldest son, Alfred Jr., had met a teenage girl at the state fair in Syracuse. After having "a bang-up gay time" for a few weeks, the youngsters married before a justice of the peace. Governor Smith had taken it as "a terrible, terrible blow," Perkins said, not because of political embarrassment but because of the wrong done to the girl and her family by marrying outside the Catholic Church.

What stayed in Perkins's mind about the incident was the stream of close friends whom Smith welcomed into his house to talk all this over. She was astonished by "how many people there were in the City of New York who rushed over to see Al and who had no qualms whatever about talking to him about this terrible tragedy in his life.

"In the circles in which I was brought up," said Perkins, a Mount Holyoke alumna and the daughter of a New England merchant, "nobody would speak to me about a thing like that. My nearest and dearest two or possibly three close friends I would tell all about it, air my grief and air my confusion and distress. But nobody else could mention it. That's the difference.

"I think FDR was the same. FDR never permitted anybody to speak to him about his affliction. That was the way you shut off the offers of intimacy."

Decades after Perkins told that story, Anna Roosevelt's son Curtis, who lived with the Roosevelts in the White House for several years, described FDR's "very keen sense of privacy" in remarkably similar terms. "The last thing he wanted was expressions of pity," Curtis Roosevelt said. "He just turned away from anything vaguely resembling that. . . . You didn't talk about that. That was plain. Everyone knew that instinctively."

So the membrane of privacy that protected Roosevelt's condition was partly built by the particular rules of his clan and his class. But it was built too by even broader and more powerful traditions of what should be public and what should be private. As the cultural historian Rochelle Gurstein has noted in *The Repeal of Reticence,* societies across history had drawn "strict boundaries between what could be seen and what must be hidden." The realm to be hidden included all the activities and states in which the human body is exposed and vulnerable: the state of nakedness; the ecstasy of sex; the unconsciousness of sleep; the act of excretion; the state of pregnancy; and the state of being physically or mentally damaged. To expose that realm, where matters both shameful and sacred dwelt together, was to break a taboo, with all the risks that breaking a taboo might entail. To violate the taboo might stir revulsion, or it might destroy the taboo itself, or it might do both.

That was the barrier Roosevelt had breached on the speaker's platform at Madison Square Garden. And that, perhaps, was the reason for the shiver that Frances Perkins had sensed in the crowd. He did not intend to address the matter in words any more than he absolutely had to. But simply by displaying his body in its new state, he had raised a silent signal: Here was a new sort of man.

In the wake of his loss at the 1924 convention, Al Smith was worried, again, about his large family, and he was eager to put away some money. His preference was to take a break from government service to lay a better foundation for a second run at the presidency in 1928. If he did so, it would be important to maintain control of the New York Democratic Party, and thus to maintain control of the governor's mansion in Albany. FDR, whose name was suddenly on many Democrats' lips, would fit that bill nicely: a popular Smith loyalist, but a crippled man who would be easy to control. So Smith asked him to run for governor. But reporters were told the answer from Hyde Park was a firm no — that Roosevelt "was compelled to devote the next few months to recovery of his shattered health." So Smith accepted another nomination for governor, was reelected in November, and began to plan for 1928.

"They have been after me to run for the Governorship in this state," FDR confided to a Harvard friend that fall, "but I have told them that the crutches must go before I run even for dog-catcher."

The sudden shower of praise after the speech for Smith, and especially the fervent calls for him to get ready for new campaigns of his own, drove FDR to reassess his situation across the board. It was clear now that he could be nominated for governor soon: 1926, 1928 — it was hard to predict with any certainty, but his moment of opportunity was nigh, and no politician can let his moment pass. Yet he remained convinced that he could not run if the public saw him as a man on crutches. He simply must find new ways to resuscitate more muscles in the crucial regions of his legs, and he must reduce and discard all obstacles and obligations that impeded that pursuit. So in the next few weeks he made swift and important decisions.

First there was the matter of money. He

could count on Van Lear Black to keep paying him $25,000 a year for an absolute minimum of time expended. But his obligations to his law partners at Emmett, Marvin & Roosevelt weighed more heavily. Grenville Emmett and Langdon Marvin had been patient, but after three years it was plain that the much-promised recovery — the "swift" recovery, the "speedy" recovery, the "complete" recovery — was still far off. They wanted more of his time, but he couldn't give it. There was now "no question," he wrote Emmett, "that I shall have to spend the greater part of the next four or five years in devoting my primary attention to my legs." He believed he could make a good deal more money if he traded the Marvin firm's fusty dealings in wills and estates for a business-oriented law practice where he could actually help to run things. And he was tired of trying to get around the firm's offices, where "the practical difficulty of locomotion" was considerable. There was a high stoop at the entrance, and "the question of even 2 steps is a very difficult one, as I have to be actually lifted up and down them."

So, with expressions of gratitude and friendship, he quit the firm.

He already had been having talks with his

new friend Basil O'Connor, the up-and-coming young lawyer who had seen him fall in the lobby of 120 Broadway. Within weeks, O'Connor's firm had a new name: Roosevelt & O'Connor.

Then there was the matter of his recovery. He saw Dr. Lovett and aired his frustrations. He told the orthopedist his recommendations had not delivered the promised results — this may have been what prompted Lovett to tell his wife that FDR would have accomplished more if he had heeded Eleanor's urgings — and he asked what else could be done. He was prepared for any regimen of any length.

Theoretically, Lovett said, "if the right treatment could be devised," FDR might continue to gain more control over his muscles until he was sixty-five or seventy.

Then why not devise it? FDR retorted. Why couldn't they invent something new?

At this point, perhaps earlier, Lovett described the good results attained by some of his young polio patients in Boston, where he had devised a tank of warm water that enhanced their ability to do exercises. Other patients, the doctor said, had made gains by swimming in Massachusetts's Buzzards Bay, south of Boston, where the Atlantic was especially warm in summer. FDR pointed out that he had spent weeks in the Gulf of Mexico — much warmer than Buzzards Bay, with only limited results to show for it.

From this point forward, FDR concluded, he must be his own doctor.

The following summer, Lovett went abroad. At the home of a friend in Liverpool, at the age of sixty-three, he died.

FDR already had a connection to Buzzards Bay, Massachusetts. It was where Louis Howe owned a tiny cottage on the lonely beach near the lovely fishing town of Westport. He and Howe went there at the end of the summer with two servants. FDR baked in the sun and went in the water. With his feet on the rocky ocean bottom, without braces or crutches, he was able to keep his balance when the water came up to his armpits, and he could pull his legs along in a facsimile of walking.

In September he made reservations for another trip south.

To Dr. Byron Stookey, the New York orthopedist who had made his latest pair of braces, FDR wrote: "I am planning to go to Warm Springs, Georgia on October 3rd to try out a remarkable swimming pool of natural highly mineralized water which comes out of the hillside at a temperature of 90 degrees. I have had such success with sunlight and swimming that I believe that in such a pool I could actually walk around at the shallow end with the water up to my shoulders, and thereby get the normal walking motion better than any other way. I can stand up without support in water just below my shoulders and I am going to take a couple of canes into the pool with me. This is a new idea in orthopedics which I think will interest you! . . .

"There is nothing like trying it out."

CHAPTER 10
"AS IF I HAD NOTHING THE MATTER"
FALL 1924 TO SPRING 1925

About the time Roosevelt became ill in 1921, a teenaged boy named Louis Joseph contracted infantile paralysis in Columbus, Georgia. He was paralyzed below the waist. The next summer his parents took the boy on a family vacation to a fading resort hotel called the Meriwether Inn in the Georgia village of Bullochville, in the Appalachian piedmont about halfway between Columbus and Atlanta. At the inn there was an outdoor swimming pool fed by water that flowed from mineral springs nearby. Louis swam in the pool often. The next year the family returned and again Louis swam. After swimming in the pool during a third vacation in 1924, Louis, using canes, could walk again. No one could explain it. Perhaps he simply experienced spontaneous recovery in his damaged muscles and helped himself by exercising. But the story of the Joseph boy went around among people who knew the resort.

The Meriwether Inn had recently been purchased by the New York banker and philanthropist George Foster Peabody. Like Louis Joseph, Peabody had been a boy in nearby Columbus. His family's business fortunes had been broken by the Civil War, and in 1866, when Peabody was fourteen, the family moved to Brooklyn, New York. There Peabody worked his way up from a job as a clerk in a dry-goods business to being one of two principal partners in the investment banking firm of Spencer Trask & Co. With substantial investments in railroads, sugar, and the Edison Electric Illuminating Company in the years when the company became General Electric, Peabody amassed a fortune, retired in 1906 at fifty-four, and started a new career in philanthropy and social activism. He became a prominent backer of education for African-Americans, treasurer of the Democratic Party, and an important supporter of Woodrow Wilson, who asked Peabody to be his secretary of commerce. Peabody declined, but he served as an informal advisor to Wilson and other members of his administration, including his fellow New Yorker Franklin Roosevelt.

When Peabody's business partner, Spencer Trask, was killed in a railroad accident in 1909, Peabody stepped in to help his widow with the Trasks' own philanthropies and service work. These included an effort to restore the mineral springs at Saratoga Springs, New York, where the Trasks had built Yaddo, their summer estate. Advancing this project, Peabody learned a good deal about the nature and management of mineral springs. He told friends he was "nerve-tired" in these years, and he found the baths at Saratoga relaxing and restorative. In 1920 he married Trask's widow, Katrina — the two had been childhood sweethearts — but she died only two years later. Now nearly seventy, heartbroken but still fit and eager to do good things, Peabody looked for new projects.

In his boyhood, Peabody's family had spent summer weeks at the resort at Bullochville, Georgia, also known in the region as Warm Springs. In 1923, he learned the old Meriwether Inn had fallen on hard times and was up for sale. He knew the lore of the place. Warriors of the Creek nation had come to the pools to soak their wounds, claiming restorative powers. American settlers who came in the early nineteenth century soaked there as well, and in 1832 a

Georgian named David Rose bought up land around the springs and built a resort. At the end of the Civil War it burned; was rebuilt; thrived for a time; then entered a long slide.

Peabody hired a chemist to test the waters and concluded that they did, indeed, possess therapeutic qualities. He bought the inn and the land around it, including the springs, and began making plans for reviving the place as a health retreat on the model of Saratoga Springs.

In the summer of 1924 Peabody got a note from a man named Tom Loyless. Loyless was an aging newspaperman, sick with cancer, who had been leasing the Meriwether Inn and trying to keep it running on the strength of a dwindling clientele. Now he was acting as Peabody's agent, keeping the place open while Peabody figured out what to do with it. Loyless was passing along another letter, one he had asked the boy Louis Joseph to write as a testimonial about the healing qualities of the water in the swimming pool.

"I was almost paralyzed with the exception of my arms," the boy said. "Discovering that I could swim in the warm water here, after someone helped me into the pool, I returned. This is my third summer. I use a cane while walking in the street, and can get about well."

Tom Loyless confirmed it. The boy had come to the place as a "helpless, if not a hopeless cripple," Loyless wrote Peabody. "This summer he seems to come and go like everyone else. Only the other night I saw him dancing in the Auditorium."

George Foster Peabody forwarded Louis Joseph's letter and Tom Loyless's letter to his friend Franklin Roosevelt.

FDR arrived at tiny Bullochville by train from Columbus, Georgia, at the end of the first week of October 1924. His retinue included Eleanor, Missy LeHand, and LeRoy Jones. With Roy's help and a cook lent by neighbors, FDR assured his mother, "we shall be quite comfortable." A little crowd of locals, having heard he was coming, were there at the station to see the man with the famous name. Few Yankees this well known had been in the area since William Tecumseh Sherman, and Sherman had reined in his marauding army short of Bullochville. The Roosevelts had a family connection to the place: Bullochville had been the home of Eleanor's grandmother Mittie Bulloch Roosevelt, the mother of Theodore Roosevelt and Eleanor's father, Elliott.

Emerging from the train at dusk, the Roosevelt party saw a tiny, forgotten farm town ten miles from the closest pavement. Meriwether County counted twenty-six thousand souls, most of them African-American, most of them poor. A lovely piedmont ridge clothed in soft autumn brown and red bordered the village, lower but not unlike the hills of Dutchess County. The scent of pine was strong. At the empty resort they found a crescent of sagging white cottages, an old dance pavilion, and the inn, a three-story Victorian dowager shedding strips of yellow and green paint, grown over in places with ivy, a mass of "spires and domes and sharp angles." It was well past the summer season, which had not been brisk to begin with. FDR claimed to find the cottages "delightful and very comfortable," but in the inn most of the crockery was broken and most of the silverware was missing. As the New Yorkers went to sleep that night, squirrels scrabbled on the roofs above their heads.

In the morning, FDR was taken to the old pool. He spoke with Dr. James Johnson, the local practitioner whose experience with infantile paralysis was limited to conversations with the teenaged Louis Joseph. Dr. Johnson told FDR what he knew: that the boy, indeed, had recovered the ability to walk, though the first effects had come only after three weeks of exercising, so FDR should not expect any miraculous turn of events simply by getting in the water.

He was helped into the pool and held upright. (By LeRoy Jones? Was a colored man allowed into this Georgia swimming pool? Almost surely not; more likely some white attendant accompanied FDR into the pool.) The water was 89 degrees Fahrenheit — delightfully warm but not the sort of steaming-hot that leaves the bather feeling enervated after twenty or thirty minutes. He stood. The water was four feet deep, several inches lower than the level of the Atlantic water in which he had stood at Horseneck Beach with Louis Howe the previous summer. He stayed standing, without braces, canes or crutches. He moved one leg, then the other.

He walked.

"I spent over an hour in the pool this a.m.," he wrote his mother that evening, "and it is really wonderful and will I think do great good, though the Dr. says it takes three weeks to show the effects."

In the afternoon, Tom Loyless took the party for a drive through the countryside. Loyless was FDR's kind of southerner, a tough progressive in the mold of Josephus Daniels. He had run the newspaper in Augusta, where he earned the Ku Klux Klan's hatred by defending the innocence of Leo Frank, a Jewish factory superintendent accused of murdering a female employee, then lynched by Klansmen. Roosevelt took to Loyless immediately, but his first impression of the landscape was mixed. "Many peach orchards," he reported, "but also a good deal of neglect and poverty." Eleanor found the sorry state of the inhabitants depressing, and the resort itself, with its broken windows and its porous roofs, seemed beyond redemption. "It won't be practical in the wintertime for a long time if it ever is," she wrote. She went back to New York after just a few days.

FDR stayed. He was enraptured by the water and increasingly interested in the countryside. As Eleanor said later, he seldom went to any new place where he did not want to buy and develop some land, and that impulse never came upon him so strongly as it did here in western Georgia. His delight in the pool fueled a fascination with Pine Mountain, where the magical water flowed out of the stone at the rate of 1,800 gallons per minute.

For three weeks FDR walked and walked

in the water — "almost as well," he told his friend Abram Elkus, an old Wilsonian and a fellow paralytic, "as if I had nothing the matter with my legs. . . . I will tell you all about it as I am convinced that it is a really remarkable cure."

FDR meant something less than literal by the word "cure"; nonetheless, the word carried powerful associations for him. When he had been a boy of nine in 1890, his father, James Roosevelt, then sixty-two, had suffered a heart attack — a mild one, but it weakened him. James and Sara were advised that the best possible treatment lay in naturally carbonated springs at the Rhineland town of Bad Nauheim, in Germany. A spa had been established there on the belief that the waters, if soaked in and drunk, could promote recovery from a variety of ills, including heart disease. Over the next decade, the Roosevelts made five prolonged visits to Bad Nauheim for James to "take the cure," with young Franklin accompanying them on four of the five trips. It was a sedate process, carried out day by day for weeks, amid gardens and parks. Hundreds of patients strolled from one station to another, first to take sequential draughts of the hot, salty water; then to repose for fifteen minutes at a time in one of the bathhouses. Immersed in the water, the body was instantaneously swathed in millions of tiny carbonated bubbles. These produced a delightful tingling sensation and were said to "dilate blood vessels, relieve the heart and circulatory system, improve blood supply."

James Roosevelt had lived for a decade after his heart attack, and he believed the waters prolonged his life. Deep in FDR's memory was the association between warm water bubbling out of the earth and the determined pursuit of good health — and not health in the abstract but the health of his beloved father.

For the time being he was agnostic on the question of whether the water's mineral properties exerted any direct influence upon healing. But there was no doubt that something about the water — if only its pleasant warmth and its buoyant properties — allowed the swimmer to stay in the water for hour after hour without fatigue. "My month down there did me more good than anything I had done before," he wrote Paul Hasbrouck, his young polio friend in Poughkeepsie. "The warm pool is splendid and you can do all sorts of exercising choosing different depths of water. The water may or may not have peculiar building up qualities, but at least you feel wonderfully after staying in for several hours and can do a great deal of exercising."

Nothing he had tried had brought so noticeable a result. "It will only be a matter of time till I can walk again, I feel sure," he told a reporter. "My physician has told me that swimming in warm water and sun baths are all that I need. (That was surely not quite what Dr. Lovett had said.) I've been greatly helped and I've only been here two weeks. My right leg I hadn't been able to move for three years. I can use it a little now. The other is much better, too.

"I have to spend as much time as I can in the water. I've turned fish-man. The doctors have a theory that exercise of all the muscles in swimming, steady warm water and sunshine will build up the nerves in my legs again. I don't think that the water of this pool has any miraculous healing powers, but it undoubtedly possesses some medicinal properties."

Before leaving Warm Springs, FDR took an hour or so away from exercising and gabbing with the locals to write what was for him a long letter. It was a response to Dr. William Egleston, a physician in South Carolina who had sent FDR a query about his first patient with polio. Egleston was perplexed about what to do and wanted to know what had happened to Roosevelt, who replied generously and at length. The doctor asked if he might seek information from FDR's own doctors, but there was no need for that, Roosevelt said, "as I have talked it over with a great many doctors and can, I think, give you a history of the case which would be equal to theirs."

He had become, in every sense, his own physician, deciding on his own therapy and professing his own history of the case.

With clinical detachment, he recounted the onset of the illness at Campobello in some detail, including the massage mistakenly administered on the advice of Dr. Keen; his passage through the acute stage and hospitalization through the next several weeks; the splinting and casting and bracing. The return of muscle power "seemed to make little progress . . . for many months," but then, with steady application, he had begun to regain strength in the affected muscles. He laid particular emphasis on the need for swimming. "I . . . found that this exercise seemed better adapted than any other because all weight was removed from the legs and I was able to move the legs in the water far better than I had expected."

He had worked along these lines steadily for two years, he told Dr. Egleston, "with the result that the muscles have increased in power to a remarkable extent and the improvement in the past 6 months has been even more rapid than at any previous time."

Roosevelt's visit to Georgia had caught the attention of several reporters, including Cleburne E. Gregory, a political writer for the *Atlanta Journal.* Gregory ran down to catch Roosevelt at Bullochville, then ran back to Atlanta, where he wrote a lengthy article for the newspaper's Sunday magazine, quoting extensively from the conversation by the pool. Not all his notes were accurate, and his interview subject may have told a stretcher or two, but Gregory must have known he would have a large audience. With Roosevelt back in the public's consciousness thanks to intense coverage of the Democratic convention in New York, the antennae of the press nationwide picked up the extraordinarily upbeat story of what appeared to be a miraculous recovery in the making. Many placed a photo of the renowned bathing beauty Annette Kellerman, who also had exercised in the pool at Bullochville, alongside the article on Roosevelt: an eye-catching display that made even more people read the story. Suddenly Roosevelt found he had not been merely shooting the breeze with a local reporter. With the syndication of the story in many papers, and adaptation to shorter articles in many others, he was speaking to a national audience of some millions.

"Franklin Roosevelt Will Swim to Health!" the *Journal and Constitution* trumpeted.

Just as his letter to Dr. Egleston had been his own first full account of his ordeal, this was the first time he had spoken about it at any length for public consumption. Readers were given a dramatic story with statements as effervescent as the waters themselves. "Mr. Roosevelt does not know how he contracted the dread disease," Gregory reported, "and does not regard himself as more outstanding or unfortunate than the hundreds of other adults who became victims at the same time by the disease usually confined to childhood. All he does know is that he was hit, and hit hard, with the result that both of his legs were immovable for many months. Gradually he acquired the skill necessary to drag himself around on crutches. . . .

The distinguished visitor has the large swimming pool all to himself for two hours

373

or more each day [Gregory continued]. He swims, dives, uses the swinging rings and horizontal bar over the water, and finally crawls out on the concrete pier for a sun bath that lasts another hour. Then he dresses, has lunch, rests a bit on a delightfully shady porch, and spends the afternoon driving over the surrounding country, in which he is intensely interested.

Not only are the swims and the sun baths delightful innovations to Mr. Roosevelt, but his method of living is enchanting, he admits. Living a full half mile from the town of Warm Springs, formerly known as Bullochville, he is protected from the intrusion of the curious, and is even favored by infrequent mail deliveries. He expressed real relief at being two or three days behind the news of the world. . . .

"I am deriving wonderful benefit from my stay here," Mr. Roosevelt said. "This place is great. See that right leg? It's the first time I have been able to move it at all in three years."

Mr. Roosevelt does not attribute any medicinal effects to the Warm Springs waters, but he gives the water credit for his ability to remain in it for two hours or more, without tiring in the least, and the rest of the credit for his improvement is given to Georgia's sunshine.

"The best infantile paralysis specialist in New York told me that the only way to overcome the effects of the disease was to swim as much as possible, and bask in the sunlight. Conditions here are ideal for both prescriptions. The water in some way relaxes muscles drawn taut by the disease, and gives the limbs much greater action. The sunshine has curative effects, I understand."

So marked have the benefits been in his case, Mr. Roosevelt plans to return to Warm Springs in March or April, to remain two or three months. At that time he will build a cottage on the hilltops that he may spend a portion of each year there until he is completely cured. Even then he plans to keep coming back, as he "likes Georgia and Georgians," he remarked.

Mr. Roosevelt has made a great hit with the people of Warm Springs who have met him, and they are extending him a hearty welcome as a prospective regular visitor. A number of Georgia's public men have also called to pay their respects and extend greetings. Georgians who attended the Democratic national convention have been especially cordial, because they appreciate the interest Mr. Roosevelt showed in them. . . .

"Say! Let's get one of the hot dogs this man makes just outside the swimming pool. They're great," Mr. Roosevelt challenged. With him everything in Warm Springs is "great" or "fine" or "wonderful." That is the spirit that has carried him to remarkable heights for a man just past his fortieth year, and it is the spirit that is going to restore him to his pristine health and vigor, for political and financial battles and successes in the years to come.

Across the United States, important Democrats read the story and took note. So did the families of adults and children paralyzed by polio.

In the weeks after the publication of the article about FDR in the *Atlanta Journal,* letters from all over the country began to arrive in Georgia and New York, some addressed to Loyless, some to FDR himself. By the spring of 1925 they had heard from some six hundred people who had read the story and wanted to know more. A few skipped the inquiry and simply came to Georgia when the resort reopened in the spring — uninvited, unheralded, the hopeful and the all but hopeless.

Roosevelt had arrived before them, and when the new guests trickled in, he found places for them to board in the village. He sized up each as if he were their doctor, making notes on the functionality of glutei, abductors, adductors, and so on. And he immediately invited them into the pool. He took the role of player-coach, participating in daily exercises he designed and supervised himself. He measured progress in each: Mrs. Steiger from Missouri, "a very bad case from the waist down"; a boy named Hersheimer whom FDR judged "a thoroughly unsatisfactory patient, largely because of his mental attitude"; a teenager from Arkansas named Philpot, who was "inclined to overdo and required constant supervision"; a young woman named Retan from outside Boston with just one leg in bad shape; and FDR's favorite, an emaciated Pennsylvanian named Fred Botts, who had been stricken in the epidemic of 1916.

Botts was twenty-five. He had spent most of his time since 1916 in a bedroom of his family's farmhouse in Elizabeth, Pennsylvania, not far from Philadelphia. As a teenager he had been a fine singer, and he had begun to take training for a career in the opera. But since the onset of paralysis he had languished, losing weight to a shocking degree. He received no treatment of any kind. The first glimmer of light he had seen was the article about Roosevelt in one of the Philadelphia papers.

Botts made the train trip to Georgia with his younger brother, hauling a homemade wooden crate, something like a cage, in which he could stand up. It was unloaded at the Bullochville depot along with Botts himself. The next morning he reached the pool. He wrote later that, in bathing trunks, he looked "so ignominiously white and angular and thin as to justify [a] most tragic end most any day." Three buoyant tubes were fixed to his body. Then he was lowered into the water. It was "of the most pleasing temperature — not so cold that it would chill a person, nor so warm that it would enervate. I paddled around with my hands and was surprised with what . . . ease I could move my legs. Because of the light mineralization of the water it was pleasant to drink, and we were told to drink it by the quart. There was also noticeable at once an extra buoyancy to the swimmer. . . . It was great sport just paddling and floating around."

Then he heard a ringing "Good morning!" It was Franklin Roosevelt. It must have been extraordinary for Botts to see this famous and powerful man displaying his body in public in a condition not unlike that of Botts himself.

They were all introduced, and Botts asked: What about doctors and nurses?

We'll be our own doctors and nurses, Roosevelt replied.

Then FDR was in the pool too, and he began to introduce Botts and the others to the workout he had developed after the model of Wilhelmine Wright's routines in Boston.

"It was 'Catch hold of the bar this way . . . now . . . swing . . . in and out. . . . Hard! Harder! That's it . . . that's fine! Now . . . again, this way . . .' " Botts wrote, "and so through the entire regime of things he had worked out that morning. It was all along the line of lending to the affected limb and muscles the normal actions as near as possible. We were told to concentrate hard on every action and movement. The gentle caress of the water as we moved our limbs through it had a most stimulating effect." The water on the limbs felt like "a gentle massage," Botts said — and that effect, plus the seeming disappearance of gravity and "a slight resistance to every movement," provided a "form of exercise most ideal" for the polio patient.

Then, out of the pool, they lay on the paved surface nearby, baking their limbs in the sun.

The workouts continued each morning for several days. Then Roosevelt gathered the newcomers and told them of plans for a new pool to be built soon — a private pool exclusively for the polio patients, away from the awkward and fleeting glances of the "normals," and with their own exercise equipment. A glass ceiling would cover the pool, so if they came in wintertime they could exercise then as well, with steam-heated locker rooms.

"What glorious news!" Botts wrote. "He, our noble mentor, had spoken. He, a man of large affairs — of international repute and who has sat high in the councils of this country's administration, had noticed the movements of our lame feet in the water, and that we were ill at ease when a strange swimmer came close to us."

Botts later ticked off the results for that summer's crop of patients. One had arrived depending on two crutches and a brace; he left using only a cane. Others were nearly able to discard their wheelchairs, including Botts himself, who "before the summer had passed was walking with crutches and was loath to use his chair."

FDR could not say as much for his own condition, but he was just as enthusiastic. After the improvements of the previous fall, he had stagnated at home, noticing no change at all despite exercising regularly. Now, in six more weeks at Warm Springs, "all muscles have undoubtedly strengthened," he wrote to a doctor in New York. "Here is a rough and ready measure. When I came here last autumn I could only stand up in water without support at level of top shoulders. When I left I could stand up with shoulders two inches out of water. Today I can stand up with shoulders four inches out of water. That represents a gain, I think, of about twenty pounds on my knees."

This was not proof. It might have resulted from a mere change in his weight. But he was utterly convinced that he had made more progress in two visits to Warm Springs than in three years of exercising.

He began to speak to Eleanor, his mother, and Louis Howe about what he wanted to do now. He wanted to purchase the resort and the land at Warm Springs.

CHAPTER 11
"IT DOES SOMETHING FOR ME"
1926 TO 1927

Of course, FDR did not need to buy the place to get its rewards. He could take the train to Georgia and exercise in the special water as much as he wanted, at least in the months when it was warm enough for swimming outdoors.

But he was yearning for a great project. He had made "a great discovery of a place," he told Sara, and, like a prospector exulting over a new claim, he yearned to own the mother lode lying at his feet.

He never had owned and run something of his own. He had bought land in Dutchess County, but the main place at Hyde Park, as deeply as he loved it, belonged to his mother and would belong to her for the foreseeable future. In the state legislature he had been one toiler among many. At the Navy Department he had worked for Josephus Daniels. Fidelity & Deposit belonged to Van Lear Black. In his law firms he had partners. Warm Springs could be his own place with its own mission, *his* mission. His work in the navy had persuaded him that his gifts were executive. His instinct was to *run* things. Not many worthy enterprises were available to be run by a man who couldn't walk.

The dilapidation of the place was part of its charm. He looked at the frowsy old buildings nodding in the sun and was enchanted by the chance not just to build but to *re*build. And in his enthusiasm to reclaim the tumble-down resort at Bulloch-ville, it's impossible to miss a strong similarity to his zest to rebuild his own body. It was as if by reflex he responded to a project that almost anyone else would give up for lost.

The landscape itself beckoned to him. "Franklin never could travel anywhere in the world without wanting to buy land . . ." Eleanor remarked later. "Land, land, land." The gushing springs, the forested ridge of Pine Mountain, the rutted roads and the stretches of pine — "it does something for me," he said.

There was a financial motive too. His circumstances were much better than comfortable, of course, but his standard of living owed a lot to the homes provided by his mother in Manhattan and Hyde Park. He (and Eleanor too) "always felt pressed for funds." When he was asked for a donation or a loan in these years, as he often was, he invariably pleaded that he was "under very heavy expense in getting over an attack of infantile paralysis," and that he was "not rich as you suppose, but must depend for my livelihood, and that of my family, on my work as a lawyer and for [Fidelity & Deposit]." A sense of insecurity surely accompanied this reliance on aid that he did not wholly earn, and he worried about not doing enough "to justify the continuation of my salary." In any case, these jobs never could give him the full freedom to do whatever he wanted.

Then too there was Sara Roosevelt's heavy hand in his financial affairs. She oversaw his inheritance from his father and awarded periodic gifts of money that often were needed for the family's expenses. In many small ways, her control of the family's fortune made her the family's head, a role she relished; and that "golden loop," her grandson James believed, was a noose that FDR yearned to throw off. He may well have yearned for it even more after his disability than before. If he could not do without physical dependence on others, he might at least be able to vanquish financial dependence.

So he had been on the lookout for a score that might yield a large income without draining precious time from his physical and political recoveries. For several years he had toyed with a series of schemes and prospects, and with several he had taken a minor plunge. Some were exotic, like air-mail service by zeppelin; some prosaic and sensible, like ideas for pooling fire insurance companies or placing ads in taxicabs — no gold mine, he acknowledged, but "the kind of airtight little business which would cost a low overhead and bring in a charming little profit." But none of these had really worked out; he had made very little or lost outright. His parents, who were very careful with their considerable resources, had raised a frugal son. (He insisted, for instance, that a mail-order shirt at two dollars was as good as what Brooks Brothers sold for several times more, and he wore clothes until they nearly fell apart.) Though he savored the hunt for profit-making ideas and hoped for a big payoff, he never allowed himself to risk enough to bring a big return, so of course none came. And because he knew his mother's funds were a backstop in any real emergency, and because he had no interest in amassing wealth for its own sake, he never directed his powerful energies to making money. That and his "Scotch" reserve — his flinty reluctance to part with coin — had kept his plunging to a safe minimum.

Still, as Eleanor said, he always found money for things he really wanted — a historic book, a rare stamp, a special print; and his desire for Warm Springs got coupled with the idea of making money — a lot of it, he suspected.

For three years he had been spending many weeks at a time in southern Florida just when that region was undergoing an enormous boom in real estate, with prosperous people from all over the country streaming southward for tropical sun. It was easy to envision Warm Springs restored to its past glory and expanded, catering not only to southerners but to streams of northerners and midwesterners "following the weather" to or from Florida. He saw new swimming pools for able-bodied and polio patients alike, golf courses, stables and riding trails, lovely terraces and picnic grounds, day trips up the mountain with "marvelous views all the way." It could be a place like other great southern resorts. With the local cotton crop withering under the depredations of the boll weevil, he also explored the possibility of developing the surrounding lands with profitable pine plantings.

Owning Warm Springs might also pay off in politics. Consider Roosevelt's position as a Democrat from New York, and not only that but a bluebood Episcopalian closely associated with Al Smith; the drinking, swearing Papist; the urban Irish Tammanyite; the archdemon Democrat in the eyes of several million southerners. FDR had very good reasons for that close association. But if and when Smith's banner fell — if Smith were to lose the fight for the Democratic nomination in 1928, or if, as the nominee, he lost the 1928 election itself — then Roosevelt meant to succeed Smith as the nation's leading Democrat. And any Democratic nominee for president absolutely needed the Solid South. How, then, would he distance himself from Smith in the eyes of southerners? A beachhead in Georgia could help. Even a friend of Al Smith's who made his second home in rural Georgia, who built a prestigious institution there with overtones of Christian charity, might win many friends in the region.

But in his close circle there were expressions of doubt. Eleanor and his mother were deeply skeptical. Louis Howe thought it made sense to seek treatment closer to home. Basil O'Connor was opposed; Roosevelt already was devoting little attention to their law practice. Only Missy LeHand supported the idea outright. "Missy . . . is keen about everything here, of course," Eleanor wrote a friend from Warm Springs — perhaps in part because time at Warm Springs was time when she was FDR's sole female support.

He tried to mollify his mother by inviting her to help him plan the improvements. "I feel you can help me with many suggestions," he told her, "and the place properly run will not only do a great deal of good but will prove financially successful."

Sara was not persuaded, but he was accustomed to brushing her fears aside. It was Eleanor's approval he really wanted, and she was just as doubtful as Sara. She continued to find the resort seedy and the region depressing. She was unnerved by the prospect of his investing the major part of his inheritance, or of turning to his mother for help. "Don't let yourself in for too much money," she warned him from New York when negotiations were under way, "& don't make Mama put in much for if she lost it she'd never get over it!"

He insisted it would be a good investment. Eleanor asked if it was fair to the children to put their inheritance in jeopardy. "Mama will always see the children through," he said, which was perfectly true.

She came down to see him and they had a long talk. She found him disconsolate — a rare state — even resentful about the family's resistance to his cherished plan. He spoke at length of what the place had come to mean to him, and she began to soften. "He feels . . . that he's trying to do a big thing which may be a financial success & a medical and philanthropic opportunity for infantile," Eleanor wrote to Marion Dickerman the next day, "& that all of us have raised our eyebrows & thrown cold water on it. There is nothing to do but to make him feel one is interested." She thought he was seriously overtaxing Van Lear Black's generosity. But her resistance was crumbling.

"I know how you love creative work," she wrote him after she had left for home. "My only feeling is that Georgia is somewhat distant for you to keep in touch with what is really a big undertaking. One cannot, it seems to me, have *vital* interests in widely divided places, but that may be because I'm old and rather overwhelmed by what there is to do in one place and it wearies me to think of even undertaking to make new ties. Don't be discouraged by me; I have great confidence in your extraordinary interest and enthusiasm."

It was a generous surrender. She was right: It *was* crazy for a man who had two jobs in New York, not to mention children still in school, not to mention a serious physical disability, with no background in managing either a resort or a sanitarium, to take on the job of turning a broken-down hotel a thousand miles from home into a profit-making spa for the rehabilitation of cripples. Of course, FDR may have smiled at his wife's warning against taking on too much at a time when she herself was teaching high-school girls in New York, starting a new household in Val-Kill cottage, supervising four sons, running the women's division of the New York Democratic Committee, and planning her daughter's wedding. She had the better of the argument. But she knew when his heart had been carried away.

As usual, he showed no reluctance to rely on others for help with projects he undertook for his own purposes.

"I hope you don't think I'm in on that, too," Basil O'Connor told him.

"I seldom am . . . able to do anything

alone," FDR replied, "so I'm counting on you."

On April 29, 1926, with O'Connor overseeing the legal details, FDR signed the papers. By the complex terms of the deal, he promised to pay George Foster Peabody $25,000 in cash up front, then $10,000 per year for ten years, plus a final payment of $20,000. By the end of 1928 he would pay $50,000 to an heir of the previous owner. These and sundry other commitments came to roughly $200,000, for which he would gain title to the springs themselves, thirteen ramshackle cottages, the Meriwether Inn, and 1,200 acres of land.

By conventional standards it was not a wise deal. In these years, his annual income ranged from $60,000 to $80,000, while his personal holdings, mostly in stocks and bonds, amounted to roughly $275,000. Thus he "had taken on an obligation in Georgia," the journalist Theo Lippman Jr. wrote later, "that many would consider out of proportion to his wealth." Wise or not, it was an enormous commitment, not only of money but of his own time and energy, since much more than money would be needed to turn the sleepy old compound into a going concern. From now on, every decision about his future must be made with his debt for Warm Springs in mind, not to mention his promise to help patients regain their mobility. They were *his* patients now.

His zeal drove everything before it.

One could easily see the situation as others did. Dying of cancer and depressed, Tom Loyless, whom Roosevelt had retained as manager of the property, had left Georgia to get treatment up north. He worried that Roosevelt's project was going to be a bust, crushing the hopes they had raised among polio patients and their families. "We have nothing to offer them," he wrote FDR, "nothing to give them in the way of proper treatment — just groping blindly in the dark and trusting to luck." He was right. The cottages stood in two sad groups — "the cheapest kind of camps," Basil O'Connor said. Only two had ceilings. The rest were covered only with thin roofs with cracks between the boards. There were no toilets, no screens in the windows, no running water, no clothes closets. The Meriwether Inn was a firetrap, though the polio patients all stayed on the first floor, since there was no elevator to the upper stories.

But where Loyless saw an abyss of unmet demands, FDR saw a list of action-ready plans to be carried out as quickly as possible. He began to recruit a staff; drew up plans to refit the existing swimming pool, refurbish the old cottages, and build new ones (with furnaces to allow year-round stays); and sketched the construction of year-round facilities for treatment, especially big new pools, one with a glass roof to trap the sun in winter. To run the operation in Loyless's absence, FDR assigned himself the job of part-time accountant and general manager. While he managed these affairs with one hand, with the other, he told his Harvard pal Livy Davis, "I am consulting architect and landscape engineer for the Warm Springs Co. — am giving free advice on the moving of buildings, the building of roads, setting out of trees, and remodeling the hotel. We, i.e. the company plus F.D.R., are working on a new water system, new sewage plant, fishing pond; and tomorrow we hold an organization meeting to start the Pine Mountain Club which will run the dance hall, tea room, picnic grounds, golf course and other forms of indoor and outdoor sports. I sometimes wish I could find some spot on the globe where it was not essential and necessary for me to start something new — a sandbar in the ocean might answer, but I would probably start building a seawall around it and digging for pirate treasure in the middle." Just weeks before her wedding, nineteen-year-old Anna ran down to see the place, where, she found, "the one & only topic of conversation is *Warm Springs!*"

He was moving with extraordinary speed and a deft touch at winning the help of others.

Money was the main challenge. To share the cost of housing and treating the current crop of patients, he secured quick promises from two wealthy fathers of polio patients, Henry Pope of Chicago and John Whitehead of Detroit. But for the long-term plan of building a health center, he would need far more, and he wanted it fast. He had no time to wait for distant profits, and in any case, even before he signed the purchase agreement, he had begun to see that Warm Springs could be either a resort or a polio center but not both. Able-bodied guests that spring were shunning the guests who had polio. And the Florida land boom was going bust, a poor augury for building a spectacular new resort in west Georgia. He was already thinking "that it would be possible for me to undertake the Warm Springs project from the purely medical angle of a sanitorium." If so, the door would open to a fund-raising campaign: he could seek donations from philanthropists who might embrace an exciting new prospect for helping crippled children.

But to make such an appeal, he would need proof of the treatment's legitimacy. Someone besides a few paralytics had to attest that Warm Springs actually worked.

Again, he took quick action. Learning that the American Orthopedic Association was about to hold its annual conference in nearby Atlanta, he dashed off a request to address the conferees about Warm Springs and to ask for "technical guidance and help."

Quite impossible, he was promptly told. The program was full and he was only a layman. This meeting was for experts.

Experts were what he needed. FDR packed Eleanor, Missy, and LeRoy Jones into a car and roared off. Within a couple of hours, he was having himself rolled into the meetings and he began to work the crowd.

Like Robert Lovett in Boston, the pillars of the American Orthopedic Association were sober, cautious professonals. Few were the type to be impressed by a famous politician with a broad smile and an extended hand, especially one who, quite uninvited, was being pushed around their hotel in a wheelchair. Dr. Michael Hoke of Atlanta, the association's president that year, was particularly irritated by Roosevelt's pushy plea for attention. Hoke was very much the traditional orthopedist — "I'm not a surgeon but a bone carpenter," he liked to say — and he was immediately suspicious of Roosevelt. "I felt it was pretty clear," he wrote a colleague, "that Mr. Roosevelt was more interested in the advertisment of his property in Georgia — getting a talking basis and using the Association as an advertising medium, than he was in idealism and philanthropy."

That may have seemed like an important difference to Hoke, but it did not to FDR, who had no choice but to promote his property if he meant to help people with polio walk. But he was colliding with an opinion broadly held among physicians.

Dr. Hoke and his colleagues had been trained in the years when "water cures," a great fad of the late 1800s, had taken on the odor of patent medicine. Some reputable physicians continued to press claims for real medical benefits. But even they conceded that hype artists and promoters had tainted the well. "We are all acquainted with the mineral spring advertising circular," wrote Dr. James K. Crook, a legitimate if unfortunately surnamed proponent of "hydriatics." "It comes to us clothed in a respectable, even elegant dress; but it too frequently portrays the virtues of the alleged healing fluid . . . in the language of absurd hyperbole. When the intelligent practitioner reads that a certain water is positively curative in an imposing list of diseases, as set forth in diverse pages of testimonials from renovated statesmen, restored clergymen, and rejuvenated old ladies, and then learns from the analysis that it contains two or three grains of lime-salts to the gallon, with the remaining ingredients requiring perhaps a third or fourth decimal figure to express, he can hardly be blamed for tossing the circular into his waste-basket, with an objurgation upon quacks generally and the mineral spring quack in particular." At first blush, Roosevelt's "warm springs" appeal sounded very much like one of these come-ons, and Hoke had no intention of seeing his association endorse it.

Yet even here, far from home, FDR found a powerful personal connection to help him. It was Dr. Robert Osgood, a Harvard medical professor who had succeeded Robert Lovett as chair of orthopedics at Children's Hospital in Boston. Osgood knew about Roosevelt's case and urged that he be heard. When Hoke still refused, Osgood proposed what FDR really needed: that the association authorize a study to see if Roosevelt's pools really did help polio patients recover their mobility. Hoke and his executive committee once more voted no. But at Osgood's urging, they said they would not object if the matter were referred, purely informally, to individual doctors willing to review Roosevelt's project. Three respected orthopedists agreed to do so, including Dr. Albert Freiberg of Cincinnati, who acted as chair. They listened as FDR outlined his plan and "were all," Freiberg said, "tremendously impressed by your fine altruistic spirit in the matter."

These three volunteers, doubtless accustomed to the stately pace of most medical research, now came under a friendly deluge of Rooseveltian pressure for immediate action. "SOMETHING MUST BE DONE PROMPTLY," he wired Freiberg. "TIME IS SHORT . . . DO NOT WAIT." FDR needed two things quickly: Approval of his candidate to conduct the study — the man he had in mind was Leroy Hubbard, just retired as chief of the public health service in New York State — and help in recruiting thirty or so polio patients to take part in a summer-long trial.

Dr. Freiberg and his colleagues promptly

delivered. Yes, they said, Leroy Hubbard was fine, though before agreeing to recruit patients, Freiberg sought Roosevelt's assurance on a delicate matter. "It is apparent to us that there is a real danger of undesirable publicity because of the great prominence of your personality," he wrote. "This, we wish to avoid if possible." If the thing did turn out to be quackery, the doctors wanted their names nowhere near it.

Of course, FDR replied: "You are quite right. . . . I can assure you that we are doing everything possible to prevent *all* publicity. One of the easiest ways to shut off the hundreds of people who have written . . . asking to come here for every known ailment, is for us to be able to say truthfully that we have filled the quota . . . for the study this summer, and can take no more."

Freiberg duly asked his colleagues to recommend patients, and, in short order, twenty-four — most of them young adults — arrived to take part, as did Dr. Hubbard. To direct the work of physical rehabilitation, Hubbard recruited a highly capable physical therapist — the term then was "physiotherapist," or "physio" for short — a New Yorker named Helena Mahoney.

Dr. Hubbard, Mahoney, and the patients went straight to work in the pool, devising underwater variants of the Wright/Lovett regimen of exercising. Dr. Hubbard was to observe the patients at work for a period of some twelve weeks, then submit a report to Dr. Freiberg and his colleagues. If the results were impressive, as FDR expected, he intended to approach major philanthropists, including John D. Rockefeller Jr., and make his case for underwriting the development of Warm Springs as a major center for polio treatment.

"Upon your report will, of course, depend my plans for the future of Warm Springs," FDR wrote Freiberg. "If you gentlemen are thoroughly and 100% convinced that it is worth while, I want, immediately after November 1st, to seek to raise the money necessary (my estimate would be $300,000) to build a fire-proof sanitarium and cottages, together with pools, equipment, etc., capable of taking care of 100 or more patients at a time." Then, he believed, Warm Springs would become a model for others to follow, a pilot case inspiring polio treatment centers across the country.

Dr. Hubbard did not use the sort of quantitative measurements of muscle function that Robert Lovett had devised. Instead, he reported his commonsense, before-and-after judgments of progress made over three months. He reported that a twenty-two-year-old Massachusetts man went from "compete paralysis" to walking with one crutch; Fred Botts, the thirty-four-year-old Pennsylvanian who had come the year before, had gone from "helpless" in a wheelchair to walking with one crutch; a four-year-old girl now "walked very much better with her brace and also without it"; a four-year-old boy, "fearless in the pool," now walked with crutches after arriving with both legs completely paralyzed; a seven-year-old girl "walks considerably better than she did when she came"; a fifteen-year-old Chicago girl had "improved considerably." Of the twenty-four cases, most of them of the "severe" type in whom little or no rapid improvement could be expected from any kind of treatment, Hubbard saw marked improvement in most. This led him to believe that "the exercises in warm water under proper supervision give a better hope for fairly rapid improvement in muscle power than any other method with which I am familiar."

"No miracles can be performed at Warm Springs," Hubbard acknowledged, and "no false hopes should be aroused in the minds of patients or their families." There was no magic or even medicine in the water. The benefits arose from its peculiar buoyancy and invigorating qualities, whatever their source might be. It could be the natural minerals, Hubbard said, or the water might be ever so slightly radioactive — in a good way. Whatever the reason, patients undoubtedly were able to exercise in Roosevelt's pool for much longer periods than they could on dry land or even in artificially heated fresh water. That was the key to it. And there was something in the air, Hubbard said — a quality of comradeship that one did not see among polio patients elsewhere, "a psychological effect due to each striving to equal the other in improvement. Also the fact that these boys and girls deprived of the usual sports are able in the water to rival the normal boy and girl and have a feeling that at least in one sport they can take part."

In November 1926, while Dr. Hubbard was assembling his final report, one member of the medical oversight committee, Dr. Frank Dickson of Kansas City, decided to have his own look at Warm Springs. He had been picking up professional scuttlebutt to the effect that "there was little faith in the treatment in the minds of the orthopedic men generally, and that Mr. Roosevelt was suspicioned of trying to put something over." If Dr. Dickson harbored doubts of his own, a couple of days with Roosevelt put them to rest. He was utterly taken by both the proprietor and the place. "I am more thoroughly convinced than ever that Mr. Roosevelt is absolutely honest and sincere in his believe [*sic*] that Warm Springs offers unusual advantages for the 'water treatment' of Polio," Dickson confided to Dr. Freiberg, "and that it is his wish to make the place available for the carrying out of this treatment to the greatest number of individuals possible. Furthermore, I am sure there is no thought of personal gain in Mr. Roosevelt's mind." Hubbard's treatment regimen struck him as effective but not overtaxing, while the patients "took their treatment seriously." Dickson echoed Hubbard's praise of "the psychical effects of the place on the patients. . . . There is a splendid morale evident in the patients there." Testing three of his own patients whom he had sent there, Dickson found "definite but not startling" improvement in muscle function; but he saw "a distinct improvement in their attitude towards working for progress." And as for the pool itself, it had "all the qualities claimed for it." Normally, Dickson said, he couldn't stay in a swimming pool for more than ten or fifteen minutes without tiring. But at Warm Springs he swam around for ninety minutes on a cool day "and came out feeling like a fighting cock. . . . What these qualities of the water are which enable so prolonged a stay I have no idea. The facts of the matter are they are there." He knew of no other place that offered more "favorable conditions for muscle training therapy."

On June 5, 1926, at St. James Episcopal Church in Hyde Park, Anna Roosevelt was married to Curtis Bean Dall, a Princeton man and a stockbroker. She had just turned twenty; Dall was twenty-nine. (Anna's veil had first been worn by a maternal ancestor, the wife of Robert Livingston, President John Adams's ambassador to France.) An alert reader of the next day's *New York Herald-Tribune* would have discerned the sort of subtle accommodation that families learn to make when one member has a disability. "She walked down the aisle on the arm of her brother, James," the story said, "but as she approached the chancel, her father took his place and gave her away."

The reception was held outdoors at the Roosevelts' home a mile down the Albany Post Road from the church. Even under

gray skies, it was a lovely setting: the dignified house with its encompassing wings;
gardens in spring bloom under old oaks;
the lawn sloping toward the Hudson.

Private rail cars hired by the Roosevelts
had brought guests up to Hyde Park from
Manhattan that morning. Other people had
motored over from estates and towns
nearby. To the knowledgeable eye, the guest
list was a kind of index to the intertwining
circles that made up the Roosevelts' lives.

Along with Roosevelt, Delano and Dall
relations, and young friends of the couple,
there were Social Register names from Sara
Roosevelt's circle (Vanderbilt, Aldrich,
Forbes); old Harvard friends of Franklin's;
associates from business, law, and politics,
from the millionaire Van Lear Black to Tom
Lynch, the Poughkeepsie florist-turned-
politico who managed that busy day to attend both the Roosevelt wedding in Hyde
Park and the wedding of Governor Smith's
daughter Emily in Albany. Eleanor's closest
women friends were there: the Democratic
activists Elizabeth Read, Read's life partner
Esther Lape, and Caroline O'Day, as well
as Nancy Cook, Eleanor's housemate at Val-
Kill (without Marion Dickerman, for some
reason). FDR's two special women admirers, Missy LeHand and Daisy Suckley, also

were there.

To guests who visited the house on such occasions, the Roosevelts seemed a boisterous and happy family. FDR would be at the center, a friend wrote, "talking to everybody, bantering with his children, teasing them and they him. The youngsters would tell preposterous stories to dignified visitors to see if they could get away with them, and would burst into gales of laughter regardless of whether the visitor fell for the story or saw through them." The four boys, another visitor said, brought "a kind of adolescent bedlam" with "high-voiced argument" and "utter scorn for each others' opinions. They regarded their mother and father as entitled to a hearing, but no more." Sara Roosevelt moved among the family's guests with the confidence and grace of an elderly ruling queen, "so handsome, so vital . . . such an indomitable and exciting personality," as a favored relation put it. Eleanor stayed at arm's length from the conversational clamor that was always arising from her husband and sons; she was the one who had a thought for each guest's feelings and special needs. To most people, the family was charming, stimulating, and comfortable company.

But beneath this happy surface, a small

number of people at the wedding — the ones genuinely close to the Roosevelts, such as Missy LeHand and Eleanor's friend Nancy Cook — were well aware of tensions. They would have known that Franklin's mother disapproved of Missy's presence wherever FDR went, with or without his wife; and that Eleanor just now was steaming at her mother-in-law for giving a Manhattan apartment to Anna and Curtis Dall without seeking permission from Eleanor and Franklin. "I am trying to be decent [to Sara]," Eleanor had written a few weeks earlier to FDR in Warm Springs, "but I'm so anxious of having her [be] nasty that I'm uncomfortable every minute!"

Close friends likely suspected what Anna herself later admitted — that the wedding itself was her ill-conceived escape from the unending friction between her mother and grandmother, and from the social conventions they imposed upon her. Anna was still angry that, a year earlier, Eleanor and Sara — agreeing, for once — had insisted that Anna make a formal debut at the high-society "Tennis Week" at Newport. Their partner in this plot was a dowager cousin, Susie Parish, who had taken the opportunity to tell Anna the tale of FDR's affair with Lucy Mercer; it was a shock that left Anna secretly disillusioned with the father she had adored and revered — a father who refused to take any hand in Anna's domestic troubles, saying, if she came to him, "That's up to Granny and Mother. You settle all this with them." Anna had made a show of falling in love with the dull and deeply conventional Curtis Dall, but very soon she would admit to herself that the wedding had been a mistake — and would later say as much: "I got married when I did because I wanted to get out."

The Roosevelt boys were not much happier. They thrived on big occasions, like the wedding, when all the members of the family were assembled. But those times had become increasingly rare, with their father far away as much as six months of the year and their mother dividing her time between Hyde Park, the Todhunter School, and her political work all over. Elliott, the middle child, now fifteen, was a congenitally unhappy boy who harbored resentments, especially of Eleanor, whom he later accused of "coldness" toward her children. It was not a family for the raising of happy, well-adjusted children. The five were eventually to have eighteen marriages between them. "By contrast with the kind of lives most young people lead, especially the poor, it's ridiculous for me to complain," James, the eldest boy, would write many years later. "Yet on a personal level there was something missing from our lives. We spent so little time alone with our parents that those times are remembered and treasured, as though gifts from gods."

Yet in spite of the fractures in the family, the marriage at its center endured. Franklin endorsed and helped Eleanor in projects that many husbands in his position, in that era, would not even have tolerated: her decision to form a household with two lesbian women, and her determined activism in party politics and public policy. She, in turn, tolerated his "office marriage" with Missy LeHand; put up with his long absences; and helped him where she could in politics.

Perhaps they would have reached this sort of accommodation if FDR had never fallen ill. But it was the polio crisis that spun their two lives into their particular trajectories. When it became clear that Franklin must depend heavily on others to do the things he wanted to do — far more heavily than if he had not been disabled — and especially when he took on the distant and weighty obligation of Warm Springs, Eleanor moved decisively into the private and political spheres she had begun to explore in the early 1920s. The favorite view of many biographers — that Eleanor took up politics in a wifely effort to "be her husband's legs" — is a candy-coated misreading of what really happened.

They had established distances, geographical and emotional, that allowed the partnership to work. As go-between, loyal to both camps — devoted to Franklin's political goals but also devoted to Eleanor — they both had Louis Howe.

That name was *not* on the list of wedding guests. This was puzzling, with no reason mentioned in the family's correspondence. No person was closer to the Roosevelts, and Grace Howe and their two children were friends of the family as well. It would have been an act of callous insensitivity not to invite them. Perhaps Anna was still nursing a grudge against him. Even after the fracas in 1922 over the room assignments at East 65th Street, Anna said later, she resented Howe for Eleanor's increasingly active life in politics; she failed to see that her mother's political life was very much of her own making.

But if Howe was not at the wedding in person, surely his influence could be detected in the way the event was portrayed to newspaper readers in New York. As FDR's press agent, Howe applied his hand to every part of his chief's presentation to the public, and on Anna's wedding day there was a small but important brushstroke in that portrait. It was the tableau setup in which the bride, the groom, and the bride's newsworthy father took their places for a press photograph. It showed that however preoccupied FDR had become with Warm Springs, he and Howe were still plotting his return to politics.

If not the first press photo since his illness to show FDR standing, it was certainly one of the first. Alongside Curtis Dall on the left and Anna in the center — and somehow dominating the image — he stands in his tails, perfectly erect, still as immaculately handsome as a man in a shirt-collar ad, though he filled out a suit much more than old friends remembered. His left hand grasps a railing. His right hand is down at his side, just visibly gripping the head of a cane. The cane's shaft is wholly hidden behind Anna's German shepherd, Chief. Unless one knew it, one would never guess this was the picture of a man who could not walk unaided.

It was one of a number of such photos taken in the mid-1920s in which much care appears to have been taken to shield or distract from the props that FDR used to stay standing without his crutches: walls, fences, gates, trees. Often a cane was shown in his hand, or part of a cane. No surviving documents explain a particular strategy behind these displays, but they were so consistent that the composition cannot be accidental. Roosevelt and Howe must have thought it through. In conversations with reporters or anyone else, neither of them would claim that FDR was more mobile than he really was. But the photographs delivered a powerful message — simply that he didn't *look* "crippled." He was up and around. He appeared to be all right after all.

Howe and FDR had been gently massaging that message into the minds of journalists — and therefore of politicians and voters — for two years, ever since Roosevelt's splash at the Democratic convention in 1924.

In that year, whenever a story about Roosevelt originated in the camp of Governor Al Smith — the stories, for example, saying that Smith had enlisted FDR as manager of his presidential campaign, or that Smith had chosen FDR to make the nominating speech at the convention — the reporter would describe FDR's physical condition with disinterested realism, emphasizing the handicap. It was: "He is obliged to depend upon crutches and will be physically incapacitated for some time" (*New York American*); or: "He is confined to a chair, except as he moves about on crutches" (*Knickerbocker Press*); or: "Mr. Roosevelt suffered an illness which caused partial paralysis, making it difficult for him to walk" (*Poughkeepsie Evening Star*).

But when a story originated in the Roosevelt camp — meaning that Louis Howe had planted it with one reporter or another, offering his chief for an interview — then the story took a distinctly upbeat direction. Now it was: "Mr. Roosevelt, who is able to use his right leg for the first time since he was stricken . . ." (*New York Evening Post,* October 1924); and: "He is gradually regaining the use of his legs and is confident of complete recovery" (*Poughkeepsie Eagle-News,* October 1924).

Reports like these — the first in a year to tell about FDR's exercise regimen at Warm Springs — were picked up and published by newspapers all across the country. It was the first time that Howe and FDR blocked out the entire polio tale as they wanted it to be understood by the general public and

413

the political fraternity. Emphasis was laid upon Roosevelt's excellent general health; his "indomitable" perseverance; his plucky humor ("If you can't stand handicaps, why go into politics?"); the "remarkable" progress he had made already at Warm Springs; and, most important, the prediction that he would come all the way back to full and independent mobility. "As he returns [to Warm Springs]," a reporter wrote, "it is with confidence that he is going to win back his old, robust health."

Of course, neither Roosevelt nor Howe could type the reporter's words for him, much as they may have wanted to. So even in positive stories, certain passages struck the wrong note. For instance, FDR was said to be tireless in his work but, "physically, was helpless as a child"; and: "The Democratic leaders were thrilled at the New York convention when, upon crutches, he made his impassioned plea for Al Smith. But they also wept."

In the tough fraternity of journalism, passages like those were known by the elegant shorthand term "sob stuff." Sob stuff entertained readers by a frank appeal to the satisfying emotion of pity, the reassuring feeling that the other fellow, even the rich fellow with the famous name, has it worse than you do, and isn't it sad how the mighty are fallen. Howe and Roosevelt liked the comeback angle. But pity was political poison. One might vote for a man who proved his strength by coming back from a grave illness — but not for a pathetic character who had to struggle to get around. So the message that Howe and FDR wanted understood was an in-between sort. They wanted FDR seen as a man in the midst of a comeback, but not yet at the end of that trail. He had not yet recovered, but he was getting better, stronger. Please come back later and ask again, Howe's planted stories said. Someday soon, he'll be ready. But not yet.

Just now, FDR's mind on that point was clear. He could not imagine running for office in his current condition. He had recently said so to an old friend, Louis Wehle, who had sent FDR a confidential note asserting that Roosevelt was "the logical Democratic nominee for President in the next election." He knew Franklin was a loyal Al Smith man, Wehle said, but after the party's debacle in 1924, he himself was quite sure Smith could not be nominated in 1928. "I am not asking you to abate one iota of your influence or energy from whatever support you intend to give Smith,"

Wehle told FDR. "I am simply suggesting that in some way your friends be permitted to organize the situation in your behalf in the event that Smith should not receive the nomination."

FDR constructed his reply piece by carefully chosen piece. He reminded Wehle that he had urged all Democrats to forswear support for particular candidates until the end of 1927; for now they should concentrate on party organization based on "really liberal" principles. He had, in fact, *not* committed himself to Smith or anyone else, he told Wehle. (Not publicly, perhaps, but he was already advising Smith on strategy for 1928.) "As to myself," he said, "I must give principle [*sic*] consideration for at least 2 years more to getting back the use of my legs. Up to now I have been able to walk only with great difficulty with steel braces and crutches, having to be carried up and down steps, in and out of cars, etc., etc. Such a situation is, of course, impossible in a candidate. I am, however, gaining greatly and hope, within a year, to be walking without the braces, with the further hope of then discarding the crutches in favor of canes and eventually possibly getting rid of the latter also. The above are necessarily only hopes, as no human being can tell whether the steady improvement will keep up."

FDR's reply was artful, even acrobatic, in the way it left the door just slightly open to a candidacy of his own in 1928. But it was unequivocal in asserting it was "of course impossible" for a man in his current state of disability to be a candidate for anything. And it was one of the few times — perhaps the only time — when he acknowedged that his plans for a fuller recovery were really "only hopes" and not a settled matter.

Yet newspaper stories about a man making an extraordinary comeback acted like a blinking beacon on influential Democrats. As the election seasons of 1926 and 1928 drew closer, from Albany to New York City to Georgia, Democrats wanted to know when the day of Roosevelt's readiness would come. Some took up the tool of the "boom": the informal public-relations campaign in which "rumors" and unnamed sources were cited to the effect that a politician's prospects were rising. In March 1926, for instance, the Hearst newspapers, hoping to derail Al Smith's drive toward the 1928 nomination, tried to "boom" FDR for president. If the boom started a wave for Roosevelt, it could bust up Smith's following and weaken their man's chances. Louis

Howe would have nothing to do with the stratagem. "Its purpose to split up the Smith backing was obvious," he wrote FDR. "It seems fatal to let it stand at this time. . . . So I saw to it that the next day one of 'Mr. Roosevelt's friends' was quoted as follows: 'You can state positively that Frank is not and will not be under any circumstances a candidate for the Presidency. He sees no political contingency in which he could be drafted to make the run.' "

In fact, Howe, and possibly FDR himself, *did* see such a contingency. Roosevelt never could challenge Smith, his ally and friend, whose popularity was soaring and whose time to be the nominee, many thought, was about to arrive at last. If Smith faltered, however, and the 1928 Democratic convention deadlocked again between urban wets and rural drys, then FDR might well be the logical compromise nominee — but only if he stayed out of the contest until the propitious moment, as Howe pointed out. "You as an active candidate just now," Howe told FDR, "would wreck the excellent chance you have of being at least one of — if not *the* one — among the leaders who all turned to [in the event of a 1928 deadlock]."

In Albany, Roosevelt had a more sincere

coterie of suitors. Edwin Corning had just taken charge as chairman of the state Democratic Party, and he was gunning to bring down U.S. Senator James Wolcott Wadsworth Jr., who would not be easy to beat. Wadsworth was the first New Yorker popularly elected to the Senate (in 1914), a Yale man (Skull and Bones), the son of a state controller and son-in-law of the late Secretary of State John Hay. And he opposed Prohibition, a good lure for independents tiring of the "Grand Experiment." Corning and his henchmen imagined a dazzling state ticket for the fall: Smith to run for a fourth term as governor, holding his power base to launch his new presidential campaign; and, for the U.S. Senate, Franklin D. Roosevelt, the unsullied star of the 1924 convention — if only he could be persuaded to run. Smith, for the moment, was playing Hamlet, saying he had not yet decided whether to run for another term as governor. So Corning put out feelers to FDR about that office too.

But Roosevelt delivered a firm no, both publicly and privately.

In the *New York Evening Post,* Howe once again planted the comeback tale, this time with the reporter Irwin Thomas, who spun an especially heroic version with the headline: "F.D. ROOSEVELT WINS LONG FIGHT."

"Friends and relatives of Franklin D. Roosevelt," the reporter wrote, "pleased beyond measure at the great fight he has made to regain his health, do not look with favor on the suggestion in some quarters that the former Assistant Secretary of the Navy become a candidate for any office this fall. Two years more and he will be fit and able to enter a campaign, but not now, say the friends of the man who has made the gamest of battles to regain his health."

Reporter Thomas told the polio tale not as "sob stuff" but in the heroic vein. For six weeks in 1921, he wrote, "the big, strong, athletic man . . . lay between life and death . . . cut down with little hope held out that he would ever walk again." (Dr. Draper's assurances that not only would his patient live but "he will not be crippled" had been forgotten.) Yet Roosevelt "had made up his mind to battle it through" with a "fighting spirit" and "the determination to do, to live."

"The legs that had been sturdy and strong continued to waste away until they were shrunken almost beyond belief," Thomas continued. "It was almost generally accepted that he was through physically.

[From] time to time came reports that he was getting along, and then he was seen out riding, and there came a time when, with light but strong braces of iron, with a couple of sturdy crutches, he swung himself along and kicked his legs. That was the beginning of the comeback physically." Then, though "people shook their heads," the crippled man proved his stamina by running Smith's campaign for president in 1924. He followed his doctors' orders to exercise, and "the little improvement that he made might have discouraged another because it was so slight, but Roosevelt plugged on." At the 1924 convention "he was a lion," and his "great speech . . . made thousands of friends." Now it was 1926. In 1928, "at the next National Convention, Franklin D. Roosevelt's friends expect him to be there with no crutches. They expect to see him nominated at a state Convention either for Governor or for United States Senator, the latter preferably. But for him to go into a campaign this year it is believed would undo the work that has been done."

When FDR and Howe had to turn down the gas, the word to reporters was: *Soon . . . but not now.* When they wanted to stoke the flame, the emphasis shifted to: *Not yet . . . but soon.* That was how FDR cast his response to a supporter at the time of Anna's wedding. "They are trying to get me to run for Governor or Senator this year," he wrote, "but I am not doing so as my legs are coming along so well that if I can devote another couple of years to them, I will be able to get about much more easily. As it is, I can walk with only one brace on, and only a crutch and a cane, and I hope, by sticking everlastingly at it, to get rid of the brace and crutch. Outside of my stupid old legs, I have never been in more robust health and on the side, I am running the New York end of a surety company, a law firm, the Boy Scouts, and a dozen other activities."

He almost surely meant it when he told friends he had "no desire to sit for six long years in the U.S. Senate!" And a Senate race could be a strategic error in his long-term pursuit of the presidency. An old friend from Hyde Park, Gustavus Rogers, remembered him calculating the benefits and costs. Imagine if he were to run and lose: What then of his prospects for the presidential nomination in some later year? It would be said that he had twice failed to carry his home state, first as Cox's running mate in 1920, then in this Senate race against Wadsworth. In that case, Rogers said, "Nationally he would cease to be a figure."

But would winning be any better? A statewide victory in New York might enhance his standing in the nominating conventions of either 1928 or 1932, after four or six years in Washington. But Senate service could imperil presidential plans, especially with the Democratic Party still in a state of war among big-city wets of the Northeast and drys of the South and West. A Senate vote on efforts to repeal Prohibition could strangle the chances of any national candidate from the Democratic Party. "If [Roosevelt] were elected and served a six-year term," Rogers recalled in a memoir written later, "he would frequently be called upon to vote on matters where the interest of the North and the South and the West were opposed. . . . If he voted for the Southern view, he would lose support in the North; if he supported the northern view, he would lose strength in the South, where he considered he was very strong; if he voted against the West, in favor of the East, he might lose the progressive strength he might have in the West."

Despite that summer's refusals and explanations, Louis Howe still worried that Roosevelt might be pressured into a Senate campaign. When FDR agreed to speak for Smith at the state convention in Syracuse in

September, Howe heard there was a plan afoot to stampede the delegates to nominate FDR for the Senate. This was another time to say: Not yet. "I hope your spine is still sufficiently strong to assure them that you are still nigh to death's door for the next two years," Howe told FDR. "Please try and look pallid and worn and weary when you address the convention so it will not be too exceedingly difficult to get by with the statement that your health will not permit you to run for anything for 2 years more."

No stampede ensued, and the Democrats, after nominating Al Smith for governor again, chose a Smith ally, Robert F. Wagner, justice of the New York supreme court, to run for Wadsworth's seat in the U.S. Senate — the opening act of a major Senate career. At the Syracuse convention, FDR took the rostrum to speak again for Smith. This time politicians watched as he walked not with two crutches but with one crutch and a cane. This was visible evidence that he had indeed made further progress since Madison Square Garden two years earlier.

For now, Howe and FDR could keep his political position in a state of delicate equilibrium, poised between the comeback story and the "health" excuse.

But how long would the political professionals remain patient? When would they say: "Look, Louis, can he run or not?" How many times could Howe and Roosevelt say "not yet" before the party quit asking? Some day soon, just as he had been promising, he must be ready. But what would "ready" mean?

CHAPTER 12
"So That They'll Forget That I'm a Cripple"
FALL 1926 TO SUMMER 1928

He had vowed to friends that he was "keeping everlastingly at it." And reporters were warming to Louis Howe's inspirational tale of the political golden boy who had been knocked down by an ugly foe but now was mounting a comeback through dogged physical labor.

But FDR was no less fallible than most people who try to stick to a dull and difficult program of exercise, year after year, especially when the rewards are very slow in coming. Often he worked diligently. Sometimes he slacked off. The great expansion of the musculature of his chest, shoulders, and arms could only have been the result of hard, sustained labor over many months. But with the lower half of his body, where many of his muscles could not be summoned at all and where others were terribly weak, it was inevitably more difficult to keep to the prescribed regimen. Evidence comes from associates of FDR's who had no stake in exaggerating the claims about a heroic recovery effort — indeed, who told the truth because they wanted him to work harder and so make the best recovery possible.

As early as 1922 his nurse, Edna Rockey, had said he was not working as hard as he should. Her report was echoed later by Mrs. William Plog, wife of the superintendent of the Hyde Park estate. Mrs. Plog had served FDR his meals that summer when, according to legend, he exerted himself day after day to reach the end of the driveway with his crutches. Mrs. Plog had found him "a wonderful patient to take care [of]. . . . He was no trouble whatsoever." But she did not see him trying to walk very much.

"I [saw] him trying walking with his crutches and his nurse [Edna Rockey] several times," Mrs. Plog told George Palmer, a historian with the National Park Service who interviewed the Plogs in 1947.

"Did he have great difficulty or not in his first attempts at walking?" Palmer asked.

"Yes, he had great difficulty in trying to walk," she said. "It was very hard for him to walk."

"Did he give up or did he keep on trying?" Palmer asked.

"I don't think he tried very often," she

said, " 'cause after a while he tried to ride horseback and he didn't do that very long either."

Eleanor Roosevelt gave a similar report to Robert Lovett in 1923.

FDR certainly worked hard with William McDonald, a physician he had heard about through his uncle Fred Delano. McDonald was helping polio patients with a difficult exercise routine of his own invention in the oceanside town of Marion, Massachusetts, near Howe's cottage on Buzzards Bay. FDR went there for a long spell in the late summer and fall of 1925 and again in 1926. McDonald believed patients should try to build up their atrophied muscles without the use of braces, and his procedures exercised entire limbs, not just isolated muscles. He had patients use the parallel bars and he had them swim. Bertie Hamlin, an old friend, and her husband saw FDR hard at work during their stay at the beach in 1925. "I watched as he made his endless rounds [of the parallel bars]," she wrote later, "for two or three hours a day — holding on to the wooden railing of a rectangular walk. Usually several of his friends were sitting around, and he talked and laughed cheerfully as he circled the platform, holding himself up by the railing and dragging his almost useless legs after him." Yet here too he seems to have been less than a perfect patient. A medical colleague of Dr. McDonald's said that when he was watching, FDR followed McDonald's regimen only when Eleanor hounded him to do so.

At Warm Springs in the spring of 1926, in a letter to her mother, Anna Roosevelt said that FDR could "handle himself better" — a reference to smaller matters of mobility, such as shifting from a wheelchair to a chair — and that he could "go up two steps." But she saw no obvious proof of her father's claims about the extraordinary benefits of exercise in the pool at Warm Springs.

"Ma," Anna wrote, "it's hard to tell whether father is walking better or not. He doesn't walk very much, & doesn't exercise over much."

In 1921, FDR had heard Dr. Lovett and Dr. Draper say that some of his muscles were beyond redemption — certainly most or all of the ones in his calves — but that above the knees, at least, other muscles might merely be dormant from prolonged inactivity. He had been less attentive when they said only time would tell how much muscle was gone for good. He had embraced the belief that improvement could go on indefinitely, given sufficient devotion to the right program of exercise, and that therefore if he simply "kept everlastingly at it," he would be able to walk again — to walk with a cane, perhaps, but not with crutches and braces. In 1924, a correspondent had urged FDR to try the treatment of Emile Coué, the French psychologist and forerunner of cognitive therapy best known for counseling people in difficulty to repeat each morning: "Every day, in every way, I am getting better and better." FDR had replied that no such strategy of autosuggestion could restore the destroyed nerves in his lower body, but that "in a way I have been following Coué's methods ever since I got this fool disease three years ago — I have been perfectly definite in my determination to throw away the crutches, and every month that has gone by has found the nerve cells and muscles returning to better control."

Now he had tried hard for two years more, tried hard but inconstantly, making progress and then falling back, regaining ground and falling back again. He did not give up everything else to pursue an unbroken course of exercise, and if any greater progress had been possible — and no one can say definitely that it *was* possible — that is what would have been required.

By 1926, his conception of the possible was changing.

One of the physiotherapists at Warm Springs was a young woman named Mary Hudson. Later in life she told Geoffrey C. Ward, one of the most astute chroniclers of FDR's life, that she always tried to teach her charges, FDR included, that "polio was a storm. You were what remained when it had passed." Ward said it took Roosevelt five years "to accept the fact that he could never again be what he had been before the storm hit." A steady refusal to accept defeat had taken him a good distance from his sickbed of 1921–1922. But now he was reframing his picture of the future.

This became clear when he began to work with Helena Mahoney, the physiotherapist recruited by Dr. Hubbard to supervise the patients in his original study at Warm Springs in 1926. Trained by Robert Lovett in Boston, Mahoney was an accomplished member of the first generation in her specialty, and she had years of experience in helping polio patients. She was thickset, straightforward, no-nonsense, and she quickly established friendly relations with both FDR and Eleanor.

According to the writer Turnley Walker, who knew Warm Springs as a patient and interviewed many other patients and members of the early staff, Mahoney asked FDR in an early meeting what he hoped to accomplish with his exercise program.

He told her he wanted to walk without crutches. He wanted, in Walker's paraphrase, to "walk into a room without scaring everybody half to death" and to "stand easily enough in front of people so that they'll forget that I'm a cripple."

Those statements mark a turning point. As with many others who find themselves disabled, it took time for him to make decisive discoveries about the very nature of disability, and these discoveries had changed his view of what he needed to do.

In the next two or three decades, in no small part because of FDR's own example, scholars would begin to articulate these discoveries in the language of social science. The social psychologist Lee Meyerson would summarize the emerging view soon after Roosevelt's death. Close observation of the lives of people with disabilities, Myerson wrote, had led to two central conclusions: that "the problem of adjustment to disability" should be seen as "a problem in creating favorable social-psychological situations"; and that it was "as much or more a problem of the non-handicapped majority as it [was] of the handicapped minority."

In other words, being *seen* as a cripple was often a bigger problem than actually *being* a cripple. Roosevelt's situation was a perfect example. He had learned that he could do a great deal without being able to walk unaided. He could work, write, travel, give speeches, run meetings. Indeed, his paralysis probably had enhanced these abilities, since it had dampened, though it did not extinguish, his tendency to do everything and go everywhere that caught his fancy. He could manage large organizations (such as Al Smith's campaign in 1924), even create large organizations, as he was doing at Warm Springs. His greatest gift — his extraordinary ability simply to *talk* persuasively and winningly, with uncanny charm — surely had been enhanced by his need to use language to distract listeners from his paralysis. In short, he had proven to himself and anyone watching that he could excel at all the work required of a person holding a high political office. What remained to be done now, in his quest for the presidency, had wholly to do with the perceptions and beliefs of other people. The goal of his physical rehabilitation, he was telling Helena Mahoney, was no longer to walk unaided. It was to give a performance that would quiet the feelings of revulsion, pity, and embarrassment that his body provoked in others. It was to act in such a way that people would "forget that he was a cripple" and toss aside the meanings that being a "cripple" held deep in their minds: inequality, inferiority, tragedy, "other"-ness, even evil. He must make of his life a continuously "favorable social-psychological situation," which simply meant a situation in which he and others were confident of his power to do the things he wanted to do.

But in 1926 he still could not give such a performance.

In the fall of 1926, Henry Pope took a special interest in Roosevelt's case. Pope was the Chicago manufacturer and backer of Warm Springs whose daughter was one of the early patients. He was determined that Roosevelt continue with the therapy he had been doing with Helena Mahoney when FDR had to return to his home in New York for the winter. He offered to pay for a monthlong visit to New York by Alice Lou Plastridge, a physiotherapist who had been working with his daughter.

Miss Plastridge, called "Lou" by her friends, was thirty-seven years old. Raised in Vermont, she had earned a degree in physical education at Mount Holyoke and taken a job teaching gymnastics. But she wanted to do something in the medical line, and a summer course in the treatment of scoliosis at the Harvard Medical School led her to the post of assistant to Robert Lovett. That was in the polio epidemic year of 1916. In Lovett's office she learned the techniques developed for recovering polio patients by Wilhelmine Wright. Lovett suggested a move to Chicago, where physical therapists were needed. There she developed a successful practice and met Henry Pope when his daughter needed help. Pope thought highly of her skills and urged FDR to work with her at his home.

Plastridge was doubtful about how much good such a trip would do with a patient so far past the acute stage of polio. "I knew [that] at the end of five years, one month was a drop in the bucket," she said later. "But they were so anxious to have someone go."

She arrived at Hyde Park in the first week of December 1926. A chauffeur picked her up at the depot and drove her to the Roosevelts'. Sara Roosevelt herself — "very cordially" — welcomed her at the front door.

"Eleanor!" Mrs. Roosevelt called. "Eleanor, come down — Miss Plastridge is here!"

A beaming Eleanor Roosevelt appeared and called, "Anna! Anna, come down! Miss Plastridge is here!"

Eleanor and her daughter led Plastridge down a long corridor to the entrance to the great library room at the end of the house, where the three women paused for a few moments, chatting.

Finally, from the far end of the room, a "very deep voice" called: "Well, aren't you ever going to speak to *me*?"

For several days she spent most of her time simply studying his movements. "Because muscles can be affected so differently," she would write, "each case is a law unto itself. It is difficult to lay down set rules to cover all conditions. Therefore, each person's individual problem must be carefully studied. The type of walking permitted may, in some cases, be unique."

She saw him applying brute force with very little finesse. He "struggled so hard," Plastridge said, "throwing himself into everything he did. . . . With crutches he would pound down on the floor. You would think the floor would break under him, his effort was so great. He would just drag his legs along."

One day he sat down too abruptly, injured

his back, and took to his bed in considerable pain. The next morning, Plastridge asked if he wanted to have a session.

"Didn't you hear I hurt my back?" he asked.

"Would it hurt your back to move your toes?"

"Yes," he said.

"Then you're not doing it right," Plastridge remarked.

"Prove it," he said.

She stretched him out on his back on a board. She was all but starting his rehabilitative work over. She was entirely sympathetic to his hope of achieving a gait that would make people "forget that I'm a cripple." To do that, he must avoid what she called the "distorted positions" and ungainly movements typical of people with polio who walked without proper training. The primary goal of her teaching, she would write, was to make "walking inconspicuous, (by moving quietly and steadily without needless body, leg or arm motions which would attract attention to the disability)."

First with his toes, she began to show him how to "localize" muscles — to concentrate on exerting still-good muscles as stand-ins for useless and weak ones. Day by day, she showed him that the "tremendously important" muscles of his upper body were "capable of indirectly moving the legs about, compensating, in a measure, for weak hip and leg muscles."

He had never really understood this before, he told her.

Slowly, he began to gain the knack of it. "He learned to use what he had — the good muscles," she would say. "He learned another way of moving."

She stayed with the Roosevelts for three weeks. Just before Christmas, sitting down to dinner with the family, Plastridge found a small, gift-wrapped box at her place. She looked up and saw everyone's eyes on her.

"Open it!" FDR said.

Inside the box she found a gold ring set with a lapis stone.

He returned to Warm Springs just five weeks into the new year of 1927 and resumed his course of therapy with Helena Mahoney, trying out in the buoyant water the techniques that Alice Lou Plastridge had taught him at Hyde Park. He went at it with new excitement, and he stuck with it week after week.

Mahoney was delighted. "He has never shown such interest and attention to this work since I have been here," she wrote

Eleanor.

By the middle of April, he was able to take steps with a single cane in one hand while the other gripped Mahoney's strong arm.

Then he took steps with only two canes — no crutches, no supporting arm.

Mahoney sought Eleanor's help. She wanted FDR to follow the course longer to be sure of cementing his progress.

"Mr. Roosevelt is doing so well that I want you to know it," Mahoney told Eleanor. "His muscles are greatly improved, his knees especially are much stronger. . . . I do dread having it interrupted and do hope he will stay just as long as possible for we always have to go back some each time he goes away. Even two weeks or so longer will establish what we have. We hope you will persuade Mr. Roosevelt to stay a bit longer."

Eleanor showed Mahoney's letter to Louis Howe, who exulted. He too urged FDR not to leave off exercising "just as you [are] going over the top. . . . I can't tell you how pleased I am, old man, at the details she gives of the way you have come back. I have always felt you would." He knew all about the prediction that FDR was years past the point when he could expect any significant improvement, and he was delighted to see his boss defy the predictions.

Roosevelt did stay a few weeks longer, then he returned again for late May and part of June. "It is good to see him walk around the house with a crutch and a cane," Mahoney told Eleanor, "and stand up to the table and do and get what he wants. His balance improves. I am sure you will find him more and more on his feet."

Still, before he could accomplish a smooth and safe gait with only canes, there was a last obstacle. Underneath his trousers he had begun to get by without the long brace on his right leg to hold the knee stiff. But when he tried to stand without the brace on his left knee, the joint would buckle every time. He could not keep his left leg straight by himself. "My own legs continue to improve, especially the waist muscles," he wrote that spring to Dr. William McDonald, "and I get about quite comfortably with canes, though I cannot get rid of that brace on the left leg yet. It is still a mystery as to why that left knee declines to lock. It is very strong, and I suppose some day I shall discover the reason why I cannot put my full weight on it."

Physical therapy took up no more than a couple of hours in the morning. He jammed the rest of the day and evening with a rolling cavalcade of activities. He spent time in the pool helping other patients with their own exercises and organizing games. Driving a Ford he had rigged up with hand controls, he charged around Warm Springs to check on the noisy construction of his new roads and cottages; took motor trips to explore the countryside; made regular pilgrimages to a rocky outlook called Dowdell's Knob, where he brought gangs for picnics. He sat with Missy to handle mail to and from scores of correspondents, including Louis Howe, who kept tabs on FDR's responsibilities at Fidelity & Deposit; with Basil O'Connor, whom FDR was dragging deeper into the legal and financial management of Warm Springs; with old pals from Harvard and the navy; with Democrats in many states; with orthopedists and health faddists; with reporters and editors; with his mother, his wife, his children, and far-flung members of the Roosevelt and Delano clans. He invited and entertained guests. Up on Pine Mountain he bought several hundred acres of pineland and hired a local farmer, Otis Moore — whom he adopted immediately as "Oat," his newest old friend — and laid plans for a little farming and forestry operation that might demonstrate the virtue of new techniques and new crops to other farmers nearby. He took an interest in Meriwether County politics, including officially changing Bullochville's name to Warm Springs.

He told friends at home that this place he had discovered was "interesting in its southern primitiveness," and it was no offhand remark. Because he was an inveterate observer and asker of questions, the problems of rural western Georgia, beset by the boll weevil and the pestilential legacies of the Civil War and Reconstruction, became his new curriculum in land use and reclamation, agriculture and animal husbandry, and the economics of the old and new South. As he did in Dutchess County at home, this son of privilege really did get to know people who worked with their hands and lived hand to mouth. It was a practical education that few politicians received. He made contacts, then friendships, among southern politicians who came to visit, and he began to develop much greater authority than the average Yankee to speak on southern issues. That spring of 1927 was the time of the greatest Mississippi River flood in the nation's history to date, and, though the damage to land and towns did not spread as far east as Warm Springs, Roosevelt was sensitive to its political implications across the region. When Louis Howe advised him to call for a special session of Congress to respond to the crisis — "Wouldn't such a move go grand in the South and make you the fair-haired boy?" — FDR did so, scoring headlines. A band of friendly southern pols took notice of this adoptive Georgian and launched another little presidential popgun on his behalf; it was less a sincere effort to promote Roosevelt than to damage Al Smith, but any publicity associating his name with big-time politics was all to the good.

Unlike Hyde Park and East 65th Street and Campobello, Warm Springs was neither Sara's home nor a family property but emphatically his own place, just as Val-Kill was Eleanor's own. It was just two days by train from New York, yet "somehow down here," he wrote his mother, "I feel just as far away as if it were Europe."

Eleanor, who regarded her husband's southern forays as "his times with Missy," as she told Anna, visited Warm Springs occasionally but seldom stayed for long. The blight of Jim Crow and Negro poverty troubled her far more than it did her husband, if it troubled her husband at all. The squalid shacks of sharecroppers drove the truth in upon her that "for many, many people life in the South was poor and hard and ugly." At the same time she was genuinely touched by southern neighborliness; "hardly a day passed that something was not brought to our door — wood for the fireplace, or a chicken, or flowers." But her emotions were taxed by the growing numbers of polio patients, ever in sight on crutches, on stretchers, in wheelchairs. She could not help being struck more by what they had lost than by what they might be gaining. "The complete gallantry of all the patients always brought a choke to my throat," she wrote later.

FDR saw them entirely differently. He wanted Warm Springs to bolster the polio people's morale and self-confidence as much as it would help their physical recovery. Financial support was provided to those who could not pay the full costs, yet he made sure no one knew which patients received such support. Not all of the polio patients had been closeted in back rooms at home, but many had, and all, like Roosevelt, had lived with the gulf that grew between themselves and the people around them. The disabled of Warm Springs were accustomed to living in a misty borderland, "neither out of society nor wholly in it," as the anthropologist Robert Murphy put it.

At home they were "undefined, ambiguous people," even "quasi-human." It was no longer so at Warm Springs. The borders disappeared and the gulf shrank, certainly among the patients and even between patients and staff, partly because patients dominated the village's population; partly because some on the staff were disabled themselves; and partly because patients had a voice in the community's governance. But the main revelation of Warm Springs was that in a community of shared experience, as Murphy wrote, "the disabled confront each other as whole individuals unseparated by social distinctions." These were values that Roosevelt, groping his way toward the kind of place he wanted for himself and the other patients, invested in the creation of Warm Springs. It had the casual comfort of the old family estates on the Hudson and of Eleanor's circle at Val-Kill. He was perfectly happy to jettison the idea of making half of Warm Springs a retreat for the rich. In fact, once he had settled on the idea of polio-only, he liked it better that way. "Oh, I do wish that you could be wafted down there and placed gently in a chair and slid gracefully down a ramp into the water," he wrote Eleanor's beloved Auntie Bye, now elderly. "You would love the informality and truly languid southern atmosphere of the place! My one fear is that this gentle charm will appeal to some of our rich friends who are suffering from nervous prosperity and that they will come down there and ruin our atmosphere."

Disabled people had been habituated to lives indoors, often deep indoors. At Warm Springs they lived in a Rooseveltian out-doors: not Uncle Ted's manly wilderness but Franklin's "country life," a gentle and genteel outdoors of picnics and summer concerts, with sparkling swimming pools at the center. If patients were depressed, he believed they should be taken to the over-look at Dowdell's Knob, where the spectacular sunsets over the Georgia forestlands would surely restore their spirits.

As 1927 passed, FDR and his Warm Springs advisors talked less and less about building a west Georgia Pinecrest alongside the center for poliomyelitis. As Louis Howe recognized, the people they were hitting up for philanthropic donations would raise an eyebrow if they thought a profit-making resort were also being planned.

And it had become perfectly clear that few able-bodied visitors wanted to share the vaunted waters with people damaged by an infectious disease, no matter how often they were told that people long past the contagious stage posed no danger to anyone. FDR was well acquainted with this species of ignorance. When a young relative of his came down with the disease in 1927, he was sorry but also relieved that he had been nowhere near the boy. "Thank the Lord I haven't seen him for months," he wrote Sara. "Otherwise some people would always feel I gave it to him."

But if there were to be no crowds of able-bodied golfers and horseback riders, then the pressure to find philanthropic donors was all the greater. By 1928, as FDR told an old friend, his "principal activities are now devoted to raising money for new improvements and paying off the mortgage by gradual stages."

Louis Howe got to work on promotion.

"My next idea for a 'stunt' for the press is to get a little amateur moving picture outfit," he wrote FDR. They could shoot footage of patients' progress over time, not "for public exhibition but for our own use. . . . I think it's a darned good idea. Wouldn't you like to have a film of how you walked . . . two years ago and how you walk now? . . . Think it over. . . . It would make a darned good story properly worked up as something new in diagnosis and treat-

447

ment. . . . There are all kinds of possibilities in the idea. You might have all the patients walk down the board and then do another 10 days later. . . . Give a showing to patients only and then have them by vote decide which one has made the greatest improvement with some kind of a little prize."

Cheesier stunts certainly had grabbed space in the newspapers. This one died on the drawing board. But FDR did allow Louis to recycle the story of his own improvement as an advertisement for Warm Springs. Their actual claims for the treatment remained responsible and accurate. There was no miraculous medicine in the water, they told reporters, only a special buoyancy that allowed patients to exercise for long periods. But the reader was left in no doubt that Patient Number One had made an extraordinary comeback indeed. Even the staid *New York Times* reported that "Mr. Roosevelt said the treatment at Warm Springs . . . has given astounding results. In his own case, he said, since taking the treatment he has been able to abandon one leg brace and substitute a stick for crutches." And in the pithy dramaturgy of New York's headline writers, his feats became downright heroic:

ROOSEVELT DEFIES DOOM OF DREAD SPINAL MALADY

F. D. ROOSEVELT IS BACK AT WORK

COMPLETELY RECOVERED FROM INFANTILE PARALYSIS AFTER NEARLY SEVEN YEARS

Those headlines and stories were read by the mothers and fathers of children with poliomyelitis across the United States, and plans were made to bring those children next year to Warm Springs. They were read by millionaire philanthropists, including Edsel Ford, who wrote a check for $25,000 to cover the cost of a glass ceiling over the biggest of the swimming pools, so the therapy could go on year-round.

And they were read by New York politicians in the corridors of the state capitol and the back rooms of Albany saloons, and in the high-altitude sanctum called the "Tiger Room," Governor Smith's favorite retreat whenever he was in Manhattan. Here he was planning his campaign for the 1928 Democratic nomination for the presidency.

All the signs pointed to Smith as the walkaway nominee. William McAdoo had quit the race before it got started, and

449

Smith's profile was on the rise in cities all over the country. But the man most likely to win the Republican nomination was Herbert Hoover, the secretary of commerce: a fine man, the "Great Engineer" who had built dams and bridges, the "Great Humanitarian" who had fed Europe's starving refugees after the Great War. Hoover would be a very hard man to beat. The nation was prospering as never before. Al Smith had won election as governor of New York four times. But in a nationwide race, the anti-Catholic wave that had denied him the nomination in 1924 would rise again, perhaps even in New York itself. New York was his great base of power. He had to hold it, and that meant he needed a strong candidate for governor on the ticket with him in 1928.

"Franklin D. Roosevelt's long fight against infantile paralysis finally has been won," the paper said.

But when Smith asked Roosevelt about running for governor, FDR said no, he needed two more years for his physical recovery.

Then at the end of June, the Democratic National Convention was held in awful heat in Houston. The delegates from New York saw Franklin Roosevelt once again approach the speaker's platform to nominate their man for the presidency. In 1924 in New York they had watched the same man struggle to the lectern with crutches — an extraordinary performance, but the man they watched that day had been a cripple. Now, four years later, they saw Roosevelt get to the dais with one hand holding the arm of one of his boys, the other hand holding not a crutch but a cane. Was he walking? Sure, he was walking. Anyway, it wasn't the hold-your-breath ordeal it had been in 1924. His gait now was rhythmic and smooth, slow but nearly natural. And then you looked up at the hulking shoulders and the massive head, the grin and the tossing chin, and you said, "That's a well man." And after a minute he was standing at the lectern like any other man, and then came the magnificent voice.

By God, that fellow *was* all right. Now, *why* couldn't he run for governor?

Chapter 13
"I Just Figured
It Was Now or Never"
AUGUST TO SEPTEMBER 1928

FDR expected to be brought into the highest echelons of the Democratic campaign, possibly directing the party's national publicity drive. "If Smith is nominated," he told Van Lear Black, "I take it I will be needed every second of the day and night, especially during the preliminary organizing period in July and August."

He was not needed. At least not for anything terribly important.

Al Smith had barely left the convention hall before his chief lieutenants took the reins of his national campaign firmly in hand, and they were no fans of Roosevelt. One of these was Belle Moskowitz, the matronly mastermind of Smith's political operation; she had pegged Roosevelt as a threat to her chief and a lightweight. The other was the steely-smart lawyer Joseph Proskauer, who had developed a deep grudge against FDR at the New York convention of 1924, when Roosevelt had nominated Smith with a speech that Proskauer had drafted, then failed to give Proskauer due credit. When Moskowitz and Proskauer were done with the campaign's organizational chart, Roosevelt's name sat among the eight figureheads on the Executive Committee and as chair of the innocuous slot labeled "Committee for Businessmen and Professionals" — hardly the heart of the Democratic campaign. When FDR asked that his nomination speech be published as a campaign tract — a standard publicity measure — Mrs. Moskowitz said no. He had to fight just to get a few minutes to talk with Smith.

In the first weeks of the campaign, he watched Smith's decisions and concluded that the governor's chances, never strong in the midst of the Republican boom, were now fading. He wanted Smith to stand up for progressive policies; to attack government by and for the wealthy; and to shift debate away from Prohibition and religion. But Smith's first big announcement — that his friend John J. Raskob would become chairman of the Democratic National Committee — placed Prohibition, religion, and wealth smack at the center of attention. Raskob was an arch-opponent of Prohibition, a leading Catholic layman, and one of the richest men in the country. At his Delaware estate he had commissioned a marble fountain graced by statues of his thirteen children. Al Smith thought Raskob's appointment would reassure businessmen that he, Smith, was no radical — a tactic that flabbergasted Roosevelt and his fellow liberals. Everybody except Smith knew that every businessman north of the Mason-Dixon line was going to vote for Herbert Hoover. The only impact the wet, Catholic Raskob might have on national opinion would be to reinforce southern fears about Smith.

FDR pleaded with Smith, saying the choice of Raskob "would make the whole situation much more difficult for the Democracy of the south," but the candidate was adamant, saying it was a bold bid for the big industrial states, which he needed to win. Of course he needed the South too. And sure enough, FDR confided to Van Lear Black, "a number of southern states are in open revolt."

For a long time he had believed that Smith would make "an unusually good president." But he had also become "very doubtful," barring a sudden crisis in the economy, "whether any Democrat can win in 1928."

Now the campaign was sliding into a pit of mudslinging over Prohibition and the pope, with Democrats leading the plunge.

"I am more and more disgusted and bored with the thought that in this great nation, the principal issue may be drawn into what we do or do not put into our stomachs," FDR said privately. And "these fool Methodist and Baptist ministers," sermonizing about Smith's slavish loyalty to the Vatican, "make my blood boil as a Protestant of a long line of wholly [*sic*] Protestant ancestry." The preachers denounced Catholic influence in secular affairs, yet "these same gentlemen are taking a deliberate and active part in American politics not just as mere individuals, but as official representatives of their own Protestant churches. Somehow that does not appeal to me as being the kind of American fair play that we preach about."

He began to suspect it was a good thing, after all, that Belle Moskowitz and Joe Proskauer were holding him at arm's length from the campaign. Smith was going to go down, with one of the death blows administered by Al's own hand. There was no sense in being handcuffed to him.

"Frankly, the campaign is working out in a way which I, personally, would not have followed and Smith is burning his bridges behind him," he remarked to Black. "It is a situation in which you and I can find little room for very active work.

"But," he added, in an oblique nod to his own plans for 1932 or 1936, "we shall be in a more advantageous position in the long run."

In mid-September he packed for Warm Springs. He wanted to be far away when New York's Democrats gathered at Rochester on October 1 to pick their nominees for the state races. He told Eleanor to quash any talk in party circles about nominating him for governor this year. If Smith was going to lose in the presidential race, then the Democrat running for governor in New York would likely lose too. And he needed more time at Warm Springs. Time to get the place on a sound financial footing. Time for more work on his legs.

As FDR was shaking his head in consternation over the foibles of Al Smith, Al Smith was hearing a good deal about the virtues of Franklin Roosevelt.

In the places where the leading Democrats of the Empire State talked and smoked and planned, from the governor's favorite haunts in New York to speakeasies and courthouses in Syracuse and Buffalo and Rochester, chills were running along spines. One way or the other, in glory or ignominy, Al Smith was about to leave the governor's chair after four terms. Their great leader and vote getter, the bringer of patronage, even of a measure of general respect for the Democratic Party, would not be leading the state ticket for the first time in ten years. And it looked as if the Republicans were about to make their smartest nomination for governor since Charles Evans Hughes in 1912.

The leading GOP candidate was Albert Ottinger, the attorney general of New York State. He was capable, smart, honest, and he was a Jew — the first, if nominated, ever to run statewide in New York. The Jews of New York City had come to trust and respect Al Smith and to vote for him as Jews had never before voted for an Irish-Catholic. But if Ottinger led the Republican ticket, many Jews who had voted for Smith were bound to vote Republican this year. Upstate, despite Democratic strength in the cities, Republicans still held a fearsome advantage. So a horse race for the vote in New York City meant deep trouble for the Democrats statewide.

The Democratic chieftains who had read story after story about Franklin Roosevelt's wonderful recovery from infantile paralysis, who had seen him walk with only a cane in Houston, were calling Smith on the phone and saying Roosevelt was the man to keep the party in power in Albany. He was the only big Democrat with any sort of base upstate; his liberal credentials would help him against Ottinger in the city; and there was always his name.

But Smith was not quite at ease with the idea of Franklin Roosevelt as governor of New York.

As a Smith man, Roosevelt had always served as a kind of stage prop, a "high type of Democrat" from the Hudson Valley who lent the governor a little of his respectability. But as a working politician, what had he done? A couple of years showing off in the assembly; then his name had gotten him a job with Wilson and a throwaway nomination for vice president. "Smith did not believe that Roosevelt had real ability," Joseph Proskauer said later.

In recent years the two had been friendly — politically friendly — but they never spent much time together. Roosevelt had all but dropped out of sight for three years; then he had come back into politics mostly via the mail. Al and Katie Smith, a Bowery beauty long since turned rotund, had accepted a couple of invitations to Hyde Park, where Roosevelt's mother looked at the governor of New York as she might look at a gardener who had invited himself to dinner — and where he never felt free to ask for a drink. Eleanor Roosevelt and Katie Smith were from different worlds, as, of course, were Al Smith and FDR. Smith liked him; who didn't? But governor? Colonel Edward House, Woodrow Wilson's old strategist, said: "Smith looks on Roosevelt as sort of a Boy Scout."

Smith himself had said to a friend: "Franklin just isn't the kind of man you can take into the pissroom and talk intimately with."

More to the point right now was Roosevelt's body. In 1921, Smith had counted FDR out of any future run for office. Of course he'd been "awfully pleased" when Eleanor told him about Franklin getting back some strength down south: "I just got all worked up about it," he wrote FDR. But he had no conception of what FDR had gone through to walk as he could now; and, like most people, he had a tin ear for how to talk about it.

A year earlier, Smith had been laid up at a time when FDR was at Warm Springs. "I certainly do envy you having a swim every day," the governor wrote. "I have been suffering with neuritis for three solid weeks. I am unable to take advantage of the bathing facilities that the Mansion affords, not to speak of a swim." If FDR had the urge to reply that he would gladly have traded the swimming pool at Warm Springs for a little neuritis, he quashed it. Unruffled, he simply invited Smith to join him in Georgia, since his water was "the finest thing in the world for the nerves."

In fact, Smith was often ill, and he blamed the physical demands of the governorship. If he, an able-bodied man, could barely handle the job, how could a cripple?

"In a certain way," Eleanor said, "I don't think Governor Smith really knew my husband very well."

But the boys in the Democratic Party wanted Roosevelt. These included some of Smith's dearest friends, men he had known since his early years in the assembly, who had helped him become governor and wanted now to make him president: older men like Norman Mack of Buffalo; George Olvany, who had succeeded Silent Charlie Murphy as head of Tammany Hall; John McCooey, the Brooklyn boss; and younger ones, the future of the state organization — Ed Flynn of the Bronx and Jim Farley from the Rockland County suburbs, both of them friendly with Roosevelt. These were smart, savvy pros, and they were telling Smith that more was riding on the nomination for governor than the governorship alone. Things were getting so bad that New York might go for Hoover, and that would be a humiliation worse for Smith than losing the presidency. To keep the state in his own column in the presidential race, the boys were saying, Smith needed the best possible candidate for governor on the ticket with him. That was Roosevelt. Maybe he was strong enough to do the work, maybe he wasn't. Right now the point was to keep a Democrat in the job.

In mid-September, as he prepared for a campaign swing through the West and Midwest, Smith turned to Ed Flynn, Democratic boss of the Bronx. Flynn was a Tammany man but he broke the Tammany mold. Quiet and bookish, he had grown up in a well-off Irish-Catholic family; he had gone to college; and he was a lawyer. He played machine politics shrewdly but he played clean, keeping the Bronx organization free of corruption.

You're his friend, the governor told Flynn. Call him down in Georgia and see what you can do.

When Flynn finally reached FDR on the phone — the call had to be scheduled by telegram — Roosevelt's refusal was "adamant."

Smith told Flynn to keep trying. Then Smith boarded his train for a two-week swing through the Midwest and West.

In Warm Springs, FDR exercised in the pool with the other patients and by himself in his cottage. He had a notion that if he stood with his back to a wall, leaning gently against it, he could talk with people and shake hands without even one cane. He wanted to try it, and he did so now. His balance was precarious. He fell again and again.

He had a neighbor named Leighton MacPherson, a man from nearby Columbus who had taken one of the cottages. One day MacPherson stepped onto Roosevelt's porch and called to see if anyone was home. He heard Roosevelt's voice calling for him to come in. MacPherson stepped into the room and saw FDR standing straight and stiff, his back against the wall, both hands empty, reaching out to his sides for balance.

"Look at me, Leighton," he said. "I'm standing alone."

Whistle-stopping through the West, Al Smith was measuring what his campaign for the presidency was really up against. By now it was clear his nomination at Houston had unlocked a Pandora's box of American fears — fear of alien immigrants in the cities, fears of gangsters and bootleggers, fear of southern blacks spreading north and west across the landscape — and the presidential campaign was becoming an ugly carnival. The Klan had slipped from its position of power in 1924, but it was still circulating outlandish tales of Smith coupling with Harlem prostitutes and warning that, if elected, he would install the pope as Washington's overlord. Protestant bishops were calling Smith the leader of "the unassimilated elements in our great cities." He was pilloried as "the papal governor of New York," king of the crooked city bosses, the immigrants, the drunkards — as a drunkard himself, and his wife as an uncouth slob. "The whole Puritan civilization which has built a sturdy, orderly nation is threatened by Smith," wrote the respected Kansas editor William Allen White. At some depots he met happy crowds of curious admirers; but by night, crosses burned along the route of his train. In Oklahoma City he tore up his prepared remarks and substituted a withering blast at the Klan. But as his train headed back east, he was shaken.

On Saturday, September 29, Smith's entourage arrived in Milwaukee. In two days New York Democrats would convene at Rochester for their nominating convention. Every slot in their statewide ticket was filled but the ones for governor and lieutenant governor. There were five weeks until the election.

Now Smith himself called Roosevelt. Again the answer was no.

New York was in trouble, Smith told him. Without the strongest possible nominee for governor, he could lose his own state; and without New York they could forget about the presidency.

He simply couldn't do it, FDR said. They had to find another man. His legs weren't ready.

"Well," said Smith, "you're the doctor," and they hung up.

The next morning Smith got a telegram from Roosevelt "confirming my telephone message." To stop any talk that FDR was making a coy play for a draft, Louis Howe handed out copies of the message to the papers.

He wished he could consider the race, FDR said, but he was perfectly sure Al Smith would carry New York on his own. Besides, he said: "My doctors are very definite in stating that the continued improvement in my condition is dependent on my avoidance of cold climate and on taking exercises here at Warm Springs during the cold Winter months. It probably means getting rid of leg braces during the next two Winters and that would be impossible if I had to remain in Albany. As I am only 46 years of age, I feel that I owe it to my family and myself to give the present constant improvement a chance to continue. I must therefore with great regret confirm my decision not to accept the nomination and I know you will understand."

With Smith's chances collapsing, Howe was more certain than ever that FDR must not run for governor, and FDR promised him that he had no intention of doing so. A *Times* man checked with Howe, then reported: "Persons who are very close to Mr. Roosevelt expressed the opinion . . . that he would stand by his decision not to run."

On Sunday FDR wrote to his mother: "I have had a difficult time turning down the Governorship — letters and telegrams by the dozen begging me to save the situation by running. But I have been perfectly firm — I only hope they don't try to stampede the Convention — nominate me and then adjourn!"

Some years later, Missy LeHand told close friends that a singular event occurred at Warm Springs on that weekend of September 29–30, 1928.

FDR, Helena Mahoney, Dr. Hubbard, and Missy were all in Roosevelt's cottage. As the others watched, Roosevelt stood, discarded his canes, and walked across the living room on his own. They were the first steps he had taken without crutches or canes in seven years. It could not have been steady or safe. But it was an extraordinary sign of how much he had accomplished. And it must have refreshed his appetite for the goal that had faded: to walk without aid.

On the next morning, Monday, October 1, Smith's train pulled into the station at Rochester. Hotels were jammed with Democratic delegates. Smith took a floor in the Seneca Hotel.

In Warm Springs, FDR got out of the village early. He had agreed to give a political talk in Manchester, Georgia, that evening, and he meant to be away from the telephone all day. Missy went along. Egbert Curtis, the young manager they had hired to run the hotel, acted as driver.

Smith went into conference. If not Roosevelt, who? They talked about half a dozen names or more. U.S. Senator Robert Wagner was only two years into his term and wanted to stay in Washington. Smith's own choice was his friend the investment banker Herbert Lehman, a serious and capable executive; a multimillionaire who could finance his own campaign; and a liberal Jew who could match Ottinger's appeal to Jewish voters. But the upstate men said nobody knew Lehman outside of New York. When Smith mentioned Townsend Scudder, a dignified justice of the state supreme court, the Tammanyites said he wasn't a man you could talk to. They kept coming back to Roosevelt, the only name the upstaters and city men could agree on.

Eleanor Roosevelt was in Rochester as head of the women's division of the Democratic State Committee. Late in the day, Smith asked her to join him and the key leaders: John Raskob, Ed Flynn, and a couple of others. They wanted to talk about Franklin.

She only had a few minutes. She was supposed to teach a class in New York the next morning and she had to make her train. She told them bluntly she would not urge her husband to run. The two of them had a firm understanding that he would make all such decisions on his own.

As she recalled the conversation later, "they began to quiz me as to whether it would really hurt Franklin's health if he were to run. I had to say I didn't think it would hurt Franklin's health, but Franklin believed that he might go further in his ability to [walk] and therefore he wanted to keep himself free to go on with his Warm Springs treatment."

That was something, at least: She was saying it wouldn't actually *harm* Roosevelt to run.

Now they tried another tack. Ed Flynn, in his phone talks with FDR, had begun to suspect that FDR's main reason for holding back was his financial obligation for Warm Springs. Flynn had said so to Smith and suggested that John Raskob might provide a solution.

So now the multimillionaire Raskob spoke to Eleanor. If her husband's health and safety were truly at risk, he said, then the party had no business asking him to run for governor. But if money was the problem, then he, Raskob, would like to offer Roosevelt financial aid. What did she think?

Recollections of her response differ slightly. Eleanor Roosevelt herself recalled that "Mr. Raskob asked if it would make a difference if [he] offered to take over some of [FDR's] investments, and I said no, I didn't think so." According to a journalist who got Raskob's version, Eleanor replied that "if her husband were to say that his health would permit him to run then Raskob could rely on it and that the real reason was the financial problem at Warm Springs" — and "everybody got the impression that Mrs. Roosevelt wanted her husband to run."

They asked her one more favor. They had been trying all day to get Roosevelt on the phone, without success. Would she try to reach him on their behalf? Didn't he owe them one last conversation? She said all right, she would try.

A call was put through from Rochester to the City Drug Store in Manchester, Georgia. Somebody at the drug store ran over to the school where FDR was speaking and told him his wife was calling. When Roosevelt got to the store and picked up the phone, Eleanor said Governor Smith wanted to speak to him, handed the receiver to Smith, and ran for her train.

FDR heard Smith's rasp. Roosevelt

shouted that the connection was bad: "It's no use . . ."

But the operator rang the store a minute later and told Roosevelt the governor would call him shortly at the Meriwether Inn in Warm Springs.

On the car ride back, Missy LeHand said: "Don't you *dare.*"

The call came. First Raskob was on the line, saying he would underwrite Roosevelt's entire investment in the Georgia Warm Springs Foundation. Then Smith: Roosevelt could spend only as much time in Albany as was absolutely necessary. He could spend nine months a year in Warm Springs if he wanted.

"Don't hand me that baloney," Roosevelt said.

Smith offered Herbert Lehman as the candidate for lieutenant governor — a man Roosevelt liked and respected, a first-rate man who could fill in whenever Roosevelt had to be away.

Then Smith put it as a personal request. He said he needed Roosevelt on the ticket in order to be elected president. He was directly asking him to do it.

Of course Roosevelt believed Smith was going to lose, and if Smith lost, he probably would lose too, especially against a strong

Republican like Ottinger. But if he refused to run in the face of Smith's extreme need, and if Smith lost New York by only a little, where would Franklin Roosevelt stand in the estimation of all those New York Democrats? What would they say when he was ready to run in 1930 or 1932? Then he would be the man who had selfishly thrown away Al Smith's only chance at the White House.

But what about his legs? What about that walk across the living room?

Dr. Hubbard said he believed Roosevelt might gain another 20 percent of his lost strength. If so — and FDR must have known it was only a guess — that was significant. But would it be enough to walk safely on his own, and without braces? Probably not. Yet it was possible.

If he gave up that chance, would the governorship, if he could win it, compensate him for the loss? Would the presidency?

Now Smith was asking a new question, the one Roosevelt had feared: If the convention nominated Roosevelt the next day, would he refuse to run?

He hesitated. Again, Missy, standing near, said: "Don't you *dare.*"

FDR said that if the delegates acted entirely on their own, he didn't know what

471

he would do.

No more questions! Smith yelled. That was good enough for him.

Outside, Egbert Curtis was waiting to drive them back to the cottage. Finally he asked: Was Roosevelt going to run?

"Curt," he said, "when you're in politics, you've got to play the game."

The next day the convention in Rochester nominated him for governor, and he wired his acceptance.

Some time later, Roosevelt told one of his sons what was probably the plain truth of it: "I just figured it was now or never."

Missy LeHand would tell friends she thought FDR would rather have walked than become president, and that the steps he took unaided that weekend showed he might have done so had he refused the call to run for governor.

But if that were true, why did he give up his chance to walk and submit to the Rochester draft?

"I didn't want it," FDR said later. "I wanted, much more, to get my . . . leg to move! But the moral pressure was too strong."

Certainly Raskob's offer of financial help had opened the door. FDR had committed a great deal of his money to Warm Springs at a moment when he thought it would be not only a center for polio but a booming resort. In the two years since, the vision of a resort had faded, and now he held a property that needed his sustained attention if he were ever to recoup his investment. He could not give it that attention as governor. Raskob was offering a way out.

Possibly there had been other phone calls. A rumor went around that Roosevelt feared that if he refused Smith in his hour of utmost need, Tammany Hall would exert its influence to steer business away from Fidelity & Deposit and Basil O'Connor's law firm. That was plausible but never proven.

But it seems more likely that for once Missy had her man wrong — that much as he would like to walk again, he wanted to be president more, and his best route to the White House went through Albany. If he said no to Smith when Smith was all but begging him, he would run a grave risk of alienating the New York Democrats for good, especially if Smith were to lose the state's electoral votes in November. He made the decision to run for governor under duress at the last possible moment. He would have preferred not to make it. But it was in keeping with decisions he had made all along. He never had pursued his recovery as diligently as he had pursued the presidency. And he had discovered ways of compensating for the loss of his mobility. If the founding and directing of the experiment at Warm Springs had given him that gift, how much more rewarding would the presidency be?

The timing was not what he had planned. This did not look like a terribly good chance to step toward the presidency. But it was the only chance he had. Now the question was not whether he ought to run, but whether, as a man who could not walk on his own, he could win.

CHAPTER 14
"DO I LOOK LIKE
A SICK MAN?"

OCTOBER TO NOVEMBER 1928

As the Democrats streamed away from the Rochester convention hall, their mood transformed, New York Republicans found themselves staring at a strange and elusive foe. Seldom if ever had there been a candidate for high office who could not stand and walk by himself. What were the Republicans going to say about *that*?

For the moment, their nominee would be no help. Albert Ottinger planned no speeches for nearly two weeks, and he promised a campaign free of "mudslinging" and "destructive criticism." But Republican editorialists could hardly stay silent about an issue as obvious as the Democratic nominee's physical condition.

A few of them — mostly in the upstate towns where the Grand Old Party was unchallenged — did not hesitate to be perfectly blunt. Roosevelt was "a sick man . . . in a sanitarium," said the editor of a little paper in Dunkirk, New York. He was "crippled," said the *Jamestown Journal,* so "he cannot stand the strain." His unfitness for the governorship was no less than "a self-evident truth."

"Republicans are as sorry as anyone could be that Franklin Roosevelt is not in robust health," said the *Albany Telegram.* "But they are not going to be misled by that fact into supposing that he ought to be elected governor."

But most editorialists who favored the GOP were more circumspect. As the *Buffalo News* put it, "mere discussion of the qualifications of Mr. Roosevelt becomes painful in the circumstances."

Why painful?

It was, at least in part, a matter of what was "sporting" and "not sporting." The "gentlemen of the press" may have included few gentlemen by the standards of Sara Delano Roosevelt, but Marquis of Queensberry rules still governed most of the nation's news columns. A boxer did not punch a man when he was down on one knee. Boy Scouts were instructed not to torment "the weak and helpless."

And most people, especially most New Yorkers, could recall with instantaneous contempt what Ty Cobb had done to a crippled man in June 1912. The Detroit Tigers had been in town to play the High-landers, predecessors of the Yankees. In center field was the Tigers' star, Cobb, the Georgia-born son of a Confederate soldier, violent on and off the field, and deeply defensive of his region's racial mores. Twelve rows up in the grandstand was one Claude Lueker, a New York fan well known for the catcalls he hurled at opposing players down on the field. In an industrial accident, Lueker had lost all the fingers of one hand and three fingers of the other. In the sixth inning Lueker called Cobb a "half-nigger," whereupon Cobb leaped into the stands and attacked Lueker with his fists. When by-standers shouted at Cobb to lay off, since the man had no hands, Cobb went on punching. He vowed afterward that he would have done the same if the man had had no feet. The beating of Claude Lueker became the most odious episode in the legend of Cobb's viciousness — not because he had responded to a racist taunt but because he had "hit a cripple."

In the code of sporting ethics, to "hit a cripple" was the unforgivable sin.

Now the Republican press was in the ring facing a man whom most people would not hesitate to call a cripple, a man who had been knocked down and was not yet fully up on his feet. If you couldn't hit a cripple, how were you supposed to run against him?

To deal with this dilemma, foes of the Democrats devised an ingenious strategem. It aimed at two for the price of one. Without "hitting a cripple," they could knock Roosevelt down with a blow at their bigger and more important enemy: Al Smith.

Franklin Roosevelt was not the villain of the drama, the GOP editorialists said. Far from it. Roosevelt was "a man whom New Yorkers respect and honor," "able and honest," "a thorough gentleman." It was *Al Smith* who had played "cruel politics" with a cripple, Al Smith who had placed a sick man in danger, his *friend.*

"There is something both pathetic and pitiless in the 'drafting' of Franklin D. Roosevelt by Alfred E. Smith," the *New York Evening Post* scolded. If he were healthy, Roosevelt "would make one of the best gubernatorial aspirants New York has ever had. . . . But even his own friends, out of very love of him, will hesitate to vote for him now. They will know that not only the 'cold climate' of Albany but also its killing hard work are no curatives for a man struggling out of one of the most relentless of modern diseases." The drafting of Roosevelt was "a reprehensible act," "almost a political crime," "a cruel physical sacrifice for the sake of helping Smith carry New York." The *Buffalo News* said "nothing has been more amazing in the career of Gov. Smith than his display of callousness with respect to his friend's health."

Smith had shown his true colors again. He was a Bowery thug, a dirty streetfighter, the sort of fellow who would hit a cripple.

And if Smith was "pitiless," then pity was the proper emotion for the likes of Franklin Roosevelt — "the poor man," "such a sad story," "too bad about him." You didn't have to punch the cripple to put him out of the fight. You could render him useless by sheer pity.

But the Democrats punched back. Smith countered the direct assault on FDR's fitness for the job. The new nominee, he told reporters, was "as strong mentally as he ever was; he is right at his prime"; and "he is as well physically as he ever was excepting that the muscles in the lower part of his legs do not function and he has trouble walking. But the governor of the state works with his head, not his feet. A governor is not elected to do backhand turns and flipflops. Ninety-five percent of his work is done at his desk. The story will be spread around that Mr.

Roosevelt will not be able to do the work. That, of course, is absurd."

FDR himself took on the more artful task of responding to the indirect blow — the accusation of cruelty leveled against Smith. He had a statement dictated to the New York papers by telephone even before he boarded the train out of Warm Springs.

"I am amazed to hear that efforts are being made to make it appear that I have been 'sacrificed' by Gov. Smith to further his own election," he said, "and that my personal friends should vote against me to prevent such sacrifice. Let me set this matter straight at once. I was not dragooned into running by the Governor. On the contrary, he fully appreciated the reasons for my reluctance and was willing to give up such advantage as he felt my candidacy might bring him in deference to my wishes. I was drafted because all of the party leaders when they assembled insisted that my often-expressed belief in the policies of Governor Smith made my nomination the best assurance to the voters that these policies would be continued. . . . I trust this statement will eliminate this particular bit of nonsense from the campaign from the very beginning."

The Democrats' allies in the press applauded FDR's retort and rushed to Smith's defense, lampooning the Republicans' "crocodile tears" for a crippled candidate. There was truth in FDR's claim that it had not been Smith himself who insisted he run — the governor had been willing to let FDR off the hook — but the clashing party leaders, who could agree only on Roosevelt and thus forced Smith's hand.

But there was logic in the Republicans' position too. *We* weren't the ones who said his health was no good, they pointed out. *Roosevelt* said it, not a week before, in a message to Smith that was sent to all the papers, and they quoted from it: "My doctors are very definite in stating that the continued improvement in my condition is dependent on my avoidance of cold climate and on taking exercises here at Warm Springs in the cold winter months." Of course he had meant what he said literally: that the governorship would put at risk only further improvement in his mobility, not his otherwise excellent health. But that was too fine a distinction to count for much in the midst of a political campaign. The guy himself had said his doctors were against him running; now he was running anyway?

FDR tried to wriggle away from the apparent contradiction, but the stubborn question stood: Was he fit for the job or not?

That was the crux of it. The only way to prove his fitness was to put himself on public display.

He had been rehearsing for this performance. He had hoped to have at least two more years to prepare. He had fought for the extra time. But circumstances and the party had forced him to yield. Now the performance was upon him.

The role he must play was a paradox. Normally the actor puts on a mask and becomes someone else. FDR's role now was to play the man he actually was — a strong man capable of leadership in the highest seats of power. The trick was to remove the mask that his audience would otherwise force him to wear. He must persuade the audience to discard its ancient, inherited belief about a man who was crippled. He must persuade them that a crippled man could be strong.

Louis Howe set up a long and adulatory feature story in the friendly *New York Sun,* politically independent but enthusiastic about FDR. Howe's chosen conduit was Edwin C. Hill, the *Sun*'s human-interest ace, who was given a couple of hours with the candidate in his study on East 65th Street. It was a lovely spot for an interview with a "high type of Democrat," an elegant retreat lined with selected prints of schooners and steamers from the candidate's magnificent collection. The headline telegraphed the campaign's key message: "F.D. ROOSEVELT, TITAN OF ENERGY, RUNS MULTIFARIOUS ENTERPRISES: LIST OF ACTIVITIES HE'S HEADING READS LIKE A BUSINESS DIRECTORY." Hill opened the door wide for Roosevelt to list all of his responsibilities — from the ownership of Warm Springs to the presidency of the Ship Model Society — and to clarify his condition, silence old suspicions, and retell the well-honed comeback narrative.

Could he really handle the physical demands of a campaign, Hill asked — travel, speechmaking, handshaking?

"Absolutely," the candidate replied. "There has been a lot of ridiculous stuff talked and printed about my physical condition. Look at me. Do I look like a sick man or one whose energy was weak?"

"Not in the least," said the visitor.

"I haven't felt so well or so vigorous in years," Mr. Roosevelt went on. "Little by little I am conquering the muscular weakness which took the use of my legs away from me in 1921. It takes a long time to

483

beat infantile paralysis, but it can be done, and I am doing it. I made up my mind that I was going to do it and I have never taken my mind off the job. But, after all, muscular weakness in one's legs has nothing whatever to do with the vigor and endurance of one's mind."

And his case had been perfectly "normal," he pointed out, "having nothing whatever to do with cerebro-spinal meningitis, bringing about muscular weakness of the legs and having no effect whatever upon mental strength or general health."

Hill's reassuring message set a tone, but Roosevelt's physical performance was the real message, and the campaign now exhibited the candidate from one end of the state of New York to the other. Traveling by auto caravan with his new African-American valet, Irwin McDuffie; Samuel Rosenman, an aide of Smith's, to help with speeches; Herbert Lehman, the nominee for lieutenant governor; and lesser candidates from down the ticket, Roosevelt raced across the southern tier of Republican farm counties, up to Buffalo and then to Rochester, where people lined the sidewalks to see the cavalcade roll into town, and where eight hundred stood in line to shake his hand at the

Seneca Hotel.

That night, October 21, with two weeks until the election, before a crowd of four thousand in the Rochester Convention Hall where he had been nominated three weeks earlier, FDR placed the issue of his disability squarely on the table.

From their seats, people could see precisely what he was: a tall, good-looking man who stood perfectly straight, not bent or bowed, and who moved with a slow, swaying gait, one hand with the cane, the other hand on an aide's arm. They saw him cross the stage, then drop into a heavy armchair, fiddle for an instant with the braces under his trouser legs, and bend his knees. They saw him listen as others spoke, tossing his head with laughter, then, when his turn came, he got to his feet with an aide's help — "and they had not failed to notice the smile on his face," the *New York World*'s reporter said.

For several days he had been choosing his topics as any other candidate would; he had talked about Al Smith, Albert Ottinger, the use of the state's rivers for the public good, Prohibition. Now he said he would speak about a new issue. He said he wished to speak about his plan to do more for the hundred thousand New Yorkers who were disabled and unable to pay for the treatments that might help them recover their mobility.

"I may be pardoned," he said, the smile gone, "if I refer to my own intense interest in the care of crippled children, and indeed of cripples of every kind."

At this, people began to rise to their feet and applaud. The *World* reporter heard women cry.

Roosevelt waited for the noise to subside, then went on: "People readily recognize that I myself furnish a perfectly good example of what can be done by the right kind of care." Cheers resumed. "I dislike to use this personal example, but do so because it fits. Seven years ago, through an attack of infantile paralysis, I was completely put out of any useful activity."

Now one woman was "sobbing audibly."

"By personal good fortune, I was able to get the best kind of medical care. The result is that today I am on my feet . . ."

Now the applause was making it impossible to hear him, and his smile came back, assured, triumphant.

"I am on my feet," he cried, "and entirely capable, at least from the physical point of view, of running any business, whether a private business or that of the government of the state of New York!"

With the deftest touch, he was learning to use his disability to his advantage. He must not seem to be asking for votes on the basis of pity — that would be disastrous. But he could, instead, show himself to be something he had never been seen as before: a fighter and, better yet, an underdog; not a man to pity, not a man to envy, but a man to cheer.

The pace of the campaign only accelerated. At stop after stop, he would blast the Republicans, reel off a list of the towns where he had spoken that day or that week, and then, with a pause and a wink, he would cry: "Too bad about this unfortunate sick man, isn't it!" or "Too bad about this helpless, hopeless invalid!"

Still, rumors surged around him. If elected, Roosevelt would serve a few weeks, then quit, letting Herbert Lehman take over as governor. Worse: Roosevelt would be dead within months. Al Smith himself was partly to blame for this buzz, since he had spoken freely and hamhandedly about how Lehman could be a historically strong lieutenant governor, filling in whenever Roosevelt needed to be in Warm Springs. And probably the Republicans did all they could to grow that seed into something more sinister.

With "sane and sensible people" writing to ask if the stories were true, FDR stomped on them hard. He tossed aside a prepared speech and powdered the Republican leaders of "both the nation and the state" as "the stupidest and most narrow-minded and most bigoted we have ever witnessed."

If anyone thought a cripple couldn't fight, he was showing them otherwise now.

"I thought that with Halloween over these ghost stories would be forgotten. . . . All I can say is that if I could keep on in this campaign steadily for another twelve months I would throw away my cane." At this the crowd erupted and William Woodford, the *World*'s man in Roosevelt's press entourage, practically cheered himself, telling his readers in an aside: "It is a fact that Mr. Roosevelt appears in better health today than he did at the outset of his campaign three weeks ago."

Now "considerably wrought up," FDR took up the resignation rumor: "I want to say in passing that if anything should happen to me, as some of my friends apparently hope it will in January, you will probably get as governor a much better man than I am in the shape and form of Herbert H. Lehman. But . . . I'd hate to see some of the Republican papers: 'Roosevelt denies he is going to resign from office.' . . .

"No, I am going to say this, that no man running for public office, be it Governor Smith or for the office of dog catcher, has the right to have in the back of his head or in the front of his head any intention whatsoever of doing anything but serving out the full term of his office." Then came his prepared blasts at Albert Ottinger and, for good measure, Herbert Hoover himself.

Then he was in the Bronx, talking up the State Federation of Labor and gaily telling the *Sun*'s reporter: "Anyone who doubts my ability to get around should have seen me clamber down the fire escape last night at the Flushing High School!"

"Independent Democrats who are against Smith because he is a Catholic are for Roosevelt," one reporter noted. "Independent Republicans who are against Ottinger because he is a Jew are for Roosevelt. Ottinger does not seem to be able to profit in this strange division along the lines of intolerance." In the ugly political atmosphere of 1928, many were prepared to base their vote on antipathies of class and creed. But it does not seem to have occurred to many to vote against a man because of his disability.

Smith lost the presidential election to Herbert Hoover in a landslide and lost his beloved home state. Roosevelt won — just by a little, but he ran well ahead of Smith statewide. He might have owed Smith his nomination, but he had won the race for governor on his own.

CHAPTER 15
"CAMPAIGN OF WHISPERS"
1929 TO 1932

Seven years into his disability, Roosevelt had proven to himself and the people who watched him at close range that he could stand the strain of a campaign for high office. And not only had he won that campaign, but he had won partly on the strength of what he had become in the public eye — a man who had overcome a terrible hardship. The thing that had seemed impossible in 1921 had been accomplished. Now he not only had the name of Roosevelt. He had staked his own claim to Theodore Roosevelt's aura.

Governing New York would demand less of his body than campaigning — a lot less. The governor's job was most difficult when the assembly was in session. But that was only three or four months a year, and it was mostly a desk job. If he could handle a month of full-tilt campaigning around the state of New York, he could handle three months a year at a desk. He had worked a lot harder at Warm Springs.

As governor of the nation's most populous state, he would execute public responsibilities second only to those of the presidency itself. That was what made the governor's chair a stepping-stone to the White House. Seven governors or former governors of New York had won their party's nomination for president. Three had gone on to the White House — one of every ten presidents to date. Even though FDR had won by less than half of one percent of all votes cast, politicians and reporters spoke of him as a leading candidate for the next Democratic presidential nomination from the moment Albert Ottinger conceded defeat — a moment Ottinger put off for twelve days until it was clear the official canvass would confirm FDR's tiny edge.

Tiny edge or no, he was delighted to be governor of New York and he meant to be a good one. But as the columnist Joseph Alsop — FDR's distant cousin on the Oyster Bay side — would write, "a memorable performance in the narrow confines of Albany was not what Roosevelt was really aiming for. He was aiming, rather, for the White House itself."

The year 1936, eight years away, still

looked like the next good chance for a Democrat to become president. Herbert Hoover was a revered figure and he had won the presidency in a landslide. If "Coolidge prosperity" lasted long enough to become "Hoover prosperity," there was every likelihood that Hoover would win a second term. That meant there was plenty of time for Roosevelt to maneuver, time to build the foundation of a strong national campaign. He would need a creditable record that appealed to key constituencies; a growing network of friendships throughout the whole party; and, eventually, a national organization. And he must find ways to close or bridge his party's fractures over Prohibition and religion.

Of course these were the problems that any hopeful Democrat faced. Roosevelt faced another. Since leaving Warm Springs in early October 1928, the problem of his physical condition had been not the condition itself but what people thought of the condition. In the campaign for governor he had surmounted that challenge by persuading a bare majority of New York voters that his infirmity should not bar him from power — and as a bonus he learned that his comeback story retained a political power all its own. Now he had to master the same challenge on the larger stage of the whole country. But that job must begin right in Albany, and even before his inauguration. It must begin with Al Smith.

Years later, FDR received a letter from Adolphus Ragan, a New York attorney who had worked for the Democratic National Committee during Smith's campaign in 1928. The letter contained Ragan's confidential account — which he insisted was "definitely and positively known by me and others to be exactly 100% true" — of a remark Smith made in his private rail car on the way home to New York City from the Rochester convention where Roosevelt was nominated. According to Ragan, "one of the delegates, namely, Daniel E. Finn, a Tammany district leader and subsequently county clerk and sheriff of New York County, took a seat beside Governor Smith and in the course of their conversation said, 'Al, aren't you afraid that you are raising up a rival who will some day cause you trouble?' Whereupon the Governor, in his rasping voice remarked: 'No, Dan, he won't live a year!' "

On its face, as Ragan said, the comment seemed to express "unbelieveable callousness." But if Ragan didn't hear the remark himself — or Smith's tone when he made it, as apparently he did not — he may have been repeating a simplified version of words that were a good deal less cold in the original than they sounded in the retelling. Smith was not a cold and callous man. His words might been spoken with a shrug of the shoulders, in a who-knows-what-might-happen tone, especially if the actual words were something more like "he *might not* live a year." But whatever Smith's exact words and tone, Ragan's tale only reinforces what was already well known: Al Smith had deep doubts about his successor's ability to endure the stress and strain of being governor of New York.

After all, it was Smith himself, more than anyone else, who had listened to Roosevelt explain again and again why he should not run for governor in his current condition. All right, the man had now endured a surprisingly good campaign and won. But Smith knew the score from Roosevelt himself, and his own exhaustion and illnesses during eight years as governor told him the job would simply be too much for a cripple. Roosevelt was his friend — not a close one, but a friend. Smith had slept under his roof. He may have felt a twinge of remorse for his role in forcing Roosevelt to run. And in the wake of the election, Smith had his own future to think of. His defeat at Hoover's hands, with all the hatred directed at his beloved Church, had left him drained and demoralized. He said he was done with politics, but what was he going to do instead? The governorship had made him a very big man. Politics was his life's work, and his large achievements in New York were his legacy. He didn't want to lose the life he loved, and he didn't want to see his legacy squandered by a weakling.

So he resolved to help. He would be around whenever Roosevelt needed him. He would see to it that the transition from the Smith to the Roosevelt administration would be seamless. Perhaps he could even keep one hand on the tiller. He would speak to FDR about reappointing the two most important members of his administration: Belle Moskowitz, his top assistant and political advisor; and Robert Moses, his secretary of state.

If FDR did not hear of Smith's specific remark on the train back from Rochester, he certainly knew such talk was going around. In his reply to Adolphus Ragan — this was ten years later — he wrote: "There were a good many people who at that time, in 1928, believed — some of them honestly and some of them because they wanted to — that I was headed for a tombstone." And if "a good many" thought that, many more must have harbored at least a doubt about FDR's stamina — probably even many who had voted for him for governor. His name had risen in the trail of Smith's comet. Will Rogers had remarked that, until now, Franklin Roosevelt had been known chiefly as "the man that any time as many as three persons met, either in conference or convention, would arise and nominate Al Smith for president. You could just wake him in the middle of the night and he would start to nominating Al." He could not continue to be known as that man.

FDR was to be inaugurated on January 1, 1929. By December 1928 both he and Smith had returned north from their southern vacations. It became known that upon his return to Albany, Governor Smith booked a suite of rooms in the city's Hotel DeWitt Clinton for the first six weeks of Roosevelt's term.

"Well, Frank," Smith said when the two spoke next, "you won't have to worry about being governor. You can come to Albany for the inauguration and stay around for a while and get the hang of things, and when you get a chance you can hop back to Warm Springs, and we'll be here to see that things go all right."

"Al," FDR replied, "did you ever leave Albany for any extended stay during a legislative session?"

"No," Smith said.

"Then I won't either."

But that was only the beginning of it.

On the evening of January 1, 1929 — the day FDR was inaugurated in the traditional ceremony in the state capitol in Albany — Eleanor invited special guests to come over to the mansion for an informal supper. One of these was Frances Perkins, whom FDR had asked to become head of the state commission on labor — in effect, the first woman to serve as a cabinet officer in New York. She was not only accomplished and brilliant but a highly perceptive judge of people. She was also married to a man who had been institutionalized with mental illness; she knew more than most about the effects of disability in the circles that revolved around a disabled man.

As the meal wound down, FDR and Al Smith retreated to a side parlor. They talked for a long time. Perkins happened to pass the open door and saw Smith pull his chair closer to Roosevelt's and lean in. On Roosevelt's face Perkins saw an expression she would come to know well during years of close contact. "Smith was telling him things and the governor was nodding in answer," Perkins said later. "I remember Roosevelt's expression. . . . He pulled his lips down, making a sort of a long lip. When he pulled his lips down in that way, later I always knew that he was evading."

A few days later, Roosevelt told Perkins what the parlor discussion had been about. Smith had urged FDR to retain Belle Moskowitz, by title Smith's secretary but in reality his chief political advisor, legislative director, and fund-raiser. When FDR asked Perkins what she thought of this, she said what everyone in Albany knew: that Mrs. Moskowitz was "terribly able." FDR remarked that Eleanor had said the same thing, that Moskowitz meant well and would do well; but also that he must realize Belle Moskowitz was smarter than most people and she enjoyed the exercise of power, and if he kept her on she would run the show for him as she had run the show for Smith. That might be good — a strong administrator to handle the daily grind of the governorship. According to Perkins, Eleanor had told FDR: "Perhaps that's the best thing to do. I don't know how strongly you feel." (Just after the election, Eleanor herself had written FDR: "Don't let Mrs. Moskowitz get draped around you for she means to be and it will always be one for you and two for Al!")

FDR already had told Smith he would not reappoint Robert Moses as secretary of state. Overbearing and ruthless, Moses, like Moskowitz, was a brilliant operator in the state's administrative labyrinth. He had engineered the overhaul and expansion of the state's parks and highways, accounting for a good deal of Smith's popularity and prestige. But Roosevelt and Moses had fought; they disliked and distrusted each other. No one expected Moses to stay on. But Moskowitz might be a different matter.

As the conversation continued, Perkins recalled, FDR said: "Right at this moment, as I am now . . . I musn't allow myself to be pushed around, because I might get into the habit. It would be easy because I haven't got my full strength." But he asked Perkins to sound Moskowitz out.

Moskowitz said she would indeed take the job if FDR asked.

Then Al Smith asked to see Perkins. He told her that if FDR wanted, he would be happy to come up to Albany a couple of days a week during assembly sessions, see people on the governor's behalf, and generally "help with a lot of things" — and the best way to make this work would be to reappoint Belle Moskowitz as secretary, since that "would enable me to help . . . so easily."

Finally Smith called FDR to ask for a meeting. Roosevelt disposed of the unsettled question right on the phone. He told Al he was very sorry, but although he was reappointing most of Smith's department heads, he had decided he could not keep Mrs. Moskowitz, since he needed a large and sturdy man in the secretary's position, one who could help him with physical accommodations, especially when traveling. He told Perkins what had happened, and she later recalled her "very real sense, as I rode home on the train that night, of this man, sick and struggling, having almost lost his will power at one time in his illness, just grabbing to keep his will power. He must do it himself. He must think it himself. He must feel it himself. He must realize it himself. It must be his."

Early in 1929 Smith went up to Albany for a couple of weekends and accepted the Roosevelts' invitation to stay over at the mansion. He would sit down to Saturday supper with the family and their other guests — Smith was especially fond of Eleanor and enjoyed her conversation about politics — but then everyone would retire and Smith would come back from Mass Sunday morning to find that FDR was still in bed. Then more people would be in and out, and pretty soon Smith would have to catch the train for New York City after snatching hardly any time for the two men to talk alone. FDR was using his expertise in diversionary tactics, Frances Perkins said, and at first Smith "didn't realize he was getting the brush-off."

Gradually, it dawned on the former governor that his protégé was giving him the cold shoulder, and he began to complain privately that Roosevelt was ungrateful: Had he not given FDR his chance? Hadn't he lifted an invalid out of his political wilderness and pushed him up to the governorship?

But FDR had his own reasons for resentment, or at least for believing he owed Al less than Al thought. Yes, the campaign had come out well and he was now governor — but hardly because of Smith's coattails. It was FDR who had run ahead of Smith statewide, not the other way around. And in his own private circle, FDR said the Republican editorialists had been right after all: Smith and his party cronies *had* dragooned FDR into running. He had wanted to stay out of the race and keep working on his recovery, but the party boys had leaned and leaned on him. FDR could not forget that he had taken his first few steps unaided just the weekend before he was drafted to run. That had been possible only because of long-sustained work with the physios at Warm Springs. He could not sustain such a regimen as a fully engaged governor, and it was a short step from that observation to the belief that he had sacrificed the possibility of walking on his own to Al Smith's yearning for the White House. FDR had done what Smith asked. So who owed whom?

Shortly after the 1928 election, when he and his aides were at Warm Springs preparing for the governorship, there was a new young secretary, Grace Tully, who had been hired during the campaign but had no idea whether she would have a job after Roosevelt's inauguration. Day after day, she heard Roosevelt speak to her of things "we would take care of in Albany" and what would happen "when we go to Albany."

Finally Tully spoke up to ask: "When *who* goes to Albany, Governor?" "Why," he replied, "I mean us, all of us. Of course you are going to Albany, child." He had not bothered to ask, and he did not expect to be turned down. He could be remiss about expressing thanks too. The politico Jim Farley, after falling out with Roosevelt years later, remarked that FDR never thanked him for his critically important work running Roosevelt's campaigns.

This presumptuous way of dealing with people whom he needed — some of whom dedicated much of their careers and even their personal lives to him — was not his most attractive trait. But in other ways he was not an ungenerous friend, and he was certainly not an unkind or unthinking boss — quite the contrary. It was the matter of always being helped that nettled him. He depended on Irwin McDuffie to help him to the toilet and to get dressed, to move from room to room and chair to chair, and on McDuffie and other men, including his sons, to keep from crashing to the floor. He was dependent enough on others. He did not care to constantly remind himself of the fact by asking and thanking people for the help they gave. And he was certainly not going to ask Al Smith or Belle Moskowitz or Robert Moses to help him be governor of New York.

Frances Perkins saw dire consequences for Democrats in the widening fracture in the Smith-Roosevelt partnership. She told her friend Belle Moskowitz that Smith had to find something else to do; he risked making a fool of himself.

"I know," Moskowitz said, "but Franklin Roosevelt can never run that show. Somebody's got to help him, and Al loves the state."

"Suppose Al had been president," Perkins retorted. "What would have happened? We all anticipated that Al wasn't going to hang around here running New York. He was going to go to Washington and be president."

"Well, he could have helped him."

Perkins went to see the former governor himself. She thought if Smith could be made to understand FDR's sensitivities, he might devise ways to help that FDR could accept. They could remain friends, and the fragile unity of the New York party — perhaps of the national party — could be protected.

Perkins told Smith "why Franklin Roosevelt, more than the average person, had to be left alone and had to have an opportunity to see what he could do without help. . . .

On account of Roosevelt's sickness and his crippledness he had a more than ordinary necessity to demonstrate himself as a political entity able to operate alone. . . . If help was to be given to him, it must be in such a subtle and impersonal way that it didn't appear to be help. It couldn't be direct advice.

"I tried to put it on the grounds of the way people feel towards their mother who likes to give them good advice," Perkins said later. "At a certain age they have to throw it off or they never learn to do it themselves.

"I remember that as the words came out of my mouth I knew that I was saying the wrong thing to Al Smith because he couldn't understand it at all. That wasn't the way he felt about his mother or supposed . . . anybody felt about their mother. Your mother is somebody you always listen to, in Al Smith's view . . . and her advice is always good and given to you for your own good. In other words, he had a perfect American-Irish mother complex that mother is always right and you always listen to her. . . .

"He would grunt and say, 'Hm, hm, yeah, well, perhaps, yeah, well, I see. Well, I've got nothing against Frank and would be delighted to see him any time.' "

FDR continued to see Smith now and then, but he kept the talk superficial and he asked Smith for nothing of substance. As Perkins had perceived, his fierce determination to be his own man surely was reinforced by his sensitivity about his physical condition, and it ignited a resentment in Smith that would grow and grow in the years to come, driving him farther into the arms of wealthy conservatives like John J. Raskob, who told him Roosevelt was a dangerous radical. It hurt and angered Belle Moskowitz, who remained a force in New York politics and fanned the flames of Smith's resentment. And in time it would spawn the single gravest threat to FDR's ambition for the presidency.

Roosevelt was now a public official with myriad public duties. In some ways this made life with disability easier to manage. In other ways it required new forms of ingenuity, new routines to cope with his immobility.

He had employed personal assistants for years, but now, with the governor's right to a full staff, he could recruit and rely on several more. To replace Belle Moskowitz in the official post of secretary to the governor, he named a former All-American basketball star at Cornell, Guernsey Cross, a New York assemblyman to whom he owed a political favor. (Of course, Louis Howe continued as FDR's chief aide and Missy LeHand carried on as his personal secretary.) Two powerful state policemen soon became members of FDR's inner circle: Gus Gennerich and Earl Miller. With the valet Irwin McDuffie, these men could share the work of making FDR mobile without draining FDR's personal funds.

Gennerich and Miller were bodyguards. But just as important — perhaps more so — they were stewards of Roosevelt's disabled body. When necessary, they carried him up and down steps and over obstacles, and, with McDuffie, they managed Roosevelt's wheelchair. This was critical.

Behind closed doors, in small gatherings with family and truly close friends — Eleanor, Sara, and his children; Louis and Missy; his personal staff and servants; close friends like Henry and Elinor Morgenthau, Nancy Cook and Marion Dickerman, and a number of others — FDR used his wheelchair without self-consciousness, though only to be pushed from room to room. As he had since the fall of 1921, he used a modest wooden chair with no arms. Once in a room, including his office, he would always shift to a regular chair, often with pads to lend extra support for his frame. He had done it this way for years and would continue to do so. Hence it has always been a maudlin exaggeration to say Roosevelt "spent his life in a wheelchair" or "was confined to a wheelchair." The wheelchair was a convenience he used for a few minutes several times a day, holding tight to the seat with one hand to keep from sliding off, and he stayed on the seat no longer than he had to.

The shift from a regular chair to the wheelchair looked easy, but it was a delicate maneuver. It took agility, upper-body strength, and a strong and experienced assistant — usually McDuffie, Gennerich, or Miller, sometimes one of the sons — who held the empty wheelchair nearly at a right angle to Roosevelt's position, bracing the chair firmly with one knee. Generally FDR would not be wearing braces on his legs. Those were only for public occasions when he needed to stand or walk. He would plant his hands on the arms of his regular chair, then thrust upward, twist his body, and land on the seat of the wheelchair. The assistant had to be not only strong but quick to react, shifting the wheelchair slightly to right or left to catch FDR as he came over. The movement in the other direction, from wheelchair to chair, was more difficult because the wheelchair had no arms, so he could not push himself up from it. His balance when sitting in the armless chair was precarious. If he leaned too far from a sitting position he risked a fall. And there was always a danger that a chair would slip or he would miss his grip — and then he would fall to the floor. His grandson Curtis Roosevelt, Anna's son, watched what he called "the flip" many times in later years. He said members of the family "always worried that 'Pa might not make it.' "

With people who were not his intimates, the possibility of a fall raised the danger not only of injury but of deep embarrassment, both to Roosevelt himself and to everyone present. FDR's "very keen sense of privacy" militated against taking the risk, Curtis Roosevelt recalled. If he fell, Curtis said, "you'd see FDR sprawled on the floor, which not only was undignified for a normal person, but absolutely impossible for somebody who was as sensitive about his infirmity [as he was]."

The fear of falling between chairs was the principal reason FDR did not use a wheelchair in public, whether outdoors or indoors. The scarcity of photographs showing him in a wheelchair suggests that he thought the chair, as a symbol, would magnify the stigma he must always fight. But he avoided displays of the wheelchair in many settings, such as private dinners and receptions, where there was little danger of being photographed. In these cases he was protecting feelings — his own and those of others — not his public image. He would have himself wheeled into the room where the gathering was to occur before others were brought in. The "flip" was done in private and the danger of a fall was put out of the way. Then guests would enter the room with FDR already comfortably seated and secure.

This was not an effort to deceive anyone. It was an effort to put people at ease who might feel embarrassed and uneasy in moments when FDR's inability to use his legs in the normal way was especially obvious. If such uneasiness was an index of the stigma associated with disability, all Roosevelt could do about that was to keep proving a disabled man could do a big job. He was not a crusader for the rights of the disabled; he was governor of New York. In that job, he would follow whatever routines he needed to follow to ease his relations with others. Deception was not the word for it. "There is no disguising the fact . . . that he is a crippled man," wrote Milton MacKaye of the *New Yorker,* "and one of the admirable things about Roosevelt is that he never attempts to disguise it." He took no pains to keep himself hidden away. "Getting in to see the Governor is hardly more difficult than dropping in on your pastor," MacKaye wrote. "He will see anyone, and by anyone I mean that even insurance salesmen have eluded his secretaries." He dropped in on staff tea parties every afternoon and brought in guests for dinner nearly every night, often as many as twenty-five.

For those who saw him often, his condition retreated to the edge of consciousness. He did not mention it; they did not ask. Reticence prevailed. The cane and crutches and wheelchair became part of the furniture, and the hours filled up with his talk: debate, decisions, gossip, political news, the trees he'd planted at Hyde Park, the fellow he'd met in Atlanta, the price of cotton, the joke an admiral had told in 1917.

Occasionally mishaps occurred. Once, during FDR's governorship, a distant cousin in the Oyster Bay branch, Nicholas Roosevelt, a Republican diplomat then serving as U.S. ambassador to Hungary, was invited for a weekend at Hyde Park. A plan was made to go for a drive in FDR's hand-controlled car. Nicholas Roosevelt stood with FDR's mother as the car was brought around from the garage. They watched "El-liot [Roosevelt] and Gus Gennerich . . . carry him down the steps and place him in the car. As they turned and left him he lost his balance . . . and he fell over on the car seat. I doubt if one man in a thousand as disabled and dependent on others would have refrained from some sort of reproach, however mild, to those whose carelessness had thus left him in the lurch. But Franklin merely lay on his back, waved his strong arms in the air, and laughed. At once they came back and helped him to his seat behind the wheel, and he called me to join him. For a moment I had seen the true spirit of the man. He was not putting on an act. Rather was it the instinctive reaction of a brave and gallant gentleman — as illuminating as it was moving and inspiring."

For the big dinners and receptions that a governor must host and attend, Eleanor and Frances Perkins devised a clever system right at the start of Roosevelt's term. On these occasions, the two women knew, he would need to shake hands and to speak with many people. He had to make new contacts and nurture old ones. He could generally afford only a few minutes with any one person, and some he would rather avoid. Yet because he had to sit in one place, he could not slip from one chatting group to another; could not hustle over to catch a committee chairman before he left the party; could not evade a windbag. So Eleanor and Perkins recruited a few intimates to act as scouts and messengers, hovering in the mingling crowd. If someone made a beeline toward the governor, a scout would intercede, striking up a conversation. Eleanor, meanwhile, kept an eye on FDR and the person he was speaking with. After a few minutes, she would deputize a messenger to seek out someone else and say: "Wouldn't you like to have a little talk with the governor?" Delighted, the invitee would come along for his reward, displacing the previous invitee. The practice kept FDR from being mobbed and it allowed him to talk with many people — and the right people.

"Of Roosevelt as Governor," his cousin Joseph Alsop would write, "it is almost enough to say that he poked no political hornet's nest for ideological reasons, yet was humane, liberal, efficient, and so popular that he won reelection by an impressive majority in 1930." He made good on his longtime aspiration to develop Democratic strength in the Republican counties north of New

York City, and he did so partly by summer tours of upstate regions by boat, using New York's network of canals and rivers. Towns that had never seen a governor in person were treated to the up-close sight of Franklin Roosevelt and his family on board a homey little houseboat, stopping at the dock in town to ask how things were going in Aurora or Watertown or Saranac Lake. For a man who was immobile on his own, it was an ingenious form of mobility to attract attention and admiration. And his majority in 1930 was not just impressive; it was the largest New York had ever seen. He won by 725,107 votes — over Charles Tuttle, the U.S. attorney for New York City — substantially bigger than any of the victories of Al Smith, who always had trouble upstate.

The triumph in 1930 enlarged Roosevelt's standing as front-runner among the prospects for the 1932 Democratic nomination for president. In 1928 FDR and Howe had looked toward 1936 as the presidential year. Then had come the great stock market crash of 1929, and now Herbert Hoover, the "Great Humanitarian," the "Great Engineer," looked vulnerable. The Democratic nomination in 1932 might be worth a great deal.

In public FDR strictly observed the etiquette that required leading aspirants to disclaim any interest in a national race. But the vote for governor in 1930 had barely been tallied when Louis Howe rented a new office in New York. Before November was out, FDR had invited Eddie Flynn to the governor's residence. Flynn, the urbane Bronx boss, who was now FDR's secretary of state, found himself sitting down to dinner with only Howe and the governor himself.

"Eddie," the governor said, "my reason for asking you to stay overnight is that I believe I can be nominated for the Presidency in 1932 on the Democratic ticket."

Shortly before FDR was reelected governor in 1930, all delegates and alternate delegates to the last Democratic national convention received an anonymous circular in the mail. A copy came to Jim Mahoney, an aide in Roosevelt's office, who passed it to Louis Howe with a note: "Honestly, I could murder for much less." The circular read:

In the home office of every life insurance company in the United States, there is on file the health examination report of every person holding a life insurance policy, no matter in what company it is held. If you will examine the health examination report of Governor Franklin D. Roosevelt, you will find that he is suffering from locomotor ataxia produced by syphilis. For almost ten years, however, Governor Roosevelt has been parading himself before the public as a victim of infantile paralysis in order to gain sympathy and to hide his real affliction. Carrying on this deception further, Governor Roosevelt has induced some men of wealth to establish at Warm Springs, Georgia, a sanitarium for the treatment of the real victims of infantile paralysis. The most disgusting, vicious and really dangerous thing about this matter is the fact that Governor Roosevelt (with his loathsome and infectious venereal disease) bathes in the same pool with these poor innocent children at the sanitarium at Warm Springs, Georgia, when he himself visits there for months at a time.

About the same time, in Marion, Massachusetts, Dr. William McDonald, the physician who had helped FDR with physical therapy in 1925 and 1926, was paid an unexpected visit by "the editor of a well known New York newspaper." The editor knew McDonald had treated FDR, and he had questions: Didn't infantile paralysis

517

sometimes have harmful effects on the brain? McDonald shut the man down: No, he had never seen the disease hurt a patient's mental powers; in fact, he thought some polio victims seemed to grow more acute.

Just as Louis Howe had predicted when FDR first became ill, the diagnosis of a paralytic disease affecting the central nervous system had let loose suspicions that grew into dark rumors and scurrilous stories. Variations on the syphilis theme flourished — though the 1930 circular's emphasis on the young innocents at Warm Springs was never quite matched for creative venom. (Only a medical expert would know that the spastic gait of a victim of syphilitic ataxia was utterly different than Roosevelt's smooth gait.) It was also said that Roosevelt's affliction had actually been a heart attack or cancer or a paralytic stroke — or it had indeed been infantile paralysis, but this was God's punishment for mysterious sins Roosevelt had committed in the past. There was also the traditional view, as a midwestern editor would later put it, that "a physical cripple is inclined to become an emotional and spiritual cripple." And the less flamboyant but more plausible charge of 1928 persisted: that Roosevelt was simply too weak for a man's job like the presidency.

The rise of any major politician provokes ugly talk on society's paranoid fringe, usually without serious consequences. But Roosevelt was well aware that paranoia had infected enough otherwise rational people in 1928 to destroy any chance Al Smith had to be president. The powerful stigma associated with paralysis would make a dangerous weapon not only for nuts but for perfectly sane and savvy political opponents. That the author of the syphilis circular had access to Democratic Party mailing lists, and money for printing and postage, reminded Roosevelt and Howe that people more powerful than a few nuts were at work in the rumor mill.

The deliberate spreading of scandalous rumors, true or false, had acquired a new name in political circles: the "whispering campaign." Of course the tactic dated at least to Thomas Jefferson and Sallie Hemings, and it had been deployed recently against Grover Cleveland (who had a mistress), Woodrow Wilson (who had a stroke), and Warren G. Harding (who was said to have "Negro blood"). Al Smith had been the most recent target, and the subterranean rumors about Roosevelt had begun to circulate as soon as he replaced Smith in

Albany and became a likely contender for president. "I find there is a deliberate attempt to create the impression that my health is such as would make it impossible for me to fulfill the duties of President," FDR wrote a friend in 1931. "To those who know how strenuous have been the three years I have passed as Governor of this State, this is highly humorous, but it is taken with great seriousness in the southern states particularly. I shall appreciate whatever my friends may have to say in their personal correspondence to dispel this perfectly silly piece of propaganda."

FDR and his team decided early that they, not their opponents, would be first to haul the issue of FDR's health out of the closet and put it squarely in the open. Simply doing the job of governing New York was Roosevelt's best retort. But as they judged it, that alone would not be enough to bury the gossip. He and his team followed a consistent strategy: They would acknowledge that people were saying his condition made him unfit to hold office — then explain why, in fact, he was perfectly fit to do so.

The first step in this effort was to take out a $560,000 insurance policy on Roosevelt's life, with the Warm Springs Foundation as the beneficiary. Twenty-two companies took a stake in the policy, a number that Roosevelt's press aides cited loudly to show that experts had confidence that FDR was full of health. The three prominent doctors who examined him declared that "his organs and functions are sound in all respects. . . . The chest is exceptionally well developed, and the spinal column is perfectly normal . . . and free of disease. He has neither pain nor ache at any time." In the wake of infantile paralysis — confined solely to his lower limbs, the doctors said — "there has been progressive recovery of power in the legs. . . . This restoration continues and will continue. . . . We believe that his powers of endurance are such as to allow him to meet all demands of private or public life."

That got some coverage, but not a great deal. Soon thereafter, an arrangement was made with a writer named Earle Looker to produce a major article in a popular magazine that would spread the news of FDR's soundness to a broader audience.

The full details of how Looker, an undistinguished writer with no special equipment for the job, snagged this assignment have never materialized. Whether Looker pitched it to the Roosevelt organization or vice versa is not known. But Looker's relationship to the Roosevelt camp was surely cozier than journalism's canon of ethics allowed. He was said to be an old friend of the Oyster Bay Roosevelts — a credential that made him more credible as a disinterested reporter, not less, since the Oyster Bay and Hyde Park Roosevelts were notoriously at odds in this era. His early contacts with FDR and Howe may have been made through Eleanor, who, as a magazine writer of growing popularity herself, knew many people in publishing. Looker was planning a book about FDR, a personal profile timed to the presidential campaign, and he had an agent seeking "the best possible publisher for the particular thing we have in mind." By December 1930 he had already done "considerable sounding," Looker told Eleanor, and he asked her to do what she could "to discourage any extended work of which [FDR's] personality — not policies — is [the] subject . . . until I am well underway with my story."

Looker researched and wrote his biographical profile as a book titled *This Man Roosevelt* and published it in 1932. But first the novel part of his research was developed into the magazine article that Roosevelt needed. With Roosevelt's agreement, Looker enlisted three physicians to conduct another examination of the governor to test his fitness for high office. The results: Yes, he was fit, confirming Looker's observation of "the alertness of his movements, the sparkle of his eyes, the vigor of his gestures . . . his strength under the strain of long working periods. . . . Merely his legs are not much good to him."

No one challenged these findings, then or later, and FDR's generally sound health for the next decade bore them out. Evidence in Looker's correspondence suggests that Roosevelt paid for the medical exams; if so, Looker's claim to a tough, no-holds-barred investigation collapses, though it does not invalidate the doctors' positive report. The project was probably exactly what it looked like: another adroit tactic engineered by Louis Howe to shape what reporters, politicians, and voters thought about Roosevelt's condition. Because of the toxic rumors, such tactics were needed now more than ever.

Looker's magazine article, "Is Franklin D. Roosevelt Physically Fit to Be President? A Man to Man Answer to a Nation-Wide Challenge," appeared in *Liberty,* a popular weekly that competed with the *Saturday Evening Post.* (*Liberty*'s signature gimmick was to estimate the reading time for every article; Looker's was promised at twenty-one minutes and twelve seconds.) But to Looker's credit, he began with a truth no one else had troubled to put squarely in print: "It is an amazing possibility that the next President of the United States may be a cripple. Franklin D. Roosevelt, Governor of the State of New York, was crippled by infantile paralysis in the epidemic of 1921 and still walks with the help of a crutch and a walking stick."

The timing — July 1931 — suited the Roosevelt campaign just about perfectly. Even before the story was actually published, Howe made hundreds of copies of the proofs and sent them to every Democratic operative in the country. Jim Farley, the campaign's key man in the field, was just concluding a month of meetings with party leaders west of the Mississippi. He found many state and county chieftains highly enthusiastic about Roosevelt. Many thought he could win, and they promised Farley they would vote for FDR at the convention — at least on the first ballot or so. But they also asked Farley about Roosevelt's health. When Farley got his copy of Looker's story — just when Democratic leaders were getting theirs — he jotted a note to Roosevelt himself: "I read the Liberty Magazine article today and think it

524

is a corker. I think it is a mighty fine time to have it appear because it fully answers the question that was put to me many times during the past three weeks."

A reader accustomed to the investigative political reporting that became common later in the twentieth century may find it strange that the unlikely Earle Looker, a second-rate freelancer, more publicist than journalist, scored a scoop on the state of Franklin Roosevelt's health just as the 1932 presidential race began. Why had working reporters not beaten him to it, especially when the ugly whispers began to circulate at the time of FDR's reelection in Albany? Why didn't the rumors catch fire in the popular press and raise a far larger cloud of suspicion?

The question seems puzzling only in hindsight. FDR had the advantage of governing a state where many of the country's best and most aggressive reporters worked, and many of them had seen a good deal of him in person. One or more of their publishers may have wanted to see Roosevelt taken down. It would have shocked no one if the "editor of a well known New York newspaper" who knocked on Dr. McDonald's door had been working for William Randolph Hearst, owner of the *New York*

Journal-American and a giant chain of other papers, a scandalmonger and mischief maker with no love for Roosevelt. But the reporters themselves, the honest ones, simply paid no heed to the health rumors. Those who had been covering FDR as governor for more than two years knew him well and liked him; and when they heard the syphilis and weakling whispers, they tagged them as what they were — transparent lies spread by Roosevelt's enemies. It was hard for any journalist with scruples to stomach what the reporter John Gunther called the "sheer defamatory wickedness" of attacks on a man admired for physical courage.

Looker no doubt had been right when he said the capital press corps in Albany thought it misleading to highlight FDR's infirmity, and the national political reporters likely felt the same way now, as the presidential campaign approached.

Some retaliated, just as reporters in 1928 had countered charges that FDR was sick or weak. One of these was Ernest K. Lindley, a Rhodes Scholar who had just shifted from the Democratic *New York World* to the Republican *Herald-Tribune*. As the 1932 campaign approached, he decided to write a biography of Roosevelt in part because he "resented the scurrilous propaganda which had been down in the fertile fields of legitimate public curiosity concerning this aspect of Mr. Roosevelt's fitness to be President. I knew from personal observation of Mr. Roosevelt during his years in Albany that it was false, and in writing this book I deliberately sought to refute it."

Undoubtedly some reporters allowed FDR's charm to blunt their critical skills. But Lindley, who became a Roosevelt confidant himself, said most reporters came to a balanced view of him in time. "I have seen three or four successive groups of newspapermen — at Albany, doing the pre-convention campaign, during the 1932 campaign, and in Washington — go through the same cycle in their reaction toward Mr. Roosevelt," Lindley wrote some years later. "They approach him with skepticism, as political reporters usually do every public man. Then they are very much smitten with his charm and personality. Then there is usually a setback when they realize that after all Mr. Roosevelt is a human being. After that there is a leveling off, and a more critical approach to him." Smitten or critical, few political reporters cared to be used to promote what they knew to be outright lies. If some felt a particular urge to protect

FDR against such lies, it was one more way in which infantile paralysis conferred an unforeseen advantage on his drive toward the presidency.

Reporters look for good stories to tell — stories comprising verifiable facts that endow their subject with clear and value-laden meanings. A potential president with infantile paralysis was a story, all right. But Louis Howe had long before perceived the meaning that most reporters would find in Roosevelt's life. It was the good old come-back story, as useful to Roosevelt now as it had been ever since it first began to appear in 1924. Earle Looker told it. Ernest Lindley told it. For American reporters raised on heroic tales of the underdog, it was the mold into which the facts fit very naturally. Jim Farley, who had been New York's boxing commissioner, later wrote that "there was a phrase for this, the supreme of all supreme accolades in the sports world: 'He got up off the deck and went on to win.' " That was always a hell of a story.

Of course the rumors of syphilis and craziness and weakness might have spread through channels other than the established press. They might have snowballed into the avalanche of sermons and church newsletters and chain letters that attacked Al Smith in 1928 as the apostle of Rome. But the disabled man has no natural antagonist in quite the way some Protestants, in 1928, felt antagonistic toward a Catholic. And it may not have been the right time for a rumor like this to catch on. By 1931, an unusually large number of people in the United States were transfixed by their own problems, and the negative energies released into political talk were nearly all aimed at the sour, self-pitying figure of Herbert Hoover.

After losing in 1928, Al Smith had said he was through with politics for good, but during the months after FDR's second inauguration as governor, Smith was talking much like a candidate for president. "Then you are not out of politics?" a reporter pressed him. "Well, not altogether," Smith conceded.

In a gesture meant to seem like goodwill, Smith had consented to nominate FDR for a second term; but in a rousing, joking attack on the Republicans at the state convention, he hardly spoke of his successor. When he did, there was a fawning condescension in what he said, as if he were praising a devoted mother rather than a strong leader. And the words "cripple" and "weak" were strangely prominent. "There is something about Frank that draws people to him," Smith said. "First, he has a clear brain, and second, he has a big heart. And all through his administration you can find running that milk of human kindness that comes from a big heart, a heart that thinks for the cripple, for the weak, for the poor, and for the afflicted."

Early in 1932, urged on by many friends, Smith declared his willingness, if not to make an active run, at least to be nominated if the party wanted him. He had been hurt by FDR and still thought him a dilettante in politics. But what Smith really yearned for, according to his biographer, Robert A. Slayton, was not so much to punish Roosevelt as to seize "the chance to redeem himself, to finally overcome the hatemongers of 1928 who had hurt him so deeply."

Smith's candidacy blocked what had looked like a clear path to FDR's nomination. Smith was still anathema in the South, but he was a far more dangerous challenger than the other hopefuls, a fairly feeble collection that included Newton Baker (Woodrow Wilson's aging secretary of war), Albert Ritchie (the too-wet governor of Maryland), and John Nance Garner (the too-dry

Speaker of the House, who liked the powerful job he already had). FDR certainly feared Smith. "Al Smith can move these city people better," he said to aides. "I can't." Party rules dating to antebellum Democratic conventions still required the party's nominee to win two-thirds of the delegates. So even with a solid majority going into the Chicago convention, FDR's powerful campaign would be vulnerable to a spoiler. The South and the West were strong for Roosevelt. But many delegates from the Midwest and the Northeast, including New York, still liked Smith. He and the others looked for any means to keep FDR's tally below two-thirds in the early ballots. Then a deadlock might tilt the delegates to some lucky alternative.

As the winter of 1932 turned to spring, the Depression was becoming a horror show. Nearly one in four workers had lost their jobs — thirteen million since 1929. By the end of the year, industrial stocks would lose 80 percent of the value they had held in 1930, and 40 percent of the banks open in 1929 would be shuttered. Hoover seemed stricken, frozen. The sculptor Gutzon Borglum wrote a friend: "I believe if a rose was placed in his hand it would wilt."

As contempt for Hoover soared, so did

the value of the Democratic nomination, and Al Smith boiled at the idea of the prize being taken from him by the rich boy he thought he had made governor. When a Roosevelt supporter begged Smith to back FDR, Smith exploded: "Do you know, by God, that he has never consulted me about a damn thing since he has been governor? He has taken bad advice and from sources not friendly to me. He has ignored me!" FDR's determination to be his own man in Albany was returning to haunt him.

"I had thought the article in *Liberty* would have stopped [the whispering campaign]," Roosevelt wrote a supporter in Illinois, "but the story is still being circulated industriously in all parts of the country, and I suppose it will have to be handled all over again."

In fact, the Roosevelt campaign already realized that the issue of FDR's physical fitness for the presidency would have to be fought every day down to the end. The office collected newspapers from all over the country and carefully tracked coverage of their man. Any report that deprecated his physical condition, even a passing negative reference in a small paper, drew a polite correction from the governor's office. When a New Jersey paper said FDR's "indispositions" had given Lieutenant Governor Lehman an especially large role in Albany, Guernsey Cross shot back: "Governor Roosevelt has had no 'indispositions' and is in extremely good health." When a Virginia paper called Roosevelt's health "still poor," FDR himself sent a tut-tutting clarification: "My health is excellent, though as you know I still have to wear braces following infantile paralysis, but that can hardly be construed as having anything to do with general health." When political reporters developed profiles of Roosevelt, they asked for and received basic information about the candidate's ability to get around. The results were generally matter-of-fact, superficial but accurate as far as they went (though the use of a wheelchair was seldom mentioned), and brief. An Associated Press report in July was typical: "Mr. Roosevelt today walks with the aid of crutches or canes. When in public he has a secretary or an escort, sometimes a friend or one of his sons, walk by his side, his arm in theirs. Patiently through the years he has taken the exercises prescribed for victims of infantile paralysis. The chief effect of the disease is that many muscles are retarded but not made useless. Exercises restore them."

The handiest retort was the shortest.

"After all," Jimmy Roosevelt said, "it's a desk job."

The Democratic convention was to be in Chicago at the end of June. Jim Farley had done his early canvassing well. With promises of support from many delegates, and victories in Democratic primaries, FDR held the advantage. A collection of contenders began to coalesce into an informal Anybody-but-Roosevelt movement, and they drew on the readiest ammunition: the fear of a cripple in the White House.

It was a quiet offensive at first. Harry F. Byrd, the former governor of Virginia, had spoken up for FDR's candidacy early. But after Byrd saw three men carry FDR up the steps of his mansion, and after he had begun to think of himself as a potential candidate, he suggested to friends that Roosevelt was not strong enough to be president. William Gibbs McAdoo, Smith's nemesis in 1924 and still nurturing hopes of the nomination, voiced the soft note of doubt that hinted at crippling without actually naming it. "I can't think of Roosevelt as being equal to the demands the White House must make on its occupants in the next four years," he wrote to the Tennessee editor George Fort

Milton. Frank Hague, mayor and boss of Jersey City, New Jersey, and a powerful ally of Al Smith, at least came right out with it, saying: "He is crippled both mentally and physically." In private, Hague even began to mimic Roosevelt's gait.

On the eve of the convention, the rhetoric became more direct. McAdoo went much farther than he had before, saying: "We don't want a dead man on the ticket." Then Al Smith himself, who had asked Roosevelt to run for governor of New York and defended him by saying the job did not require an acrobat, joined the crowd. In the *Saturday Evening Post,* Smith declared that a national campaign "requires a man of great vigor and bodily strength to stand the physical strain of it, to make no mention whatever of the tax he has to put upon his mental qualities to permit him to conduct the campaign intelligently over so long a period." "Alfalfa Bill" Murray, governor of Oklahoma, went all the way to the bottom: "How much less can a man think who has locomotor ataxia, a nervous disease that affects the spinal column, and ultimately the brain? I know they say it is infantile paralysis, but locomotor ataxia never came from that source." It came from syphilis, as everyone knew, including those who had first read the charge in the anonymous smear sheet circulated a year earlier to Democratic leaders around the country.

The columnist Walter Lippmann thought Roosevelt himself was not above raising doubts about a candidate's health; he believed FDR had started whispers about the heart condition of Newton D. Baker, a perennial back-up in Democratic contests since the war.

But Roosevelt never relinquished his lead, and after a complicated series of deals and promises that gave the vice-presidential nomination to "Cactus Jack" Garner of Texas, the Speaker of the House, he was nominated. Al Smith refused to concede, and his delegates refused to make the nomination unanimous.

The next morning, July 2, Hoover's chief aide, James MacLafferty, entered the president's office to congratulate him on the news that the Democrats had nominated Roosevelt. It was what Hoover had been hoping for.

"Well," Hoover said. "I suppose of all those mentioned he will be the easiest one to beat."

They discussed the news just announced: that Roosevelt would break precedent by taking an airplane from New York to Chicago to accept the nomination in person. MacLafferty said that was another blunder, since "the audience would see Roosevelt's physical helplessness. . . . I marveled at their willingness to put a man as physically incapacitated as he at the head of the government."

No, Hoover said, they'll never be allowed to see Roosevelt as he actually was. Hoover believed that when Roosevelt visited the White House for a conference of governors several months earlier, his aides had shielded his legs from photographers.

MacLafferty recorded the conversation with Hoover in his diary that evening. But as he wrote the last of it, the radio brought news. "It turns out Mr. Hoover was wrong [about Roosevelt concealing his condition from the delegates]," McClafferty wrote, "for it has just been announced over the radio that Mr. Roosevelt is being helped to arise to his feet so that he may address the convention and the whole country is now hearing as to his physical affliction."

The name Roosevelt they knew, but to many Americans the new man by that name remained vague even now, with the nomination secured. James Thurber's tongue-in-cheek observation in the *New Yorker* in July

537

probably contained a large kernel of truth: "It seems that a lot of people in Darke County, Ohio, and in Kansas, Louisiana, Oregon, etc., think that one of the candidates for President this fall is the late Theodore Roosevelt, a man who, they feel, is greatly needed at the helm of State in these times." That was no disadvantage, of course. But it meant Roosevelt remained in danger of being defined by others, and of being defined once and for all not as the man who had come back from crippling but simply as a cripple, a man too weak for the job.

Party leaders were advising against any difficult campaign tours of the country. Louis Howe agreed. The race was all but in the bag: Hoover was a dead man walking. Why take the chance of a grueling trip with chances at every stop for unforeseen trouble or a terrible tumble caught on camera?

The party men in New York asked Jim Farley to go up to Hyde Park on a steaming afternoon in August to talk to the nominee. Farley was supposed to say that everyone thought the smart play was for FDR to stay near home and make a few speeches on the radio.

Roosevelt listened to Farley deliver this message, then asked: "Jim, what do you think yourself?"

"I think you ought to go," Farley said. "And I know you are going anyway."

"That's right," Roosevelt said.

Hoover had to force himself to go out and give speeches. He was exhausted and afraid of angry crowds. "Lou, I do not know whether I will be able to weather this trip," he told his wife. "I have reason to doubt that I will live through it."

Meanwhile, a six-car "Roosevelt Special" set off on September 12 for a tour of eighteen cities: St. Louis, Kansas City, Topeka, Denver, Cheyenne, Salt Lake City, Butte, Spokane, Seattle, Portland, San Francisco, Los Angeles, Albuquerque, Omaha, Sioux City, Milwaukee, Chicago, and Detroit. And those were just the major stops for big speeches. There were dozens of "tank-stops" along the way, when people in small towns could come to see Roosevelt standing on the platform of the rear car, waving, reaching down to shake a few hands, saying a few words, cracking a joke or two, asking about crop prices. They could see that he stood stiffly and held on to railings or an aide's arm, but he was obviously the picture of good health — a big, vivacious man with a powerful voice and a winning smile.

In mid-September, a reporter for one of the news syndicates described it:

A sympathetic silence invariably descends as the specially built gangplank or ramp is hauled from the baggage car ahead to the rear platform so that he may alight. The fact that Gov. Roosevelt was stricken with infantile paralysis after maturity is generally known. His descent from the train is made by grasping two brass handrails anchored at either edge of the runway, and his son precedes him by a step. As he comes back aboard, Roosevelt climbs alone, leaning far forward and virtually pulling himself up with one strong arm after another.

It is generally believed that the New York Governor decided to make this trip against the almost unanimous judgment of his advisers for two purposes: First, to present a personal appeal for the suffrage of the people, and second, to convince them that he is not a wheelchair invalid incapable of meeting the physical ordeals of the Presidential Office. The Governor gives the impression of a man in excellent physical condition, capable of meeting as strenuous campaigning as anyone else. To the great body of the people, who see him first standing at the microphone behind tables which cut off sight of his body from the hips down, he is visioned as a man of broad shoulders and tremendous vigor. His youthful, vibrant voice carries the impression of strength. Almost invariably, however, when he must stand or walk, he is supported on the arm of his son, with a cane in his other hand. He moves slowly, cautiously, but with great composure.

This was the tableau he had aimed to create when he told the physiotherapist Helena Mahoney in 1926 what he wanted to do if he could not walk by himself. He wanted to recover enough strength and agility so as not to frighten people. He wanted people to be able to "forget that he was a cripple."

Near the end of the campaign, the *New York Times* columnist Anne O'Hare McCormick spent time with both candidates.

She had covered Hoover's race in 1928. Even then, "when the sky seemed cloudless and all the signs were fair," she had thought him "an uncomfortable office-seeker, awkward and uncertain in an irksome role." Now he struck her as "thinner, grayer, harder, older — ten years older — than the Hoover of four years ago." McCormick found him firm in his confidence that he had acted properly throughout the crisis. He was hurt by accusations that he had been unfeeling in the face of suffering. Think of General Pershing, he told her — Pershing, the commander of U.S. forces during the war, who was deeply grieved by his soldiers' suffering in battle. "But wasn't it his duty not to crumple up at the front," Hoover demanded, "and have all the men crumpling up with him? The place to show his feeling was at headquarters, working over maps and plans and supplies, so that the men were properly quartered and fed, the wounded had ambulance service, and there was the least possible sacrifice of life."

Some days later, at the house on East 65th Street in New York, McCormick was one of several reporters invited to dine with the Roosevelts. As the meal wound down, FDR rapped the table for quiet and began to say something, but Eleanor shushed him: "Franklin, I said there would be no speeches." He barreled over her, laughing loudly: "As I was saying before I was so rudely interrupted . . ." After more banter, McCormick said, he "turned grave."

"No man can cross the continent in these times and remain the same," he said. "I find conditions different and worse than I expected. I have looked into the faces of thousands of Americans and they are the faces of people in want. I don't mean the unemployed alone. Of course, they would take anything. I mean those who still have jobs and don't know how long they'll last. They have the frightened look of lost children. And I don't mean physical want alone. There is something more. I was in Paris when Wilson first went over. I watched the crowds in the streets and I noticed there, particularly in the faces of women, the same expression I see here today. A kind of yearning. Then they were thinking of the war. Perhaps this man, their eyes were saying, can save our children from the horror and terror we have known. Now they are saying: We're caught in something we don't understand; perhaps this fellow can help us out."

Finally McCormick rose to go. At the front door she bumped into a taxi driver. He had stopped his car out front and run up in hopes of shaking hands with the governor. She and the driver went down the steps to the street together.

"I tell you, lady," he said, "the day Roosevelt is elected will be a national holiday — like Armistice Day, you know? I figure . . . that if we get rid of old Gloom and put in a feller that can laugh and act human, the depression will be half over."

EPILOGUE

The great Hollywood director Frank Capra was a Republican who disapproved of the New Deal. But in the late 1930s, when Capra was at work on *Mr. Smith Goes to Washington,* a friend in the press corps invited him along to a White House news conference, and the skeptical filmmaker found himself in thrall to the figure behind the desk.

"Through three rows of standing reporters I caught glimpses of FDR," Capra recalled. "A long cigarette holder tilted up rakishly from his massive face as he scanned the reporters with a roguish, challenging smile. My first thought: He is *not* crippled."

Roosevelt was aware of this effect — keenly aware of it.

"You know, Orson," he is reported to have said once to Orson Welles, "you and I are the two best actors in America."

Who was Franklin Roosevelt after 1921? Was he a man transformed by hardship? Was he different than he would have been if the poliovirus had left him alone?

That was what his wife thought. "Franklin's illness proved a blessing in disguise," she wrote during his presidency, "for it gave him strength and courage he had not had before." When a friend asked her once if FDR would have been elected president had he not been handicapped, she said: "He would certainly have been President, but a president of a different kind."

Frances Perkins, who first met him as a state legislator and became the only Cabinet secretary to serve through his entire presidency, also thought polio changed FDR. When she saw him in 1924 for the first time since his illness, she wrote, "I was instantly struck by his growth. . . . He was serious, not playing now. . . . He had become conscious of other people, of weak people, of human frailty." She added: "He was not born great, but he became great," and polio had been the turning point.

If some, like Perkins, saw a tougher Roosevelt, others saw a softer one. Thomas

Leonard, a political crony in Hyde Park, said that after 1921 FDR "seemed to be more interested in . . . the friendship of other people. I'd say [he felt more] affection for the people generally after his accident." Guernsey Cross, FDR's secretary during the governorship, thought the ordeal of polio "deepened and mellowed a naturally aggressive personality."

I incline toward the idea of the Roosevelts' eldest son, James, who said he did not "believe the ordeal of being crippled built father's character. I believe he had the basic strength of character to overcome his handicap." The story told here suggests that the man he became was the man he had been all along, but only the brush of chaos summoned his best traits and his underlying strength. People saw that and learned who he really was, as perhaps he did himself. His comeback from polio proved to everyone that he was not merely the rich and polished heir to a famous name but a man of extraordinary character. One didn't have to like him or approve of his politics to recognize that.

Of course, Eleanor's view and James's view can both be true, and probably both are. But Roosevelt's transformation had more layers than either of those views admits. It also borrowed from the legerde-main of stage and screen, as FDR acknowl-edged with a wink to the maker of *Citizen Kane.* It was, at least in part, a kind of masquerade — not a deception but a *perfor-mance* in which actor and audience tacitly agreed to go through a drama together, with the audience suspending its ability to distin-guish between the actor and the character. As Dr. Draper said of the entire Roosevelt family, the disabled FDR was himself "a complex tapestry" indeed.

The particular way in which Roosevelt came back from his illness exhibited the es-sential habits of mind and action that he would deploy during the Great Depression and World War II: improvisation, experimen-tation, and perseverance in the face of enormous trouble. His assertion in 1933 that fear was a greater obstacle than any material peril was not just a rhetorical trick. Through personal experience, he had come to believe it. The way he fought against his paralysis, trying one thing, then another when the first thing failed, and then a third, was perfectly reflected in his pragmatic response to the crises of his presidency.

The temptation to give up had been the greatest threat to his extraordinary ambi-tion, and if he ever felt that temptation —

no one knows if he did or not — he overcame it. For years he thought that to run for president he would have to walk without assistance, and he tried to do that for five years. When Al Smith pressed the nomination for governor on him, he gave up the effort to walk; and when he won that election, he came to realize he could govern New York and run for president *without* walking. However many people were unaware or unsure of his inability to walk without help, the example he set transformed ancient assumptions and beliefs about disability.

The conventional wisdom is that FDR became president *in spite of* polio. I think the evidence suggests an alternative truth — that he became president *because* of polio. Instead of grabbing Al Smith's coattails, an FDR who could stand and walk in 1922 might well have contested with Smith for supremacy in New York politics — and Smith probably would have won. That might not have killed FDR's career in politics. But it is hard to imagine him rising to national power with Smith as an enemy all the way. Instead, disability kept Roosevelt on the sidelines of the Democratic Party's intramural bloodbath of the mid-1920s, and he recovered just enough by 1928 to seize the now-or-never chance that Smith offered him, much to Smith's later chagrin. Polio also gave Roosevelt a story to tell — the story of the man who came back. Without that story, his odds of being nominated and elected to the presidency would have been longer. He would have been more widely seen, as Walter Lippmann said in 1932, as merely "a pleasant man who, without any important qualifications for the office, would very much like to be President." Many agreed with Lippmann, but it was partly because of polio that many didn't.

The urgency of the Hundred Days — the period in 1933 when FDR hurled a storm of bills at Congress to fight the causes and effects of the Great Depression — may be attributable in part to a belief that he had to be more and do more than any previous president simply to ward off the likely charge that he was not fit for his office. But the habit of masquerade that disability often encourages may also have nurtured his reputation for trickiness and duplicity, a reputation he deserved.

The more troubling sequel to FDR's fight with polio in the 1920s came in 1944. Several historians — chief among them Robert Ferrell, in *The Dying President* — have made a thoroughly persuasive case that

FDR ran for reelection that year when he should not have done so. His health was in grave decline, his energy was flagging, and his life was in jeopardy. He was losing the wherewithal to exercise power in the final and critical stage of World War II.

The parallels between his handling of polio and his handling of cardiovascular disease are striking. Both times he nodded to his doctors' instructions but took his own view of his prospects. Both times he denied the power of disease to end his career. It worked the first time but not the second. His cardiovascular crisis was a graver threat to his life, and the stakes were far higher. One can view his decision to run for a third term in 1940 — when his standing and his leadership were arguably indispensable for the coming crisis — far more sympathetically than his decision to run in 1944, when the war was all but won. Perhaps the presidency had become so central to the life he had reclaimed in the 1920s that he simply could not bear to give it up. But by refusing to relinquish his grip on the office, he put the good of the country at risk. He chose a new candidate for vice president carelessly, and it was only by a stroke of luck that his successor was as good a president as Harry Truman.

During the debate over the Roosevelt Memorial in Washington, D.C., much rhetoric was deployed for and against the proposition that a statue of Roosevelt should show him in a wheelchair, and many people claimed to speak for "what FDR would have wanted." That is both a harder and an easier question than it may have seemed to either side.

For one thing, we know precisely what Roosevelt wanted as a memorial because he said so explicitly: the simple, unadorned obelisk that was installed according to his wishes next to the National Archives. It's possible that he envisioned this plain piece of stone precisely because he foresaw the problem of whether to show him sitting or standing. (Of course, the able-bodied Abraham Lincoln is seated in his own memorial. There is no way of showing in a statue that Lincoln was handicapped by chronic depression.) The wheelchair made it into the memorial, but the reader will recognize it as misleading, since Roosevelt used his wheelchair for only a few minutes each day. The British, actually, are the ones who got the imagery right: The noble statue of FDR in

Grosvenor Square, London, where he stands in his naval cape with his cane plainly visible, precisely captures the picture of himself that he presented to the American public.

The fact that FDR shrouded the extent of his disability in his own time does not mean he would have wanted it shrouded in another time, when the meaning of disability has changed a great deal — partly because of his own example. He tacked with the wind then — that was an essential part of his nature and his skills — and he would likely do so now, with the wind blowing in new directions. As president he seemed to feel regret about his inability to walk, but not the embarrassment he had felt about it in the early years. He kept most people, from politicians to the broad public, from seeing how crippled he was because that made it easier to do his business with them. That was his main concern — to do his business — and he did what he thought was necessary to get it done.

If there was a "splendid deception," it certainly did not fool the unnumbered thousands of disabled people and their families who were fully aware of what Roosevelt had overcome, and his example not only fueled their hopes and their efforts but opened the door that would lead, in time, to the transformational Americans with Disabilities Act of 1990. Hundreds of disabled people and members of their families wrote to FDR in the White House. One of them was Mary Louise Ray, a young woman in Milton, Massachusetts, whose husband had contracted polio at the age of eleven. He had trained to become an electrical engineer and in 1943 was preparing for a commission in the navy.

"The story of your life, President Roosevelt, has been an inspiration and solace to us both," she wrote. "We have seen you hurdle the insurmountable. You have given to my husband, and to many less fortunate, a challenge, which is, after all, the best of life itself. It is the struggle to catch the challenge that gives life its zest."

If a person's sense of self — his belief about who he really is — is the story of his own life that he carries in his mind, then FDR, as president, must have drawn power from the turn his story took between 1921 and 1932. He knew he had done something terribly difficult. Through exercise, practice, and compromise with his own highest hopes, he had recovered some of the strength and mobility he had lost to the poliovirus. But more important and more difficult, he had defeated the stigma that prevented people with disabled limbs from participating fully in life's struggles. That victory required a fierce will, many wiles, and a lot of help. The wiles and the will lay somewhere inside the thirty-nine-year-old man at the moment he became ill. He might have retreated into a comfortable retirement. Instead he chose to exert his will and exercise his wiles, and that act of choosing, more than anything else, revealed who he was. His close aide and friend of the later presidential years, Harry Hopkins, once said: "The guy *never* knows when he is licked." Hopkins said that was a defect. Perhaps it was. But obviously it was also a strength. As the journalist John Gunther put it, "Because he had beaten his illness, Roosevelt thought that he could beat anything."

Nearly half a century after Roosevelt died in 1945, the anthropologist Robert Murphy told the story of his own paralysis in an extraordinary memoir, *The Body Silent.* Murphy observed that because all of us are wounded, visibly or invisibly, the struggle of the disabled represents the struggle of every man and woman. It stands for "the battle of life's wounded against isolation, dependency, denigration and entropy, and all other things that pull them backward out of life into their inner selves and ultimate negation. This struggle is the highest expression of the human rage for life, the ultimate purpose of our species — paralytics, and all the disabled, are actors in a Passion Play, mummers in search of Resurrection." One cannot help but see FDR's pursuit of the presidency as the embodiment of Murphy's idea.

Roosevelt's best epitaph may be an off-hand remark he made when an aide, listening to him spin yet another grand plan, said: "Mr. President, you *can't* do that."

The president looked at him and said: "I've done a lot of things I can't do."

ACKNOWLEDGMENTS

It's a pleasure to acknowledge the help of many.

For financial support, I'm grateful to Karen Maitland Schilling, former dean of the College of Arts and Science at Miami of Ohio; to the White House Historical Association; and to the National Endowment for the Humanities.

I had good advice and strong support from colleagues at Miami, including Richard Campbell, Cheryl Gibbs, Cheryl Heckler, Stephen Siff, Edward Arnone, Ann Hagedorn, Allan M. Winkler, Mary Kupiec Cayton, and Marguerite S. Shaffer.

In two long conversations, Curtis Roosevelt, the grandson of Franklin and Eleanor Roosevelt, elaborated upon the memories and insights that appear in his rich memoir, *Too Close to the Sun* (2008). His help was essential.

Several authorities on Franklin Roosevelt

and the Roosevelt family were generous with their insights and time. I'm especially indebted to Allida M. Black, founding editor of the Eleanor Roosevelt Papers Project and executive director of the fdr4freedoms Digital Initiative; F. Kennon Moody, author of *Franklin Roosevelt and His Hudson Valley Neighbors* (2013); and Diane Lobb Boyce of the National Park Service. My hearty thanks go also to Robert Ferrell, author of *The Dying President* (1998) and many other works on the Roosevelt-Truman era, who shared his insight on FDR's personality and allowed me to examine his research files at Indiana University's Lilly Library; Dr. Richard Thayer Goldberg of Boston's Spaulding Rehabilitation Hospital, author of *The Making of Franklin D. Roosevelt: Triumph Over Disability* (1982); and Geoffrey C. Ward, author of the definitive two-volume biography of the young FDR. Daniel J. Wilson of Muhlenberg College, our leading authority on the American experience of polio, very graciously provided me with original documents from his own research files.

At the historic sites associated with the Roosevelts, fine public servants help others to understand the members of that "complex tapestry" of a family and why they matter. Among those who helped me were Herman Eberhardt, supervisory museum curator of the Franklin D. Roosevelt Library and Museum in Hyde Park, who allowed me to examine FDR's braces; Deborah S. Gardner, curator of Roosevelt House at Hunter College, City University of New York, who introduced me to the beautifully restored twin town houses at 47-49 East 65th Street in Manhattan and answered many questions; Michele Ballos of the National Park Service; Anne Newman and Stephen Smart at Roosevelt Campobello International Park; and Tara McGill of the Roosevelt-Vanderbilt National Historic Site. Staff members and associates of the White House Historical Association generously shared ideas and sources: John Riley; Emily Soapes; Sally Stokes; Bill Bushong; and Martha Joynt Kumar.

I had skilled assistance from several professional researchers: Frederic Alan Maxwell, who searched several libraries for obscure sources; Emily Victorson in Chicago; Peggy Ann Brown in Washington, D.C.; Ann Trevor in Palo Alto; and Corey Goettsch in Atlanta.

Many archivists answered queries, dug up sources and provided guidance, including, at the Franklin D. Roosevelt Library, Virginia H. Lewick, Alycia Vivona, Mark Renovitch, Matthew C. Hanson, and supervisory archivist Robert Clark, who did me many favors; David Rose, archivist at the March of Dimes in White Plains, New York; Helmi Raaska at the Gerald R. Ford Library in Ann Arbor; Jessica Murphy at Harvard's Francis A. Countway Library of Medicine; Matthew Schaefer at the Herbert Hoover Presidential Library; Douglas Brown at Groton School; and Allen Packwood at the Churchill Archives Centre. I'm also grateful to these librarians: Jenny Presnell at Miami of Ohio and my friends Barbara Beaton, Judith Avery, and Bryan Skib at the University of Michigan.

To this stranger in the world of medical science, the help of experts was indispensable. My special thanks go to two neurologists, Dr. John D. Segall and Dr. James W. Albers, who steered me through the complexities of polio; and to Dr. James K. Richardson of the University of Michigan, a specialist in physical medicine who answered many questions about FDR's condition and recovery. Other medical specialists who responded to queries and offered suggestions include Dr. Howard Markel; Dr. Arno K. Kumagai; Dr. Claire Z. Kalpakjian; Dr. Robert W. Lash; Dr. Ann T. Laidlaw; and Sunny Roller, M.A., all of the University of Michigan; and Robbie Leonard, former director of physical therapy at the Roosevelt Warm Springs Institute for Rehabilitation in Warm Springs, Georgia. Anne Brantley Segall, M.S.W., helped me to develop a better understanding of the emotional difficulties of people who undergo traumatic injury.

Of all these people in the healing professions, I'm especially grateful to Dr. John D. Segall, who patiently read intermediate drafts of the manuscript in search of my errors. Any that remain are my fault, not his.

I'm grateful to Dr. Herbert Levine, son of Dr. Samuel Levine, who allowed me to see his father's unpublished notes about FDR's case, and to Dr. Bernard Lown, who steered me to the younger Dr. Levine.

Of everything I read about the experience of disability, the late Robert F. Murphy's memoir, *The Body Silent: The Different World of the Disabled* (1987) was the most powerful, the most beautiful, the most insightful. Murphy's account of his own illness had a great deal to do with the shape this book ultimately took. Christopher Clausen's essay in the *The Wilson Quarterly,* "The President and the Wheelchair" (Summer 2005), also had a seminal effect on my research.

Important tips, ideas, sources, and insights

came from, among others, Hank Meijer, author of the forthcoming *America's Senator,* the definitive biography of Arthur S. Vandenberg; Kevin Boyle of Ohio State University; Sam Walker of the *Wall Street Journal;* Jean Patteson of the *Orlando Sentinel;* Harlan Crow; Samuel Fore; Scott Ellsworth, and Dr. Sally Stein, who graciously helped with an important photograph of FDR.

John T. Gorham of the U.S. Secret Service spoke with me at length about his experiences in the Roosevelts' White House during World War II.

I'm grateful to Columbia University's Center for Oral History for permission to quote from the Reminiscences of Frances Perkins.

It's harder to be specific about personal debts than professional ones, but then again, I think these creditors already know what I owe them.

At Fletcher and Company, my agent, Christy Fletcher, not only rendered excellent service but saved my bacon more than once — probably more often than I know, certainly more than I had a right to expect. Thank you, Christy. Thanks to Melissa Chinchillo, too.

At the Free Press, Bruce Nichols got the project going and Webster Younce helped it along with excellent suggestions. Both were crucial.

I'm deeply grateful to all those at Simon & Schuster who brought the book into the world — the wise and good Alice Mayhew; the smart and hard-working Jonathan Cox; and their first-rate colleagues, including Michael Accordino, Paul Dippolito, Robert Castillo, and Lisa Healy.

At a tough moment, a small band of friends hurried to answer my call for help with key tasks, a good deed I won't forget — Dianna Campbell; Arlene and John Shy; and Jonathan Marwil.

I can only acknowledge, not repay, the dear friends named in the dedication, who did much to keep the work and the author afloat when storms moved through. Other friends were in the boat, too: Anne and Tom Segall; John Lofy; Patti Milgrom; Dave Coverly; Rick Ratliff; David Stringer; Gerald S. Linderman; and the late Douglas Evett.

No writer could have a more loving and supportive family. Claire Tobin and Lizzie and Jon Keller have been mainstays — the source of fun, laughter, meaning, encouragement, and love. And I'm grateful to the extended tribe of Tobins, Wilsons, LaFaves,

Fischers, and Richardsons, who managed to be encouraging even as they learned that "How's the book?" was not my all-time favorite question.

Leesa Erickson Tobin gave everything she had for this costly work of mine, even as she seemed to be giving everything she had to everyone else in our lives. Her sacrifices to help the book come into being and her responses to the slowly growing manuscript meant and continue to mean everything to me. She is my one and only — the strongest, the smartest, the most beautiful, the best.

NOTES

Abbreviations

Persons
FDR: Franklin D. Roosevelt
ER: Eleanor Roosevelt
SDR: Sara Delano Roosevelt
MAL: Marguerite A. LeHand

Sources
FDRL: Franklin D. Roosevelt Library, Hyde Park, New York
FBP/Correspondence: Papers Pertaining to Family, Business, and Personal Matters — General Correspondence File, 1904–1928, Papers of Franklin D. Roosevelt
FBP/Subject: Papers Pertaining to Family, Business, and Personal Matters — Subject File, 1904–1928, Papers of Franklin D. Roosevelt
Papers Donated by the Children: Papers

Countway Library: Francis A. Countway
Library of Medicine, Harvard University
CCOH: Columbia Center for Oral History,
Columbia University. Where ellipses have
been used in quotations from oral history
interviews, every effort has been made to
remain faithful to the interviewee's meaning.

Prologue

Franklin D. Roosevelt sat in a plain chair:
"Roosevelt Busy From Dawn to Night,"
New York Times, 3/5/1933; James A.
Hagerty, "Roosevelt Address Stirs Great
Crowd," *New York Times,* 3/5/1933; John
Herrick, "100,000 Cheer First Address of
President," *Chicago Tribune,* 3/5/1933;
Robert C. Albright, "Broad Powers Are
Wanted by New President," *Washington
Post,* 3/5/1933.
Indeed, when many in the Capitol crowd:
Francis Perkins oral history interview, pt.
4, session 1, 26, CCOH.
"This nation will endure": The most thorough
account of FDR's first inaugural address

is Davis W. Houck, *FDR and Fear Itself: The First Inaugural Address* (College Station: Texas A&M University Press, 2002). The notion of blaming the nation's economic paralysis on collective fear may have come to FDR or his aides from a letter by Austin E. Griffiths published in the *New York Times* of 4/11/1932, which said: "What underlies this calamitous world depression? Fear! Banish fear and confidence will flourish again." The letter came to my attention in an undergraduate honors thesis in history at the University of Michigan: Abigail Meert, " 'And For What?': Anti-War Sentiment in America, 1918–1941," 2013.

"A man in Cleveland": quoted in Houck, *FDR and Fear Itself,* 10–11.

"Millions will say": "Press Hails Stout Words of President as Augury," *Washington Post,* 3/5/1933.

"one of the central problems": Joseph Alsop, *FDR 1882–1945: A Centenary Remembrance* (New York: Viking, 1982), 73–74.

"I tried continually": Robert E. Sherwood, *Roosevelt and Hopkins: An Intimate History* (New York: Harper & Brothers, 1948), 9.

"It is hard to imagine": Maureen Dowd, "Not-So-Splendid Deception," *New York Times,* 5/2/1996.

"He relentlessly, obsessively hid": Charles Krauthammer, "FDR in a Wheelchair? No," *Washington Post,* 6/14/1996.

FDR *"was a credit to Western Union":* Richard Rovere, "Books: A Matter of History," *New Yorker,* 12/23/1950.

Chapter 1: Infection

poliovirus resembles a distant planet: My description of the poliovirus is derived chiefly from Robin Marantz Henig, *A Dancing Matrix: Voyages Along the Viral Frontier* (New York: Knopf, 1993); Leslie Collier and John Oxford, *Human Virology* (Oxford: Oxford University Press, 2000); Ann Giudici Fettner, *Viruses: Agents of Change* (New York: McGraw-Hill, 1990); and Andrew Scott, *Pirates of the Cell* (Oxford: Basil Blackwell, 1985).

whole Northeast had been roasting: "One Dies, Five Prostrated, by Heat and Humidity," *New York Times,* 7/26/1921; "Storm Fear Leads to Double Tragedy," *New York Times,* 7/27/1921; "Heat Kills Five, Score Overcome, No Relief Today," *New York Times,* 7/29/1921.

They mingled in paneled rooms: Helen Worden, *Round Manhattan's Rim* (Indianapolis: Bobbs-Merrill, 1934), 207–211;

Robert A. Caro, *The Power Broker: Robert Moses and the Fall of New York* (New York: Knopf, 1974), 503.

Roosevelt heartily approved of the Scouts: FDR, "How Boy Scout Work Aids Youth," *New York Times,* 8/12/1928.

"a product of the streets": Ibid. For FDR's involvement with the Boy Scouts of America, and the influence of that relationship on the founding of the Civilian Conservation Corps, see Neil M. Maher, *Nature's New Deal: The Civilian Conservation Corps and the Roots of the American Environmental Movement* (New York: Oxford University Press, 2008), 31–41.

he certainly looked like an athlete: James Roosevelt with Bill Libby, *My Parents: A Differing View* (Chicago: Playboy Press, 1976), 72–73.

"a beautifully built man": Roosevelt with Libby, *My Parents,* 40–41.

he often jogged or ran: Elliott Roosevelt and James Brough, *An Untold Story: The Roosevelts of Hyde Park* (New York: Putnam, 1973), 82.

"two, three, or four at a time": Frank Freidel interview with Shannon Allen, 5/21/1948, Small Collections, FDRL.

A reporter who compared: W. A. Warn, "Senator F. D. Roosevelt, Chief Insurgent at

Albany," *New York Times,* 1/22/1911.

"There used to be satin handkerchief boxes": Herman Hagedorn interview with Mr. and Mrs. Sheffield Cowles and Mrs. Joseph Alsop Sr., Theodore Roosevelt Association.

"a kind of feminine intuition": Marquis Childs oral history interview, CCOH.

"the most androgynous man": Thomas Corcoran quoted by Marquis Childs, ibid.

"weak as a kitten": FDR to Felix Frankfurter, 11/17/1932, Max Freedman, ed., *Roosevelt and Frankfurter: Their Correspondence* (London: Bodley Head, 1968), 96.

"You couldn't make him unattractive": Marion Dickerman oral history interview, CCOH.

"quiver[ed] with animation": John Gunther, *Roosevelt in Retrospect: A Profile in History* (New York: Harper & Brothers, 1950), 24.

"all the categories": "What Is to Become of Us?" *Fortune,* 12/19/1933.

"No! No! I won't hear of it!" Frances Perkins, *The Roosevelt I Knew* (New York: Viking, 1946), 11.

"amiably insistent force of his personality," Earle Looker, *This Man Roosevelt* (New York: Brewer, Warner & Putnam, 1932), 14.

"particularly susceptible": Eleanor Roosevelt, *This I Remember* (New York: Harper &

Brothers, 1949), 2.

"He was fantastically sensitive": Notes from interview with Mrs. Amyas Ames, Joseph Lash Papers, FDRL.

"a big friendly smile": Frank Capra, *The Name Above the Title: An Autobiography* (New York: Macmillan, 1971), 346.

"the bitterest moment": Gunther, *Roosevelt in Retrospect,* 176.

well-lubricated mock trial: "Big Business Men Visit Boy Scouts in Summer Camp," *New York World,* 7/28/1921; "Enright Framed in 'Wet' Case, But Wins Acquittal," *New York Daily News,* 1921.

poliovirus passes from person to person: Suellen Hoy, *Chasing Dirt: The American Pursuit of Cleanliness* (New York: Oxford University Press, 1995), 7–15; Edwin G. Burrows and Mike Wallace, *Gotham: A History of New York City to 1898* (New York: Oxford University Press, 1999), 588–589.

"almost in the same manner": John R. Paul, *A History of Poliomyelitis* (New Haven: Yale University Press, 1971), 2.

cleanliness crusades were seen to work: Hoy, *Chasing Dirt,* 62–72.

New York's first cases: "269 Poliomyelitis Cases Here in a Year," *New York Times,* 9/18/1921; "Infantile Paralysis Cases

Increasing," *New York Times,* 9/25/1921.

children were struck in Westchester County: "Infantile Paralysis Is Spreading Upstate," *New York Times,* 8/23/1921.

The park sits in the Hudson Highlands: Palisades Interstate Park Commission, *60 Years of Park Cooperation: A History, 1900–1960* (New York[?], 1960), 15–33; William J. Myles, *Harriman Trails: A Guide and History* (New York: New York-New Jersey Trail Conference, 1991), 354–356, 459–470. Bear Mountain and Harriman State Parks were established as part of the Palisades Interstate Park, which includes properties in both New York and New Jersey.

"greatest playground in the world": George D. Blauvelt, "Bear Mountain," *Proceedings of the New York State Historical Association with the Quarterly Journal,* vol. XIX, 1921, 31–32.

a highlight of the season: for usage of Bear Mountain/Harriman State Parks, see *Annual Report of the Commissioners of the Palisades Interstate Park,* 1919 (Trenton, NJ: State of New Jersey, 1920), 16–17; *Annual Report of the Commissioners of the Palisades Interstate Park,* 1921 (Albany: J. B. Lyon, 1922), 307; *"Boy Scouts Hosts* of City Leaders," *New York Times,* 8/25/ 1921.

by 1920 the water: Sanitary conditions at Bear Mountain are reviewed in *Annual Report of the Commissioners of the Palisades Interstate Park,* 1921 (Albany: J. B. Lyon Co., 1922), 10; New York [State] Department of Health, *Annual Report for the Year Ending December 31, 1921* (Albany: J. B. Lyon, 1922), 320–24.

"keen country": Quoted in Ronnie Clark Coffey, *Images of America: Harriman State Park* (Charleston, SC: Arcadia Publishing, 2010), 50.

quick to shake hands: Geoffrey C. Ward, *A First-Class Temperament: The Emergence of Franklin Roosevelt* (New York: Harper & Row, 1989), 116.

Like a seed: Dorothy Crawford, *The Invisible Enemy: A Natural History of Viruses* (New York: Oxford University Press, 2003), 19–20.

Chapter 2: Symptoms

"The first thing for a private secretary": quoted in Doris Kearns Goodwin, *No Ordinary Time: Franklin and Eleanor Roosevelt: The Home Front in World War II* (New York: Simon & Schuster, 1994), 21.

"I thought he looked quite tired": MAL to ER,

8/23/1921, FBP/Correspondence, FDRL.

ordeal that shook his confidence: The best account of the Newport scandal is in Geoffrey C. Ward, *A First-Class Temperament: The Emergence of Franklin Roosevelt* (New York: Harper & Row, 1989), 568–574.

"spoke of the presidency": Rexford G. Tugwell, *In Search of Roosevelt* (Cambridge, MA: Harvard University Press, 1972), 52–53.

"For twenty years": Quoted in John Gunther, *Roosevelt in Retrospect: A Profile in History* (New York: Harper & Brothers, 1950), 262.

"he thought he might one day be president": Geoffrey C. Ward, *Before the Trumpet: Young Franklin Roosevelt, 1882–1905* (New York: Harper & Row, 1985), 253.

"anyone who is governor of New York": "Franklin Delano Roosevelt, 1882–1945: Five Harvard Men Pay Tribute," *Harvard Alumni Bulletin,* 4/28/1945, 451–452.

"I always thought he had this in mind": Oral history interview with Josephus Daniels, 5/29/1947, Frank Freidel, Small Collections, FDRL.

His vaulting ambition: Geoffrey C. Ward, the leading authority on FDR's youth and early career, describes FDR's veneration of Theodore Roosevelt, makes the comparison between James Roosevelt and T.R., and presents the idea that FDR, though genuinely in love with ER, also hoped to use the marriage as a way of strengthening his connection to her uncle. See *Before the Trumpet,* 194, 314–15.

FDR hung a portrait: S. J. Woolf, *Drawn from Life* (New York: Whittlesey House, 1932), 368–369.

"the ghostly procession": Henry F. Pringle, *Alfred E. Smith: A Critical Study* (New York: Macy-Masius, 1927), 297.

"1932 will be our year": Rexford G. Tugwell, *The Democratic Roosevelt* (Garden City, NY: Doubleday, 1957), 129. Tugwell noted: "This bit of forecasting I might doubt if Tom Lynch himself, with Mrs. Lynch corroborating, had not related it to me with utterly convincing circumstantial description. I am compelled to accept it."

"Not sent": Quoted in Ward, *First-Class Temperament,* 574–575. Ward notes the depth of Roosevelt's alarm over the incident in this reflection: "A dozen years later, he was still fearful of the potential political damage his career might suffer if the opposition chose to rake up the old Newport scandal. Running for President in 1932, and working closely with Earle Looker,

his extravagantly admiring campaign biographer, Roosevelt and [Louis] Howe made sure that Franklin's lengthy press release written to refute the [Republican senators'] charges was included in the text, word for word. Of the eighteen pages devoted to Franklin's almost eight years at the Navy Department in Looker's *This Man Roosevelt*, nearly half are devoted to his version of what happened at Newport."

Emotional stress can weaken: Suzanne C. Segerstrom and Gregory E. Miller, "Psychological Stress and the Human Immune System: A Meta-Analytic Study of Thirty Years of Inquiry." *Psychological Bulletin*, 2004, vol. 130, no. 4, 601–630.

long history of medical troubles: Ward, *Before the Trumpet*, 122–123, 150, 177, 185–186, 198–200; Ward, *First-Class Temperament*, 19, 63, 156, 187–188, 196, 199, 307–308, 310, 326, 368–369, 407–410, 413–414, 466. Tonsillectomy has been noted to have a high correlation with poliomyelitis, though a causal link has not been proven. See Noah D. Fabricant, "Franklin D. Roosevelt's Tonsillectomy and Poliomyelitis," *Eye, Ear, Nose and Throat Monthly,* vol. 36 (June 1957), 348–349.

"I never should allow:" Quoted in Ward, *Before the Trumpet*, 139–141.

And water for the Roosevelt kitchen: John F. Sears, F. Kennon Moody, and John Auwaerter, *Historical Resource Study for the Roosevelt Estate,* vol. 1, "An Operational History" (draft manuscript, National Park Service, 2004), 35.

associates at both firms: FDR's employment with the law firm and Fidelity & Deposit are described in Ward, *First-Class Temperament,* 560–562; and Frank Freidel, *Franklin D. Roosevelt: The Ordeal* (Boston: Little, Brown, 954), 92–93.

"laughed as much as we all did": FDR to Van Lear Black, 3/6/1925, FBP/Correspondence, FDRL.

many wealthy New Yorkers: Interview with Anna Eleanor Roosevelt, Robert D. Graff Papers, FDRL. See also Alden Nowlan, *Campobello: The Outer Island* (Toronto: Clarke, Irwin, 1975), 89–92.

Hay fever and asthma: Ibid.

"logy and tired": ER, *This Is My Story* (New York: Harper & Brothers, 1937), 329–330.

"delicate manifestations": George Draper, *Acute Poliomyelitis* (Philadelphia: P. Blakiston's Son & Co., 1917), 62–63.

job of baiting hooks: Earle Looker, *This Man Roosevelt* (New York: Brewer, Warner & Putnam, 1932), 111; see also Robert

Lovett to George Draper, 9/12/1921, Lovett Papers, Countway Library, Harvard University.

"old salt": Elliott Roosevelt and James Brough, *An Untold Story: The Roosevelts of Hyde Park* (New York: Putnam, 1973), 138.

If a person has had the virus: Dorothy Horstmann, "Acute Poliomyelitis: Relation of Physical Activity at the Time of Onset to the Course of the Disease," *Journal of the American Medical Association,* 142:4, 1/28/1950, 236–241.

"Father loved life on the island": James Roosevelt with Bill Libby, *My Parents: A Differing View* (Chicago: Playboy Press, 1976), 52.

"wild, whooping, romping": James Roosevelt and Sidney Shallet, *Affectionately, FDR: A Son's Story of a Lonely Man* (New York: Harcourt, Brace & Co., 1959), 141.

His activities on Wednesday: Anna Roosevelt Boettiger, "My Life with FDR: How Polio Helped Father," *The Woman,* July 1949, 53–54. James Roosevelt and Sidney Shalett describe the swimming, sailing, and forest fire in *Affectionately, FDR,* 141–142. Elliott Roosevelt and James Brough closely mirror James's account in *An Untold Story,*

139. The Roosevelt children's accounts differ as to whether they fought the fire with their father on the same day that he first reported feeling ill, August 10, or the day before. Anna, writing some years closer to the event, and in greater detail, said the fire was August 9. James and Elliott said it was August 10. Eleanor Roosevelt also put it on August 10, in *This Is My Story*, 329–330. Thus, out of four participants who referred to a date, the vote was three to one in favor of the fire occurring on August 10, the day that Roosevelt said he was ill and went to bed. So I have written as if the events all happened on one day. But it's possible the fire occurred the day before.

"I didn't feel the usual reaction": Looker, *This Man Roosevelt,* 111. Only one firsthand account of the onset of his polio by Roosevelt himself survives. It came in a letter to a physician, William Egleston, who inquired about his case in 1924, 10/11/1924, FBP/Correspondence, FDRL. FDR also gave an account of the incident to the journalist Earle Looker, who published a campaign biography, *This Man Roosevelt,* in 1932. Looker's account contains errors; the Egleston letter is more trustworthy.

If he had a cold: Elliott Roosevelt and James

Brough, *An Untold Story,* 139.

"There was no fuss": Anna Roosevelt Boettiger, "My Life with FDR: How Polio Helped Father," *The Woman,* July 1949.

first hint that something is wrong: See, for example, Tony Gould, *A Summer Plague: Polio and Its Survivors* (New Haven: Yale University Press, 1995), 230.

When Anna came upstairs: Roosevelt and Brough, *An Untold Story,* 139.

"whine about trouble": Ibid., 142.

"stabbing pains": Ibid., 139.

Eleanor directed Calder: Ibid., 139.

Only one treatment in the early stage: "Serum Treatment of Acute Poliomyelitis," *The Medical Council,* 21:1, August 1916, 57; George Draper, *Infantile Paralysis* (New York: Appleton-Century, 1935), 146–147.

"our faithful friend": Eleanor Roosevelt, *This Is My Story,* 331.

He found the recent nominee: ER to James Roosevelt Roosevelt, 8/14/1921 and 8/18/1921, ER papers FDRL; Eleanor Roosevelt, *This Is My Story,* 331; FDR to Dr. Lloyd Egleston, 10/11/1924, FBP/Correspondence, FDRL; ER interview with Robert D. Graff, Graff Papers, FDRL.

Adult patients have compared: Daniel J. Wilson, *Living with Polio: The Epidemic and Its*

Survivors (Chicago: University of Chicago Press, 2005), 19–20, 35, 43–44.

When he awoke: FDR to Egleston, 10/11/1924, FBP/Correspondence, FDRL.

Chapter 3: Diagnosis

basic skills in nursing: Eleanor Roosevelt, This Is My Story (New York: Harper & Brothers, 1937), 332.

"She had been hurt": Marion Dickerman oral history interview, CCOH, 345.

"That was her story": notes of interview with Esther Lape, Joseph Lash Papers, FDRL.

only a few undisputed facts: Joseph E. Persico combines the various scraps of information with informed guesses to create a credible account of the relationship between FDR and Lucy Mercer in Franklin and Lucy: President Roosevelt, Mrs. Rutherfurd, and the Other Remarkable Women in His Life (New York: Random House, 2008).

"The war had made": The Autobiography of Eleanor Roosevelt (New York: Harper & Brothers, 1961), 112.

The doctor . . . was "mystified": ER interview with Robert Graff, Graff Papers, FDRL.

Her husband too was now: ER to James Roosevelt Roosevelt, 8/18/1921, ER Papers,

FDRL. FDR's state of mind at this point is indicated by ER's statement a few days later that he was "getting back his grip & a better mental attitude."

"who, thank heavens, is here": ER to James Roosevelt Roosevelt, 8/14/1921, ER Papers, FDRL.

"a very little and very ugly man": Notes on interview with George Marvin, Rexford Tugwell Papers, FDRL.

"looked like a singed cat": Oral history interview with John Mack (George Palmer), 2/1/1949, Small Collections, FDRL.

His father had been a newspaper editor: S. J. Woolf, "As His Closest Friend Sees Roosevelt," *New York Times,* 11/27/1932.

"wear out his hams": Russell Baker, *The Good Times* (New York: Morrow, 1989), 8–9.

Josephus Daniels said Howe: Oral history interview with Josephus Daniels (Frank Freidel), 5/29/1947, Small Collections, FDRL.

"harder, racier, more down to earth": Elliott Roosevelt and James Brough, *An Untold Story: The Roosevelts of Hyde Park* (New York: Putnam, 1973), 120.

Dr. Keen had been practicing: James L. Stone, "W. W. Keen: America's Pioneer Neurological Surgeon," *Neurosurgery,* vol.

17, no. 6, 1985, 997–1009; Richard L. Rovit and William T. Couldwell, "A Man for All Seasons: W. W. Keen," *Neurosurgery,* vol. 50, no. 1, January 2002, 181–190.

"great discouragement": ER to James Roosevelt Roosevelt, 8/18/1921, ER Papers, FDRL.

"a most careful, thorough examination": ER to James Roosevelt Roosevelt, 8/14/1921, ER Papers, FDRL.

"excruciating" procedure: Roosevelt and Brough, *An Untold Story,* 141.

"chill and exposure": The words are ER's, reporting Dr. Keen's view to Rosy. ER to James Roosevelt Roosevelt, 8/18/1921, ER Papers, FDRL.

Keen gave Eleanor graver news: ER to James Roosevelt Roosevelt, 8/14/1921, ER Papers, FDRL. Later, ER either forgot the specificity of Keen's diagnosis or chose to cover his error. In the mid-1930s, she wrote: "Doctor Keen decided that it was some form of paralysis but could not explain it," *This Is My Story,* 331.

"his judgment seems at its very best": James L. Stone, "W. W. Stone: America's Pioneer Neurological Surgeon," *Neurosurgery,* 17:6 (1985), 997–59 1009.

But he should have known: I am indebted to

the neurologist John Segall, M.D., for this insight.

"could surely go down": ER to James Roosevelt Roosevelt, 8/14/1921, ER Papers, FDRL.

"I hope you will think": Ibid.

"ill from the effects of a chill": Ibid.

"had a severe chill": ER to MAL, undated, FBP/Correspondence, FDRL.

"The doctor feels sure": ER to James Roosevelt Roosevelt, 8/14/1921, ER Papers, FDRL.

"We have really had a very anxious time": ER to Endicott Peabody, 8/19/1921, Groton School Collections.

"a severe chill . . . very weak": Louis Howe to "Mr. Washburn," 8/19/1921, FBP/Correspondence, FDRL.

"sooner or later I": Alfred B. Rollins, Jr., *Roosevelt and Howe* (New York: Knopf, 1962), 172.

Howe decided to tell Fred Delano: This contention is borne out by ER's memory that she first learned that polio was suspected only when Frederic Delano told her so when he telephoned her at Campobello several days later. ER interviews with Robert D. Graff, Session 4, Graff Papers, FDRL.

"I dread the time": ER to James Roosevelt

Roosevelt, 8/18/1921, ER Papers, FDRL.

chiefly by providing opium: Geoffrey C. Ward, *Before the Trumpet: Young Franklin Roosevelt 1882–1905* (New York: Harper & Row, 1985), 70–78.

"how often we see young men": Frederic A. Delano to FDR, 7/30/1899, FBP/Correspondence, FDRL.

Delano showed Dr. Levine: Samuel A. Levine, "Some Notes Concerning the Early Days of Franklin D. Roosevelt's Attack of Poliomyelitis . . . ," unpublished manuscript, copy made available to the author by Dr. Levine's son, Dr. Herbert J. Levine.

And Levine was hardly accustomed: Herbert J. Levine, "Samuel A. Levine (1891–1966)" *Clinical Cardiology,* 15 (1992), 473–476.

He was troubled by the thought: Levine, "Some Notes . . ."

It is hard to know: J. F. Ditunno, Jr. and G. J. Herbison, "Franklin D. Roosevelt: Diagnosis, Clinical Course, and Rehabilitation from Poliomyelitis," *American Journal of Physical Medicine & Rehabilitation,* vol 81, no. 8, August 2002. Ditunno and Herbison say: "There are no prospective clinical trials in the literature . . . devoted to poliomyelitis that support [Levine's] claim, and there is no mention of this as a recommended treatment in review articles in the 1940s and 1950s."

Over dinner at the Harvard Club: Levine, "Some Notes."

Lovett made his examination: Robert Lovett to George Draper, 9/12/1921, Lovett Papers, Countway Library, Harvard University.

"I learned that when Dr. Lovett": Levine, "Some Notes." In Lovett's surviving papers on the Roosevelt case at the Countway Library of Medicine at Harvard, neither he nor George Draper, whose letters to Lovett about the case are in Lovett's collection, refer explicitly to the performance of a lumbar puncture to test Roosevelt's cerebrospinal fluid for the level of white blood cells, then the more or less definitive test for poliomyelitis. But Samuel Levine's unpublished note on the case indicates that the procedure, though delayed, was indeed performed. The complete reference to the procedure in Levine's note is as follows: "I . . . learned that when Dr. Lovett saw the patient [on August 24–25] the lumbar puncture had not been done and it was not done till Wednesday [August 24] (four days after I advised it). I did not find out the cause of

the delay — whether the suggestion was not delayed by Mr. Delano or whether no one could be found to do it or possibly it was thought by the local physicians to be inadvisable. During those several days further paralysis had taken place. It never will be known whether a more prompt removal of spinal fluid would have altered the outcome." In 2003, several researchers contended, based on a statistical analysis, that Roosevelt's symptoms were more likely to have been caused by Guillain-Barre syndrome (GBS), an autoimmune disorder, than by poliomyelitis. (Armond S. Goldman, et al, "What Was the Cause of Franklin Delano Roosevelt's Paralytic Illness?" *Journal of Medical Biography*, 11 [2003], 232–240.) But the authors apparently were unaware of Dr. Levine's unpublished note; they say: "FDR's cerebrospinal fluid was not examined." As the authors themselves note, cerebrospinal fluid taken from a patient with GBS contains "few leucocytes [white blood cells] but a high concentration of protein. This was the opposite of the cerebrospinal fluid findings in paralytic poliomyelitis." But Dr. Levine's private note indicates that Dr. Lovett did examine the cerebrospinal fluid and knew very well that a high level of white blood cells was consistent with poliomyelitis. If Lovett had discovered a low white blood cell count, he would have doubted that poliomyelitis was the cause of FDR's illness. Yet Lovett wrote George Draper that "I thought [the diagnosis] was perfectly clear as far as the physical findings were concerned." Lovett to George Draper, 9/12/1921, Lovett papers, Countway Library of Medicine, Harvard University. Absolute certainty about the diagnosis is impossible without the laboratory tests later developed to distinguish between polio and GBS. But the existing evidence, taken together, indicates that poliomyelitis was by far the most likely cause of Roosevelt's illness and the resulting paralysis.

Near the end of her life: Geoffrey C. Ward, *A First-Class Temperament: The Emergence of Franklin Roosevelt* (New York: Harper & Row, 1989), 591.

Chapter 4: "To Keep Up His Courage"

"some uncertainty in their minds": Robert Lovett to George Draper, 9/12/1921, Lovett Papers, Countway Library, Harvard University.

"by instinct an aristocrat": "Robert William-

son Lovett, 1859–1924," *Boston Medical and Surgical Journal,* 2/19/1925, 374–375.

So he could only state what he knew to be the facts: Robert Lovett to George Draper, 9/12/1921, Lovett Papers, Countway Library, Harvard University.

Lovett was well prepared: Robert W. Lovett, *The Treatment of Infantile Paralysis* (Philadelphia: P. Blakiston's Son & Co., 1917), 17–26.

Lovett put his confidential view: Robert Lovett to George Draper, 9/12/1921, Lovett Papers, Countway Library, Harvard University.

"no more than two or three cases": Lovett, *Treatment of Infantile Paralysis,* 20.

Roosevelt could expect "considerable" improvement: E. H. Bennet to Robert Lovett, 9/1/1921, Lovett Papers, Countway Library, Harvard University. Dr. Bennet asked Lovett: "When you stated that the improvement in 2 weeks would be considerable, did you mean *above* or *below* waistline?" Lovett answered Bennet's letter but not his question.

there must be no more massage: Robert Lovett to W. W. Keen, 9/12/1921, Lovett Papers, Countway Library, Harvard University.

later studies: J. F. Ditunno Jr. and G. J. Herbison, "Franklin D. Roosevelt: Diagnosis, Clinical Course, and Rehabilitation from Poliomyelitis," *American Journal of Physical Medicine & Rehabilitation,* vol 81, no. 8, August 2002, 562.

"disease is too serious": Frederic A. Delano to ER, 8/20/1921, FBP/Correspondence, FDRL. See also Eleanor Roosevelt, *This Is My Story* (New York: Harper & Brothers, 1937), 332.

Eleanor felt "great relief": Eleanor Roosevelt, *This Is My Story,* 332.

He suggested that Dr. George Draper: Robert Lovett to George Draper, 9/12/1921, Lovett Papers, Countway Library, Harvard University.

Before Lovett left the island: Lela Stiles, *The Man Behind Roosevelt* (Cleveland, OH: World, 1954), 81–82.

"The handling of [FDR's] mail": Eleanor Roosevelt, *This Is My Story,* 333.

"the fact of his illness": W. W. Keen to Robert Lovett, 9/14/1921, Lovett Papers, Countway Library, Harvard University.

Howe released a statement: "Franklin D. Roosevelt Ill," *New York Times,* 8/27/1921.

a bad cold: Earl Harding to ER, 9/8/1921, FBP/Correspondence, FDRL. Harding wrote: "I had no idea Mr. Roosevelt was so ill — the office only said he had a bad cold."

"Dear Lang": FDR to Langdon Marvin, 9/3/1921, FBP/Correspondence, FDRL.

"It is perfectly marvelous": Annie Delano Hitch to ER, 9/2/1921, Papers Donated by the Children, FDRL. No letter survives in which ER asks friends and relatives to keep the diagnosis secret, but that she made the request is evident, given replies from Annie Delano Hitch and others. ". . . the secret has been pretty well kept considering all the telegraphing, etc.," Frederic Delano wrote her. "Of course I shall say nothing," a friend of Eleanor's replied in early September. Frederic A. Delano to ER, 8/28/1921, FBP/Correspondence, FDRL; unidentified correspondent to ER [September 1921], ER Papers, FDRL.

"to feel that we know": ER to Robert Lovett, 8/24/1921, Lovett Papers, Countway Library, Harvard University.

"only a few glimpses": James Roosevelt and Sidney Shalett, *Affectionately, FDR: A Son's Story of a Lonely Man* (New York: Harcourt, Brace & Co., 1959), 142.

"the most dangerous instrument,": W. W. Keen to Robert Lovett, 9/14/1921, Lovett Papers, Countway Library, Harvard University. For FDR's bladder infection, see ER

to W. W. Keen, 9/26/1921, Small Collections, FDRL.

He had diarrhea: FDR to Dr. William Egleston, 10/11/1924, FBP/Correspondence, FDRL.

"Atrophy increasing power lessening": E. H. Bennet to Robert Lovett, 8/31/1921, Lovett Papers, Countway Library, Harvard University.

"When you stated that the improvement": E. H. Bennet to Robert Lovett, 9/1/1921 Lovett Papers, Countway Library, Harvard University.

"Cannot add anything": Robert Lovett to E. H. Bennet, 9/2/1921, Lovett Papers, Countway Library, Harvard University.

FDR's mother arrived at Campobello: SDR to Frederic Delano, 9/2/1921, FBP/Correspondence, FDRL.

"controlled herself remarkably": Roosevelt and Shalett, *Affectionately, FDR,* 142. James Roosevelt said his mother gave him this report of SDR's composure.

"He looks well": SDR to Dora Delano Forbes, 9/3/1921, Papers Donated by the Children, FDRL.

"greatest authority we have": SDR to Dora Delano Forbes, 9/3/1921, Papers Donated by the Children, FDRL.

"some 'fatherly' advice": Frederic Delano to

592

FDR, 9/4/1921, FBP/Correspondence, FDRL.

Sara settled the point: Lyman Delano to ER, 9/1/1921, Box 17, Papers Donated by the Children, FDRL; E. H. Bennet to Robert Lovett, 9/8/1921, Lovett Papers, Countway Library, Harvard University.

As soon as Sara reached New York City: George Draper to Robert Lovett, 9/9/1921, and Robert Lovett to George Draper, 9/12/1921, Lovett Papers, Countway Library, Harvard University.

"trouble with his legs": "Roosevelt's Legs Affected," *Brooklyn Citizen,* 9/10/1921; "Franklin D. Roosevelt Oddly Ill," *Oswego Times,* 9/10/1921.

Down the stairs they lugged him: Eleanor Roosevelt, *This Is My Story,* 333–334.

Upon reaching the mainland: Geoffrey Ward gives a complete account of the trip from the cottage to New York in *A First-Class Temperament: The Emergence of Franklin Roosevelt* (New York: Harper & Row, 1989), 598–602.

"said that some weeks ago": "Roosevelt Much Better, Starts Back to New York," *New York World,* 9/14/1921.

"he managed to wave": John Gunther, *Roosevelt in Retrospect: A Profile in History*

(New York: Harper & Brothers, 1950), 223.

"stood the journey finely": E. H. Bennet to Robert Lovett, Lovett Papers, Countway Library, Harvard University.

Draper stood on the platform: Ernest K. Lindley, *Franklin D. Roosevelt: A Career in Progressive Democracy* (New York: Blue Ribbon Books, 1931), 203.

Chapter 5: "The Psychological Factor Is Paramount"

"such a serious illness": George Draper, *Infantile Paralysis* (New York: Appleton-Century, 1935), 143.

Fear of the cripple: Herbert C. Covey, *Social Perceptions of People with Disabilities in History* (Springfield, IL: Charles C. Thomas, 1998), 45–88; Alexander Horwitz, "The Cripple's Place in Society Through the Ages," *The Nation's Health* (August 1923).

Barnum freak show: Douglas McMurtrie, *The Care of Crippled Children in the United States* (New York, 1912), 8.

"Physical weakness or inferiority": Horwitz, "Cripple's Place in Society."

survey of 600 U.S. employers: Henry H. Kessler, *The Crippled and the Disabled:*

Rehabilitation of the Physically Handicapped in the United States (New York: Columbia University Press, 1935), 22–23.

"The repugnance and distaste": Kessler, *Crippled and Disabled,* 22.

everyone equated disability with weakness: Alan M. Kraut, "Plagues and Prejudice: Nativism's Construction of Disease in Nineteenth- and Twentieth-Century New York City," in David Rosner, ed., *Hives of Sickness: Public Health and Epidemics in New York City* (New Brunswick, NJ: Rutgers University Press, 1995); Naomi Rogers, *Dirt and Disease: Polio Before FDR* (New Brunswick, NJ: Rutgers University Press, 1992), 30–71. See also Andrew Mc-Clary, "Germs Are Everywhere: The Germ Threat as Seen in Magazine Articles, 1890–1920," *Journal of American Culture,* vol. 3, no. 1, 33–46, Spring 1980.

"a little too loose": quoted in Betty Boyd Caroli, *The Roosevelt Women: A Portrait in Five Generations* (New York: Basic Books, 1998), 302.

In his office on Manhattan's Upper East Side: William O. Douglas, *Go East, Young Man: The Early Years* (New York: Random House, 1974), 177. Douglas, whom Roosevelt appointed to the U.S. Supreme Court in 1939, was George Draper's patient and friend.

Few doctors of the era: Sarah W. Tracy, "George Draper and American Constitutional Medicine, 1916–1946: Reinventing the Sick Man," *Bulletin of the History of Medicine* 66:1 (Spring 1992), 53–89; George Draper, "A New Point of View in Approaching the Diagnosis and Treatment of a Patient," *Endocrinology,* vol 3, no. 2, April–June 1919, 164–172.

"remember that the healing force": George Draper, *Infantile Paralysis* (New York: D. Appleton-Century, 1935), 151.

Louis Howe may also have told: Geoffrey C. Ward makes the point about Howe's possible intention in *A First-Class Temperament: The Emergence of Franklin Roosevelt* (New York: Harper & Row, 1989), 603.

Rates of recovery from paralysis: Draper, *Infantile Paralysis,* 143.

"paralyzing injury": Ibid., 136–137.

Draper had to say something *definitive:* "F.D. Roosevelt Ill of Poliomyelitis," *New York Times,* 9/16/1921; "F.D. Roosevelt in Hospital Here, Infantile Paralysis the Diagnosis," *New York World,* 9/16/1921 "F.D. Roosevelt Suffers a Mild Paralysis Attack," *New York World,* 9/16/1921.

"would hasten the return" and "the attack was so slight": New York Times, 9/16/1921.

"My dear Eleanor:" Adolph Miller to ER, 9/16/1921, ER Papers, FDRL.

"Of course he will regain": Mary Sprague Miller to ER, 9/16/1921, ER Papers, FDRL.

"I thought it would please": Van Lear Black to ER, 9/16/1921, ER Papers, FDRL.

"an illness of that kind": Corinne Robinson Alsop to FDR, 9/16/1921, ER Papers, FDRL.

No visitors were allowed: Louis Howe to Louis B. Wehle, FBP/Correspondence, PFDRL; cards from well-wishers, "Infantile Paralysis" file, ER papers, FDRL.

"I appreciate your little note": FDR to Daniel C. Roper, 9/29/1921, FBP/Correspondence, FDRL.

"You drive the thought of it": Turnley Walker, *Rise Up and Walk* (New York: Dutton, 1950), 21.

"While the doctors were unanimous": Quoted in Ward, *First-Class Temperament,* 603.

"In their own eyes": Daniel J. Wilson, *Living with Polio: The Epidemic and Its Survivors* (Chicago: University of Chicago Press, 2005), 50.

"The idea that you": Anne Walters and Jim Marugg, *Beyond Endurance* (New York: Harper & Brothers, 1954), 138.

Roosevelt in his hospital room: FDR to

Henry Morgenthau, Jr., 9/22/1921; FDR to A. R. Mansfield, 9/22/1921; FDR to Thomas McRae, 9/20/1921; FDR to Manton Wyvell, 9/28/1921, all FBP/Correspondence, FDRL; FDR to Walter Camp, 9/28/1921, in Elliott Roosevelt, ed., *FDR: His Personal Letters, 1905–1928* (New York: Duell, Sloan and Pearce, 1948), 530.

"that state of nervous collapse,": George Draper to Eben Homer Bennet, quoted in John Gunther, *Roosevelt in Retrospect: A Profile in History* (New York: Harper & Brothers, 1950), 226.

When Dr. Draper permitted: Ward, *First-Class Temperament,* 606.

"a very trembling signature": ER interview with Robert D. Graff, Robert D. Graff Papers, FDRL.

"They assume a Papa-knows-best attitude," Isadore Snapper, "Other Times, Other Fears," in Samuel Standard and Helmuth Nathan, *Should the Patient Know the Truth?* (New York: Springer, 1955).

"I feel so strongly": George Draper to Robert Lovett, 9/24/1921, Lovett Papers, Countway Library, Harvard University.

"I do not know whether you use it": Robert Lovett to George Draper, 9/26/1929, Lovett Papers, Countway Library, Har-

vard University.

"had much more power": George Draper to
Robert Lovett, 10/11/1921, Lovett Papers,
Countway Library, Harvard University.

"There is power," Robert Lovett to E. H.
Bennet, 10/17/1921, Lovett Papers, Countway Library, Harvard University.

He directed that the move be made: Rita
Halle Kleeman, *Gracious Lady: The Life of
Sara Delano Roosevelt* (New York:
Appleton-Century, 1935), 277.

"a physical impairment's meaning": Davis W.
Houck and Amos Kiewe, *FDR's Body
Politics: The Rhetoric of Disability* (College
Station, TX: Texas A&M University Press,
2003), 6.

Chapter 6: "Perfectly Definite in My Determination"

"very cheerful," Eleanor Roosevelt, *This Is
My Story* (New York: Harper & Brothers,
1937), 335.

"It's a lovely region": Lily Norton to Miss
Whidden, 11/14/1921, Small Collections,
FDRL.

"the most natural insistence": George Draper,
Infantile Paralysis (New York: Appleton-
Century, 1935), 161–162.

"exceedingly ambitious," George Draper to

Robert Lovett, 11/19/1921, Lovett Papers, Countway Library, Harvard University.

Roosevelts' adjoining town houses: A full description of the residence on East 65th Street appears in Deborah S. Gardner, *Roosevelt House at Hunter College: The Story of Franklin and Eleanor's New York City Home* (New York: The Gilder Lehrman Institute of American History and Hunter College, 2009). The Roosevelts gave the residence to Hunter College in 1942. After a thorough restoration, it became the home of Hunter's Public Policy Institute in 2009.

"He was tall and heavy": Eleanor Roosevelt, *This Is My Story,* 335.

As to physical pain: FDR to William Egleston, 10/24/1924, FBP/Correspondence, FDRL.

According to a reporter: Ernest K. Lindley, *Franklin D. Roosevelt: A Career in Progressive Democracy* (New York: Blue Ribbon Books, rev. ed., 1934), 205.

reprise of high fever: John Gunther, *Roosevelt in Retrospect: A Profile in History* (New York: Harper & Brothers, 1950), 227.

"I am back in my own house": FDR to Robert Marx, 12/2/1921, FBP/Correspondence, FDRL.

"The price for normal relations": Robert F. Murphy, *The Body Silent* (New York: W.W. Norton, 1990), 107, 171.

"As cheerful of demeanor": Hugh Gregory Gallagher, *Black Bird Fly Away: Disabled in an Able-Bodied World* (Arlington, VA: Vandamere Press, 1998), 45–46.

"everything look[s] big": Arnold R. Beisser, *Flying Without Wings* (New York: Doubleday, 1989), 23.

"When the small child": Turnley Walker, *Rise Up and Walk* (New York: Dutton, 1950), 37.

"Each person simply accepts": Murphy, *Body Silent,* 12.

"The alien intruder": Ibid., 108.

"this other body": Lorenzo Wilson Milam, *CripZen: A Manual for Survival* (San Diego: MHO & MHO Works, 1993), 131.

"my legs": FDR to William Egleston, 10/24/1924, FBP/Correspondence, FDRL.

"I have tried hard": Unknown to ER, [n.d.], ER Papers, FDRL.

"a fixture of the consciousness": Ibid., *Body Silent,* 64–65.

"It was a kind of inner reserve": ER, oral history interview with Robert Graff, Graff papers, FDRL.

"a person without privacy": Gallagher, *Black*

Bird Fly Away, 46.

"It's hard to ask": Milam, *CripZen,* 130.

"If you require the help": Gallagher, *Black Bird Fly Away,* 77.

"a diminution of everything": Murphy, *Body Silent,* 85.

"Mr. Pell had better wake up": "a trifle optimistic": quoted in Frank Freidel, *Franklin D. Roosevelt: The Ordeal* (Boston: Little, Brown, 1954), 102.

Howe was a disappointed dramatist: Alfred B. Rollins, Jr., *Roosevelt and Howe* (New York: Knopf, 1962), 71–73.

"I was impressed": S. J. Woolf, "As His Closest Friend Sees Roosevelt," *New York Times Magazine,* 11/27/1932.

Howe's *"bony body":* Rexford G. Tugwell, "The Fallow Years of Franklin D. Roosevelt," *Ethics* (January 1956), 98–116.

"He couldn't be . . . natural": Frances Perkins oral history interview, pt. 4, session 1, 455–57, CCOH.

"this stupid way of living": Louis Howe to Grace Howe, 11/15/1922, Howe Personal Papers, FDRL.

"Is it possible": Louis Howe to Grace Howe [undated; July 1915], Howe Personal Papers, FDRL.

"you told me": Louis Howe to Grace Howe,

7/10/1922, Howe Personal Papers, FDRL.

But he was getting bigger offers: Howe's biographers differ on the particulars of his decision about what job to take in 1921, but they agree on the key point — that he had substantial offers from various employers and turned them down to stay with Roosevelt. See Lela Stiles, *The Man Behind Roosevelt* (Cleveland, OH: World, 1954), 75; Albert B. Rollins, Jr., *Roosevelt and Howe* (New York: Knopf, 1962), 128, 174, 177; Julie M. Fenster, *FDR's Shadow* (New York: Palgrave MacMillan, 2009), 126–128.

"This is my job": James Roosevelt and Sidney Shalett, *Affectionately, FDR: A Son's Story of a Lonely Man* (New York: Harcourt, Brace & Co., 1959), 144.

"It was the closest thing": Quoted in Geoffrey C. Ward, *A First-Class Temperament: The Emergence of Franklin Roosevelt* (New York: Harper & Row, 1989), 615.

"flung [a] challenge": Stiles, *Man Behind Roosevelt,* 82–84.

"The house was not overlarge" and room arrangements: Eleanor Roosevelt, *This Is My Story,* 335, 336–337.

Eleanor took this to heart: ER, interview with Frank Freidel, Small Collections, FDRL;

Eleanor Roosevelt, *This Is My Story,* 340; Ward, *First-Class Temperament,* 617.

"I do hope that he'll keep": Frances Perkins oral history interview, pt. 2, session 1, 330, 463, CCOH.

"vociferous in her demands": Anna Roosevelt Boettiger, "My Life with FDR: How Polio Helped Father," *The Woman,* May 1949.

She offered to provide: Eleanor Roosevelt, *This I Remember* (New York: Harper & Brothers, 1949), 13.

"treated the entire affair": S. J. Woolf, "As His Closest Friend Sees Roosevelt," *New York Times Magazine,* 11/27/1932.

"Franklin had no intention": Sara Delano, *My Boy Franklin* (New York: Ray Long & Richard R. Smith, Inc., 1933), 101–102.

"what really happened": Gunther, *Roosevelt in Retrospect,* 227–228.

"many men and women": Richard Thayer Goldberg, *The Making of Franklin D. Roosevelt: Triumph over Disability* (Cambridge, MA: About Books, 1981), viii.

Chapter 7: "A Tower of Blocks"

"Wherever there is . . . the ability": Wilhelmine Gerber Wright, *Muscle Training in the Treatment of Infantile Paralysis* (Boston: Ernest Gregory, 1916), 3.

"Please tell him": Annie Delano Hitch to ER, 9/27/1921, ER Papers, FDRL.

"My body was still rigid": Hugh Gregory Gallagher, *Black Bird Fly Away* (Arlington, VA: Vandamere Press, 1998), 52–53.

"He himself is quite pleased": Kathleen Lake to Robert Lovett [fragment, apparently 1/4/1922], Lovett Papers, Countway Library, Harvard University.

"He is a wonderful patient": Kathleen Lake to Robert Lovett, 12/17/1922, Lovett Papers, Countway Library, Harvard University.

"She remarked with some pride": Kathleen Lake to Robert Lovett, 1/22/1922, Lovett Papers, Countway Library, Harvard University.

"The stretching of his knees": Kathleen Lake to Robert Lovett, 1/13/1922, Lovett Papers, Countway Library, Harvard University. FDR refers to the emergence of foot drop at this point in his treatment in his letter to William Egleston, 10/11/1924, FBP/Correspondence, FDRL.

"the most important feature": Robert Lovett to Arthur Krida, 1/31/1922, Lovett Papers, Countway Library, Harvard University.

"He appeared extremely relieved": Kathleen Lake to Robert Lovett, 2/12/1922, Lovett Papers, Countway Library, Harvard University.

"It depressed me to find": Bentz Plagemann, *My Place to Stand* (New York: Farrar, Straus & Co., 1949), 237.

"pulling myself up": Charles Mee, *A Nearly Normal Life* (Boston: Little, Brown, 1999), 97–98.

Roosevelt would fall: James Roosevelt and Sidney Shallet, *Affectionately, FDR* (New York: Harcourt, Brace & Co., 1959), 157.

"Counsel him not to try": Robert Lovett to Kathleen Lake, 3/20/1922, Lovett Papers, Countway Library, Harvard University.

"interesting thread in the complex tapestry": George Draper to Robert Lovett, 3/25/1922, Lovett Papers, Countway Library, Harvard University.

"I am writing without any talking": Robert Lovett to SDR, 6/7/1922, Lovett Papers, Countway Library, Harvard University.

"I have had such enormous": FDR to F. D. Pryor, 7/10/1922, FBP/Correspondence, FDRL.

"I am inclosing": FDR to Milo T. Bogard, 1/15/1924, FBP/Correspondence, FDRL.

"Below the knee": George Draper to Robert Lovett, 3/25/1922, Lovett Papers, Countway Library, Harvard University.

"stopped to analyze": Eleanor Roosevelt, *This I Remember* (New York: Harper & Brothers, 1949), 25.

"the most trying winter": Eleanor Roosevelt, *This Is My Story* (New York: Harper & Brothers, 1937), 336.

"I should judge": Robert Lovett to George Draper, 5/5/1922, Lovett Papers, Countway Library, Harvard University.

"They gave us self-respect": Regina Markel Morantz-Sanchez, et al., *In Her Own Words: Oral Histories of Women Physicans* (Westport, CT: Greenwood Press, 1982), 104–105.

"It is hard to tell": Wilhelmine G. Wright, "Crutch-Walking as an Art," *American Journal of Surgery,* December 1926.

"to get hold of him": Robert Lovett to SDR, 6/7/1922, Lovett Papers, Countway Library, Harvard University.

"I think [he] has made some gain": Robert Lovett to George Draper, 6/5/1922, Lovett Papers, Countway Library, Harvard University.

"Jim's eyes filled with tears": FDR to Adolphus Ragan, 4/6/1938, "Reminiscences by Contemporaries," Small Collections, FDRL.

By striving for years: "W. F. Sheehan Dies; Ex-Lieut. Governor," *New York Times,* 3/15/1917.

his ticket out of the trap: Rexford Tugwell develops this explanation of Roosevelt's escape from Tammany's shadow via "the Sheehan business" and the ascendency of Woodrow Wilson in *The Democratic Roosevelt* (Garden City, NY: Doubleday, 1957), 74–87.

Al Smith talked to New Yorkers: Smith has had many biographers, but the best short portrait of Smith's early career appears in Robert Caro, *The Power Broker: Robert Moses and the Fall of New York* (New York: Random House, 1974.)

"Of course, the word had spread around": Frances Perkins oral history interview, pt. 2, session 1, 328, CCOH.

"take care of yourself": Quoted in Geoffrey C. Ward, *A First-Class Temperament: The Emergence of Franklin Roosevelt* (New York: Harper & Row, 1989), 644.

George Draper may not have understood: George Draper to Robert Lovett, 6/9/1922, Lovett Papers, Countway Library, Harvard University.

"this vile burgh!" FDR to Livingston Davis, 4/10/1923, FBP/Correspondence, FDRL.

"I wish you would change": Quoted in F. Kennon Moody, "F.D.R. and His Neighbors: A Study of the Relationship Between Franklin Delano Roosevelt and the Residents of Dutchess County (doctoral dissertation, Department of History,

State University of New York, 1981), 3.

"Look what I can do": Edna Gurewitsch interview, *The American Experience,* "FDR: Part 2: Fear Itself," Public Broadcasting System.

two parallel bars: Oral history interview with Louis Depew (January 1948), National Park Service, FDRL.

"that he was passing": Sidney Gunn to FDR, 8/24/1924, FBP/Correspondence, FDRL.

"Don't worry about my getting fat": FDR to Sidney Gunn, 9/4/1924, FBP/Correspondence, FDRL.

"I'm not going to be conquered": Geoffrey C. Ward, ed., *Closest Companion: The Unknown Story of the Intimate Friendship Between Franklin Roosevelt and Margaret Suckley* (Boston: Houghton Mifflin, 1995), xvii.

"the water got me where I am," Oral history interview with Louis Depew, National Park Service, Small Collections, FDRL.

"I'd never felt anything": Earle Looker, *This Man Roosevelt* (New York: Brewer, Warren & Putnam, 1932), 111.

the nurse confirmed: Edna T. Rockey to Robert Lovett, Lovett papers, Countway Library, Harvard University.

Walking with crutches: The techniques used by polio patients in the 1920s to walk with crutches are described in Wilhelmine G. Wright, "Crutch-Walking as an Art," *American Journal of Surgery,* December 1926.

O'Connor recognized the crippled man: Basil O'Connor told the story to Turnley Walker, who retold it in *Roosevelt and the Warm Springs Story* (New York: A. A. Wyn, Inc., 1953), 6–9.

Chapter 8: "The Limits of His Possibilities"

He had fallen: James Roosevelt and Sidney Shalett, *Affectionately, FDR: A Son's Story of a Lonely Man* (New York: Harcourt, Brace & Co., 1959), 157.

the wheelchair would symbolize: Nick Watson and Brian Woods, "No Wheelchairs Beyond This Point: A Historical Examination of Wheelchair Access in the Twentieth Century in Britain and America," *Social Policy and Society,* 4:1 (January 2005), 97–105.

But Kathleen Lake told Dr. Lovett: Kathleen Lake to Robert Lovett, 3/17/1922, Lovett Papers, Countway Library, Harvard University. FDR refers to the difficulty of getting around the office of Emmett, Marvin & Roosevelt in a letter to Grenville Emmett, 9/24/1924, FBP/Correspondence, FDRL.

"A gentleman always rises": Emily Post, *Etiquette in Society, in Business, in Politics and in the Home* (New York: Funk and Wagnall's, 1922).

"It was his friends": Frances Perkins oral history interview, pt. 2, session 1, 328, CCOH.

"He never complained": Oral history interview with Eleanor Roosevelt, Robert Graff Papers, FDRL.

"I only wish": FDR to Frank N. Chapman, 3/22/1923, FBP/Correspondence, FDRL. In 1934, as president, Roosevelt would sign the enabling act for the establishment of Everglades National Park, though it would be thirteen more years before the land was assembled and the park actually dedicated.

"I read the History": FDR to John Lawrence, 4/12/1923, FBP/Correspondence, FDRL.

"The result has been most satisfactory": FDR described his activities aboard *Weona II* to Robert Lovett, 4/27/1923, Lovett Papers, Countway Library, Harvard University.

"I have found . . . for myself": FDR to Paul Hasbrouck, 10/17/1923, FBP/Correspondence, FDRL.

"He came back immensely improved": Kath-

leen Lake to Robert Lovett, 5/24/1923, Lovett Papers, Countway Library, Harvard University.

"I can't help feeling": FDR to George Marvin, 8/10/1922, FBP/Correspondence, FDRL.

"I have never specialized": Quoted in S. J. Woolf, *Drawn from Life* (New York: Whittlesey House, 1932), 369.

he built: Frank Freidel, *Franklin D. Roosevelt: The Ordeal* (Boston: Little, Brown, 1954), 114–115.

resumed work on an earlier program: Charles W. Snell, "Franklin D. Roosevelt and Forestry at Hyde Park, New York, 1911–1932," National Park Service, 1955.

He deplored the destruction: Thomas W. Patton, "The Forest Plantations at Hyde Park," in Nancy Fogel, ed., *FDR at Home* (Poughkeepsie, NY: Dutchess County Historical Society, 2005). See also John F. Sears, F. Kennon Moody, and John Auwaerter, "Historic Resource Study for the Roosevelt Estate," National Park Service, 2004.

"T.R. was the Roosevelt": Quoted in Woolf, *Drawn from Life,* 370.

"He could not drive his car": Samuel Rosenman, *Working with Roosevelt* (New York: Harper, 1952), 37–38.

"We are so busy": FDR to Charles McCarthy, 8/13/1923, FBP/Correspondence, FDRL.

"It dispels boredom": Quoted in Otis L. Graham, ed., *Franklin D. Roosevelt: His Life and Times* (New York: Da Capo Press, 1985), 400.

"Roosevelt was a walking": Frances Perkins oral history interview, pt. 3, session 1, 309–310, CCOH.

he once spent an entire morning: FDR to U. P. Hedrick, 3/28/1922, FBP/Correspondence, FDRL.

"I am very well satisfied": Robert Lovett to ER, 6/1/1923, Lovett Papers, Countway Library, Harvard University.

"recall her husband having said": Geoffrey C. Ward, *A First-Class Temperament: The Emergence of Franklin Roosevelt* (New York: Harper & Row, 1989), 665n.

"very long drawn out": FDR to Kathleen Lake, 7/23/1923, FBP-Subject/Infantile Paralysis, FDRL.

he reported good results: FDR to Paul Hasbrouck, 10/23/1923, FBP-Subject/Infantile Paralysis, FDRL.

He had been looking into every possibility: Ward, *First-Class Temperament,* 644–646.

"aero-therapeutic" method: FDR to B. P. Bagby, 12/5/1922; FDR to George

Draper, 11/17/1922; Draper to FDR, 1 1/27/1922, FBP-Subject/Infantile Paralysis, FDRL; "The Cunningham Tank Treatment," *Journal of the American Medical Association,* 5/5/1928. Cunningham's work was a forerunner of hyperbaric oxygen therapy, a legitimate treatment for some problems, but not for poliomyelitis.

"an entirely new life": Anna Roosevelt Boettiger, "My Life with FDR," *The Woman,* August 1949.

"Dear Father, I hope you are well": FDR Jr.'s letters are in Papers Donated by the Children, FDRL.

her relationship with FDR: So much has been written about FDR's sex life — very little of it based on any substantial evidence — that I have felt no need or wish to say anything more. His doctors said at one or two points that he was capable of intercourse in the sense that his paralysis did not prevent an erection. That is about all anyone really knows. I lean toward the view of Charles McGrath, who, in reviewing Joseph Persico's *Franklin and Lucy: President Roosevelt, Mrs. Rutherfurd, and the Other Remarkable Women in His Life* (New York: Random House, 2008), wrote: "[T]he evidence suggests that his real idea of pleasure at the end of the day was just to smoke a cigarette, have a couple of drinks and bask in the attention of some admiring females. That we want to read sex into this probably says more about us than about him." "The End of the Affair," *New York Times,* 4/20/2008.

"She was always so cheerful": Egbert Curtis quoted in Doris Kearns Goodwin, *No Ordinary Time: Franklin and Eleanor Roosevelt: The Home Front in World War II* (New York: Simon & Schuster, 1994), 117–118.

"without any background": Quoted in Bernard Asbell, *The FDR Memoirs* (Garden City, NY: Doubleday, 1973), 247.

"lovely throaty voice": Fulton Oursler, *Behold This Dreamer!* (Boston: Little, Brown, 1964), 368.

"banishing distrust and bitterness," Raymond Moley, *After Seven Years* (New York: Harper & Brothers, 1939), 297.

"she was just too devoted": Barbara Muller Curtis quoted in Asbell, *FDR Memoirs,* 248.

"I am very much disheartened": George Draper to Robert A. Lovett, 2/11/1924, Lovett Papers, Countway Library, Harvard University.

"there were days on the Larooco*":* Freidel, *Roosevelt: The Ordeal,* 191.

Chapter 9: "If You Will Get It Right"

They found out how far: Marion Dickerman oral history interview, CCOH.

Madison Square Garden: Preparations in Madison Square Garden are described in Robert K. Murray, *The 103rd Ballot: Democrats and the Disaster in Madison Square Garden* (New York: Harper & Row, 1976), 97–98, 116. See also "13,500 Flags in Big Arena," *Evening Star,* 6/21/1924.

Perkins sensed a collective shiver: Frances Perkins oral history interview, pt. 2, session 1, 325–28, CCOH. Perkins's recollections of Roosevelt's speech are the most detailed of all those left by eyewitnesses.

He reached the lectern: James Roosevelt and Sidney Shalett, *Affectionately, FDR: A Son's Story of a Lonely Man* (New York: Harcourt, Brace & Co., 1959), 204–206.

"In one huge burst": "Demonstration for Gov. Smith Well-Prepared," *Poughkeepsie Eagle-News,* 6/27/1924.

"Marion, I did it!" Marion Dickerman oral history interview, CCOH.

"He is hopelessly an invalid": Kyle D. Palmer quoted in Davis W. Houck and Amos Kiewe, *FDR's Body Politics: The Rhetoric of Disability* (College Station: Texas A & M University Press, 2003), 32.

"There was nothing at the Democratic conven-tion": Louisville *Courier-Journal* quoted in Houck and Kiewe, *FDR's Body Politics,* 30.

"It was one of the very best nominating speeches": Mark Sullivan, "Smith's Chances Slim in Spite of Huge Ovation in Convention," *Philadelphia Evening Star,* 6/27/1924.

"The one man to whom the contending fac-tions": "Looker-On" [James Montague], "Party Turning to Roosevelt as Sole Hope," *New York Herald-Tribune,* 7/1/1924.

delegates afterward told their own stories: Quoted in Frank Freidel, *Franklin D. Roosevelt: The Ordeal* (Boston: Little, Brown, 1954), 178n, 179–180n.

"I have heard it on every hand": Quoted in Houck and Kiewe, *FDR's Body Politics,* 34.

"I met your friend": Quoted in Freidel, *Roosevelt: The Ordeal,* 180.

"could not realize": Isabella Greenway to FDR, [undated] FBP-Subject/Infantile Paralysis, FDRL.

Perkins once told a story: Frances Perkins oral history interview, pt. 3, session 1, 344–347, CCOH.

"very keen sense of privacy": Author's inter-view with Curtis Roosevelt, 11/7/2011.

"strict boundaries between": Rochelle Gur-

stein, *The Repeal of Reticence: A History of America's Cultural and Legal Struggles over Free Speech, Obscenity, Sexual Liberation, and Modern Art* (New York: Hill and Wang, 1996), 10–11.

"was compelled to devote": "Democrats Hunting a Man for Governor to Suit All Factions," *New York Times,* 8/28/1924.

"They have been after me": FDR to Sidney Gunn, 9/4/1924, FBP/Correspondence, FDRL.

"I am planning": FDR to Byron Stookey, 9/4/1924, FBP/Correspondence, FDRL.

Chapter 10: "As If I Had Nothing the Matter"

teenaged boy named Louis Joseph: For the Louis Joseph and Tom Loyless letters, see Earle Looker, *This Man Roosevelt* (New York: Brewer, Warner & Putnam, 1932), 118–119.

"we shall be quite comfortable": FDR to SDR [October 1924], Elliott Roosevelt, ed., *FDR: His Personal Letters* (New York: Duell, Sloan and Pearce, 1948), 564–565.

"spires and domes": G. Fred Botts, "Where Infantile Paralysis Gets Its Walking Papers," unpublished manuscript, Small Collections, FDRL.

most of the crockery was broken: "Extemporaneous Remarks to Patients at Warm Springs, Ga., March 24, 1937," Master Speech File, FDRL.

"I spent over an hour": FDR to SDR [October 1924], *Letters,* 564–565.

"It won't be practical": Quoted in Blanche Wiesen Cook, *Eleanor Roosevelt,* vol. 1 (New York: Viking, 1992), 335.

"as if I had nothing the matter" FDR to Abram Elkus, 10/24/1924, FBP/Correspondence, FDRL.

prolonged visits to Bad Nauheim: Geoffrey C. Ward, *Before the Trumpet: Young Franklin Roosevelt, 1882–1905* (New York: Harper & Row, 1985), 143–147.

"My month down there": FDR to Paul Hasbrouck, 1/12/1925, FBP-Subject/Infantile Paralysis, FDRL.

"It will only be a matter of time": "Roosevelt at Warm Springs for Treatment," [Buffalo?] *Courier,* 11/16/1924.

It was a response to Dr. William Egleston: FDR to William Egleston, 10/11/1924, FBP/Correspondence, FDRL.

The distinguished visitor: Cleburne Gregory, "Franklin Roosevelt Will Swim to Health," *Atlanta Journal,* 10/26/1924.

"so ignominiously white": G. Fred Botts, "Where Infantile Paralysis Gets Its Walk-

ing Papers," unpublished manuscript, Small Collections, FDRL.

"all muscles": FDR to Ober, 4/1/1925, Robert Lovett Papers, Countway Library, Harvard University.

Chapter 11: "It Does Something for Me"

"Franklin never could travel": ER remarks, typescript highlights of interviews at Warm Springs by Rexford G. Tugwell, Small Collections, FDRL.

"always felt pressed": Marion Dickerman oral history, CCOH. On the effect of the Roosevelt estates on FDR's standard of living, see F. Kennon Moody, "FDR and His Neighbors: A Study of the Relationship Between Franklin Delano Roosevelt and the Residents of Dutchess County" (doctoral dissertation, State University of New York at Albany, 1981), 51.

"under very heavy expense": FDR to Milo T. Bogard, 1/15/1924, FBP/Correspondence, FDRL.

"not rich as you suppose": FDR to J. Cliff, FBP-Subject/Infantile Paralysis, FDRL.

"to justify the continuation": FDR to Annie Delano Hitch, 7/29/1922, FBP/Correspondence, FDRL.

"golden loop": James Roosevelt and Sidney

Shalett, *Affectionately, FDR: A Son's Story of a Lonely Man* (New York: Harcourt, Brace & Co., 1959), 26. Eleanor Roosevelt said her mother-in-law enjoyed the matriarchal power of the purse, even to the point of regretting that both Eleanor and Franklin had any independent resources at all. Eleanor Roosevelt, *This I Remember* (New York: Harper & Brothers, 1949), 12–13.

on the lookout for a score: On FDR's money-making efforts in 1920s, see ER oral history with Frank Freidel, Small Collections, FDRL; ER oral history with Robert D. Graff, FDRL; Eleanor Roosevelt, *This I Remember,* 12–16; Alva Johnston, "Mr. Roosevelt as a Businessman," *Saturday Evening Post,* 10/31/1936; John Gunther, *Roosevelt in Retrospect: A Profile in History* (New York: Harper & Brothers), 74–76.

"airtight little business": FDR to Van Lear Black, 6/16/1926, FBP/Correspondence, FDRL.

"following the weather": Rexford G. Tugwell typescript, "Franklin D. Roosevelt at Warm Springs, Georgia," 4/8/1958, Speech and Writings File, Rexford G. Tugwell Papers, FDRL.

"marvelous views": FDR to SDR, 2/1/1926,

Papers Donated by the Children, FDRL.

profitable pine plantings: Tugwell, "Roosevelt at Warm Springs."

"Missy . . . is keen": ER to Marion Dickerman, quoted in Kenneth Sydney Davis, *Invincible Summer: An Intimate Portrait of the Roosevelts* (New York: Atheneum, 1974), 61.

"I feel you": FDR to SDR, 3/7/1926, Papers Donated by the Children, FDRL.

"Don't let yourself": ER to FDR, 4/26/1926, Papers Donated by the Children, FDRL.

"Mama will always see": ER oral history with Frank Freidel, Small Collections, FDRL.

"He . . . feels that he's trying:" ER to Marion Dickerman, 4/25/1926, quoted in Davis, *Invincible Summer,* 62.

"I know how you love": ER to FDR, 5/4/1926, quoted in Davis, *Invincible Summer,* 62.

"I hope you don't think": Marion Dickerman recalled this exchange in her oral history, CCOH. Basil O'Connor went on to make Roosevelt's project at Warm Springs the great work of his life, becoming chairman of the National Foundation for Infantile Paralysis and a crucial figure in the virtual eradication of polio.

complex terms of the deal: This accounting appears in Theo Lippman, Jr., *The Squire of Warm Springs: FDR in Georgia, 1924–1945* (Chicago: Playboy Press, 1977), 42–43.

"We have nothing": Tom Loyless to FDR, quoted in Earle Looker, *This Man Roosevelt* (New York: Brewer, Warner & Putnam, 1932) 129.

"the cheapest kind of camps": Basil O'Connor, "The Glory in the Limited Life," address at Warm Springs, GA, 4/12/1951.

accountant and general manager: This and other details of FDR's management of Warm Springs in 1926 appear in an undated "Memorandum," Freiberg Family Papers, Jacob Rader Marcus Center of the American Jewish Archives, Cincinnati, OH.

"I am consulting architect": Quoted in Frank Freidel, *Franklin D. Roosevelt: The Ordeal* (Boston: Little, Brown, 1954), 195.

"the one & only topic": Anna Roosevelt to ER, 4/12/1926, quoted in Bernard Asbell, ed., *Mother and Daughter: The Letters of Eleanor and Anna Roosevelt* (New York: Coward, McCann & Geoghegan, 1982), 43.

"that it would be possible": FDR to Charles Foster Peabody, quoted in Looker, *This Man Roosevelt,* 129.

FDR packed Eleanor: The impromptu visit

to the conference is described in Turnley Walker, *Roosevelt and the Warm Springs Story* (New York: A. A. Wyn, 1953), 84–86.

"I'm not a surgeon": Quoted in Ruth Stevens, *Hi-Ya Neighbor* (New York: Tupper and Love, Inc., 1947), 24.

"I felt it was pretty clear": Michael Hoke to Albert Freiberg, 4/7/1927, Freiberg Papers, Marcus Center.

"We are all acquainted": James K. Crook, *The Mineral Waters of the United States and Their Therapeutic Uses* (New York: Lea Bros. & Co., 1899), 34.

"all tremendously impressed": Albert Freiberg to FDR, 4/29/1926, Freiberg Papers, Marcus Center.

"Something must be done": FDR telegram to Albert Freiberg, 5/2/1926, Freiberg Papers, Marcus Center.

"It is apparent to us": Albert Freiberg to FDR, 4/29/1926, Freiberg Papers, Marcus Center.

"You are quite right": FDR to Albert Freiberg, 5/3/1926, Freiberg Papers, Marcus Center.

"Upon your report": FDR to Albert Freiberg, 8/3/1926, Freiberg Papers, Marcus Center.

"I am more thoroughly convinced": Frank

Dickson to Albert Freiberg, 11/29/1926, Freiberg Papers, Marcus Center.

"She walked down the aisle": "Anna E. Roosevelt Becomes Bride of Curtis Bean Dall," *New York Herald-Tribune,* 6/6/1926.

Social Register names: "Anna E. Roosevelt Weds C. B. Dall," *New York Times,* 6/6/1926.

"talking to everybody": Frances Perkins, *The Roosevelt I Knew* (New York: Viking, 1946), 63.

"adolescent bedlam": Rexford G. Tugwell, *In Search of Roosevelt* (Cambridge, MA: Harvard University Press, 1972), 38–39.

"so handsome, so vital": Corinne Robinson Alsop to FDR, 9/9/1941, Papers Donated by the Children, FDRL.

"I am trying": ER to FDR, 4/6/1926, Papers Donated by the Children, FDRL.

Anna was still angry: Asbell, ed., *Mother and Daughter,* 32–33, 39–41.

"By contrast with": James Roosevelt with Bill Libby, *My Parents: A Differing View* (Chicago: Playboy Press, 1976), 58.

"the logical Democratic nominee": Louis Wehle's exchange with FDR is quoted in Wehle's memoir, *Hidden Threads of History: Wilson Through Roosevelt* (New York: MacMillan, 1953), 90–92.

"Its purpose to split": Louis Howe to FDR, 3/7/1926, quoted in Freidel, *Roosevelt: The Ordeal,* 216.

Roosevelt, the unsullied star: "F. D. Roosevelt Urged to Enter Race this Fall," *Poughkeepsie Eagle-News,* 5/1/1926.

"Friends and relatives": Irwin Thomas, "F. D. Roosevelt Wins Long Fight," *New York Post* [June 1926], Roosevelt Scrapbooks, FDRL.

"They are trying": FDR to Thomas Craven, 6/2/1926, FBP/Correspondence, FDRL.

"Nationally he would cease": Gustavus Rogers, untitled typescript; Gustavus Rogers Papers, Small Collections, FDRL.

"I hope your spine": Louis Howe to FDR [undated, August or September 1926], quoted in Freidel, *Roosevelt: The Ordeal,* 216–217.

Chapter 12: "So That They'll Forget That I'm a Cripple"

"I [saw] him trying": Oral history interview with Mr. and Mrs. William A. Plog, 12/19/1947, National Park Service oral histories, Small Collections, FDRL.

McDonald believed patients: FDR to George Draper, 9/30/1925, FBP-Subject/Infantile Paralysis, FDRL.

"I watched as he made": Mrs. Charles Hamlin, "An Old River Friend," *New Republic,* 4/15/1946.

"handle himself better": Anna Roosevelt to ER, 4/12/1926, in Bernard Asbell, ed., *Mother and Daughter: The Letters of Eleanor and Anna Roosevelt* (New York: Coward, McCann & Geoghegan, 1982), 43.

"in a way": FDR to S. R. Bertron, 9/24/1924, FBP-Subject/Infantile Paralysis, FDRL.

"polio was a storm": Mary Hudson Veeder quoted in Geoffrey Ward, *A First-Class Temperament: The Emergence of Franklin Roosevelt* (New York: Harper & Row, 1989), 669.

he wanted to walk without crutches: Turnley Walker, *Roosevelt and the Warm Springs Story* (New York: A. A. Wyn, 1953), 94. In a style common to popular nonfiction of the midtwentieth century, Walker composed his narrative with a good deal of dramatic license taken in the presentation of scenes and conversations. One cannot believe that such passages are verbatim reconstructions. But a comparison of Walker's reports with documentary evidence suggests that he was a reliable and thorough researcher. So I tend to credit his assertions about events at Warm

Springs even while disregarding his imaginative reconstructions of conversations. One cannot be positive that Roosevelt made these statements to Mahoney. But they are in keeping with statements he made in writing to friends and associates.

"the problem of adjustment": Lee Myerson, "Physical Disability as a Social Psychological Problem," *Journal of Social Issues* 4 (2–10), 1948.

"I knew": Alice Plastridge Converse interview with Rexford G. Tugwell, Tugwell oral histories, Small Collections, FDRL.

She arrived at Hyde Park: For Plastridge's work with FDR, see Alice Lou Plastridge, "Corrective Walking," *The Polio Chronicle,* October 1932; L. Caitlin Smith, "Alice Plastridge-Converse," *PT Magazine,* October 2000; Jay Schleikhorn, "Physical Therapist, 98, Recalls Rehabilitating Franklin Roosevelt," *P.T. Bulletin,* 3/16/1988; Alice Lou Plastridge to Frank Ober, 12/15/1926, Lovett Papers, Countway Library, Harvard University; Theo Lippman, Jr., *The Squire of Warm Springs: FDR in Georgia, 1924–1945* (Chicago: Playboy Press, 1977), 56–57.

"He has never shown": Helena Mahoney to ER, 4/23/1927, Papers Donated by the Children, FDRL.

"It is good": Helena Mahoney to ER, 5/27/1927, Papers Donated by the Children, FDRL.

"My own legs": FDR to William McDonald, 5/20/1927, FBP/Correspondence, FDRL.

"interesing in its southern primitiveness": FDR to Abram Elkus, 8/6/1926, FBP/Correspondence, FDRL.

"Wouldn't such a move": Louis Howe to FDR [April or May 1927], Louis Howe Official Papers, FDRL. For press coverage of FDR's statement on the Mississippi River flood, see, for example, "Finds South Wants Congress Called," *New York Times,* 5/13/1927.

"somehow down here": FDR to SDR, 3/7/1926, Papers Donated by the Children, FDRL.

troubled her far more: For ER's comments on Warm Springs, see Eleanor Roosevelt, *This I Remember* (New York: Harper & Brothers, 1949), 26–28.

"neither out of society" and *"the disabled confront"*: Robert F. Murphy, *The Body Silent* (New York: W. W. Norton, 1990), 110, 131–134.

"Oh, I do wish": FDR to Mrs. Sheffield Cowles, 6/29/1927, Elliott Roosevelt, ed., *F.D.R.: His Personal Letters, 1905–1928* (New York: Duell, Sloan and Pearce,

1948), 623–624.

If patients were depressed: Ward, *A First-Class Temperament,* 83.

"Thank the Lord": FDR to SDR, 11/18/1927, Papers Donated by the Children, FDRL.

"My next idea": Louis Howe to FDR [no date], Louis Howe Official Papers, FDRL.

"Mr. Roosevelt said": "Offers Spa to Push Fight on Paralysis," *New York Times,* 8/13/1927.

"Roosevelt Defies Doom": Undated newspaper clipping, Roosevelt Scrapbooks, FDRL.

"F. D. Roosevelt Is Back at Work": Undated newspaper clipping [February 1928], Roosevelt Scrapbooks, FDRL.

Chapter 13: "I Just Figured It Was Now or Never"

"If Smith is nominated": FDR to Van Lear Black, undated, FBP/Correspondence, FDRL.

He had to fight: FDR to Harry Byrd, 8/20/1928, quoted in Frank Freidel, *Franklin D. Roosevelt: The Ordeal* (Boston: Little, Brown, 1954), 247.

"very doubtful": FDR to Josephus Daniels, 6/23/1927, FBP/Correspondence, FDRL.

"I am more and more disgusted": FDR to Jo-

sephus Daniels, 7/20/1928, FBP/Correspondence, FDRL.

"these fool Methodist": FDR to Josephus Daniels, 7/26/1928, FBP/Correspondence, FDRL.

"Frankly, the campaign": FDR to Van Lear Black, 7/25/1928, FBP/Correspondence, FDRL.

He told Eleanor to quash: Interview notes, Frank Freidel interview with ER, 9/3/1952, Small Collections, FDRL.

"Smith did not believe": Joseph Proskauer oral history, CCOH.

"Smith looks on Roosevelt": E. M. House quoted in Robert A. Slayton, *Empire Statesman: The Rise and Redemption of Al Smith* (New York: Free Press, 2001), 351.

"Franklin just isn't": Al Smith quoted in Robert A. Caro, *The Power Broker: Robert Moses and the Fall of New York* (New York: Knopf, 1974), 285.

"awfully pleased": Al Smith to FDR, 1/1/1926, FBP/Correspondence, FDRL.

"I certainly do": Al Smith to FDR, 3/22/1927, FBP/Correspondence, FDRL.

"the finest thing": FDR to Al Smith, 5/20/1927, FBP/Correspondence, FDRL.

Maybe he was strong enough: For Smith's judgment on FDR's fitness, see Slayton, *Empire Statesman,* 352–353.

FDR standing straight: Turnley Walker, *Roosevelt and the Warm Springs Story* (New York: A. A. Wyn, 1953), 139–141.

Pandora's box of American fears: On bigotry against Smith, see Slayton, *Empire Statesman,* xi–xv, 305–317; Richard O'Connor, *The First Hurrah: A Biography of Alfred E. Smith* (New York: Putnam, 1970), 206–215.

"Persons who are very close": "Democrats Press Roosevelt to Run," *New York Times,* 9/27/1928.

"I have had": FDR to SDR, 9/30/1928, Papers Donated by the Children, FDRL.

walked across the living room: Grace Tully, *FDR: My Boss* (New York: Charles Scribner's Sons, 1949), 36. Tully shifted from Eleanor Roosevelt' staff to FDR's during the campaign for governor and served as one of his secretaries until the end of his life. Missy LeHand, who was Tully's close friend, told Tully the story of FDR's unaided steps. The incident has been mentioned in several published sources, but Tully's appears to be the only published account based on the report of an eyewitness.

"I didn't want it": Quoted in Emil Ludwig, *Roosevelt: A Study in Fortune and Power* (New York: Viking, 1938), 119–120.

Chapter 14: "Do I Look Like a Sick Man?"

"a sick man": "His Name Is Needed," *Dunkirk Grape Belt,* undated clipping, Roosevelt Scrapbooks, FDRL.

"cannot stand the strain": "Franklin D. Roosevelt," *Jamestown Journal,* undated clipping, Roosevelt Scrapbooks, FDRL.

"a self-evident truth": "Acrobats and Alibis in Politics," *Gloversville Republican,* undated clipping, Roosevelt Scrapbooks, FDRL.

"Republicans are as sorry": "The Truth About Roosevelt," *Albany Telegram,* 10/7/1928.

"mere discussion": "People's Problem," *Buffalo News,* undated clipping, Roosevelt Scrapbooks, FDRL.

"hit a cripple": It is notable that in the archaic lexicon of baseball, a "cripple" was a pitch thrown when the count on the batter was three balls and no strikes, and the pitcher is all but forced to throw a hittable pitch. Nothing is easier, the phrase says, than to "hit a cripple." It was said as a witticism, reminding us of a tradition as ancient as tales of the lame Greek god Hephaestus — the cripple as a butt of jokes.

"There is something": New York Evening Post quoted in "Roosevelt Lauded by Mayor Walker," *New York Times,* 10/3/1928.

"nothing has been": "Cruel Politics," *Buffalo News,* undated clipping, Roosevelt Scrapbooks, FDRL.

"as strong mentally": "Smith Is Happy Over Choice of State Ticket," *New York Sun,* 10/3/1928.

"My doctors are": "More Whispering," *New York Herald Tribune,* undated clipping, Roosevelt Scrapbooks, FDRL.

"F.D. Roosevelt, Titan": Edwin Hill, "F. D. Roosevelt, Titan of Energy, Runs Multifarious Enterprises," *New York Sun,* undated clipping, Roosevelt Scrapbooks, FDRL.

"the stupidest": "Health Improving, Roosevelt Shows," *New York World,* undated clipping, Roosevelt Scrapbooks, FDRL.

Chapter 15: "Campaign of Whispers"

Seven governors or former governors: The seven were Martin Van Buren, Horatio Seymour, Samuel Tilden, Grover Cleveland, Theodore Roosevelt, Charles Evans Hughes, and Al Smith.

"a memorable performance": Joseph Alsop, *FDR 1882-1945: A Centenary Remembrance* (New York: Viking, 1982), 99.

"definitely and positively known": Adolphus Ragan to FDR, 3/28/1938, FDRL.

"There were a good many": FDR dictated a reply to Ragan in which this remark was included. He never mailed the full reply but amended the letter to form a short thank-you. But he kept the full draft as a memo titled "Written for the record." Elliott Roosevelt, ed., *F.D.R.: His Personal Letters,* 1928–1945, vol. 2 (New York: Duell, Sloan and Pearce, 1950), 771–773.

"the man that any time": "Roosevelt Nomination Leads Will Rogers to Rumination," *New York Times,* 10/3/1928.

"Well, Frank": James Kieran, "Roosevelt and Smith," *New York Times Magazine,* 6/28/1936.

Perkins happened to pass: Perkins's fascinating and insightful recounting of the relationship between Roosevelt and Smith appears in her oral history, pt. 3, session 1, 1–86, CCOH.

"Don't let Mrs. Moskowitz": Quoted in Blanche Wiesen Cook, *Eleanor Roosevelt,* vol. 1 (New York: Viking, 1992), 387.

And in his own private circle: Elliott Roosevelt, *A Rendezvous with Destiny: The Roosevelts of the White House* (New York: G. P. Putnam's Sons, 1975), 194. Elliott reported a meeting, apparently in the late 1930s, in which FDR spoke of the matter to his close presidential aide Harry Hopkins: "According to the scribbled notes which Hopkins kept of their meeting, Father repeated to him something that he had previously, I believe, confided only to the family: that if he had been able to continue treatment at Warm Springs after 1928, use of his left leg would have been restored. When he yielded to Al Smith's urging to run for governor of New York, Father sacrificed the opportunity of ever walking alone again."

When who goes to Albany: Grace Tully, *FDR: My Boss* (New York: Charles Scribner's Sons, 1949), 40.

always worried that 'Pa might not make it' ': Author's interview with Curtis Dall Roosevelt, 11/7/2011. Mr. Roosevelt explained in detail the maneuver he called "the flip" and FDR's fear of falling among people he did not know well.

There is no disguising: Milton MacKaye, "The Governor, II," *New Yorker,* 8/22/1931.

Occasionally mishaps occurred: Nicholas Roosevelt, *A Front Row Seat* Norman: University of Oklahoma Press, 1953), 224.

Eleanor and Frances Perkins devised: Frances Perkins oral history interview, pt. 3, session 1, 3–4, CCOH. Perkins said: "That practice went on all through the

Roosevelt administration at all kinds of social occasions."

"Eddie," the governor said: Edward J. Flynn, *You're the Boss* (New York, Viking, 1947), 82.

In the home office: Quoted in Ted Morgan, *FDR: A Biography* (New York: Simon & Schuster, 1985), 337.

"the editor of a well known": Mrs. Charles Hamlin, "Some Reminiscences of Franklin D. Roosevelt," Small Collections, FDRL.

Just as Louis Howe had predicted: Theo Lippman, Jr., *The Squire of Warm Springs: FDR in Georgia, 1924–1945* (Chicago: Playboy Press, 1977), 178, 192–197.

Variations on the syphilis theme: Richard Thayer Goldberg, *The Making of Franklin D. Roosevelt: Triumph over Disability* (Cambridge, MA: About Books, 1981), 173–174

"I find there is": Quoted in Frank Freidel, *Franklin D. Roosevelt: The Triumph* (Boston: Little, Brown, 1956), 210.

"The three prominent doctors": John Gunther, *Roosevelt in Retrospect: A Profile in History* (New York: Harper & Brothers, 1950), 266–267.

"I read the Liberty": James Farley to FDR, 7/17/1931, Howe Personal Papers, FDRL.

"I have seen three or four": Ernest K. Lindley, *Half Way with Roosevelt* (New York: Viking, 1937), 80–81

"Then you are not out of politics?": Quoted in Robert A. Slayton, *Empire Statesman: The Rise and Redemption of Al Smith* (New York: Free Press, 2001), 365.

"There is something about Frank": "Ex-Gov. Smith's Speech Nominating Gov. Roosevelt," *New York Times,* 10/1/1930.

"the chance to redeem": Slayton, *Empire Statesman,* 366.

"Al Smith can move": Quoted in Slayton, *Empire Statesman,* 366.

"I believe if a rose" Quoted in Robert E. Sherwood, *Roosevelt and Hopkins: An Intimate History* (New York: Harper & Brothers, 1948), 59.

"Do you know": Quoted in Slayton, *Empire Statesman,* 370.

"I had thought": Quoted in Steve Neal, *Happy Days Are Here Again: The 1932 Democratic Convention, the Emergence of FDR — and How America Was Changed Forever* (New York: Morrow, 2004), 171–172.

"Governor Roosevelt has had" and *"My health is excellent"*: Quoted in Davis W. Houck and Amos Kiewe, *FDR's Body Politics: The Rhetoric of Disability* (College Station:

Texas A & M University Press, 2003), 58.

"Mr. Roosevelt today walks": "Franklin Roosevelt Thrives on Rigors of Campaigns," *Milwaukee Sentinel,* 7/4/1932.

The handiest retort: Charles Norman, "The Man in the White House," *St. Petersburg Times,* 6/30/1936.

It was a quiet offensive: Neal, *Happy Days Are Here Again,* 78, 125, 171–174.

"Well," Hoover said: James MacLafferty Diary, July 2, 1932, in Timothy Walch and Dwight M. Miller, eds., *Herbert Hoover and Franklin D. Roosevelt: A Documentary History* (Westport, CT: Greenwood Press, 1998), 45.

"It seems that a lot": James Thurber, "Notes and Comment," *New Yorker,* 7/23/1932.

"Jim, what do you think": Quoted in James A. Farley, *Jim Farley's Story: The Roosevelt Years* (New York: Whittlesey House, 1948), 28.

"Lou, I do not know": Quoted in Donald A. Ritchie, *Electing FDR: The New Deal Campaign of 1932* (Lawrence: University Press of Kansas, 2007), 127.

"A sympathetic silence": James L. Wright, "Spellbinding Mode Changes," *Los Angeles Times,* 9/20/1932.

Near the end of the campaign: Anne O'Hare

McCormick, "The Two Men at the Big Moment," *New York Times,* 11/5/1932.

Epilogue

"Through three rows": Frank Capra, *The Name Above the Title: An Autobiography* (New York: Macmillan, 1971), 259.

"You know, Orson": Quoted in John Gunther, *Roosevelt in Retrospect: A Profile in History* (New York: Harper & Brothers, 1950), 62.

"Franklin's illness proved": The Autobiography of Eleanor Roosevelt (New York: Harper & Row, 1961), 142.

"He would certainly": Quoted in John Gunther, *Roosevelt in Retrospect,* 243.

"I was instantly struck": Frances Perkins, *The Roosevelt I Knew* (New York: Viking, 1946), 30, 5.

"seemed to be more interested": Quoted in John F. Sears, F. Kennon Moody, and John Auwaerter, "Historic Resource Study for the Roosevelt Estate," National Park Service, 2004, 121.

"deepened and mellowed": "Roosevelt Secretary Lauds Qualities of Incoming President," *Evening Independent* (St. Petersburg, FL), 1/24/1933

"believe he had the basic strength of character": James Roosevelt with Bill Libby, *My*

Parents: A Differing View (Chicago: Playboy Press, 1976), 94–95.

It was, at least in part, a kind of masquerade: The cultural critic Tobin Siebers offers a different and fascinating interpretation of masquerade among the disabled in "Disability As Masquerade," *Literature and Medicine* 23(2004), 1–22.

"The story of your life": Mary Louise Ray to FDR, 3/13/1943, President's Personal File, FDRL.

"Because he had beaten": Gunther, *Roosevelt in Retrospect,* 243.

"the battle of life's wounded": Robert F. Murphy, *The Body Silent* (New York: W.W. Norton, 1990), 230.

"I've done a lot of things": John Gunther's notes of an interview with Dr. Howard Bruenn, John Gunther Papers, Special Collections Research Center, University of Chicago Library.

PHOTO CREDITS

Franklin D. Roosevelt Library, Hyde Park, NY: insert pages 1, 2, 3, 5 (bottom), 6, 7, 8, 9, 10, 11, 12, 13, 14

Olin Dows, *Franklin Roosevelt at Hyde Park (American Artists Group, 1949)*: insert page 4

National Library of Medicine: insert page 5 (top left and right)

ABOUT THE AUTHOR

James Tobin won the National Book Critics Circle Award in biography for *Ernie Pyle's War* and the J. Anthony Lukas Work-in-Progress Award for *To Conquer the Air: The Wright Brothers and the Great Race for Flight*. Educated at the University of Michigan, where he earned a Ph.D. in history, he teaches narrative nonfiction in the Department of Media, Journalism, and Film at Miami of Ohio.

The employees of Thorndike Press hope you have enjoyed this Large Print book. All our Thorndike, Wheeler, and Kennebec Large Print titles are designed for easy reading, and all our books are made to last. Other Thorndike Press Large Print books are available at your library, through selected bookstores, or directly from us.

For information about titles, please call:
(800) 223-1244

or visit our Web site at:
http://gale.cengage.com/thorndike

To share your comments, please write:
Publisher
Thorndike Press
10 Water St., Suite 310
Waterville, ME 04901